D1483362

The Foundations of
American Economic Freedom
Government and Enterprise
in the
Age of Washington

Published with assistance from the Roger E. Joseph Memorial Fund for greater understanding of public affairs, a cause in which Roger Joseph believed

The
Foundations of
American Economic
Freedom

*Government and Enterprise
in the
Age of Washington*

by
E. A. J. Johnson

University of Minnesota Press
Minneapolis

© Copyright 1973 by the University of Minnesota.
All rights reserved.
Printed in the United States of America
at Kingsport Press, Inc., Kingsport, Tennessee
Published in the United Kingdom and India by the Oxford University
Press, London and Delhi, and in Canada
by the Copp Clark Publishing Co. Limited, Toronto

Library of Congress Catalog Card Number: 72-92336

ISBN 0-8166-0664-1

To

Arthur H. Cole

whose explorations of the
entrepreneurial aspects of economic history
have opened up new vistas of knowledge
and provided new insights
for understanding american culture

Preface

Iₙ CALLING THIS BOOK *The Foundations of American Economic Freedom,* I will no doubt be accused of attempting to fractionalize something essentially holistic, and incur the wrath of advocates of civil rights, protagonists of the freedom of worship, and defenders of the freedom of speech and of the press. I will probably be criticized for failing to stress freedom of assembly or of association, freedom to bear arms, or freedom from false imprisonment or forced labor. All these potential critics can aver that my concept of freedom is too limited, and that at best I am only describing some of the origins of our so-called "free" enterprise system. I readily admit that such arguments are plausible, for indeed all the foregoing are extremely important aspects of liberty. Yet I believe that, to most Americans, "freedom" means the right to earn a living in the way of one's own choosing, to launch an enterprise, to save and invest, to own property, and, above all, to share in the income and wealth that a progressive economy generates. I think the quintessential aspect of freedom that we Americans cherish is much more economic than political, and that such rights as freedom of worship, once so controversial, have lost importance, as indifference toward religion increases, as a result religious freedom is today far less consequential than the right to strike for higher wages, shorter hours, or additional fringe benefits.

Liberty has meaning in the context of some social process; its content, as Harold Laski pointed out many years ago, is always changing with conditions of time and place. In one age the dominant demand may be for religious toleration, in another the emphasis may be on political enfranchisement. But in the long sweep of history the struggle for freedom has tended to emphasize economic improvement: for slaves, underprivileged persons, trade unions, or ethnical minorities. Moreover freedom has come to be less an individual quest and more a demand of groups of persons. In our history we have sought liberty largely through an emphasis on pluralism, and out of group inter- actions has come the American way of life. It is the modest object of this book to explain, in some rather precise detail, the origins of this American pluralistic concept of economic freedom.

Completion of this study, begun under the auspices of the Council on Research in Economic History, now a standing committee of the Economic History Association, has been long delayed. The basic re- search and much of the composition had been done when my aca- demic career was interrupted by twelve years of military and govern- mental duties that took me to England, Scotland, Norway, Korea, Japan, Greece, and Yugoslavia, years of such demanding duties that there was no time available for completing unfinished manuscripts. When I returned to the academic fold, new priorities intruded, first the revision and enlargement of a book on the American economy and then the preparation and publication of two books dealing with economic development: *Market Towns and Spatial Development in India* and *The Organization of Space in Developing Countries.* These three books plus a fourth—a volume of memoirs—together with about a dozen articles prepared for American, Italian, Indian, and Polish journals, meant that another decade passed before I could find time to devote to this study. Fortunately the subject is as timely now as when I began my research. Moreover my enthusiasm for this inquiry has not flagged; indeed the long interregnum has deepened rather than diminished my conviction of the importance of such an inquiry as this. Were I younger I would further delay publication pending the completion of the *Documentary History of the First Federal Congress of the United States of America,* which, at long last, has been begun by the Johns Hopkins Press. But that worthy project will not be finished in much less than a decade, and so many years, I fear, will not be allotted me. It is better, therefore, that I publish now, however partial and inadequate the sources for my chapters VIII and IX.

Having confessed my sins let me now acknowledge my indebtedness to gracious friends and critics. To Arthur H. Cole I am doubly be- holden. As the chairman of the Council on Research in Economic History, he urged me to undertake an examination of the ideational relations of government and enterprise in the early national period. As my work progressed he read and criticized each chapter, and I have richly benefited from his helpful suggestions. To Fred Henrich, who carried on parallel research on the state level, I am deeply indebted. He supplied me with the detail on state legislation that enriched my data, particularly for chapter IX. I must also record my obligation to the late James O. Wetterau, whose untimely death robbed us of a masterful study that no one else could ever complete or duplicate. He read several of my chapters and gave me the benefit of his wide knowledge and deep insight. Two other excellent scholars, Joseph Dorfman and Stuart Bruchey, read my manuscript and gave me very helpful suggestions. The foibles that remain must all be laid at my door.

E. A. J. Johnson

Barnaby Woods
Washington, D.C.

Contents

The Foundations of
American Economic Freedom

Government and Enterprise
in the
Age of Washington

I

The
Great Synthesis

It was indeed next to a Miracle that there should have been so much unanimity, in points of importance, among such a number of Citizens, so widely scattered, and so different in their habits in many respects as the Americans were.

George Washington

Challenge and Response

DURING the century and a half that preceded their war for independence, the American colonists had been busily engaged in converting forests, and what little open land there was, into farms; laying out villages, towns, and a few cities; building houses, ships, docks, workshops, warehouses, mills, and other business structures; constructing roads; and addressing themselves to the many tasks necessary for the economic development of the Atlantic seaboard and the Piedmont. While this dramatic chapter in capital formation and in the creation of productive facilities was being enacted, a fragmentary body of economic thought gradually took form, a cluster of tentative ideas occasionally remarkable for insight but seldom comprehensive and often lacking in consistency.[1] Many of the basic concepts and much of the analysis reflected British or European precedents, although problems created by a different environment, by changing trade patterns, and by a chronic scarcity of hard money provided intellectual problems that elicited a few original ideas and a great many heterodox opinions. For the most part, however, no really sharp appreciation of macro-economic policy or the role of government in economic development occurred before the colonists became involved in a war of liberation, as a consequence of which they found themselves outside a colonial system in which they had so long and for the most part rather comfortably existed. Out of this new challenge came a welter of ideas, particularly after it became painfully evident that the makeshift government under the Articles of Confederation had signally failed

---

1. I have tried to organize, explain, and criticize this body of thought up to about 1700 in my *American Economic Thought in the Seventeenth Century* (London, 1932). A very competent appraisal of the growing body of American economic thought in the eighteenth century will be found in Joseph Dorfman, *The Economic Mind in American Civilization*, I (New York, 1946), 111–344.

to integrate the new nation politically or to unify the seaboard economy.[2] The circumstantial factors that had led to independence, and the very unsatisfactory first decade of political emancipation, called for a careful reconsideration of the proper relations that should exist between enterprise and government. Out of a most troublesome situation, in which the very future of the American nation often hung in the balance, fortunately there emerged a great synthesis of political and economic ideas, one that resulted not merely in the American Constitution but in a body of thought that essentially determined the American way of life.

The following chapters will describe how an acceptable form of federal government and a national public policy that could promote the general welfare were ultimately agreed upon after violent disagreement and acrimonious debate. Through a number of concessions, bargains, and compromises, a comparison of ideas about the proper relations between government and enterprise occurred; during the course of these debates, areas of common ground were found that made it possible for divergent "interests" to reconcile enough of their differences to permit a tolerable degree of cooperation. For the American nation was pluralistic from its very beginnings, with a government created by farmers, merchants, professional men, mechanics, and speculators all valiantly trying to ensure that their respective groups would retain the "freedom" which they had sought through insurrection. Little attempt was made to conceal the egocentric nature of the arguments. Very realistically the American writers and legislators recognized that society is not atomistic but composed of various forms of association, and that each such grouping tends to have a collective opinion that stems from the desires and aspirations of its members.[3]

2. Edward Channing's account of the interstate disagreements, conflicting policies, and mutual stultification is still one of the most graphic descriptions of this chapter in American history. See chap. XV, "Four Years of Confusion, 1783–1787," in *A History of the United States*, III (New York, 1926), 463–491.

3. Only perfectly homogeneous societies can escape the pressures originating in the ambitions of social segments. Such perfect homogeneity is seldom found; it is approximated most nearly in primitive societies where customary conduct is expected from all and is enforced by the collective conscience of the entire society. But this "mechanical solidarity," as Émile Durkheim has called it, is normally weakened in the course of social evolution. Cohesion of society therefore calls for some process that will reconcile the egocentric groups. See *De la division du travail social* (Paris, 1893), trans. George Simpson as *On the Division of Labor in Society* (New York, 1933). This translation is based on the first and fifth editions.

Moreover there was a deep-seated conviction that each group had rights which the other groups and the government must respect.

The Theory of Interests

In the eighteen-century literature the term used to designate basic occupational groupings was the word *interest,* and the debates in the Constitutional Convention and the contemporary political and economic tracts teem with references to the major or influential "interests" that presumably existed in the American economy. How many such groups there actually were is rather hard to say, and although Forrest McDonald asserts that "there were in the United States in 1787 at least twenty basic occupational groups having different economic characteristics and needs,"[4] the consensus of contemporary writers and legislators seems to be that there were eight well-recognized interests: agricultural; mercantile; manufacturing; mechanic; professional; financial; corporate; and foreign. To this list might be added two more: the consumers' interest and the propertied interest; and, to complete the classification, the "public," "general," or "common" interest.

However egocentric the demands of a particular interest may have been, all the groups seem to have recognized that some balance had to be found between the several claimants to political and economic privilege, and that an emergent national government would of necessity have to be an arbiter of inter-group conflicts. But there was a general belief that government ought to be much more than an umpire; and because it was feared that a government, by the exercise of discretionary power, might favor particular interests and discriminate against others, it became extremely important that the several interests should be accorded proper legislative representation. Nor was the fear merely that an oligarchical government, such as John Adams advocated, might neglect the poor or that a revolutionary government, such as demanded by the Shaysites, might plunder the rich; there was a far more likely possibility that one interest or another might be overrepresented and capable of dominating the legislative procedure.

A number of writers were hopeful that in framing a new national government the people of the United States could make a fresh start, and thereby balance all the interests ab initio. Accordingly they pro-

4. *We the People: The Economic Origins of the Constitution* (Chicago, 1958), p. 398.

posed that a government be formed that would represent all constituent interests, and to ensure some measure of parity they proposed
that small or weak groups, such as mechanics, seamen, or fishermen,
should pool their strength in "amalgamated interests" in order to
achieve power commensurate with that of the larger and stronger
interests such as farmers or merchants. The difficulty, of course, lay in
actually making such a fresh start for any new system of group enfranchisement would have to be made in the face of power already
possessed by entrenched existing interests. Moreover power might
quickly gravitate toward some heretofore relatively small interest, so
that regardless of any formally agreed upon balance an *imperium in
imperio* might circumstantially emerge—for example, a powerful
speculative or "stockjobbing" interest. One thing that articulate members of the Constitutional Convention clearly realized was that in a
republic a government could not be a wholly neutral agency, separate
and distinct from a society's major economic interests. Yet if large and
powerful interests were accorded proportionate representation, how
could such a government serve as an impartial arbiter and protect
smaller and weaker interests? The problem in short was how to ensure
inter-group harmony in a pluralistic society, how to prevent a dominant
interest from acting oppressively toward less powerful groups or
toward the public at large. Out of this dilemma arose a somewhat
vague notion of the state as a protector of the smaller and weaker
interests.[5]

Because Charles A. Beard rather dramatically called attention to
certain interests represented at the Constitutional Convention, it has
sometimes been assumed that he was the first to discover that these
interests existed,[6] an inference both unfair and unwarranted. For there
was an unmistakable awareness by the Founding Fathers of the
pluralistic nature of American society and a very forthright recognition that the several interests would have to be accorded some
measure of political representation. Alexander Hamilton, for example,
made no effort to conceal the fact that public creditors, whether
original holders or shrewd speculators, "had a considerable agency in
promoting the adoption of the new Constitution, for this peculiar
reason . . . that it exhibited the prospect of a government able to do

5. This responsibility has been recognized by all the leading proponents of
pluralistic doctrine: Otto von Gierke, Harold Laski, A. D. Lindsay, J. Neville
Figgis, Léon Duguit, Ernest Barker, and Joseph Paul-Boncour.
6. In his *Economic Interpretation of the Constitution of the United States*
(New York, 1913).

justice to their claims."[7] An unashamed advocate of funding the national and state debts, Hamilton saw no reason why the "financial interest" ought not be as well cared for as the agricultural or the commercial interest.[8]

Property, Private Enterprise, and Market Forces

This honest defense of pluralism, which is basic to the American idea of freedom, rested essentially on a preference for private enterprise and a profound respect for private property. If the social philosophy of the Founding Fathers can be called "democratic," it rested unambiguously on a belief in what Joseph Dorfman has called "the democracy of property owners."[9] John Adams put the issue sharply: civil society must find a mean between tyrannical despotism and democratic anarchy. Hence "a society to be stable must be based on property" because ownership of things always "breeds responsibility."[10] But if an unfair dominance by an aristocracy is to be prevented—in short, if the "general welfare" is to be safeguarded—property must be relatively widespread.[11] For that reason there seems to have been general agreement that the structure of government, and its impact on society, should be such as to guarantee freedom for all citizens to choose their occupations, to invest or to launch enterprises, to buy and sell, and, by these means, to acquire, transfer, or bequeath property. Nor were these views confined to conservative-minded Federalists; Jefferson, for example, was equally convinced that "enterprise thrives best when left to individual initiative,"[12] although he admitted that government might properly intervene to protect citizens from casual embarrassments.[13]

The idea that free enterprise would need to be guided if a truly wholesome economic development was to be fostered had been clearly stated before the Constitutional Convention began its deliberations. An

7. *The Works of Alexander Hamilton,* ed. Henry Cabot Lodge (New York, 1885–1886), VIII, 437.

8. For a summary of the arguments in favor of funding all debts in full face value, see Broadus Mitchell, *Alexander Hamilton: The National Adventure, 1788–1804,* II (New York, 1962), 64–68.

9. *Economic Mind in American Civilization,* I, 405.

10. Ibid., I, 421. The central place that property occupied in eighteenth-century thought has been carefully analyzed by Paschal Larkin in *Property in the Eighteenth Century with Special Reference to England and Locke* (Dublin, 1930).

11. For a searching analysis of John Adams's political views, see Page Smith, *John Adams,* 2 vols. (Westport, Conn., 1962).

12. Dorfman, *Economic Mind in American Civilization,* I, 440.

13. Ibid. For details concerning Jefferson's belief in the social utility of property, see Dumas Malone, *Jefferson and His Time,* 2 vols. (Boston, 1948–1951).

anonymous author[14] summarized the argument succinctly: although agriculture (which can readily expand under free private enterprise) is the foundation of a nation's wealth, the value added by processing is four times that of the raw produce. Consequently if a nation hopes to develop, it must encourage manufacturing by some form of assistance or subvention because a far more profitable and specie-yielding commerce can be supported by selling manufactured goods than by exporting unprocessed or semi-processed agricultural produce. Moreover if manufacturing is encouraged, a nation's population can more rapidly increase so that the total of disposable incomes can enlarge, hence animating the whole economy.[15]

Although the climate of opinion favored a reliance on market forces wherever possible, this preference of the eighteenth-century Americans very seldom led to a doctrinaire commitment to a policy of *laissez-faire*. Almost to a man there was agreement that government should aid in the building of internal improvements, such as roads and canals,[16] whether by lending money to construction companies or by joint ventures.[17] Nor should government confine its "fostering hand" to infrastructure. A large proportion of the American publicists favored government assistance for nascent manufactures by tariff protection, bounties, land grants, or capital advances,[18] and there was almost general agreement that the public domain should be reserved for American settlers[19] and alienated in a manner calculated to quicken the nation's economic development and promote the general welfare. Commerce should also be stimulated by judicious governmental as-

14. Dorfman thinks it might have been Colonel James Swan. See his *Economic Mind in American Civilization*, I, chap. XII, p. xvii, n. 47.

15. *Observations of the Agriculture, Manufactures and Commerce of the United States* (1789).

16. For a concise analysis of this aspect of American economic history, see Carter Goodrich, "American Development Policy: The Case of Internal Improvements," *Journal of Economic History*, XVI (December 1956), 449–460. For a more detailed account, see Carter Goodrich, Julius Ruben, and Harvey H. Segal, *Canals and American Economic Development* (New York, 1961).

17. Milton Heath has shown very precisely how such joint action later materialized in Georgia. See his *Constructive Liberalism: The Role of the State in Economic Development in Georgia to 1860* (Cambridge, Mass., 1954).

18. For details see chap. IX below. Alexander Hamilton's vigorous advocacy of such a program has been well described by Mitchell in his *Alexander Hamilton*, II, chap. 8.

19. In an *Essay on the Extent and Value of Our Western Unlocated Lands, and the Proper Method of Disposing of Them*, which Pelatiah Webster published in Philadelphia in 1781, the argument was that these hitherto "crown lands" now belonged to the thirteen states, and hence Webster abhorred "the very idea of strangers having their paw on any of our lands." This "essay" was reprinted in Webster's *Political Essays* (Philadelphia, 1791), pp. 485–501.

sistance. Whether the central government should charter a national bank became a far more controversial issue. The followers of Hamilton vigorously argued in favor of this widening of governmental activity while the agrarian factions, led by John Taylor and Thomas Jefferson, bitterly opposed the bank charter as incompatible with the American concept of equal rights and stigmatized Hamilton's proposal as an entering wedge for monopoly and special privilege for the favored few. The question therefore was how to determine the proper sphere for governmental intervention; or as Loammi Baldwin so forthrightly said, to decide "what should be done by statute and what should be left to [the] good sense" of individuals. Because the whole American economic situation was so different, and the new federal type of government so essentially experimental, Baldwin felt that "European models and experience" could provide little guidance, and for that reason in America "everything in relation to political economy must be original."[20]

Actually of course this wasn't true. A considerable portion of the great synthesis represented borrowed and imported ideas. The worship of property, for example, rested squarely on the political theory of James Harrington[21] and John Locke,[22] a dependence very clearly evident in the writings of John Adams. Alexander Hamilton borrowed many ideas from Malachy Postlethwayt, David Hume, and Matthew Decker;[23] he had read Adam Smith, as Thomas Jefferson, George Logan, and James Madison also had done. John Taylor cited Malthus, and James Logan quoted Arthur Young. James Madison, however, seems to have covered a wider literature than most of his contemporaries since he refers not only to English writers such as Hume, Smith, Malthus, and Godwin, but to a number of French writers: Montesquieu, Raynal, Condorcet, Turgot, Necker, and de Tracy.

The Chief Contributors to the Great Synthesis

Who were the leading American writers, pamphleteers, thinkers, legislators, or petitioners who circumstantially put together a theory of interests, a doctrine of economic freedom, and a philosophy of governmental intervention into a crystallizing synthesis? Everyone knows about the three authors of the *Federalist* Papers, but Alexander Hamilton, John Jay, and James Madison owe their fame largely to the amaz-

20. *Thoughts on the Study of Political Economy* (1809), quoted by Dorfman, *Economic Mind in American Civilization*, I, 340.
21. For a compact analysis, see George Sabine, *A History of Political Theory* (New York, 1937), pp. 498–508.
22. Ibid., pp. 526–540.
23. See below, p. 131.

ing facility with which they expressed their ideas. Their contemporaries were in many ways their equals. From all walks of life came the participants to the great debates that preceded and followed the adoption of the Constitution: plantation owners such as Thomas Jefferson and John Taylor; merchants like James Bowdoin and Pelatiah Webster; Princeton preachers; frontier farmers; Boston, New York, and Philadelphia lawyers; clergymen living in small towns as well as in cities; scholars and lexicographers; manufacturers; and financiers. The problems of war, liberation, and postwar adjustment, the patent need for a better integrated form of government, the constant threat of domestic fissiparous movements, and the danger of diplomatic impotence contributed to the ferment of thought and the search for some common ground, for some agreed principles not only on which to restructure the federal government, but on which to rest the foundations for a durable system of political and economic freedom.

Despite the different regions from which the main actors in this drama came, and despite their varied intellectual preconceptions, contrasting income levels, or occupational differences, the participants to the earnest discussions and debates that charged the atmosphere in the Age of Washington, for all their wrangling, ultimately found essential agreement on three main issues. There was, first of all, an explicit and forthright recognition of the existence of interests and a hope at least that the more important interests would, by one means or another, obtain appropriate legislative representation. This honest recognition of the pluralistic nature of society is surely basic to our American idea of freedom. A second area of general agreement was a uniform respect for private property and a consistently declared preference for giving wide scope to private enterprise. As a corollary, there pervades the literature a great, although by no means an exclusive, reliance on market forces as a means for organizing the economy and promoting the growth and development of the nation; not an exclusive reliance, however, since almost every writer or legislator recognized that for an underdeveloped country such as the United States the rational and constructive use of public authority was required to assist economic growth and to improve and "happify" society by a wide range of activities. Agreement on these three major principles reflected a melding of the ideas of several groups whose characteristics and composition deserve notice.

THE SCHOLARS

Because so many of the eighteenth-century plantation owners, merchants, clergymen, and lawyers were well educated, it is difficult to select a few writers who can properly be called "scholars." Yet because of their primary concern with intellectual problems, James Madison, Noah Webster, John Witherspoon, and William Barton probably deserve such designation. Of these four, Madison was clearly outstanding; and although he is too often remembered merely as a joint author of *The Federalist,* he ought to be judged not by a particular partisan appeal to an influential group in New York[24] designed to win its support for the Constitution, but by the whole fabric of his political thought, a great deal of which, to be sure, was expressed in *The Federalist.* Madison received a solid classical training as an undergraduate at Princeton[25] (where John Witherspoon was president) and followed this with postgraduate study under Witherspoon of the writings of Montesquieu, Hobbes, Locke, Sidney, Pufendorf, and many other authorities on philosophy and government. He was, as has been aptly said, "essentially a scholar in politics" who blended together "vast knowledge and profound insight into human nature."[26] In *The Federalist* he justified the proposed Constitution as a means for reconciling an adequate measure of democracy with the security of private property[27]—an adequate measure of democracy because, in his opinion, the central problem was not to achieve equality but to preserve liberty. Government must therefore regulate the "various and interfering interests" and curb the proliferation of "factions" which Madison thought constituted an ever-present and insidious danger to good government. His ideal centered on a proper balance of a limited number of basic "interests," a doctrine he tried to materialize when he was president of the United States (1809–1817).

Noah Webster, who graduated from Yale with a "complete stock of respectable opinions,"[28] and who was much more than a lexicographer,[29] repeatedly and very effectively contributed to the pre-

24. The main purpose of *The Federalist* was to undermine the opposition of George Clinton and Robert Yates to the Constitution.
25. Then called "The Presbyterian College of New Jersey."
26. William Seal Carpenter, in *Encyclopaedia of the Social Sciences,* X (New York, 1933), 34.
27. Like Hamilton, John Adams, and other contemporaries, Madison subscribed to John Locke's labor theory of property, the basic thesis of which was that property had been originally created by human labor. Although Madison thought that in a good society, property rights ought not have priority over personal rights, by reason of the wide diffusion of property in the United States he thought the likelihood that property owners would encroach on the liberty of the mass of people was remote.
28. Vernon Louis Parrington, *Main Currents in American Thought: An Interpretation of American Literature from the Beginnings to 1920,* I (New York, 1927), 382.
29. Webster first attracted attention by his famous *Spelling Book* (1783), of

Constitutional and post-Constitutional debates. A convinced and loyal Federalist, he agreed with Hamilton that the rich and wellborn must be accorded a wide measure of governmental responsibility and freedom of enterprise. "What would become of the poor," he asked, "without the rich? How would they subsist without employment, and how could they be employed without the capital of the rich? Who but the wealthy can pay the public expenses?"[30] Who else can furnish the funds needed for public improvements? The ways in which government can unwittingly frustrate the fruitful activities of businessmen must be clearly recognized, Webster insisted; his vigorous assault on laws intended to regulate usury is a classic example of his devout belief in the beneficence of market forces. Webster lent his assistance to many other crusades,[31] serving often as a "journalist hack for the Federalists." Yet he sometimes displayed striking independence, stubbornly refusing, for example, to accept the Federalist condemnation of the followers of Daniel Shays, who to him represented "the substantial yeomanry of the country"[32] whose complaints deserved sympathetic consideration.

John Witherspoon's (1723–1794) contribution to the intellectual climate of the late colonial period and the first decade of American independence was both profound and pervasive. From Scotland he brought the philosophic principles that had been developed by Thomas Reid, professor of moral philosophy at Glasgow University, which opposed the skepticism of David Hume with "common-sense" beliefs. There are, said Reid, "principles which the constitution of our nature leads us to believe and which we are under the necessity to take for

which sixty-two million copies ultimately were printed and sold (by 1889). Then, beginning with his *Examination of the Leading Principles of the Federal Constitution* (1787), he rapidly increased his reputation as a publicist. He founded a daily newspaper (*The Commercial Advertiser*) and a weekly journal (*The Spectator*), both in support of the Federalists. In 1799 his two-volume *History of Epidemic and Pestilential Diseases* was published, while three years later two more books, *Historical Notices of the Origin and State of Banking Institutions* and *The Rights of Neutral Nations in Time of War,* appeared. After 1807, when his *Philosophical and Practical Grammar of the English Language* was completed, he turned his attention almost exclusively for the next twenty years to his *American Dictionary of the English Language.* Once that tremendous task was finished, he began his *History of the United States,* which was published in 1832. *A Collection of Papers on Political, Literary and Moral Subjects* (1843) was Webster's last publication.

30. Letter of Noah Webster to Daniel Webster, quoted by Dorfman, *Economic Mind in American Civilization,* II, chap. XXIII, p. vi, n. 9.

31. For his role in organizing the Hartford Convention that threatened New England's secession from the Union if the War of 1812 was not ended, see Dorfman, *Economic Mind in American Civilizaton,* I, 345–346.

32. Ibid., I, 312, 293, 270.

granted in the common concerns of life without being able to give a reason for them."[33] These are the "self-evident truths" that were to play such an important role in Jefferson's thinking and writing. As president of the Presbyterian College of New Jersey, Witherspoon, in his *Lectures on Moral Philosophy,* indoctrinated his students with conservative principles of government and economics, which strongly opposed efforts at price-fixing[34] and trade monopoly.[35] Bitterly antagonistic to paper money to finance the Continental Army, Witherspoon urged the use of loans from private persons in anticipation of taxes. But, as a strong believer in the sanctity of property and of contract, he insisted that interest must be promptly and regularly paid on all borrowed funds. Ready to wrestle with almost any problem, Witherspoon "was more of an academician than a man of commerce," yet his *Essay on Money* (1786) had wide circulation and great influence during the bitter debates concerning how the nation's debts should be refunded.

The fourth of our scholars, William Barton (1755–1817), the son of an Episcopal clergyman and the nephew of David Rittenhouse, the astronomer, was educated in England. Parting company with his distinguished Tory father, Barton joined the Continental Army. Later he studied law, but it was as a scholar that he was honored by the University of Pennsylvania, the College of New Jersey (now Rutgers), and a number of learned societies. Beginning his economic writings with his *Observations on the Nature and Use of Paper Credit* (1781), Barton soon became one of the foremost advocates of a "balanced economy" which would ensure the development of agriculture, commerce, and manufacturing. As secretary of the Pennsylvania Society for the Encouragement of Manufactures and the Useful Arts, Barton explained in his *True Interest of the United States, and Particularly of Pennsylvania Considered* (1786) how a home market for agricultural produce could be developed by stimulating the growth of manufactures by tariff protection, import prohibitions, and bounties. Like James Bowdoin, Jr., Barton argued in favor of protection for American shipping by means of navigation acts that would discriminate against foreign vessels. Although an advocate of a strong national government and of a balanced economy, Barton never allowed partisan politics to control his loyalties, and in his *Dissertation on the Freedom of Navigation* (1802), which he dedicated to Jefferson, he argued that both

33. Ibid., I, 113.
34. Ibid., I, 121, 214–215.
35. Witherspoon argued that Britain might gain, rather than lose, from American independence. For details, see ibid., I, 208–209.

the agricultural and the manufacturing interests would benefit from the protection of American maritime rights.

THE LAWYERS

Just as James Madison was outstanding among the American scholars who took part in the great debates of the 1780s and 1790s, Alexander Hamilton towered above his lawyer compatriots not so much because of his exceptional legalism but because of his extraordinary capacity to comprehend complex political, economic, and administrative problems.[36] Like other leading lawyers who contributed to the great synthesis—John Adams, Fisher Ames, and John Jay—Hamilton associated good government with an elite leadership and unhesitatingly stated his reservations about the political utility of democracy. Born on the island of Nevis, he began work in a countinghouse on St. Croix when he was twelve and showed such exceptional natural ability that two years later he became the controller of a sizable wholesale mercantile enterprise. With borrowed funds he studied in a New Jersey grammar school before he entered King's College (now Columbia University) where, as a freshman, he wrote two well-reasoned tracts supporting the cause of the American colonies. With the outbreak of hostilities he joined the Continental Army, serving, as a captain of artillery, with distinction in the battles of Long Island, White Plains, Trenton, and Princeton. In March 1777 Washington appointed Hamilton his aide-de-camp and confidential secretary. His marriage to the daughter of General Philip Schuyler brought him into contact with the rich and wellborn whom he so much admired. At the close of the war he studied law in Albany, served a term in Congress (1782–1783), and then became one of the leading New York City lawyers.[37]

As a delegate to the Annapolis Convention (1786) and to the Constitutional Convention, and as an indefatigable pamphleteer[38] and propagandist advocating a strongly centralized government, Hamilton made signal contributions to the great debate before he was appointed secretary of the treasury. In that capacity, with unflagging persistence,

36. Parrington has described Hamilton as "a man of quite remarkable ability, a lucid thinker, a great lawyer, a skillful executive, a masterly organizer, a statesman of broad comprehension and inflexible purpose." Yet for all these virtues, Parrington noted Hamilton's "intellectual arrogance," his "cynical contempt," and his incapacity to manifest even a "shred of idealism." *Main Currents in American Thought*, I, 292, 295.

37. Although there are several biographical studies of Hamilton's meteoric career, by far the best account is that of Broadus Mitchell's two-volume work *Alexander Hamilton*.

38. Fifty-one of the eighty-five essays in *The Federalist* were written by Hamilton.

14

he succeeded in persuading the new Congress to fund the national and the state debts, and his two reports on public credit, which were written to justify his fiscal program, are among the more famous of our state papers.[39] Consistently Hamilton favored the "propertied interest" not only by his insistence on full payment to all holders of public debt, whether original purchasers or speculators, but by his advocacy of the need for "mutual support between business and government."[40] For this reason he favored governmental assistance for industrial development (a thesis he warmly endorsed in his *Report on Manufactures*) and joint private and governmental participation in a national bank.

Scornful of plain and ordinary people, Hamilton believed "that governmental power should be concentrated and kept at a distance from the people."[41] His whole concern might be described as macro-economic or macro-political in that he thought always in terms of national wealth, strength, security, order, and authority. These worthy ends could not, in his judgment, be achieved unless wealthy citizens were given responsibility for ensuring good government; the property-less he considered feckless and irresponsible,[42] unmindful of a nation's development. Indeed Hamilton seems to have held a very simplified view of society; to him there were really only two interests: the rich and the poor, and in his opinion "liberty is freedom to acquire and keep wealth; equality is nonsense."[43] His prescriptions for policy savored more of mercantilism than of Adam Smith and foreshadowed the thinking of Friedrich List; yet for all the strictures of the Jeffersonians, it was Hamilton's concept of a mixed economy, one that combined public and private resources, that was to shape the future of the American economy.

Next to Hamilton John Adams must be accorded high marks for his contribution to the great synthesis. He too was "a sound lawyer, a capable statesman, a vigorous thinker and courageous debater."[44] Like

39. For a vivid account of the reasons for Hamilton's report, the origin of some of the ideas it contained, and the stormy reception it received, see Mitchell, chap. III, "Rescue of Public Credit," in *Alexander Hamilton*, II, 32–56, and chap. IV, "Conflict over Funding," in ibid., II, 57–85.

40. Dorfman, *Economic Mind in American Civilization*, I, 407.

41. Allan Nevins, "Alexander Hamilton," in *Encyclopaedia of the Social Sciences*, VII, 251.

42. But surely, said Parrington, there is a fallacy in this argument. For if men are motivated by self-interest, as Hamilton believed, why would "this sovereign motive abdicate its rule among the rich and well born? . . . Do the wealthy betray no desire for greater power? Do the strong and powerful care more for good government than for class interests?" *Main Currents in American Thought*, I, 302.

43. Dorfman, *Economic Mind in American Civilization*, I, 409.

44. Parrington, *Main Currents in American Thought*, I, 308.

Hamilton he had risen from obscurity to high positions,[45] and in the process he became increasingly conservative, pragmatic, self-important, and tactless. But he had made a systematic study of various forms of government, reaching the conclusion that some form of aristocracy had been a dominant force in every variety of stable and successful government. Bluntly rejecting the idealism of Tom Paine and Thomas Jefferson, Adams "refused to be duped by fine dreams or humanitarian panaceas."[46] His *Defense of the Constitutions of Government of the United States of America,* although revealing his wide reading and rigorous analysis, nevertheless reflected his Machiavellian preconceptions. The great mass of people he considered selfish, indolent, incapable of long-range planning, turbulent, irresponsible, shiftless, and ignorant. Since every society inevitably consists of patricians and plebeians, there is no mystery why the former tend to control governments and use them for their own purposes. They are better educated, more class conscious, and therefore more unified; above all, they maintain their power by control over property. The fundamental problem of government, said Adams, much in the spirit of Aristotle, is to find a midway point between tyranny and anarchy. To do this, factional strife must be suppressed, for it is wholly unwarranted to assume that the people are the best judge of their liberties. Good government must be a judicious system of balanced interests in which the selfishness of one group will be neutralized by the counter-selfishness of other groups. The predominance of power, however, should be accorded to the owners of property, to the aristocratic elements, for there can be no stability in government unless the security of property is guaranteed, simply because property always breeds a sense of responsibility. But to prevent too narrow an aristocracy from becoming a callous ruling class, property should be as widespread as possible.

For the "natural aristocracy," consisting of persons who could prove their right to govern by acquiring and increasing their property, Adams advocated a large measure of freedom: from price-fixing schemes and from embargoes or other restraints on trade. The function of government should be to maintain public faith and confidence so that business will flourish. For these reasons Adams endorsed Hamilton's program for funding the national debt and for raising taxes so that interest

45. Adams was a member of the Continental Congress; a signer of the Declaration of Independence; commissioner to France (1778); negotiator of treaty with Holland (1782); ambassador to Court of St. James (1785); vice-president of the United States (1788–1796); president of the United States (1796–1800).
46. Parrington, *Main Currents in American Thought,* I, 307.

could be unfailingly paid. That taxes might be regressive and fall with greater severity on the poor than on the rich did not distress this successful shoemaker's son. Whatever repressed luxury among the unpropertied masses he thought desirable. Constantly fearful that the poor or propertyless might despoil the rich, the ambitious, and the foresighted, he thought the structure of government must be so designed as to control the "popular" assemblies which the enfranchisement of the small-propertied would bring into office. An upper house, a senate, composed of the rich and wellborn would, in his view, provide the nation with a "guardian of liberty and property and prevent a thoughtless process of leveling."[47] Yet this was not enough. Because of the danger of factional disputes between the House and the Senate, or among the aristocrats themselves, Adams advocated a strong executive who would have sole power to appoint civil and military officers[48] and would be able to prevent fissiparous factions and disputes.

For all of Adams's realism, there is in his political philosophy a surviving medievalism.[49] He conceived of society as made up of contrasting "orders"; and stability and social harmony required that each person should know his place and be made to accept it. Since most people would have to work to subsist, only a few men of property would have the leisure time needed for study. Differences in wealth, income, education, and privilege would therefore persist; thus, the first and foremost function of government should be to balance the orders and thereby "restrain their rivalries, so that all [orders] can enjoy their liberty and property."[50]

John Jay had a truly remarkable career. Like Hamilton he was educated at King's College, but unlike his self-made associate, Jay had wealth and aristocratic friends from birth. Admitted to the New York bar in 1768, he allied himself a few years later with the New York merchants who protested British trade restrictions. When he was elected to the First and Second Continental congresses (1774 and 1775), he first opposed the more radical groups, although he vigorously supported their program after the Declaration of Independence had been signed. Soon thereafter he distinguished himself in numerous ways. He drafted the Constitution of the State of New York[51] and was appointed chief justice of that state in 1777. The next year he was not only

47. Dorfman, *Economic Mind in American Civilization*, I, 427.
48. Ibid.
49. For this characteristic of New England thought, see my *American Economic Thought in the Seventeenth Century*, especially chaps. V, VI, VII, and XI.
50. Dorfman, *Economic Mind in American Civilization*, I, 428.
51. The first of the new constitutions to provide for the election of governors by popular vote.

elected to the Continental Congress but chosen president of the Congress. Two years later he went to Spain to seek recognition for the American Confederation. In 1782, in Paris, he acted as one of the commissioners who negotiated peace terms with Britain. When he served as secretary for foreign affairs (1784–1789), he realized how ineffective the government under the Articles of Confederation actually was, and this intimate experience convinced him of the need for a strong national government. It is therefore understandable why he joined forces with Hamilton and Madison and contributed five articles to *The Federalist*. Once the new Constitution had been adopted and the new government formed, President Washington appointed Jay the nation's first chief justice of the Supreme Court, a position he held until he went to England in 1794 to negotiate an agreement now known as "Jay's Treaty."[52] Finally before he retired from public life, Jay served as governor of New York from 1795 to 1801. Although a Federalist, he has been described as a "moderate conservative with democratic sympathies."[53]

A graduate of Harvard, so respected by his alma mater that he was offered the presidency of that institution in 1804, an honor that he declined, Fisher Ames achieved distinction as a lawyer, a political essayist, and an orator. Elected to the House of Representatives of the First Congress under the new Constitution, he soon became one of the prominent members of the Federalist party who led the legislative maneuvers for many of President Washington's policies. A fiery orator, Ames bitterly assailed the ideas and program of Thomas Jefferson. Long before he came to Congress he had inveighed against democracy, writing caustic newspaper essays lambasting the leaders of Shays's Rebellion. Ancient history, he argued, had convincingly shown the dangers of tyranny, a perverted form of government that had its origins in democracy. Because his philosophy began with the premise that all men are naturally evil, ever hungering for wealth and fame, democracy would perforce be government by the worst elements and must lead either to anarchy or, as a counter measure, to tyranny. A doctrinaire conservative, Ames had favored harsh measures to suppress Shays's Rebellion, and this Massachusetts experience deepened his conviction that only an "energetic" national government could

52. So designated by American friends of France who were highly critical of the provisions of the treaty and who wished to disassociate themselves from the agreement because Jay made too many concessions and because the treaty favored Britain against the French revolutionists. The best study of this diplomatic episode is still Samuel Flagg Bemis, *Jay's Treaty: A Study in Commerce and Diplomacy* (New Haven, Conn., 1923).
53. William MacDonald, in *Encyclopaedia of the Social Sciences*, VII, 377.

ensure "the greatest permanent happiness of the greatest number of people."[54]

THE SOUTHERN PLANTERS

Although a considerable number of plantation owners were legislators, who in many ways contributed to the congressional discussion of appropriate public policies, two planters, Thomas Jefferson and John Taylor of Caroline, were by all odds the most influential representatives of southern agrarian opinion. Both were well informed, conversant with history, politics, and philosophy, and felicitous and persuasive writers. Of the two, Jefferson demonstrated more originality, a wider range of knowledge, and, for all of Taylor's criticism of the "paper aristocracy," a deeper and more sincere idealism. Although admitted to the bar following his graduation from William and Mary College, Jefferson only briefly practiced law. After his election to the Virginia House of Burgesses (1767) he devoted most of his energy and talents to politics, diplomacy, agriculture, education, and, not least important, to study.

One of the ablest exponents of the eighteenth-century philosophy of enlightenment, Jefferson was a passionate defender of democracy not only against the tidewater aristocracy but against Federalists like Hamilton and Ames who doubted whether the rank and file of common people could be trusted with affairs of government. Because the estate he had inherited lay on the Virginia frontier, Jefferson had come to appreciate the inherent wisdom that poorly educated or illiterate small farmers and frontiersmen possessed. He envisioned an ideal society consisting of communities of farmers, enlightened by free schools, able to govern themselves through democratic institutions; and he felt that the main duty of a benevolent gentry, such as he represented, should be to widen and deepen the democratic process. His residence in France brought him into personal contact with leading members of the physiocratic school of economic thought and gave him a philosophical affirmation for his instinctive preference for an agrarian economy, making him even more reluctant than before to envisage an America blemished with all the ugly by-products that industrialization had produced in Europe. Bitterly opposed to the social dualism that aristocratic government had created in Europe, he was fearful of great cities peopled with a hapless proletariat that industrialization might bring. A free yeomanry should, in his opinion, be the mainstay of American freedom, and since this seemed so eminently desirable and so feasible in a country that possessed a vast public domain, he looked

54. Dorfman, *Economic Mind in American Civilization*, I, 270.

with disfavor on the Federalist program with its emphasis of tariffs, banks, funding operations,[55] and the stimulation of manufacturing.[56]

From the time of the Virginia convention of 1774, for which he prepared resolutions subsequently published as a pamphlet,[57] Jefferson became one of the most ardent advocates of revolution. Elected to the Continental Congress in 1775, he wrote an initial draft of the Declaration of Independence which proved so acceptable that it was adopted essentially unchanged. But Jefferson was not content with a program that called for mere political separation from Britain; he thought it necessary that American state government should also be cleansed of aristocratic taint. First as a member of the state legislature and then as governor, Jefferson turned his attention to reforming the laws of Virginia, spearheading the movement that led to the abolition of entail and primogeniture, the guarantee of freedom of religion by the disestablishment of the state church, the extension and improvement of public education, and more particularly, the establishment of the University of Virginia. When in 1783 he was elected to the United States Congress, he drafted a plan for the political organization of the Northwest Territory before he went to Europe where he succeeded Benjamin Franklin as minister to France. He returned in 1789 to become Washington's secretary of state. In 1796 he was elected vice-president of the United States, and then, in 1801, when he was tied with Aaron Burr in the presidential election, he was chosen president by the House of Representatives after Alexander Hamilton had given him rather unexpected support.[58]

Although, as will presently be shown, far too much has been made of the differences between Hamilton and Jefferson, there were some really sharp contrasts in their outlook. Whereas Hamilton distrusted the people, Jefferson, who thought men were inclined to be good unless corrupted by bad institutions, sought to create the schools, the legal arrangements, and the forms of government which would make

55. Jefferson agreed to support Hamilton's funding and state debt assumption program on condition that the United States capital be located on the Potomac, although he later alleged he had been tricked into making this bargain. For details, see Mitchell, *Alexander Hamilton*, II, 79–83.

56. As president, however, he was compelled to modify his views when interference with American import and export trade by both the British and the French convinced him of the political need for domestic manufactures in order to ensure the continued independence of the United States. For details of the circumstances that led to this change of opinion, see Dumas Malone, *Jefferson the President: First Term, 1801–1805* (Boston, 1970).

57. *A Summary View of the Rights of America.*

58. Hamilton, who had long feuded with Burr in New York State politics, chose to throw his support to Jefferson because he respected the Virginian's integrity and distrusted Burr's ruthless ambition.

possible the fullest development of the talents of all the people. His view of freedom was therefore based on a concept of becoming that reflected both his idealism and his optimism. Yet it was actually in this very concept of becoming that Jefferson's philosophy proved inadequate. By reason of its amazing variety of resources, the versatility of its native and immigrant population, and its strategic location, the United States was destined to develop a far more complex and diversified economy than Jefferson had foreseen. The advocates of industrialization, whose program Jefferson rather unwittingly assisted by his Embargo Act,[59] understood more accurately than the sage of Monticello that the United States would not long remain a simple agricultural society. Yet even though his hope that America could remain essentially agrarian was not to be realized, certain values of Jeffersonian thought have permanently and profoundly influenced the American climate of opinion: limited government; the accountability of public officials; the dispersal of power among federal, state, and local governments; a respect for individual rights; a "canny knowledge of man's fallibility and government's weakness";[60] but above all a "conviction that here in America, through the instrumentality of political democracy, the lot of the common man should somehow be made better."[61]

John Taylor shared Jefferson's preference for an agrarian economy and even more vigorously defended the "states' rights" doctrine that was to play such a role in the nineteenth-century conflict between North and South. A master of vitriolic prose, Taylor castigated the Federalists, branding them as "parasitic, aristocratic, stockjobbers," who "by means of their law-created privileges filched their gains from the industry of the sole productive class of farmers."[62] His writings, published at Fredericksburg, Richmond, Washington, and Georgetown, made a deep impression on southern public opinion, intensifying the antagonism of the South toward centralized government, industrialization, and the "moneyed aristocracy." Although he greatly admired Jefferson, whose life-span and life-style paralleled his,[63] Taylor's views were far more radical on some issues than Jefferson's, more con-

59. This legislation placing a ban on all foreign commerce was recommended by Jefferson and enacted by Congress on December 22, 1807.
60. William V. Shannon, "Mr. Jefferson's Return," *New York Times* (October 17, 1971), pp. 4, 11.
61. Parrington, *Main Currents in American Thought*, I, 343.
62. Dorfman, *Economic Mind in American Civilization*, I, 360.
63. Taylor (1750–1824), like Jefferson (1743–1826), attended William and Mary College, served ten years in the Virginia legislature, practiced law, managed a large plantation cultivated by a slave work force, and served for short periods in the United States Senate.

servative on others. He vigorously opposed Hamilton's funding program, challenged the loose construction of the Constitution, and went so far as to advance the idea of interposition by states when the federal government encroached on their rights.[64] With blistering contempt he attacked John Adams's arguments in favor of government by a "natural aristocracy," and branded Hamilton's ill-concealed efforts to create a "paper aristocracy" as a shameful attempt to transfer legislative power from "natural interests" to "artificial interests," from legitimate groups of farmers, merchants, and manufacturers to illegitimate interests created by public debt, incorporated banks, and the monopolization of public offices. He asserted that by the machinations of a new aristocracy of stockjobbers, five million people composing natural interests were being oppressed by five thousand members of artificial interests.

The reasons why southern planters opposed tariffs, bounties, or any other aid for nascent industries were, of course, quite understandable. Their agricultural staples—tobacco, rice, grain—could not benefit from protective duties since they were priced in overseas markets. Duties could only raise the prices of manufactures. Consequently the export-oriented farmers were best served by free trade and the territorial division of labor. Against this planter contentment for the short run, Hamilton explained how the development of manufactures would, in the long run, make possible a fuller utilization of America's natural and human resources. "As the finance minister of a rising empire," Hamilton[65] "broke the tables of the law and substituted for them discretion." It was precisely such "discretion" that infuriated John Taylor. He charged that Hamilton had formed "a ministerial corps" that was "polluting every operation of the government." What Taylor failed to appreciate was that the secretary of the treasury had to be a policy maker and not merely a clerk who received and paid out public funds.

Whereas Jefferson might be described as an apologetic slaveholder,[66] Taylor staunchly defended the "peculiar institution," arguing that it would gradually atrophy since, as the white population increased, the wages of white labor would fall to such an extent that it would no longer be profitable to own slaves. Until that equilibrium was reached,

64. This doctrine was most vigorously articulated in his *Construction Construed* (Richmond, 1820) and further developed in his *New Views of the Constitution of the United States* (Washington, 1823).

65. Mitchell, *Alexander Hamilton*, II, 141, 267.

66. As a young legislator Jefferson had proposed a plan for the abolition of slavery, but he reluctantly abandoned this hope when he realized how enmeshed the institution of slavery was with the general laws of property and a range of political, social, and economic issues.

a spatial diffusion of slavery would lead to better subsistence for the slave population since in the newer soil-rich states the per slave productivity would rise, while in the old states slaves would be relatively fewer. Whatever liberalism Taylor may have had deserted him when he discussed the increasingly controversial subject of slavery. After employing every possible justification for the denial of freedom for slaves (until slavery became clearly unprofitable), he rested his case on a "most rigid defense"[67] of property. Oddly enough the writer who had most bitterly assailed the aristocratic doctrines of John Adams agreed completely with the New Englander's belief in the sanctity of property, and, since slaves were property, not even the state, in Taylor's view, could interfere with such valuable private assets. When Taylor, in the guise of a Jeffersonian democrat, branded Adams an "aristocrat," Adams's response was that no one could be more aristocratic than a southern planter who owned a great estate and a large number of slaves.

THE MID-ATLANTIC GENTRY

In much the same way that Thomas Jefferson and John Taylor reflected the opinions of southern plantation owners, George Logan and John Beale Bordley served as spokesmen for mid-Atlantic large-scale agriculture, although both were involved in a variety of other activities. Logan, whose life-span (1753–1821) paralleled that of Jefferson and Taylor, was the grandson of James Logan, William Penn's agent in Pennsylvania; he inherited the Logan estates and other investments from his father, a wealthy Philadelphia merchant. After schooling in England, George Logan was apprenticed to a Philadelphia merchant and received the customary training. Finding the mercantile world too routine, he returned to Europe and entered the medical school of the University of Edinburgh from which he received the M.D. degree in 1779. Meantime he had visited the Continent and found time to read the works of Adam Smith and the physiocrats. When he returned to Pennsylvania in 1780, he established himself as an estate farmer and became a leader in undertaking agricultural experiments, making careful efforts to farm his ancestral estates scientifically.

Like Jefferson, Logan was profoundly influenced by the French physiocrats, and in his writings, especially his *Letters to the Yeomanry,* he propagated Quesnay's doctrine that agriculture is the sole "productive" employment because it alone creates a surplus over and above the costs of subsistence. The amount of this surplus varies with the investments that are made and with the agro-technical methods

67. Dorfman, *Economic Mind in American Civilization,* I, 402.

that are employed. Most American farms he considered too small, with the result that farmers could not make the necessary investments from their meager "net product." Unlike Richard Henry Lee and William Findley, both of whom championed the cause of small-scale or frontier farmers, Logan insisted that large estates had superior efficiency because their owners or administrators were better educated and because the scale of operations would permit the investments needed to maximize the "net product."

Although Logan, an ardent Republican who helped Jefferson to win his struggle with the Federalists, might be described as an agrarian liberal, he considered the right of property to be absolute and sacrosanct. Every property owner, he said, ought to have complete freedom to do whatever he wished with his property. Civil law should enforce contracts but ought never attempt to restrict entrepreneurial freedom. Competition and free trade will result in just prices for all commodities and ensure the best rewards for human endeavor. Arbitrary commercial regulations, preferential navigation laws, subsidies, and all such interventions distort the workings of a "natural order" and result in monopoloid situations and unfair gains. Following the physiocratic prescription, Logan considered all indirect taxes, such as excises or tariffs, unjust and pernicious. They usually confiscate some of the net product that farmers have produced and lead to inflation not only of prices but of wages, thereby damaging a country in its international trade relations. He opposed Hamilton's funding plan because a public debt will inevitably lead to the use of indirect taxes to service it. He was equally antagonistic toward Hamilton's attempt to stimulate manufactures, arguing that the livelihood of thousands of mechanics would be sacrificed in order to increase the gains of a few factory owners.

Logan, who served six years in the Pennsylvania legislature, went to France in 1798 to promote better relations between that country and the United States. Bitterly criticized for this venture, he was treated with contempt by George Washington; moreover, in 1799, Congress passed the "Logan Act" which forebade private citizens from undertaking paradiplomatic negotiations.[68] Nevertheless Logan was appointed United States senator in 1801 and was reelected when his term expired. His friendship with Jefferson and his familiarity with French physiocratic thought made him a forceful protagonist of the agricultural interest. He was one of the founders of the Philadelphia Society for Promoting Agriculture and was elected a member of the American Philosophical Society in 1793.

68. For further details about the "Logan Act," see Mitchell, *Alexander Hamilton,* II, 312–313.

While Logan shifted his attention from medicine to agriculture, his Maryland compatriot John Beale Bordley forsook a notable career in law so that he could carry out experiments with new crops and new rotations on his landed estate. He had been the prothonotary of Baltimore County in 1753, judge of the Maryland Provincial Court in 1766, and judge of the Admiralty in 1767. From 1770, however, Bordley devoted all his attention to scientific farming. His operations comprehended much more than field-crop farming and animal husbandry, since on his estate brewing, salt-making, and the firing of brick also constituted important activities. In 1791 he moved to Philadelphia, where with Logan he helped to establish the Philadelphia Society for Promoting Agriculture. His *Essays on Husbandry* (1794) described an immutable "natural order" so inexorable that it ultimately frustrates all the foolish efforts of legislators to "warp employment against its natural bent."[69] Lawmakers who with the best of intentions wish to assist the manufacturing interest may discover they have done so at the expense of the basic national agricultural interest. Bordley recognized that manufacturing enterprises would ultimately be established in the United States since skilled artisans would gradually come from Europe. What he opposed, as did most agrarians, was any effort to speed up this "natural" process by means of tariffs and bounties. But although Logan and Bordley disparaged any and all efforts to hasten the development of manufactures, they unabashedly advocated both governmental and cooperative assistance for agriculture. Bordley, for example, recommended the establishment of "pattern farms" to demonstrate better farming methods and the dispatch of "ingenious persons" to Europe who could observe the more advanced agricultural techniques practiced there.[70]

Although Logan and Bordley were the most articulate and persuasive representatives of the mid-Atlantic and northern agrarians, a number of other writers made useful contributions in the shaping of public policy, particularly Francis Adrian van der Kemp, George Clymer, Richard Peters, Timothy Pickering, and Dr. S. L. Mitchell.

SPOKESMEN FOR SMALL FARMERS AND FRONTIERSMEN

The great mass of small farmers had few advocates in the Constitutional Era for two main reasons. Many were illiterate, and those who were not were normally too busy with their insistent farm duties to

69. *Essays on Husbandry,* p. 378.
70. Ibid., pp. 444, 445, 447. For more details about Bordley's proposals, and a survey of recommendations by other agrarian writers for governmental intervention on behalf of the agricultural interest, see pp. 202–204.

write books or pamphlets. Fortunately a few publicists emerged who spoke on their behalf, the foremost of whom were Richard Henry Lee and William Findley. Although born a Virginia patrician on a large plantation, Lee nevertheless proved to be a staunch defender of small farmers. From his maiden speech in the Virginia House of Burgesses (1758), when he proposed a resolution restricting the importation of slaves, Lee boldly voiced his liberal views. A member of the Virginia Committee of Correspondence that organized resistance to British restrictions on colonial freedom, and a delegate to the Continental Congress (1774–1779), Lee, like Jefferson and John Witherspoon, signed the Declaration of Independence.

The debates that antedated the adoption of the Constitution, however, elicited the mature and memorable opinions of Richard Henry Lee. When Hamilton, Jay, and Madison, in *The Federalist,* were pressing for the prompt approval of the Constitution, Lee in carefully reasoned essays criticized their undue haste, denying that the political and economic situation was as critical as the triumverate averred, and counseled careful consideration of all the possible consequences of the degree of governmental centralization that the Constitution might produce. Like John Taylor, he felt that the rights of the states were being unduly infringed, but, unlike Taylor, he argued that this erosion of states' rights would have its greatest impact upon the small farmers, the "men of middling property" who constituted the "weight of the community," because they were the majority of American citizens.

Lee's *Letters from the Federal Farmer*[71] asserted that the proposed Constitution was patently undemocratic and an instrument that would result in the subjection of the majority of the American people to the control of a minority. He granted that the Articles of Confederation needed revisions, but he felt that the enemies of democracy were "making undue capital out of the shortcomings of an emergency government."[72] Rejecting Hamilton's arguments in favor of government by an elite and John Adams's advocacy of a "natural aristocracy," Lee in many ways anticipated Lincoln's conception of government of the people, by the people, and for the people. He reached this conclusion by his analysis of the occupational composition of the economy of eighteenth-century America. The agitation over the Constitution, he said, could be ascribed to "two very unprincipled parties." One party "is

71. The full title was *Observations Leading to a Fair Examination of the System of Government Proposed by the Late Convention; and to Several Essential and Necessary Alterations in It. In a Number of Letters from the Federal Farmer to the Republicans* (1787). Reprinted in P. L. Ford, *Pamphlets on the Constitution* (1888).

72. Parrington, *Main Currents in American Thought,* I, 290.

composed of little insurgents, men in debt who want no law and who want a share of the property of others." But these Shaysites or levelers Lee considered less dangerous than the extremists at the opposite ideological pole, men who "avariciously grasp at all power and property," aristocrats and their sycophants who dislike "free and equal government," and who "go systematically to work" to mold governmental institutions that will solidify their power and influence.[73] To favor the first of these groups would mean anarchy; to accede to the demands of the latter group would mean "a transfer of power from the many to the few." Neither group truly represented the American people, said Lee, for between these two parties are "the men of middling property, men not in debt," people "content with republican government" who are "not aiming at immense fortunes, offices and power."[74]

While Richard Henry Lee questioned whether the new Constitution would ensure political and economic freedom for the middle classes— the small farmers, mechanics, and other people with but little property —another critic, William Findley, emerged as the advocate, dragoman, and paladin for the frontiersmen. Born in Ireland of Scottish ancestry, Findley came to America in 1763. Versatile and industrious he worked as a weaver, taught school, and operated a farm before he entered the Continental Army. At the close of the war he settled in western Pennsylvania where as a champion of the frontiersmen he became one of the leaders of the Whiskey Rebellion. Indeed it was his connection with that revolt against the federal excise taxes that led him, in 1796, after he had become an advocate of a compromise settlement of the rebellion, to publish his *History of the Insurrection in the Four Western Counties of Pennsylvania*.[75]

As a member of Congress Findley had openly and energetically attacked Hamilton's entire fiscal program, castigating the secretary of the treasury as an agent of the "monied interest" whose members "have no common interest with the citizens otherwise than to oppress

73. *Letters from the Federal Farmer*, p. 43.
74. Ibid.
75. As part of his fiscal program, Hamilton proposed the use of excise taxes, and, following his recommendation, Congress imposed a number of such indirect taxes including an excise on spirituous liquors. In western Pennsylvania distillers refused to pay the tax, and in this action they had the support of the majority of farmers who, owing to their distance from wholesale markets, could only find a cash crop by converting their grain into whiskey which could be transported by pack horses over mountain trails. The political leaders of the region—Findley, Hugh Brackenridge, and Albert Gallatin—branded the whiskey excises as unfair and discriminatory. The stubborn efforts of the government to collect the excises led to violence in 1794. Troops were dispatched to suppress the rebellion, and Hamilton himself accompanied the expedition. For a compact account of this unhappy episode, see Mitchell, *Alexander Hamilton*, II, 308–330.

them."[76] Caustically Findley alleged that Hamilton's funding and debt assumption program would enable the wealthy seaboard speculators to absorb the property of the frontier farmers. An aristocracy "supported by public revenue," said Findley, is far more vicious than a feudal aristocracy because it has no integral connection with any natural interest. A truly republican government must, above all, protect the native dignity and the equal rights of all citizens.[77]

THE MERCHANTS

Quite a number of the members of the Constitutional Convention no doubt reflected the views and hopes of the mercantile interest;[78] moreover, once the new Congress had been elected, the large number of petitions from merchants showed very clearly that the government would be expected to consider the wishes of this important occupational group. But very few merchants wrote books or pamphlets, although two merchants, one from Philadelphia, the other from Boston, did put their thoughts into print. The most prolific of the two, Pelatiah Webster, was born in Lebanon, Connecticut, went to Yale, studied theology, and was ordained. At the age of twenty-nine, he became a merchant in Philadelphia, a profession that he seems to have followed for the next twenty years. Just how successful he was is not known but he had his share of trouble during the Revolution. En route to Boston in 1777, his shipload of flour and iron was seized by the British and he was clapped into a Newport prison. The next year brought equally bad luck: this time much of his Philadelphia property was confiscated while he languished in another jail. Yet in his writings, Webster fulminated far more against American price-fixing laws than against the British government.

From 1776, when he published "An Essay on the Danger of Too Much Circulating Cash in a State,"[79] he wrote extensively on a wide range of subjects,[80] his last essay appearing in 1795, the year of his death. Webster probably did more than any other American writer of

76. *A Review of the Revenue System Adopted by the First Congress* (Philadelphia, 1794), pp. 52–53.
77. Ibid., p. 128.
78. It should be remembered that the Annapolis Convention of 1786, which helped spawn the idea of a convention to propose the amendment or the replacement of the Articles of Confederation, was called to improve the domestic and foreign trade of the United States.
79. Reprinted in his *Political Essays.*
80. Thus, in 1783, he published *A Dissertation on the Political Union and Constitution of the Thirteen United States of North America,* a thoughtful and imaginative essay which anticipated some of the fundamental ideas that were later incorporated into the Constitution. For details, see Channing, *History of the United States,* III, 475–477.

his generation to justify and defend "a free open market" as the most efficient means for providing a nation with the largest possible supply of high quality goods. All efforts at price-fixing he branded as "abridgements of natural liberty."[81] Since competition is the best way to prevent the exploitation of consumers, all governmental attempts to regulate trade by embargoes, tender acts, or price-fixing are not only irritating but counter-productive; "laws should conform to the natural cause of things." Only when every man can make his own decisions, only when every man can "taste and enjoy the sweets of that liberty of person and property" will social contentment be maximized. Business can never flourish in despotic countries,[82] said Webster, because despotism threatens the security of property and discourages people from making investments. The vigor of enterprise depends on entrepreneurial freedom.

During the troubled years of the war, when the Continental Congress resorted to the issue of paper money to finance its military forces, Webster was able to offer sound advice. At his suggestion, in March 1780, Congress devalued the continental bills of credit forty to one for specie in payment of state quotas of taxes. Following another of Webster's proposals, Congress provided a scale of depreciation for loan-office certificates, based on their value at date of issue. In 1781 still another of Webster's proposals was adopted—the appointment of a superintendent of finance to systematize the government's fiscal program. Two years later Webster rather modified his objections to governmental interference with trade by arguing in favor of an interstate agreement to impose import duties. He did, however, propose that the enforcement of the Tax Act should be entrusted to merchants who would have the "professional honour" to collect the prescribed duties. Once a truly national government was established, said Webster, one essential component should be a chamber of commerce composed of merchant delegates from the trading towns.[83] Here then was a very concrete proposal for the legislative representation of the commercial interest.

While Pelatiah Webster dealt almost exclusively with problems of domestic trade, his contemporary James Bowdoin, Jr., a Bostonian merchant, raised questions about the tactics that the United States

81. *Political Essays,* p. 24.
82. Ibid., p. 439.
83. Under Webster's plan, the chamber of commerce would not only collect revenue for the government but would give advice on all problems of trade. The details were given in his *Dissertation of the Political Union and Constitution of the Thirteen United States.*

government should adopt concerning foreign trade.[84] He thought it absolutely necessary to protect "native" American merchants against "alien" British merchants and their agents. Rejecting David Hume's criticism of the balance of trade as too abstract, he pointed out that unless a nation such as the United States had an import surplus of specie, the value of property would fall, precipitating unrest and injustice. Yet, unless American traders were favored by some preferences, the indebtedness of Americans to British shipowners and factors would increase, and a colonial relation would be restored despite the political independence of the United States. Since the United States had no gold or silver mines, American merchants were the only source of the nation's money supply. By finding markets for American products, they provide domestic employment; moreover, whatever they earn from their business, they spend in the United States as contrasted with British merchants who engross the trade of the southern states but spend their profits in England and Scotland. The proper policy that the American government should follow should be to enact navigation acts[85] that will give preferences to American shipowners. Although Bowdoin's recommendations were rejected by Jefferson, who advocated reciprocal arrangements with foreign nations, it will be shown[86] that Bowdoin's recommendations bore some legislative fruit when the Congress decided to enforce discriminatory tonnage duties.

In his advocacy of government assistance for the American merchant marine, James Bowdoin, Jr., was reiterating a demand that had been made a decade earlier by his father, Governor James Bowdoin. Fearful that the Constitutional Convention would not grant control over commerce to the federal government, the senior Bowdoin had attempted to persuade the states, one by one, to adopt navigation acts modeled on those of Great Britain.

THE ECONOMISTS

Problems arising from monetary, fiscal, credit, and balance of payments difficulties engaged the attention of a large number of late eighteenth-century American scholars, lawyers, merchants, bureaucrats, and businessmen. The contributions to this range of topics made by John Witherspoon, William Barton, Alexander Hamilton, and Pelatiah Webster have been briefly noted. Three other writers deserve

84. In his *Opinions respecting the Commercial Intercourse between the United States of America and the Dominions of Great Britain* (Boston, 1797).

85. *Observations upon the Necessity and Importance of the American Navigation Act* (Boston, 1797).

86. See below, p. 259.

special mention: Samuel Gale, a Tory who served as a cashier and assistant paymaster with the British armies; James Sullivan, a leading businessman of Massachusetts; and James Swan, a skillful albeit unscrupulous enterpriser, whose checkered career undoubtedly weakened the influence that his writings might otherwise have had.

Samuel Gale joined the British forces at Sandy Hook in 1776 after troubled and unhappy employment as a deputy surveyor in Cumberland County, New York. Born and well educated in England, he came to Philadelphia in 1770. Just why he was befriended by the surveyor general of New York is not clear, but his assignment as a surveyor soon threw him into bitter controversy over the "New Hampshire Grants." Driven out of disputed territory by the Allen brothers in 1773, he became a marked man when the Revolution broke out.[87] He was arrested and brought to Connecticut where he was imprisoned until he was released on parole after intercession by James Duane, an influential New York State landowner and revolutionist. Soon thereafter, however, Gale was believed to be in correspondence with the British, as he probably was, since before he could be arrested again he joined the British forces.[88] It was during the time he served with the British in South Carolina and Florida that he began to write his four essays *On the Nature and Principles of Public Credit* to explain how the British government could utilize the public debt to animate the British economy.

His essays, which have been very skillfully summarized by Dorfman,[89] reflect Gale's thoughtful reaction to the controversies concerning the utility and the hazards of paper money that raged in the colonies before and during the Revolution. His most important argument, and one which may well have influenced Alexander Hamilton,[90] asserted that a public debt not only was a proper means for financing a war but could compel, by taxation to service it, an increase in the fraction of incomes saved. By the proper administration of a public debt, an entire economy could be stimulated, since an increase in commerce and industry depends upon the rate of capital formation.

The second writer, James Sullivan, whose views on money, credit, and banking had, beyond any doubt, a profound influence on the climate of opinion in the Constitutional Era, had served as attorney

87. Dorfman, *Economic Mind in American Civilization*, I, 2–29.
88. Ibid.
89. Ibid., pp. 229–238.
90. The parallel reasoning between Gale's *Essays* and Hamilton's *Reports on Public Credit* is so striking that it seems likely that Hamilton might have been familiar with Gale's writings.

general of Massachusetts.[91] A successful businessman who had made a fortune from canal and bridge investments, Sullivan proved to be also a persuasive publicist even though his *Path to Riches* (1792) lacks the rigorous logic found in Gale's *Essays*. Sullivan's thesis was that commerce was the "path to riches" and commerce requires money as a medium of exchange. Although the "real money" is specie, paper money can serve as a representative of real money provided its issue is strictly controlled by a central bank as was the case in England. Unfortunately, said Sullivan, in the United States the several states permit the establishment of private banks designed to benefit a few favored stockholders. The issue posed by Sullivan therefore raised the question of the societally desirable boundaries of entrepreneurial freedom, an issue that centered temporarily on bank charters, but one that had far wider implications.

The career of James Swan was so bizarre that the impact of his *National Arithmetick* is difficult to appraise in view of the characterization of him by the American minister to France as a "corrupt, unprincipled rascal."[92] Swan came to Boston from Scotland, began his career there as an apprentice, but soon, after an advantageous marriage, embarked on a variety of profitable enterprises. He was one of the "Indians" who staged the Boston Tea Party, after which he served in the Revolutionary Army where he rose to the rank of a colonel. Combining politics and business, he became a member of the Massachusetts legislature, while meantime engaging in trade, privateering, insurance, toll-bridge ventures, army contracts, and speculation in real estate, continental securities, and sequestrated Tory property. He obtained some publicity when he proposed to end slavery by the creation of exclusive trading companies to employ black labor in Africa, compensating the Negroes with American manufactured goods.

Although quite a number of Americans had read Hume, Adam Smith, James Steuart, Locke, or Harrington, James Swan seems to have been the only American resident who had studied the writings of Sir William Petty. Following Petty's methodology,[93] Swan published, in 1786, an analysis of the economic difficulties of the American Confederacy (and of Massachusetts) which he called *National Arithmetick*. In it he recommended that indentured servants rather than slaves be used to enlarge the American work force, and he proposed that the immigration of persons who would become free (after they had com-

---

91. He later was elected governor of Massachusetts.
92. Dorfman, *Economic Mind in American Civilization*, I, 311.
93. First articulated in his *Political Arithmetick* (London, 1690), and further explained in his *Political Anatomy of Ireland* (London, 1691).

pleted their temporary servitude) should be stimulated by tax exemptions. But as the labor force expanded, businessmen should be assisted, so that appropriate investments would be made that would increase employment. The fishing industry, maritime commerce, and domestic manufacturing should be the most important sectors of the economy to be favored.[94] Meantime luxury and useless expenditures should be curtailed.[95] Taxation should be used not only to raise revenue but to compel proper utilization of national resources[96] and to stimulate new branches of production.

Unfortunately this talented man, who had a more comprehensive view of macro-economics than any of his countemporaries, proved to be a reckless international adventurer, and his sly operations destroyed confidence in him. Finding himself bankrupt from overextended speculative ventures, he moved to France in 1788, where he offered to put the principles of his *National Arithmetick* at the service of the successive revolutionary governments. By speculating in American public debt, soliciting French government contracts, and by a variety of other transactions, Swan seems to have "evolved an elaborate far-flung organization"[97] capable of all manner of double-dealing with the French and the British. Of his integrity there may have been some doubt, but not of his keen insight into economic problems.

THE INDUSTRIAL ADVOCATES

The most carefully reasoned arguments in favor of governmental assistance for nascent industries in the Age of Washington is to be found in Alexander Hamilton's *Report on Manufactures,* a study which had been requested by the House of Representatives in 1789 and which was submitted to that body in December 1791. A great deal of investigation had been necessary to obtain data on existing industries, and the opinions of businessmen and other knowledgeable persons had been solicited.[98] Since the precise recommendations Hamilton made will be discussed in some detail in a later chapter, it need only be pointed out here that the basic argument of the *Report* was that the development of a wide range of industrial enterprises would benefit several interests—agricultural, commercial, financial—and not merely the industrial groups.

94. *National Arithmetick,* pp. 10, 13–16.
95. Ibid., pp. 21–22, 61–62.
96. Thus Swan proposed that timber producers should be taxed enough to compel them to convert cutover land into arable fields. Ibid., pp. 18–19.
97. Dorfman, *Economic Mind in American Civilization,* I, 311.
98. For details, see Arthur H. Cole, ed., *Industrial and Commercial Correspondence of Alexander Hamilton Anticipating His Report on Manufacturing* (Chicago, 1928).

Although the existence of three drafts of the *Report* in Hamilton's handwriting indicates that he wrote the document himself,[99] he was by no means the only advocate of governmental stimulants to foster industrial development. It will be recalled that William Barton and James Swan warmly recommended such a policy. Next to Hamilton, however, the most energetic advocate of a policy of industrialization was Tench Coxe (1755–1824). With distinguished ancestors, a good education at the College of Philadelphia, and sound mercantile training in his father's countinghouse, Coxe had both valuable contacts and business experience when he served as a delegate to the Annapolis Convention in 1786 and as a member of the Continental Congress in 1788. Although he had engaged in a variety of business ventures—trade, banking, and real estate transactions—he eagerly sought governmental posts since he had not been too successful in business. His ambition seemed to be realized when he was appointed assistant secretary of the treasury in 1790, but his political opportunism soon led to disagreement with Hamilton.[100] When his office was abolished, he was appointed commissioner of the revenue in 1792, a position he held until 1798, when he was dismissed by President John Adams who was outraged that Coxe had become a Republican. He returned to Philadelphia where Jefferson appointed him a purveyor of public supplies, a post he held from 1803 to 1812.

Although his politics may have lacked consistency, his constancy in trying to advance industrial development never wavered. Like William Barton, Coxe advocated a "balanced" national economy, and he devoted much of his energy to the Philadelphia Society for the Encouragement of Manufactures and the Useful Arts. Interested in new projects, Coxe helped publicize Samuel Slater's introduction of British-type machinery in the cotton textile industry. He urged that public commissioners be provided with government-supplied funds to attract foreign businessmen to the United States. Like Hamilton, he was convinced that the development of manufactures would create such a sizable nonagricultural population that important home markets for agricultural produce—food and fibers—would thereby be created. Navigation and the fishing industry would likewise be stimulated, while employment would increase and investment opportunities grow in number and variety. But to overcome temporary disadvantages, public assistance for nascent industries was necessary; in addition to tariff duties, Coxe recommended the payment of bounties and the free importation of necessary raw materials. Like Bowdoin, he urged the

99. Mitchell, *Alexander Hamilton*, II, 151.
100. For details, see ibid., pp. 287–289.

enactment of an American navigation act to reduce the excessive importation of foreign goods which he alleged were dumped in the American market at less than cost prices in order to frustrate American industrial ventures.

A vivid and felicitous writer, Coxe indefatigably helped spread the new gospel of economic progress by means of occupational diversification. In a series of publications written between 1789 and 1814,[101] he explained his theories of economic development. Agriculture, he urged, cannot absorb all the manpower available from the growth of population and immigration because many people are too poor to engage in farming. Suitable investments in machinery not only will provide employment but will increase the productivity of workers. Meantime geographical division of labor will be facilitated; the South could produce cotton and other raw materials, the West grain and meat, the East and Northeast manufactured goods. All the regions would benefit from the exchange of their productions.

Hamilton and Coxe were advocates of mechanized, factory-type industrialization. As will be explained,[102] their proposals ran afoul of the strong objections of the defenders of the mechanics interest. George Logan, for example, condemned "that baneful system of European Management which dooms the human facilities" and converts men into machines.[103] Jefferson had fully as strong misgivings. But there were only a few spokesmen for the mechanics, and Absalom Aimwell's[104] Lecture Containing a Short History of Mechanics[105] is, for that reason, a particularly welcomed document.

THE PREACHERS

By the last quarter of the eighteenth century the influence of the clergy on public policy had been reduced far below what it had once been in the days of John Cotton.[106] Yet the "enlightenment" that Jeffer-

101. *An Enquiry into the Principles on Which a Commercial System for the United States of America Should Be Founded* (Philadelphia, 1789); *A Brief Examination of Lord Sheffield's Observations on the Commerce of the United States of America* (Philadelphia, 1791); *A View of the United States of America* (Philadelphia, 1794); *An Essay on the Manufacturing Interest of the United States* (Philadelphia, 1804); and *A Statement of the Arts and Manufactures of the United States of America for the Year 1810* (Philadelphia, 1814).

102. See below, chap. III, p. 90.

103. *Letter to Citizens* (1800), p. 17.

104. The pen name used by Andrew Adgate.

105. Catskill, 1795.

106. When a preacher could, by exposing a businessman's sharp practices, induce the colonial government to humble, harass, and penalize a leading citizen. For details see my *American Economic Thought in the Seventeenth Century*, pp. 123–127.

son reflected was by no means typical; whereas the direct effects of church doctrine on public policy had been eroded, the preachers still played an important role in molding public opinion, particularly in New England where election sermons provided opportunities for clergymen to deal with current political and economic issues. But with the weakening of the Calvinist faith, whether from the gradual spread of English deistic thought, the teachings of Rousseau, or the everyday experience of frontier communities which demonstrated that the doctrine of original depravity was not borne out by the decent conduct of the majority of people, the clergy lost its influence. Despite the melodramatic attempts of Jonathan Edwards to revive a belief in the "landscape of hell," the old Calvinist system was crumbling, and with the rise of new sects the separation of church and state resulted more from the refusal of Baptists, Methodists, Quakers, and other sects to support churches from which they had seceded than from any intellectual movement. As a result of this attrition of ecclesiastic authority, the preachers perforce had to speak more guardedly in the 1780s and 1790s than they had fifty years earlier. Nevertheless their voices were still influential, and a survey of the groups whose views helped crystallize the great synthesis must include mention of at least the more articulate members of the clergy.

To say that most preachers were conservative would be an understatement. The medieval thesis that society was made up of hierarchical orders was reflected in the repeated admonition that divine wisdom had assigned "a place, a business and a duty" for each person.[107] Jealousy and envy therefore constituted sins since, by the very nature of things, there must be "inequality in personal talents and property . . . so long as the world exists."[108] Recognizing these inevitable differences, government must defend and preserve property;[109] on this score the preachers were completely in agreement as can readily be seen from such examples as the sermons of Samuel Langdon[110] and Jeremy Belknap[111] in New Hampshire, Timothy Stone[112] and Nathan Strong[113] in Connecticut, and Daniel Foster[114] in Massachusetts. Within a "well-organized civil community," people must accept the places that "God assigned them" and refrain from coveting the property

107. Nathan Strong, *A Sermon* (Hartford, 1790).
108. Azel Backus, *Absalom's Conspiracy* (election sermon, May 10, 1798).
109. Ibid.
110. *The Republic of the Israelites: An Example to the American People* (Exeter, 1788).
111. *An Election Sermon* (Portsmouth, 1785).
112. *A Sermon* (Hartford, 1792).
113. *A Sermon.*
114. *A Sermon* (Boston, 1790).

that others possess—a doctrine that must have given great comfort to the defenders of things as they are. Yet it would not be quite fair to accuse the clergy of ignoring the inequities of the marketplace. Self-interest ought not be allowed to compromise the common good,[115] a thesis no doubt often conveniently interpreted to coincide with the economic interests of the majority of the members of a church congregation.[116] Yet the ecclesiastical views were basically utilitarian: each member of civil society should be free to promote his own well-being provided his action was "not attended with injury to the community."[117] The object of government should not be to equalize fortunes, for that is impossible, but to give each citizen an opportunity to become rich and respectable.[118]

The ecclesiastical concept of liberty was therefore a qualified one. Liberty, said Timothy Stone, "is one of the most important blessings which men possess," but the idea that liberty is synonymous with complete freedom from restraint "is a most unwise, mistaken apprehension." True liberty depends upon proper governance, on controls that will lead all members of society "to unite their exertions" for the common welfare.[119] Often the clergy specified just what types of intervention were required for achieving the "common good." For example, Samuel Deane, a Portland preacher, thought it appropriate to recommend "new manufactures to be erected and fostered by the hand of government,"[120] a concrete proposal Jeremy Belknap had made in an earlier election sermon,[121] in which he also urged governmental responsibility for providing adequate transportation facilities, a task he considered appropriate for government because the benefits would be shared, in some degree, by all members of society.

The theological content of the American concept of freedom derives largely from Puritan roots. Despite all the ferment created by Thomas Paine and other Americans who were stirred by French revolutionary ideals, the majority of the thinkers whose ideas were melded in the great synthesis clung to the basic tenets propagated by the Puritan churches. The right to rise in the world, provided one did not defile that privilege by shameful luxury or by insolent disregard of the social lamination necessary for social stability, represented the most sacred of

115. Peres Fobes, *A Sermon* (Boston, 1795), p. 12.
116. Thus Timothy Dwight in his Connecticut election sermon, *Virtuous Rulers a National Blessing,* urged the government to deal with the nation's creditors "with scrupulous fairness" (Hartford, 1791).
117. Robert Gray, *A Sermon* (Dover, New Hampshire, 1798).
118. Backus, *Absalom's Conspiracy,* pp. 24–25.
119. *A Sermon,* pp. 9–10.
120. Samuel Deane, *A Sermon* (Boston, 1794), p. 25.
121. *An Election Sermon,* p. 27.

human rights. Work, thrift, and diligence reflected true virtue. The duty of legislators should be to provide the political framework within which every citizen could fulfill some useful function thereby benefiting himself, his family, his community, and his country.

THE LEGISLATORS AND THE CONGRESSIONAL PETITIONERS

When the First Congress under the new Constitution convened, the nation's representatives, duly elected to express the wishes and the will of the American people, were given a first opportunity to appraise the adequacy of the ideas and governmental policies that had been promulgated in the forum of public debate (and by less public agreements and compromises) among the scholars, lawyers, gentry, industrialists, farmers, merchants, economists, and clergy. In a sense these groups, whose leading members have been briefly described, were the inventors of a new system of republican government. Invention, however, is seldom a complete definitive act; it is rather a process that consists of four, quite separate and distinct, stages. First emerges an awareness of some unsatisfactory *Gestalt* or phenomenal configuration, a frustration shared by many people. Then comes, to a few persons who possess exceptional insight, an appreciation of the essential elements of the problem, out of which, by an even smaller number of people, there is crystallized a visualization of a better solution to some besetting problems. When the First Congress convened, these three stages of the great American political invention had essentially been achieved.

New devices, arrangements—all innovations and inventions—are, at first, tentative, essentially primitive, and imperfect. Only as their shortcomings are realized can they be improved and perfected.[122] This fourth stage is therefore in many ways the most important, since it involves a continuous process of "critical revision."[123] Ever since 1789 our legislators have been attempting to improve and better adapt the American governmental institutions to current needs, circumstances, and emergent ideals. All that can be done in this study is to show that this ceaseless process was begun by the First Congress; the specific proposals that were made by more than two dozen legislators will be detailed in chapter VIII.

But it was not only the elected representatives who set about modi-

122. Contrast, for example, the efficiency of the original Daimler-Benz automobile with its modern counterpart.

123. For the expression "critical revision" I am indebted to Abbott Payson Usher, whose penetrating analysis of the nature of invention is detailed in his *History of Mechanical Inventions* (Cambridge, Mass., 1954).

fying our governmental instruments. Despite the hopes of those architects of the Constitution who realized the nature of a pluralistic society,
territorial representation in the Congress (which the Constitution provided) did not ensure the degree of participation in government that
all interests thought necessary. From the first, therefore, petitions were
presented to the Congress by groups of persons who asked that special
attention be given to their demands. What were the first groups of
petitioners and what interests did they consider underrepresented? The
cordage manufacturers wanted lower duties on hemp and high duties on
imported rope, cord, and twine. Sharply opposed to these proposals
stood the hemp growers who insisted "that equal attention should be
paid to the agricultural interests" as to the manufacturing interest.
Other petitions for higher tariffs came from the mustard manufacturers of Philadelphia, the paint makers of New Jersey, and the
snuff grinders of Baltimore. The "Maritime interest" asked that the
tonnage duties on foreign ships be raised, detailing the reasons in a
stream of petitions prepared by the merchants of Philadelphia, New
York, and Rhode Island. Nail makers and glass manufacturers importuned the government to help them, as did the hat makers and stocking
knitters. The whole story of the activities of the quickly formed
pressure groups will be described in chapter IX. Every interest asked
for governmental intervention on their behalf, showing by their action
degrees of dissatisfaction with the simplistic theory of representation
that compromise had provided. Better than any fancy theory the
forthright petitions revealed the pluralistic nature of the emergent concept of American freedom.

II

The Few and the Many
The Theory of Interests

A landed interest, a manufacturing interest, a mercantile interest, a moneyed
interest, with many lesser interests, grow
up of necessity in civilized societies, and
divide them into different classes,
actuated by different sentiments and
views.

James Madison

The Recognized Interests

ONE NEED only read *The Federalist* to appreciate how clearly the existence of separate interests was recognized in the Constitutional Era. The passage quoted from Madison's essay reveals his recognition that interests could introduce divisive tendencies in any society.[1] The resulting segmentation was viewed as an unmistakable social process not only by Madison but by Jay, who warned against forming several American confederations because the resulting differences in commercial policy "must create different interests."[2] Much as Durkheim did later, the authors of *The Federalist* associated the emergence of interests with the division of social labor; interests were conceived to "grow up of necessity" and since "the causes of faction cannot be removed . . . relief is only to be sought in the means of controlling its effects."[3]

Conflict between interests was therefore regarded as inevitable; the citizens of every state, wrote Madison, will inevitably divide "into different classes," and these, in turn, will "give birth to contending interests and jealousies."[4] But the proliferative tendency which alarmed Madison and Jay seems not to have disturbed Hamilton. Provided a nation's representative assembly included "landholders, merchants, and men of the learned professions," he felt confident that all interests would be adequately protected. "Where is the danger," he asked, "that the interests . . . will not be attended to by these three descriptions of men? Will not the landowner know and feel whatever will promote or insure the interest of landed property? . . . Will

1. *The Federalist* (Lodge), X, 54 [1787].
2. Ibid., IV, 25 [1787].
3. Ibid., X, 55 [1787].
4. Ibid., XXXVII, 221 [1788].

not the merchant understand and be disposed to cultivate, as far as may be proper, the interests of the mechanic and manufacturing arts . . . ? Will not the man of the learned profession . . . be likely to prove an impartial arbiter?"[5] In spite of the persuasiveness of the argument, George Logan did not share this optimistic view. Instead of cherishing Hamilton's belief that three interests would not only guard and protect their own groups but also ensure the well-being of lesser interests, Logan was fearful that a ruling class would emerge which would disregard the "liberties" of all major interests, one that would "strip the farmer, the mechanic, the manufacturer, and useful laborer, of all importance."[6] A decade earlier Pelatiah Webster had voiced a similar misgiving about the government's ability to protect the several interests: "when the trade, agriculture, and mechanic arts . . . are properly encouraged, the government is good"; but when faulty legislation or injudicious administration weakens any one of these fundamental interests, "the government must be bad indeed"[7]— which is what he thought it was in 1781.

That eighteenth-century writers recognized a process of social segmentation based upon economic function is therefore quite clear. That agriculture, commerce, and manufacture were considered the major interests is also evident. Often some categories were conceived as compound interests comprising lesser interests; thus Tench Coxe said that commerce "including our exports, imports, shipping, manufactures and fisheries, may be properly considered as forming one interest." Yet even in this aggregative sense, the commercial interest could not compare in importance with the agricultural interest, since Coxe said that his calculations did "not raise the proportion of property, or the number of men employed" in the compound commercial interest "to one-eighth of the property and people occupied by agriculture."[8] George Logan's estimate was even lower; grouping all gainfully employed in three major interests, he believed that 90 percent of the population belonged to the agricultural interest, 5 percent to the commercial interest, and 5 percent to the mechanic-manufacturing interest.[9] But whatever their relative importance, agriculture, commerce,

5. Ibid., XXXV, 205–206 [1788].
6. George Logan, *Five Letters Addressed to the Yeomanry of the United States* (Philadelphia, 1792), p. 8.
7. Webster, *Political Essays on the Nature and Operation of Money, Public Finances, and Other Subjects*, p. 195 [1781].
8. Coxe, *A View of the United States of America*, p. 7 [1787].
9. George Logan, *An Address on the Natural and Social Order of the World, As Intended to Produce Universal Good; Delivered before the Tammany Society* (Philadelphia, 1798), p. 8.

manufacturing, mechanic arts, and the professions were clearly distinguished as separate interests, each deserving of governmental recognition.[10] These five, as will presently be shown, were construed as "natural interests"; emerging spontaneously, they were presumed to create a naturalistic functionalism within society, pleasing to God and useful to men.[11]

Whether the "artificial" or "unnatural" interests, as they were censoriously designated, had an equally spontaneous origin became a matter of acrimonious dispute. On the one hand writers typified by James Sullivan found a natural enough explanation for the emergence of the financial or "monied" interest. Men always dislike labor, he said, but whereas in a state of nature hunger compels them to work, in civilized societies men are torn between two attractions: avarice urges them to exertion, while an instinctive indolence tempts them to avoid the irksomeness of labor. Faced with this unpleasant choice, "we find everyone, who can drive a bargain to advantage, forsaking the plough to do it."[12] Hence the origin of all arbitrage, a type of transactional activity distinct from commerce. For although the "commercial interest" carried on an exchange of goods for money and of money for goods, it produced net social benefits by making goods abundant. Stockjobbing, on the other hand, merely meant an exchange of ownership. The dubious social utility of the "monied" interest could therefore be emphasized, even though the "natural" motivation to arbitrage was understandable.

John Taylor of Caroline, however, categorically denied the naturalness of the monied interest. To him the whole business of trading in representations of wealth was unnatural in origin and deleterious in effects. Whenever an oligarchy controls a state, he argued, ways and means will be found to make the rest of society subservient. Stock-

10. This recognition is to be found in legislative preambles as well as in political tracts. Thus a Pennsylvania statute (1785) for erecting a loan office was avowedly passed "to promote and establish the interests of internal commerce, agriculture and mechanc arts." *11 Pennsylvania Statutes at Law,* 560, ch. 1159, sec. 1–3.

11. Part of the vindication of natural interests represents a fusion of vestigial medievalism with eighteenth-century concepts of natural law. In the election sermons, for example, the medieval doctrine of social classes was often stated. Thus one preacher asserted: "Every man is a member in the political body; and every member hath a place in which it may be useful. If any are not useful, it is their fault; for divine wisdom hath so organized the body [that] there is a place, a business, and a duty for all." This being so, "no order, possession, or employment, may say to another, there is no need of thee." Strong, *A Sermon,* p. 22.

12. James Sullivan, *The Path to Riches: An Inquiry into the Origin and the Use of Money* (Boston, 1792), p. 43.

jobbing is merely one of these "factitious" devices,[13] and hence the financial interest is unnatural. Because the indictment which Taylor levied against the unnatural interests will be examined in detail in a later chapter, it is only necessary here to point out that the "monied" interests were recognized as a separate social segment, and that doubts were entertained about the social utility of a separate interest which specialized in the business of arbitrage. Members of such a group, said William Findley, "not being engaged in the pursuit of active industry . . . have no common interests with the citizens otherwise than to oppress them."[14] But, as we shall see, such strictures did not go unchallenged.

The corporate interests, in Taylor's opinion, were equally factitious, although more dangerous, because they "neither live nor die naturally; they only live or die by law."[15] Their emergence must therefore depend on legislative favor and their continued existence on "exclusive rights and legislative weight."[16] Being "successional bodies," corporate interests are less exposed to the divisive tendencies that often weaken natural interests; moreover, since they are systematically organized, they can acquire special privileges "by seducing the representatives of the states from their natural allegiance."[17] Corporate interests supply the stock in trade of the "monied" interests, monopolize banking, and foster speculation. All these things, said the enemies of high finance, make corporate interests unnatural and illegitimate. The defenders of the corporate interests said very little, but they were not unmindful that they were under attack.

In addition to the financial interests and the corporate interests, one other group, the foreign interests, was bitterly assailed. In this onslaught patriotism, chauvinism, and egoism were blended in unknown proportion. Thus George Logan, although he had been one of Adam Smith's best American disciples in the early 1790s, was preaching national self-sufficiency in 1800 and berating the "British interests."[18] Merchants whose markets had narrowed after American independence

13. Taylor's rancorous condemnation of the financial interest, although it pervades his earlier writings, is most elaborately developed in his *Inquiry into the Principles and Policy of the Government of the United States* (Fredericksburg, 1814).

14. Findley, *Review of the Revenue System*, pp. 52–53.

15. *Principles and Policy*, p. 259 [1814].

16. John Taylor, *A Definition of Parties* (Philadelphia, 1794), p. 16.

17. John Taylor, *An Enquiry into the Principles and Tendency of Certain Public Measures* (Philadelphia, 1794), p. 37.

18. Logan, *Letter to the Citizens of Pennsylvania on the Necessity of Promoting Agriculture, Manufacture, and the Useful Arts*, pp. 16–17.

had rather more personal reasons for criticizing the foreign interests,[19] although they were by no means alone in their contention that restrictions should be imposed on alien interests. Meantime the enemies of the Bank of the United States bemoaned the infiltration of foreign financial interests, and Taylor alleged that "America has defeated a nation, but is subdued by a corporation."[20]

At least eight distinct interests were therefore recognized by the late eighteenth-century political theorists. Five of them—agriculture, commerce, manufacture, mechanic arts, and the professions[21]— were willingly conceded to be "natural interests," but grave doubts were entertained about the naturalness and the utility of the financial and the corporate interests. The foreign interests represented a rather vague gather-all, and the concept reflected not only the age-old suspicion of aliens, but a particular hatred of British factors, merchants, and financiers.

To the eight clear-cut interests may be added two more: the "propertied interests" and the "consumers' interest." Both are only indistinctly described, although there is probably enough evidence to justify their inclusion as recognized "interests." In both cases, overlapping would occur: the propertied interest would include farmers, merchants, manufacturers, and financiers, while the consumers' interest was obviously even more comprehensive. These two interests are, for the time, merely added to the list. Further discussion of the propertied interest will be found in the section of this chapter devoted to "wealth and political priority." The consumers' interest will be examined in chapter III.

19. See, for example, Bowdoin's *Opinions respecting the Commercial Intercourse between the United States of America and the Dominions of Great Britain Including Observations upon the Necessity and Importance of the American Navigation Act.*

20. *Enquiry into Certain Public Measures*, p. 22.

21. Hamilton regarded the members of learned professions as unusually impartial and civic-minded persons. "The learned professions," he wrote, "form no distinct interest in society." *The Federalist* (Lodge), XXXV, 204 [1788].

Like many seventeenth-century British Writers, Noah Webster believed that too many persons were crowding into the professions. "The number of professional men in a State," he argued, "should be as few as possible; for they do not increase the property of the State, but live on the property acquired by others." Like Nehemiah Grew (see my *Predecessors of Adam Smith*, New York and London, 1937, chap. VII), Webster believed that, by eliminating the complexity of common law, statute law could reduce the need for lawyers. "An artful Legislature," said Webster, "will take away some of the causes of litigation, and thus curtail the number of lawyers." See his *Collection of Essays and Fugitive Writings* (Boston, 1790), p. 117.

The Problem of Representation

The claims of the several interests to political representation led to proposals which ranged all the way from Richard Henry Lee's frank espousal of pluralism to John Taylor's stubborn opposition to any political recognition of interests whatever. The problem of according political power to interests became far more complicated after the adoption of the Constitution. Representation in the Continental Congress had been by states whereas under the Constitution the plan ultimately chosen for the House of Representatives provided for representation in terms of population aggregates. No doubt the several interests had sought representation in the Continental Congress; when Tench Coxe, for example, was appointed to Congress in 1788, the purpose was said to be to give Pennsylvania "a mercantile representative."[22] But since the Continental Congress was more of a continuous diplomatic conference than a genuine legislative body,[23] the problem of interest representation was never a central issue. The Constitutional Convention, on the other hand, stemming as it did from the Annapolis Convention where representatives of the commercial interest were in the majority, brought to the forefront the arguments for political representation of the several interests.

Since every interest is of necessity egoistic, said Richard Henry Lee, no one of them can be trusted to enact laws for the general good: "merchants alone would never fail to make laws favorable to themselves and oppressive to farmers," and "farmers alone would act on like principles."[24] Other interests would be equally self-centered: manufacturers would "contend for monopolies," professional men would endeavor to keep their fees high, whereas "the people who pay them [consumers' interest?]" would "endeavor to lower them." Each interest would be equally untrustworthy. Hence the only safe and "fair representation" would be one wherein "every order of men in the community . . . can have a share in it." Since a fresh start was being made, Lee proposed that the new government ought to recognize the interests quite frankly and "to allow professional men, merchants, traders, farmers, mechanics, etc. to bring a just proportion of their best informed men respectively into the legislature."[25]

22. See Harold H. Hutcheson, *Tench Coxe* (Baltimore, 1938), pp. 15–16.
23. For a vivid and comprehensive chronicle, see Edward C. Burnett, *The Continental Congress* (New York, 1941).
24. Richard Henry Lee, *An Additional Number of Letters* (New York, 1788), p. 61.
25. *Observations Leading to a Fair Examination of the System of Govern-*

Hamilton took at least two different positions on the issue. In Number XXXV of *The Federalist,* he argued that landholders, merchants, and men in learned professions would adequately and impartially represent all interests,[26] while in Number LX he contended that territorial representation by virtue of the "diversity in the state of property" would result in proper representation of the different interests.[27] Those regions primarily agricultural would ultimately become more differentiated as domestic manufactures developed, and since this differentiation would be "the fruits of a more advanced population," such a region would be accommodated by "a fuller representation," and for this, said the author of the *Federalist* Number LVI, the convention had provided.[28] But this argument really evaded the issue; "fuller representation" would not necessarily ensure ratable occupational representation. Yet apparently most members of the Constitutional Convention were of the opinion that territorial representation would safeguard all legitimate interests. For that reason, John Adams advocated territorial congressional districts rather than the selection of representatives at large. A representative drawn from a particular region, he said, would be "much better acquainted with its wants and interests."[29]

That members of Congress would tend to plead the cause of particular interests was nevertheless to be expected. Legislators, said Madison, are "advocates" of particular causes, and for that reason the legislative process, if it is to be just, must "hold the balance" between importuning interests.[30] In the much later language of Durkheim, the interests would need to be reconciled by "restitutive law."[31] This is certainly what Noah Webster apparently had in mind when he insisted that law must establish the boundaries of self-interest.[32] But law depends on the lawmakers; if the legislative assembly is made up of the "advocates" of particular interests, how can law constitute a regulating force? Madison signalized "the regulation of these various and interfering interests"

---

ment (New York, 1787). Reprinted in P. L. Ford's *Pamphlets on the Constitution* (1888), p. 10.

26. *The Federalist* (Lodge), XXXV, 205–206 [1788].

27. Ibid., LX, 375 [1788].

28. Ibid., LVI (Hamilton or Madison), 354 [1788].

29. *A Defense of the Constitutions of Government of the United States of America* (London, 1787), p. 155.

30. *The Federalist* (Lodge), X, 54–55 [1787].

31. *Division of Labor in Society,* chap. III.

32. "Each individual pursues his own interest; and consults the good of others no farther than his own interest requires. Hence the necessity of laws which respect the whole body collectively, and restrain the pursuits of individuals when they infringe the public rights." *Sketches of American Policy* (Hartford, 1785), p. 6.

as "the principal task of modern legislation,"[33] but he gave no clear answer as to how a legislature, which represented interests, could regulate them. He did make it plain that if one "faction [interest] consists of less than a majority, relief is supplied by the republican principle, which enables the majority to defeat its sinister views by regular vote."[34] And here the authors of *The Federalist* rested their case. The normal divisive tendency was thought to be persistent enough to fragmentize society "into so many parts, interests and classes of citizens, that the rights of individuals, or of the minority, will be in little danger from interested combinations of the majority."[35] Fear of combinations of interests nevertheless persisted,[36] and as the Hamiltonian program was unfolded, many people began to believe that a dangerous coalition of interests had quite promptly been effected.

John Taylor gave more sustained thought and attention to this eventuality than any of his contemporaries. His penetrating analysis of minority rule, which anticipated much of Gaetano Mosca's theory of the ruling class, will be examined presently. Here it need only be pointed out that Taylor rejected completely the whole idea of interest representation. Groping for a concept similar to Durkheim's "organic solidarity," Taylor insisted that law, if it is to be benevolent, must be sanctioned by the public will. Laws engineered "by the will of a combination among parties of interest," he contended, can never advance the public good.[37]

Should Interests Be Balanced?

Since social segmentation is inevitable and since interests will ceaselessly bid for political power, John Adams proposed that a deliberate attempt ought to be made to sanction a limited number of interests and to balance them once and for all. For unless some sort of an equilibrium is arbitrarily established, "where the riches are, there will be the power."[38] And what would be the consequence? "If a few be as rich as all the rest," said Adams, "a few will have as much power as all the rest; in that case the commonwealth is unequal, and there can be no end of staving and tailing till it be brought to equality." Like Richard Henry Lee, Adams thought that the United States had an opportunity

33. *The Federalist* (Lodge), X, 54 [1787].
34. Ibid., 55.
35. Ibid., LI (Madison or Hamilton), 325–326 [1788].
36. See Findley's *Review of the Revenue System*, p. 128 [1794], and Sullivan's *Path to Riches*, pp. 6–7 [1792], for particularly trenchant illustrations.
37. See *Principles and Policy*, pp. 575, 602 [1814].
38. *Defense of the Constitutions*, p. 165 [1787].

48

to make a fresh start in the allocation of power to various interests. "It is of great importance," he insisted, "to begin well," since "misarrangements now made, will have great, extensive and distant consequences."[39] But just what interests were to be balanced,[40] or how it was to be done, Adams never made precisely clear. The very rich, whom he considered the most power-hungry interest, should, he thought, be allowed to monopolize the Senate where they could do little harm. For, like Harrington, Adams believed that revolutions were caused by inequalities in property; governmental stability, therefore, required that some restraints should be imposed on groups that engross property to the disadvantage of other groups. What Adams hoped to create was equilibrium among interests as measured by property. In this ambition he was definitely a follower of Harrington and Locke.

Against Adams's proposal for establishing an equilibrium among interests, John Taylor of Caroline launched a fierce, albeit belated, attack. In the first place, said Taylor, "a specific balance of property among orders, or separate interests" is impossible "in the present state of commerce and manners."[41] It is absurd even to suppose that property in land can be equalized "by assigning to each order or interest" its aliquot share. Moreover, the history of colonial America had shown that "property and good order" can be ensured without dividing society into interests; indeed Taylor argued that the vitality of colonial economic life could be explained "by the absence of jealous and rival orders; by the absence of the system of balancing power and property between such orders."[42] What was called for, Taylor insisted, was solidarity not segmentation, mutuality not distinctness. As opposed to this oneness, "the system of a balance of orders, is bottomed upon the idea of some natural or political enmity, between the one, the few and the many."[43]

Taylor was attacking the interest principle itself. Instead of Harrington's hierarchy of property-owning orders, he advocated a type of individualism resembling that of Bentham, insisting again and again that each individual should count as one. "Mr. Adams proposes," he said, "an equality or balance of property, power, and understanding

39. Ibid., p. 380.
40. Although Adams sought to achieve a stable equilibrium between interests, he did not use the word *balance* to express this idea. He used *balance* in the same sense that Harrington did, that is, to mean a predominating share. Thus the rich and highborn tend always to hold the "balance of property." But in America, said Adams, "the balance of property is nine-tenths on the side of the people." Ibid., p. 165.
41. *Principles and Policy*, pp. 117, 403 [1814].
42. Ibid., p. 135.
43. Ibid., p. 231.

between orders comprising a nation. And yet all the disciples of the theory will exclaim against the mischief, folly and impossibility, of levelling or balancing property among individuals."[44] The right policy, the one which will vitalize enterprise and guarantee justice, said Taylor, should balance one individual with another, not by the leveling force of law but by the equality of opportunity which will result from universal education and the right of free and unrestrained alienation of property. There can be only one consequence of "separate interests warily balanced": it will make it easy for the few to exploit the many.[45] Instead of neutralizing one interest by some "coequal power," as Adams asserts, combinations of wealthy groups[46] will divide society into but two classes, the rich and the poor. Hence the vaunted stability that a balance of interests promises is entirely illusory. True stability can only be achieved by rejecting the whole idea of interests. "It was reserved for the United States to discover," Taylor said, "that by balancing man with man, and by avoiding the artificial combinations of exclusive privileges, no individual of these equipoised millions would be incited by the probability of success, to assail the rest."[47] Taylor was uncompromising; whereas Adams would balance the interests, Taylor would root them out. But although he condemned Adams's proposal as "only a theory" and a "phantom of the imagination," his own recommendations could hardly be called realistic. "Balancing man with man" called for the elimination of all interests, all group cohesion!

Adams blundered by oversimplifying his political solution for the conflict of interests. Moreover, he erred in supposing that a balance could be effected which would be permanent. Less doctrinaire writers saw the balancing of interests as a continuous social and legislative process, one which called for many small adjustments. Legislators may wish to assist the manufacturing interest, said John Beale Bordley, but if they are wise "they will be cautious how they favor the one at the expense of the other."[48] The controversy between Adams and Taylor had neglected economic considerations; indeed in their preoccupation

44. Ibid., p. 404.
45. "I object to the levelling principle [by law] itself, whilst they [the defenders of balanced interests] approve of its application to their theory." Ibid.
46. The argument advanced in Number LI of *The Federalist* is that social segmentation can be counted on to divide society "into so many parts, interests, and classes of citizens, that the rights of individuals, or of the minority, will be in little danger from interested combinations." See *The Federalist* (Lodge), LI (Madison or Hamilton), 325–326 [1788].
47. *Principles and Policy*, p. 422.
48. Bordley, *Essays and Notes on Husbandry and Rural Affairs* (Philadelphia, 1799), p. 385 [1794].

with political matters, they failed to appreciate that some economic balance between interests is a functional necessity. Noah Webster, on the other hand, made this perfectly clear. "In every trading nation," he said, "there ought to be a due proportion between the commercial interest, the agricultural and the manufacturing." For if "the farmers and manufacturers are too numerous for the merchants, produce and manufactures will be plentiful and cheap,"[49] although trade will be unduly "lucrative"; similarly, if merchants are too numerous, markets will be glutted, profits will fall, and the proper operation of the entire economy will be jeopardized. But Webster failed to say how the interests should be balanced in this functional sense, and what if anything the government should do to maintain the proportionality of interests.

There is implicit in Webster's argument, however, the idea that interests should be balanced in such a way that income streams would reflect some satisfactory degree of parity between interests. This is apparently what George Logan also had in mind when he argued that the American manufacturer "should have such an equivalent for his labor as to enable him to live with comfort; to educate his children, and to preserve something for the support of his family in case of unavoidable accident."[50] This is probably what Madison was thinking of when he said that government must "hold the balance" between debtors and creditors.[51] This is what Richard Henry Lee was discussing when he urged that taxes be levied in such a way that the several interests would be "balanced." It was this idea of balance that the Delaware legislature had in mind when it repealed the earlier legislation governing intestates which had given a double portion of inheritance to the eldest son, stating in the preamble to the law that it was "the duty and policy of every republican government to preserve equality amongst its citizens by maintaining the balance of property."[52] This principle, seven years earlier, had been incorporated in the Ordinance of 1787, probably at Jefferson's suggestion.

Wealth and Political Priority

The problem of interests was crystal clear to one group of eighteenth-century writers who said quite frankly that the property and the enterprise opportunities of the group Hamilton called the "rich and well-born" should be protected by government. The defenders of this

49. Noah Webster, *Collection of Essays*, pp. 119–120 [1785].
50. Logan, *Address before the Tammany Society*, p. 10 [1798].
51. *The Federalist* (Lodge), X, 55 [1787].
52. *2 Delaware Laws* 1122, ch. 53 C [January 29, 1794].

doctrine of political priority for the propertied classes were for the most part politicians and preachers. The ecclesiastical view may be gleaned from election sermons, the political argument may be sampled in the writings of Hamilton and Adams.

In seventeenth-century America, especially in New England, the theologians had been by far the most articulate critics of contemporaneous economic activity. Their opinions were unambiguous, their proposals specific. Striving valiantly to create a Christian commonwealth in the new world, they attempted to exercise surveillance over prices, wages, and interest rates, land policy and commerce, foreign trade and taxation.[53] Little by little, their control over economic affairs weakened as secular influence spread over business and presently over politics. By the closing years of the eighteenth century, clergymen had come to be generally what they are today—specialists in theology and moral philosophy: as arbiters of the proper economic role of government they had been superseded by men of affairs, professional men, or practical politicians.

Yet with undisguised nostalgia, the preachers looked back to the days when the churches had exercised a great deal of control over economic activity, to the time when the ideal had been a society modeled on the Old Testament hope that every man might sit under his own fig tree. Hence, in spite of the property accumulations which a secularized business community had acquired, often by means which the seventeenth-century clergy had condemned in withering language, the eighteenth-century clergy still staunchly defended property. Moreover, they looked with disapproval upon any and all political doctrines which seemed to threaten property rights. "So long as the world exists," Azel Backus told the members of the Connecticut legislature, "there will be an inequality in personal talents and property, which will be a source of continual envy and jealousy to those who do not possess them."[54] What should government do in the face of this envy and jealousy? It should defend and preserve property; this duty was specifically imposed upon government in practically every election sermon preached during the last quarter of the eighteenth century.[55]

53. See my *American Economic Thought in the Seventeenth Century,* especially chaps. V, VI, and VIII.
54. Backus, *Absalom's Conspiracy,* pp. 24–25.
55. See as examples, Samuel Langdon, *The Republic of the Israelites: An Example to the American People* (New Hampshire election sermon, Exeter, 1788), p. 11; Timothy Stone, *A Sermon* (Connecticut election sermon, Hartford, 1792), p. 19; Daniel Foster, *A Sermon* (Massachusetts election sermon, Boston, 1790), pp. 13–14; Jeremy Belknap, *An Election Sermon* (Portsmouth, New Hampshire, 1785), p. 20; Nathan Strong, *A Sermon* (Connecticut election sermon, Hartford, 1790), p. 20.

Supported by the waning authority of the preachers, more practical men took an even bolder attitude toward the relation of government to the propertied classes, grounding their argument in favor of political priority for wealthy and successful people on a sociological theory which presumably justified their governmental proposals. That theory was based on the idea that a "natural aristocracy" always differentiated itself from the mass of the people and on the political doctrine that governmental stability required the protection of these elite members of society. Hamilton stated the thesis succinctly when he said: "All communities divide themselves in to the few and the many. The first are rich and well-born, the other the mass of the people. The voice of the people has been said to be the voice of God; and however generally this maxim has been quoted and believed, it is not true in fact. The people are turbulent and changing; they seldom judge or determine right."[56]

Even greater confidence characterized John Adams's belief in the inevitable rise to power of the so-called "natural aristocracy," although Adams was by no means as certain that the rich and wellborn should have an exclusive right to govern. Replying to Turgot's argument that republics are founded on the equality of citizens, Adams asserted that "in every state . . . there are inequalities which God and Nature have planted there, and which no legislator ever can eradicate."[57] These inequalities of wealth, birth, and talent "have a natural and inevitable influence in society."[58] The emergence of a "natural aristocracy" will provide society with "a body of men which contains the greatest collection of virtues and abilities," and this elite group can "be made the greatest blessing of society, if it be judiciously managed . . . But if it is not, it will always be the most dangerous."[59] Adams therefore proposed that "the most conspicuous" members of the "natural aristocracy" should be allowed to monopolize the Senate[60] and that senators should be deprived of "all pretentions to the executive power"[61] lest "their ambition and avarice" diminish "the privileges of

56. *Works of Alexander Hamilton,* I, 401.
57. *Defense of the Constitutions,* pp. 106–107 [1787].
58. Ibid., p. 107.
59. Ibid., p. 114.
60. Although Edward Channing (*History of the United States,* IV, 171n) characterized Adams's proposal that the Senate be made up of representatives of the rich and wellborn as "innocuous," the issue was a fundamental one. Tench Coxe, before he became a Jeffersonian (see Hutcheson, *Tench Coxe,* pp. 16–17), praised Adams for being a "friend of property" whereas Adams's political enemies branded him not only as a defender of a ruling class but as a monarchist.
61. *Defense of the Constitutions,* p. 137.

the people."[62] Despite the abuse Adams's enemies heaped on this proposal (which they interpreted as proof of his solicitude for the "rich and wellborn"), there is no reason to suspect Adams's sincerity. He did not say that the wealthy and successful should have exclusive political power; he said they would seize and hold such power unless they were prevented from doing so[63] or were induced to accept a position of honor in a politically feeble Senate where the nation might "have the benefit of their wisdom without fear of their passions."[64]

The notion of a natural aristocracy, which formed an integral part of the political theory of Hamilton and Adams, but which aroused the fears of Richard Henry Lee,[65] encountered a blistering attack. Once again the heavy artillery was forged by John Taylor of Caroline. A remarkable thing about Taylor's critique was its similarity to the theory of the ruling class which Gaetano Mosca expounded seventy years later.[66] Mosca traced a succession of ruling groups whose power was based respectively on monopoly of priestly functions, military organization, landholding, and money.[67] In Taylor's writings we find virtually the same explanation for the continuity of minority rule. "For the sake of perspicuity," he wrote, "I shall call the ancient aristocracy, chiefly created and supported by superstition, 'the aristocracy of the first age'; that produced by conquest [which merges Mosca's second and third ruling classes], known by the title of the feudal system, 'the aristocracy of the second age'; and that erected by paper and patronage, 'the aristocracy of the third or present age.' "[68] This historical sequence, Taylor said, proves that "aristocracy is artificial and not natural" and that the ruling class never was a "natural aristocracy"[69] despite all the pretensions of John Adams. The diffusion of knowledge destroyed the minority rule based on superstititon; the ex-

62. Ibid., p. 361.
63. "Riches," said Adams, "will hold first place, in civilized societies at least, among the principles of power, and will often prevail . . . over the principles of authority." Ibid., p. 156.
64. Ibid., p. 138.
65. "If we make the proper distinction between the few men of wealth and abilities, and consider them, as we ought, as the natural aristocracy of the country, and the great mass of the people, the middle and lower classes, as the democracy, this federal representative branch will have but very little democracy in it." *Observations of the System of Government*, p. 17 [1787].
66. Taylor's *Principles and Policy* appeared in 1814 whereas Mosca's first statement of his theory of the ruling class was contained in his *Sulla Teoria dei Governi e sul Governo Parlementare*, published in 1884.
67. Gaetano Mosca, *Elementi di Scienca Politica* (1896); translated as *The Ruling Class* (New York, 1939), pp. 59–69, 80–82, 141–144.
68. *Principles and Policy*, pp. 20–21 [1814].
69. Ibid., p. 82.

pansion of commerce and the alienation of land gradually overthrew the feudal aristocracy.[70] Just how Taylor thought the financial aristocracy, which he said the Federalists were creating, could be destroyed will be pointed out in chapter IV.

Full of confidence that a genuine democracy could be established in the United States, Taylor looked forward to a time when government would represent the "natural or general interest of a nation"[71] rather than "factitious aristocracies" of special or exclusive interest. In his opinion, the history of minority rule proved that all government based upon interests was baneful and vicious. For no interest can transcend its egoism; it will therefore use its power to exploit other groups in society, pretending the while that it is conducting a government for the benefit of all. "All separate factitious interests," claimed Taylor, "pretend that they benefit nations in some mode, too intricate to be investigated by the mass of mankind."[72] These deceptions, employed by all minorities to justify their political power, Mosca later called "political formulas," concluding that they not only served to consolidate the power of a ruling minority but also provided a unifying force which helped to hold society together.[73] Taylor denied categorically that these pretenses, these "great superstitions" as Herbert Spencer later called them, could be socially benevolent. True unity, Taylor insisted again and again, must come from a genuine solicitude for the public good; and in this Rousseauistic belief he anticipated the concept of organic solidarity later developed by Émile Durkheim.

Taylor was not another David fighting alone against the Philistines. Denial of the political priority of the "rich and wellborn" became a central part of the Republican attack upon the Federalist party. But whereas the 1790s teem with anti-Federalist literature, very few of the tracts are philosophical enough to throw much light on the theory of interests. Government "perverted to serve the ambition and avarice of the few" is, to be sure, violently condemned;[74] so is "the preference

70. Ibid., p. 14.
71. *Enquiry into Certain Public Measures*, p. 59.
72. *Principles and Policy*, p. 338 [1814].
73. This thesis was more explicitly developed by Mosca when he said, "Ruling classes do not justify their power exclusively by *de facto* possession of it, but try to find a moral and legal basis for it, representing it as the logical and necessary consequence of doctrines and beliefs that are generally recognized and accepted." *The Ruling Class,* p. 70. Mosca argued that political formulas are not "mere quackeries aptly invented to trick the masses into obedience"; instead "they answer a real need in man's social nature" because they give the impression that people are governed "not on the basis of mere material or intellectual force, but on the basis of a moral principle." Ibid., p. 71.
74. George Logan, *Five Letters to the Yeomanry*, p. 4 [1792].

of partial to general interests."[75] Precise views about property and political priority, however, are less conspicuous than these blanket indictments. Moreover, even ardent Republicans admitted that government must give some measure of preferential attention to property owners: George Logan, for example, argued that "property alone can stimulate to labor" and hence it was not property per se but only its "excess" that "is the great malady of civil society";[76] for that reason, although laws cannot equalize men, they ought not "aggravate the inequality which they cannot cure."[77]

That possession of property did give a measure of political priority in all the states is attested by the property qualifications which restricted the number of people who could vote. Moreover, the minimum property qualifications required for eligibility to several of the state legislatures were astonishingly high.[78] Although important beginnings of political democracy occurred in the Federalist period,[79] an aggressive attack on the political priority of the possessors of property had to await the democratic movement of the Jacksonian era; in the Age of Washington, the controversy mostly centered on the question of how much political preference the rich should have.

Controversies about more or less political power are bound to be both violent and vague. Each disputant forms his own opinions about the meaning of "enough" or "too much." The result is a great deal of heat but very little light, and that this was the case in the 1790s will be abundantly clear from just one example. Here, for instance, is the way James Sullivan stated the issue: "Whenever the laws, or the measures of state policy, give to one man, or one order of men, an exclusive right to acquire property, or a greater or more advantageous opportunity to improve his, or their talent, than is given to all, there is just cause of complaint."[80] An "exclusive right" would seem to be easily recognizable; yet it apparently was not. The critics of Hamilton's funding and assumption program bitterly condemned it as an exclusive right "enabling those who were more wealthy to absorb the property of those who were less so."[81] On the other hand, the defenders of the program construed it as a measure giving all possessors of liquid prop-

75. Ibid., pp. 11–12.
76. Ibid.
77. Ibid., p. 12.
78. For examples see Richard B. Morris, *Government and Labor in Early America* (New York, 1946), pp. 503–507.
79. For details see Richard P. McCormick, *The Second American Party System* (Chapel Hill, N.C., 1966).
80. *Path to Riches,* p. 7 [1792].
81. Findley, *Review of the Revenue System,* p. 38 [1794].

erty an equal opportunity to share in the appreciation of the public securities. Admittedly transactions in public securities resulted in profit opportunities only for the possessors of money, but this preference was regarded as entirely legitimate since it represented a customary priority available to the possessors of property.

To John Adams and his property conscious countrymen, the political priority of the propertied interest was inevitable; "riches," he said, "will hold first place, in civilized countries at least, among the principles of power."[82] Hence, although government should always protect and preserve property, it ought nevertheless temper the autocratic tendencies of the propertied classes. Whenever government is weak, said the authors of the *Federalist* Number LXII, the resulting economic and political instability will give an "unreasonable advantage" to "the sagacious, the enterprising and the moneyed few," since "every new regulation . . . affecting the value of the different species of property, presents a new harvest to those who watch the change." Thus unless government referees a nation's business, a state of things will emerge "in which it may be said with some truth that laws are made for the few, not for the many."[83] But this circumstantial power of the rich Noah Webster thought far less dangerous than the political preeminence which might be permanently acquired by an hereditary propertied class. Business fortunes, he pointed out, cause great inequalities in property holding, but since "this inequality is revolving from person to person," it does not create a hierarchy of politically dominant property owners.[84]

A quite different argument for special political privilege of some members of the propertied interest was advanced by another Webster, the sagacious Pelatiah. Governments, he argued, by granting corporate charters, by alienating unimproved lands, and by other acts, "vest a right or interest in an individual or company of men." These acts of the government constitute "bargains or contracts" with men of property, under the implied terms of which the propertied interests expend money "in prospects of great benefits" to both the investors and the public.[85] Once the propertied interests have fulfilled their part of the bargain by investing money, the legislature on its part cannot right-

82. *Defense of the Constitutions*, p. 156. In proof of this assertion, Adams quoted from Harrington: "Men are hung upon riches, not of choice . . . but of necessity, and by the teeth; for as much as he who wants bread, is his servant that will feed him; and if a man thus feeds a whole people, they are under his empire."

83. *The Federalist* (Lodge), LXII (Hamilton or Madison), 390 [1788].

84. *Sketches of American Policy*, p. 18 [1785].

85. *Political Essays*, pp. 456–457 [1786].

fully repeal or abrogate such agreements since "all acts of this kind vest such rights, privileges or interests in the grantees."[86] What Webster stated was therefore an early variant of the due process controversy which was to create such a complicated legal and economic tangle in the nineteenth century.

Natural Interests and Natural Justice

The whole course of democratic thought is hard to trace; for whereas it thunders through the rocky gorges of political controversy and foams conspicuously through the narrow defiles of constitutional quarrels, it meanders almost unobserved through the rich and prosperous meadowlands of business enterprise. And yet it seems no overstatement to say that American democracy as it unfolded was as much an economic as a political phenomenon. Here was the emergent freedom par excellence; here was the magnet that drew millions of immigrants to the American continent. It is this phase of democratic thought that most needs clarification. Too often it has been assumed that "pure competition," "*laissez-faire*," or some other compact phrase tells the story. Such is not the case. The democracy of American enterprise was much more than an experiment with Adam Smith's "obvious and simple system of natural liberty"; it was a militant, pragmatic variety of libertarianism. But since action rather than theory characterized the American democracy of enterprise, the theoretical literature is minute in the 1790s, and even when it does begin to grow, in the 1820s, the writings are devoted to particular aspects of entrepreneurial democracy rather than to the total movement.

There is enough theoretical literature, however, to indicate that American economic liberalism in the 1790s represented an opposition to certain interests which not only were allegedly predatory and therefore unjust, but which also operated as restraining influences on the economic efficiency of the enterprise system. The blameworthy interests were both historical and emergent. Thus the British "landed interest" represented a historical exploitative agency as did the British factorage system. The "monied interest," the "paper interest," or the "banking interest," in contrast, represented new "factitious" interests; they were conceived to be recent perversions of an otherwise wholesome economic society. Democratic thought waged war, therefore, on two fronts: against the older propertied interests (which defended their privileges by a "political formula" which asserted that social stabil-

86. Ibid., p. 457.

58

ity required social stratification),[87] and against the newer "unnatural,"
"factitious," financial interests which threatened to create different
forms of exploitation and to generate new forms of inefficiency within
the enterprise system.

The true democratic course lay between these old and new perversions. It was a "natural" course in the sense that it called for no
government to generate it, although it ought not to be confused with
absolute concepts of *laissez-faire*.[88] "The natural interest of a country," wrote John Taylor of Caroline, "includes whatever may subsist,
without the direct aid of municipal law, as commerce, manufactures
and [mechanic] arts."[89] And this "natural interest . . . ought exclusively to legislate,"[90] because it represents those social segments that
are genuinely productive and hence socially beneficient. Indeed it was
the fundamental and quintessential productiveness of the natural interest that gave it a moral priority to legislate. For unlike all "factitious"
or "unnatural" interests that subsist upon the natural interests by ap-
propriating the product of "industry and talent" for the benefit of a
law-protected minority, the natural interest is nonexploitative. It
divides property and the fruit of labor not by chicanery, fraud, or
onerous taxation, but by a natural process which is just and meliorative.
Above all, the natural interest is inclusive; "because of this, every individual participates,"[91] whereas all "factitious" interests are exclusive and therefore provide greater "temptation to injustice and partiality."[92]

Europe, it was claimed, had been enslaved by "laws for enriching
parties of [unnatural] interest, by tythes, offices, sinecures, and
stock."[93] Against all these forms of exploitation, as well as against
any new forms of servitude, the natural interests must be ever vigilant.
Government by the natural interest must therefore be something
more than *laissez-faire*; it must protect the individuals who compose
the natural interests against the exploitative proclivities of all "artifi-

87. The best examples are to be found in the election sermons. "The members
of a well-organized civil community . . . have no more reason to complain, of
the station alloted to them," the Reverend Nathan Stone told the Connecticut
legislature, "than the members of the natural body, have of the place by God
assigned them in that." *A Sermon*, p. 20.

88. James Logan, who was probably the only writer of the 1790s who defended a simon-pure *laissez-faire* policy, quoted with approval the reply of "an
old experienced Merchant [Legendre]" to Colbert, "Let us alone." *Five Letters
to the Yeomanry*, p. 19 [1792].

89. *Principles and Policy*, pp. 56–57 [1814].

90. Ibid., p. 58.

91. Taylor, *Enquiry into Certain Public Measures*, p. 59 [1794].

92. Ibid.

93. Taylor, *Principles and Policy*, p. 621 [1814].

cial," "unnatural," or "factitious" interests.[94] Entrepreneurial democracy in this sense is not something achieved once and for all; rather, it is a continuous defensive action, an eternal war of good against evil, a natural interest "forever resisting . . . frauds against its rights."[95]

What are these rights which must be so zealously guarded? "Every member of civil society," said James Sullivan, "has a clear right to gain all the property which vigilance and industry, regulated by the laws of the state, can bestow upon him."[96] He has this right by virtue of a utilitarian sanction, since "everything he acquires in this way, advances the interest of the public." Moreover, freedom to enjoy the fruits of industry not only creates "a beneficent excitement of effort," but it also makes available a share "sufficient to preserve a free government."[97] This is necessarily so because "labor is in fact the great fund for human existence"; this productive agent produces a surplus of subsistence which "abridges the necessaries" of others.[98] The rights that a democratic government must protect are therefore the right to engage in socially useful labor unhindered by restraints imposed by any artificial interest, and the right to retain the fruits of such labor. Whatever income is acquired by virtue of industry and talent should belong to the producers "except what they owe to society," which is their aliquot contribution "equivalent to the necessities of government."[99]

The ethical qualities of a society based on natural interests reveal themselves in several ways. By emphasizing industry, such a society leads men to follow "the honest and painful methods of earning fortunes" and dissuades them from pursuing "chimerical ways and means of obtaining wealth by sleight of hand."[100] By compelling men to expect not quick speculative profits, but "slow and regular gains," such a society preserves morality by "keeping men employed."[101] By leaving distribution to the free play of "industry and talents," each producer receives what he contributes to the nation's stockpile of produce, less only his share of the public burdens.[102] If the exploitation by "unnatural" or "factitious" interests is eliminated, the incentives to

94. Ibid., pp. 388–389.
95. Ibid., p. 638.
96. *Path to Riches*, pp. 5–6 [1792]. See also John Taylor: "Civil liberty depends upon leaving the distribution of property to industry." *Principles and Policy*, pp. 282, 634 [1814].
97. Taylor, *Principles and Policy*, p. 620 [1814].
98. Taylor, *Definition of Parties*, p. 9 [1794].
99. Taylor, *Principles and Policy*, p. 282 [1814].
100. Pelatiah Webster, *Political Essays*, p. 290 [1785].
101. Noah Webster, *Collection of Essays*, p. 106 [1787].
102. Taylor, *Principles and Policy*, p. 282 [1814].

industry and application are increased, thereby augmenting a nation's total production. Finally, by protecting individuals from the oppression of "unnatural" interests, a government consisting exclusively of natural interests will not only elicit maximum exertion, but will generate that natural type of justice which distributes property in proportion to "industry and talents."[103]

From whence will this government by natural interest draw its personnel? In answering this question, American democratic thought again reveals its natural law origins. Neither wisdom nor wealth are construed as monopolies of an elite group in society, because "the wise men made by nature, are eternally overturning those made by law."[104] Moreover, "with the intervention of education," variations in talents will prove to be "numberless," and the developing abilities of the rank and file of the population[105] will demonstrate the artificiality of the so-called "natural aristocracy" of the "rich and wellborn."

The Importunity of Partial Interests

Since every society is composed of interests, every government will constantly be under pressure to enact legislation advantageous to particular groups. If the general well-being of an entire nation is to be advanced, however, the government must be able to resist "the clamorous importunity of partial interests" and especially the "contemptible cunning of Financiers, who seldom possess any intention to promote the general welfare."[106] The object of all pressure groups is always the same: they are formed to bring about "a transfer of private or public property, or both, from individuals or nations, to orders, corporations or to other individuals."[107] Because of the "depravity of human nature,"[108] the love of money and property "possess[es] almost an unbounded influence over the human mind."[109] In moments of great national emergency, the avarice and selfishness of interests may tem-

103. Ibid., pp. 561, 631; *Enquiry into Certain Public Measures*, p. 59 [1794]; Sullivan, *Path to Riches*, pp. 5–6 [1792].
104. Taylor, *Principles and Policy*, p. 634 [1814].
105. Hamilton admitted, rather grudgingly, that "there are strong minds in every walk of life that will rise superior to the disadvantages of situation," and for that reason, "the door ought to be equally open to all." But he did not think such cases would be frequent; indeed he concluded that "occasional instances of this sort will not render the reasoning, founded upon the general course of things, less conclusive." *The Federalist* (Lodge), XXXV, 207–208 [1788].
106. Logan, *Five Letters to the Yeomanry*, p. 23 [1792].
107. Taylor, *Principles and Policy*, p. 365 [1814].
108. Findley, *Review of the Revenue System*, p. 128 [1794].
109. Taylor, *Principles and Policy*, p. 112 [1814].

porarily be supplanted by "public spirit, heroic virtue, and love of country";[110] but only for a time, since once the moment of peril is past, patriotic enthusiasm subsides "and is absorbed in the general steady principle, private interest."[111]

The moral blemish which gives rise to such group egoism is therefore a universal one. Although it is more pronounced in the "unnatural interests," it nonetheless infects the "natural" interests as well. The mercantile interest, for example, although inherently "natural," may nevertheless persuade a government to enact commercial regulations "highly injurious to the agricultural interests of our country."[112] Local interests may seek special legislative advantages and thereby prejudice general or national well-being;[113] in the absence of federal regulation of commerce, merchants in particular ports, for instance, might persuade state governments to institute local legislation inimical to the nation as a whole.[114]

But the "unnatural interests" constitute the worst enemies of good government. By such devices as funding systems, bank charters, or excise laws, said George Logan, the Federalists have allowed "the property and rights of meritorious citizens" to be "sacrificed to wealthy gamesters and speculators."[115] The particular indictment which Republicans brought against Federalists need not concern us; only the basic contrast between legislation in behalf of partial interests and legislation intended to further the general interest is essential to the argument of this chapter. The technique employed by the financial interest, said Logan, is to induce the government to pass laws designed to favor "a few monied men . . . under a false pretext of serving the agricultural interest"[116] or some other "natural interest." Since any one pressure group may be unable to obtain legislative favor, "combinations will be formed, and interests combined."[117] Here is to be found the real danger to republican government; for even though one admits that "the rules and regulations, adopted by civil society, ought always to be such, as not to afford to any individual, or particular company of men, an accidental opportunity, or a superior privilege for the acquirement of property,"[118] how shall such favoritism be avoided? In 1794 Taylor

110. Webster, *Collection of Essays,* p. 83 [1787].
111. Ibid.
112. Logan, *Five Letters to the Yeomanry,* p. 6 [1792].
113. Findley, *Review of the Revenue System,* p. 82 [1794].
114. Jay, *The Federalist* (Lodge), IV, 25 [1787].
115. *Five Letters to the Yeomanry,* p. 6 [1792].
116. Ibid., p. 26.
117. Findley, *Review of the Revenue System,* p. 128 [1794].
118. Sullivan, *Path to Riches,* pp. 6–7 [1792].

proposed that the money changers be driven out of the temple.[119] But who will do the driving if one interest trades votes with another? Perhaps it was because he realized the impossibility of cleansing Congress of all partial interests that Taylor, when he wrote his *Principles and Policy of Government* in 1814, rejected the whole idea of interests; at any rate he then declared that law sanctioned "by common consent or public will" was wholly irreconcilable with law sanctioned "by the will of a combination among parties of interest."[120]

How government could resist pressure groups, therefore, became the dilemma. All critics of importuning interests agreed with Logan that the "preference of partial to general interests is the greatest of all public evils."[121] No doubt they also agreed with Taylor that "a separate interest, drawing wealth from a nation, and able to gain an influence in a government," could not be construed as a bona fide republican[122] institution, and consequently legislative favoritism met with rancorous and bitter condemnation. How much of this represented the political opportunism of the Republican party and how much a sincere revulsion against pressure groups cannot be measured. A great deal of it no doubt reflects the rising sentiment in favor of more democratic government. But there are no scales on which political sentiments can be weighed.

In the discussion of pressure groups, the problem of interests had to be faced with complete political realism. For it one admits the omnipresence of interests, as the eighteenth-century writers did, then it follows that interests cannot be driven out of legislative halls. That they can be permanently balanced is unlikely. That individuals can transcend their interests is conceivable but improbable. Hence all legislation will be tinctured with partiality for one interest or another because public policy is formulated not by objective and disinterested lawgivers, but by legislators confronted by the "importunity of partial interests," by men who themselves represent particular interests. Taylor hoped that a solicitude for the general interest could be generated by educational forces, and, as his political thought matured, he admitted the impossibility of controlling interests "by the restraints of political law."[123]

119. "The expulsion of paper men [speculators in public securities] out of Congress" was his solution for ridding Congress of one pressure group. *Enquiry into Certain Public Measures*, p. 61 [1794].
120. *Principles and Policy*, p. 602 [1814].
121. *Five Letters to the Yeomanry*, pp. 11–12 [1792].
122. "To the term 'republican,' the Americans have annexed the modern meaning of general good." *Principles and Policy*, p. 575 [1814].
123. Ibid., p. 654.

Patricians and Plebeians

The inescapable consequences of well-organized legislative blocs were depicted vividly by the Republican critics of "unnatural and factitious" interests. "There can be but two [classes] under a system of paper," John Taylor prophesied: "creditor and debtor, patricians and plebeians, or masters and slaves."[124] The consolidation of a powerful "monied" interest, he said, had been encouraged by Hamilton's financial policies. But whereas the motives were veiled by a smoke screen of insincere patriotism, the whole program constituted an invasion of "the correct and honest principle of private property."[125] For in the final analysis, there can be but "two modes of invading private property: the first, by which the poor plunder the rich is sudden and violent; the second, by which the rich plunder the poor, slow and legal."[126] Was it not clear, Taylor asked, that the Bank of the United States tended to make the "rich, richer; and the poor, poorer"? The poor, having no savings with which to buy bank stock, were as effectively excluded from participating in banking profits as they would have been if they had been forbidden to subscribe to bank shares.[127] Yet by virtue of the very nature of the economic system, the profits of banking are "paid out of labour," and since in all countries it is the poor who labor, "will it not make this class poorer?" Since the net effect then of the machinations of the paper interest had been to create an annuity, "conjured up by law," for the exclusive benefit of the rich, "will it not make them richer?"[128]

Conflict between rich and poor had been foreseen by Richard Henry Lee at the time when the Constitution was being drafted. Much in the spirit of John Adams, Lee thought the poor and the rich equally "unprincipled." The poor consisted of "little insurgents, men in debt, who want no law, and who want a share of the property of others"; these, he contended, "are called levellers, Shayites, etc."[129] The rich comprised "a few but more dangerous men" because they "avariciously grasp at all power and property." Like Aristotle, Lee believed the

124. Ibid., pp. 264–265.
125. Ibid., p. 280.
126. "One begets ferocity and barbarism, the other vice and penury, and both impair the national prosperity and happiness." Ibid.
127. *Enquiry into Certain Public Measures*, p. 15 [1794].
128. Ibid., p. 15.
129. Hamilton agreed with this description of the poor: "If Shays had not been a desperate debtor," he wrote, "it is much to be doubted whether Massachusetts would have been plunged into a civil war." *The Federalist* (Lodge), VI, 28.

highest political morality resided in the middle class, "in men of middling property, men not in debt . . . and not aiming at immense fortunes, offices and power."[130] How would this class fare in the inevitable conflict of interests?

Lee feared that if the middle-class "yeomanry" could not "negative" laws designed to benefit the rich, "they may in twenty or thirty years be . . . totally deprived of their boasted weight and strength."[131] George Logan shared Lee's concern; moreover he pointed out that the efficiency of agriculture demanded the preservation of the American yeomanry. From a careful study of crop rotation, he concluded that farms should not be less than two hundred acres.[132] Farms of that size, however, could not be equipped and stocked by a "poor tenantry"; hence land policy should be planned for the purpose of maintaining the middle-class farmers.[133] Speculation in land, carried on by a "monied interest," was therefore condemned. "Where are the blessed efforts" of Hamilton's financial program? asked William Findley. "Is the princely estates accumulated by speculators . . . a national blessing?" "Is the changing the state of society by a rapid increase of wealth in the hands of a few individuals, to the impoverishing of others, by the artificial aid of law . . . a national blessing?"[134] If the "monied interests" can become richer by molding legislation to their advantage, said John Taylor, popular indignation will surely lead to "the pernicious and impractical idea of equalizing property by law."[135]

So went the controversy about the rich and the poor. Anti-Federalists like John Taylor felt certain that the monied interests in Congress would widen the gulf between patricians and plebeians. Legalistic minds saw the conflict as one between debtors and creditors.[136] Preachers gave comfort to the defenders of things-as-they-are by assuring their listeners that there would always be rich and poor "so long as the world exists."[137] Believers in a "natural aristocracy" rested their case for the political priority of the "rich and wellborn" on the grounds of

130. *Observations of the System of Government,* p. 43 [1787].
131. Ibid., p. 27.
132. *Fourteen Agricultural Experiments, to Ascertain the Best Rotation of Crops: Addressed to the Philadelphia Agricultural Society* (Philadelphia, 1797), p. 33.
133. Ibid., pp. 36–37.
134. *Review of the Revenue System,* p. 40 [1794].
135. *Principles and Policy,* p. 563 [1814].
136. "Is a law proposed concerning private debts? It is a question to which creditors are parties on one side and debtors on the other." Madison, *The Federalist* (Lodge), X, 54–55 [1787].
137. Backus, *Absalom's Conspiracy,* pp. 24–25 [1798].

special competence.[138] Advocates of a bill of rights admitted that although "laws cannot equalize men," they must be so devised that they will not "aggravate the inequality which they cannot cure."[139] Amateur social psychologists predicted that the luxury of a law-favored plutocracy would "corrupt" the tastes of the humble and produce a "spirit of envy" which would make people "disquiet" and "unhappy" who "before had been quite contented."[140] On only one thing did the social theorists seemingly agree, that "those who hold and those who are without property have ever formed distinct interests in society."[141]

The Solidarity of Equilibrium

With genuine insight, Hamilton or Madison, whichever wrote the *Federalist* Number LI, indicated two alternative ways in which government might deal with conflicting interests. One was to create "a will in the community independent of the [legislative] majority."[142] This method (which John Taylor later espoused) the Federalists rejected, placing their trust in the emergence of so many separate interests "as will render an unjust combination . . . very improbable."[143] Unreasonable demands, or overtly selfish schemes, said the author of the *Federalist* Number LI, will be neutralized by the other interests represented in the Congress; hence it was contended that a coalition of interests "could seldom take place on any other principles than those of justice and the general good."[144] Moreover, an understanding of the mutual interrelations of the several interests will be appreciated, said Hamilton: merchants will understand the need of guarding the well-being of manufacturers and mechanics; professional men will serve as impartial arbiters.[145] A variety of solidarity would therefore emerge, originating in the self-interest of particular interests, but leading nevertheless to an equilibrium between interests. This idea of inter-interest checks and balances may be designated as the solidarity of equilibrium.

138. Alexander Hamilton, *Works*, I, 401; Lee, *Observations of the System of Government*, p. 17; Adams, *Defense of the Constitutions*, pp. 106–107.
139. Logan, *Five Letters to the Yeomanry*, pp. 4, 12 [1792].
140. Sullivan, *Path to Riches*, pp. 7, 40 [1792]; Taylor, *Principles and Policy*, p. 167 [1814].
141. Madison, *The Federalist* (Lodge), X, 54 [1787].
142. *The Federalist* (Lodge), LI, 325 [1788].
143. "The diversity in the faculties of men," wrote Madison in *The Federalist* (Lodge, X, 53), "is . . . an insuperable obstacle to a uniformity of interests."
144. *The Federalist* (Lodge), LI, 327 [1788].
145. Ibid., XXXV, 205–206 [1788].

Rational Solidarity

The lawmaking process during Washington's administration, however, revealed little evidence of such solidarity. Fierce controversies raged over the wisdom and the justice of funding the public debt, assuming the state debts, chartering a bank, and imposing excise taxes. The Republican opposition denied that any such thing as an equilibrium of interests existed; they alleged that a powerful financial interest had come into being under the aegis of Federalist leaders. Some Republicans rejected the whole idea of inter-group equilibrium. Instead of group egoism, they said, there must be nurtured a sincere and intense solicitude for the general welfare. Only this "common will," essentially the equivalent of Rousseau's *volonté générale,* transcending the egoism of interests, can generate a national solidarity which will be rational and hence permanent.

The leading exponent of such rational solidarity was, of course, John Taylor of Caroline. "A nation cut up into orders or separate interests," he asserted, "cannot exert national self-government, because the national self no more exists than a polypus, after being cut into four or five pieces, which forage in different directions or upon each other."[146] The true function of government should be to advance the prosperity of the entire nation. This can only be accomplished by the "exclusion of separate interests, able to create factions."[147] For whenever combinations of interests coalesce in Congress, a "spurious" government emerges, which intrudes itself upon the lawful government and the common will.[148] The framers of the Constitution intended to create a government that would be responsible to the "will of numbers," not to the "will of wealth." Yet there has grown up a financial interest, representing no more than 5000 persons, which has taken government out of the hands of the 5,000,000 citizens.[149] Instead of national unity, a feeling of "oppression and hatred" has been generated.[150] "Only the one thousandth part of the nation retains in reality a political existence"; indeed the power to influence legislation, which is the essence of political life, has been engrossed by the 5000, while "the 5,000,000 are only allowed, once in two years, a kind of political spasm."[151] Favoritism rather than impartiality, said another critic of

146. *Principles and Policy,* p. 444 [1814].
147. Ibid., p. 346.
148. *Definition of Parties,* p. 5 [1794]; *Principles and Policy,* p. 282 [1814].
149. *Definition of Parties,* p. 4 [1794].
150. *Principles and Policy,* p. 39 [1814].
151. *Definition of Parties,* p. 14 [1794].

the Federalists, has honeycombed legislation in spite of a constitutional provision "that no man, or company of men, should have any legal exclusive right or privilege."[152]

For these perversions, said the advocates of rational solidarity, there can be but one remedy. Every individual must assume the full responsibility which democratic government involves; for "the salutary restraint of accountableness" is the only recipe for national welfare. Each individual must learn to understand that "all human interests are the same," that "nothing which is vicious or wrong, can be really beneficial" to anyone.[153] The idea that individuals can benefit by forming legislative blocs or by organizing pressure groups is illusory. Hence "all false and factitious interests" which are "eternally seducing men from true and natural interests" must be rejected.[154] The common will must assert itself; it must learn to detect all legislation tinctured with selfishness. It must first understand, however, that "principles dictated by public good, can never unite with motives of private interest."[155] Every rational individual must ultimately perceive that "a government for advancing the prosperity of the entire nation" is preeminently superior to one which allows society to be fragmented into hostile camps.[156] All law must therefore serve general, not separate, interests. The only way whereby this utilitarian end can be achieved, said the advocates of rational solidarity, is through the "representation and responsibility" of alert, public-spirited, rational individuals.[157]

The Solidarity of Benevolence

A third way whereby the public or common good might be promoted may be designated the solidarity of benevolence. The founders of the Massachusetts Agricultural Society asserted, for example, that they had "no other interest than the benefit of the human species at large." The only rewards they sought for their labors, so they alleged, was "the satisfaction of being beneficial" to themselves and the community.[158] Such an aggregate test of action, said Noah Webster,

152. Sullivan, *Path to Riches*, p. 73 [1792].
153. Taylor, *Principles and Policy*, p. 436 [1814].
154. Ibid., p. 349.
155. Taylor, *Definition of Parties*, p. 15 [1794].
156. *Principles and Policy*, p. 640. "A chain," said George Logan, "does not derive its strength and utility from being composed of a few heavy links, and the remainder weak and ill-conditioned." In the same way, "a state is rendered more respectable and powerful by the prosperity of all its citizens than by the overgrown wealth of a few." *Five Letters to the Yeomanry*, p. 21 [1792].
157. See Logan, *Five Letters to the Yeomanry*, pp. 19–20 [1792]; John Taylor, *Definition of Parties*, p. 5 [1794].

should dominate the "whole art of governing"; if it did, it would succeed in "binding each individual by his particular interest, to promote the aggregate interest of the community."[159] George Logan thought social benevolence would necessarily result if government were based on the rights of man: "from the very nature of this [social] compact, every act of Government should be equally favorable to all the citizens without distinction."[160] But whereas government ought to protect equally "the person and property of every one of its members," each individual citizen must, in turn, assume certain social responsibilities. "Useful employment and comfortable support" must be provided for the "weakest and most miserable fellow-citizens." This responsibility is individual, not governmental: "duty as well as interest, oblige the members of the same society to assist each other."[161] Good citizenship therefore demanded two things: an honest performance of one's economic function[162] and a solicitude for one's fellows. The motto of every American, said Logan, should be that of the French economists: "faire le bien c'est le recevoir"; moreover this motto is as applicable to nations as to individuals because nations merely succeed in injuring themselves "by circumscribing or destroying the advantages of their neighbors."[163]

The Solidarity of Self-Interest

The solidarity originating in benevolence merges almost imperceptibly, in late eighteenth-century social theory, with a concept of solidarity based on self-interest. This fusion is well illustrated in the writings of George Logan. In civil society, said Logan, man is a member of

158. *Laws and Regulations of the Massachusetts Society for Promoting Agriculture* (Boston, 1793), p. iv.

159. *Collection of Essays*, pp. 73, 94, 114 [1787]. "The object of a law is to prevent positive evil or produce positive good to the whole State; not merely to a particular part."

160. *Five Letters to the Yeomanry*, p. 7 [1792]. See also his *Address before the Tammany Society*, p. 12 [1798]. A few of the later election sermons also contain samples of Benthamite philosophy. Thus the Reverend Worcester admonished rulers "in all matters of property or privilege" to consider carefully "the greatest good of the greatest number." *An Election Sermon* (Concord, New Hampshire, 1800), p. 4.

161. Logan, *Five Letters to the Yeomanry*, pp. 7, 22 [1792].

162. Coxe called "usefulness in their proper sphere" the "most valuable characteristics of good citizens." *View of the United States*, p. 359 [1792].

163. Logan, *Five Letters to the Yeomanry*, p. 24 [1792]. Noah Webster used the same argument for interstate commercial unity in 1785. The states, he said, "ought to encourage the commerce of each other—they ought to promote such an intercourse as will conciliate rather than alienate each others' affections." *Sketches of American Policy*, p. 45 [1785].

a political family; within this family he "is connected with his Fellow-citizen, by ties of interest and benevolent attachment."[164] Each citizen's "social affections must extend to the whole Community of which he is a Member." But benevolence interacts with self-interest; each citizen "should feel the Safety, and the Common Welfare, intimately connected with his own."[165] Public good and private well-being are, in fact, so "closely united" that "it is incumbent on us to do everything in our power to enrich our Country."[166] National enrichment, however, cannot be advanced by governmental action;[167] it springs from the "independence and prosperity" of all citizens, and hence "it becomes not only the duty, but the interest of every individual to promote the prosperity and independence of his Fellow-Citizens."[168]

It is this ethical aspect of self-interest that differentiates American libertarianism from its British counterpart. "Self-interest," wrote Noah Webster, "is and ought to be the ruling principle of mankind; but this principle must operate in perfect conformity to social and political obligations." It must be enlightened self-interest, because "a selfishness which excludes others from a participation of benefits is, in all cases, self-ruin."[169] True patriotism, therefore, "is nothing but self-interest, acting in conjunction with other interests for its own sake," and "public good is but the aggregate sum of individual interests."[170] Boundaries of self-interest must nevertheless be established to "restrain the pursuit of individuals when they infringe the public rights."[171] How this doctrine was reflected in legislation will be explained later; here one example will suffice. In 1795, the Pennsylvania legislature forbade the construction of wooden buildings east of Tenth Street in Philadelphia, stating in the preamble that it was the duty of the legislature "to strengthen the security of property [by reducing fire hazards] whenever the same can be done without violating the rights of private persons."[172]

Self-interest cannot be sovereign. Even though every person "has a

164. *Letter to the Citizens*, p. 5 [1800].
165. Ibid.
166. Ibid.
167. Until 1798, when he admitted that government ought to stimulate manufacturing, Logan was as ardent a disciple of Adam Smith as any of his contemporaries. He always insisted, however, that self-interest alone could not promote the public good.
168. *Address before the Tammany Society*, p. 8 [1798].
169. *Sketches of American Policy*, p. 48 [1783].
170. Ibid., p. 3 [1785].
171. Ibid., p. 6.
172. The preamble alleged that brick or stone construction was no more costly than wood, and hence the law infringed no rights. *15 Pennsylvania Statutes at Large*, 354–355, ch. 1860.

clear right to gain all the property which vigilance and industry . . . can bestow upon him,"[173] this right must not infringe the well-being of the community. The good of the whole must take precedence; hence, whereas individuals "are not bound to sacrifice all private views,"[174] the common good cannot be achieved "without injury or inconvenience to some individuals."[175] The goal of social policy must therefore be to "promote the general interests with the smallest injury to particular ones";[176] it must seek "so to unite and combine public and private interests, that they may mutually support, feed and quicken each other."[177]

The history of ideas is always a complex and baffling subject, and the cardinal sin of most historians is oversimplification. The forgoing analysis of "the few and the many" has demonstrated how the problem of interests challenged the political ingenuity of the eighteenth-century social theorists. The existence of interests was accepted as a sociological fact; moreover it was clearly appreciated that some political representation of the several interests was not only proper but inescapable. Yet political realism created serious obstacles to any neat, effective, and stable equilibrium between conflicting interests; the fear of secret representation leading to the political dominance of combinations of interests bred distrust, suspicion, and antagonism between political parties. Should the propertied interests have special political privileges? Or should natural interests monopolize legislative power? Would the lobbying activities of particular interests jeopardize the common good? Could combinations of interest be prevented, or would they coagulate into a "ruling class" and divide society into but two classes, the rich and the poor? The disagreement which these questions reveal seriously complicated not only political theorizing but the practical business of lawmaking. And although four roads to the common good are discernible in eighteenth-century social theory, no agreement seemed possible as to which road should be taken. The Federalists asserted that their public policies were uniquely capable of advancing the common good, and they justified their policies by their own brand of social theory. The Republicans condemned not only Federalist policies but Federalist social theory. The conflict of parties, however, was comparatively simple; it represented mainly a disagreement centered on natural versus factitious interest. This subject must therefore be further explored.

173. Sullivan, *Path to Riches*, p. 5 [1792].
174. Gray, *A Sermon*, pp. 13–14.
175. Fobes, *A Sermon*, p. 12.
176. Coxe, *View of the United States*, p. 29 [1787].
177. Pelatiah Webster, *Political Essays*, p. 499 [1781].

III

The Natural Interest and the Common Good

Cultivators . . . are the most valuable
citizens. They are the most vigorous, the
most independent, the most virtuous, and
they are tied to their country, and
wedded to its liberty and interests by
the most lasting bounds.

Thomas Jefferson

Agriculture, the Mother Which Suckles All

THE FOUNDER and the standard-bearer of the Republicans, Thomas Jefferson, not only denied the legitimacy of the unnatural interest of finance and arbitrage, but in his earlier writings even questioned the social desirability, in the United States, of manufacturing enterprise. Good government, he argued quite unambiguously, depends largely upon control by agriculturalists. Commerce and the professions ought to be represented, but the agrarian element should predominate. Oddly enough the justification was essentially theological. "Those who labor in the earth," said Jefferson, "are the chosen people of God"; they possess more "substantial and genuine virtue" than any other class of people, because their incomes depend not "on the casualties and caprice of customers," but on their own industry.[1] Being historically uncorrupted and naturalistically incorruptible, the agricultural interest should have political priority.

With less religiosity but with equal certitude, other writers stressed the primacy of the agricultural interest. Agriculture, said Tench Coxe, furnishes outward cargoes for all American and many foreign ships, pays for American imports, supplies the entire population with food, and provides raw materials for manufacturers.[2] Since he estimated that it employed nine-tenths of the population,[3] Coxe called the landed interest "an irresistible power"[4] whose political representation would be guaranteed by virtue of the numerical voting strength of the farmers. Hamilton similarly assured his readers, in 1788, that "the landed

1. *Notes on the State of Virginia* (Paris, 1785), pp. 302–303 [1781].
2. *View of the United States,* pp. 6–7 [1787].
3. Ibid. George Logan estimated that, in 1798, agriculture still employed nine-tenths of the American working population. *Address before the Tammany Society,* p. 8.
4. *Pennsylvania Herald* (December 29, 1787).

interest must, upon the whole, predominate in the government,"[5] and he promised that the Constitution would not make the agricultural interest subservient to the mercantile interest. But although "agriculture is predominant," said Hamilton, it needs no special legislative representation since in proportion to its importance "it will be conveyed into the national representation."[6] Moreover Hamilton thought that, in a political sense, the agricultural interest was "perfectly united from the wealthiest landlord down to the poorest tenant,"[7] a thesis that other writers vehemently denied.[8]

John Taylor's attitude toward the agricultural class, in sharp contrast with Hamilton's, was physiocratic. "Those who furnish the subsistence" of society, he argued, "pay all the taxes";[9] nor can the agricultural interest, he said, shift the tax. Its capacity to provide society with food and its alleged responsibility for paying all taxes gave agriculture a clear right to political priority; "from her other interests diverge, like rays from the sun, but she is the center of them all." Whatever laws "operate against her" automatically injure all other groups since she is "the mother which suckles all other interests."[10] James Swan, the Boston political arithmetician, agreed with this fulsome praise of agriculture. "The husbandman's labour," he contended, is the most beneficial to a state because it provides food for seamen, merchants, and mechanics, thus permitting a state to have a larger population and yet be ensured against the "danger of famine in peace and blockade in war."[11] George Logan, himself a progressive farmer, willingly added his approbation, and ventured the opinion that "notwithstanding the glare of her commerce and manufacturing," England "owes all her real wealth and greatness to the prosperity and independent situation of her farmers."[12]

With the sureness that stems from conviction, the defenders of the primacy of the agricultural interest emphasized its beneficent contributions to the common good. Its industrious and incorrupt[13] personnel

5. *The Federalist* (Lodge), LX, 377 [1788].
6. Ibid., p. 376.
7. *The Federalist* (Lodge), XXXV, 205 [1788].
8. See Claude G. Bowers, *Jefferson and Hamilton* (Boston, 1925), especially chaps. VII and XVII for abundant evidence.
9. *Principles and Policy,* p. 333 [1814].
10. Ibid., p. 618 [1814].
11. *National Arithmetick* (Boston, 1786) pp. 6–7.
12. *Fourteen Agricultural Experiments,* pp. 40–41 [1797].
13. "Corruption of morals in the masses of cultivators is a phaenomenon of which no age nor nation has furnished an example." Thomas Jefferson, *Notes on Virginia,* p. 303 [1785]. "The proportion which the aggregate of the other classes of citizens bears in any state to that of its husbandmen, is the proportion of its unsound to its healthy parts, and is a good enough barometer whereby to measure its degree of corruption." Ibid.

74

provide a nation with food, with raw materials for domestic consumption and for exportation. It protects a nation against famine or the inconveniences resulting from blockades, yet, withal, it increases population and pays all taxes. To this list of social contributions, John Taylor added still another: the agricultural interest, unlike the financial interest, does not tend toward monopoly. "Land," said Taylor, "cannot in interest be at enmity with the public good—paper money is often so. Land cannot be incorporated by law, or by an exclusive interest, into a political junto—paper money may. Land is permanent, paper fluctuating. A Legislature, by a paper legerdemain, may transfer to themselves the lands of their constituents—a landed interest does not admit of intricate modifications."[14]

The claims that agriculture provided greater social utility than any other interest did not go unchallenged. Hamilton in his *Report on Manufactures* admitted that farmers provided a nation with food and raw materials. He conceded also that agriculture was "most favorable to the freedom and independence of the human mind." He granted that it made possible an increase of population. He even acknowledged that agriculture "has intrinsically a strong claim to pre-eminence over every other kind of industry."[15] Yet despite all this, Hamilton denied that the agricultural interest could lay claim to being more useful than other interests. Manufacturing, in his opinion, was no less productive, and he took great pains to demonstrate this vividly.[16] He therefore concluded that the functional efficiency of an economy demands reciprocal interrelations between the several interests; hence it is a "maxim, well established by experience and generally acknowledged, . . . that the aggregate prosperity of manufacturers and the aggregate prosperity of agriculture are intimately connected."[17]

Hamilton's contention that the prosperity of the agricultural interest depended on a nation's industrial development found vigorous endorsement in the writings of Tench Coxe.[18] "The creation of a ready, near, and stable market" for agricultural products by the development of domestic manufactures, claimed Coxe, "is the most effectual

14. *Definition of Parties*, p. 9 [1794].
15. Alexander Hamilton, *Papers on Public Credit, Commerce and Finance*, ed. Samuel McKee (New York, 1934), p. 180 [1791].
16. Ibid., pp. 181–190.
17. Ibid., p. 230.
18. There is such striking similarity between Coxe's and Hamilton's arguments in favor of developing manufactures that it seems not unlikely that Coxe assisted Hamilton in the *Report on Manufactures*. It should be recalled that Coxe succeeded William Duer as Hamilton's assistant in the Treasury (May 4, 1790) and that he held this post when the *Report* appeared (December 5, 1791). See Hutcheson, *Tench Coxe*, pp. 19–28. But for an opposite opinion, see Mitchell, *Alexander Hamilton*, II, 151.

method to promote husbandry, and to advance the interests of the proprietors and cultivators of the earth."[19] Frontier agriculture is especially dependent on markets fostered by domestic manufactures, although even near the seacoast "the all-important landed interest would languish" were even the limited "present [1793] manufactures . . . abolished."[20] Furthermore, Coxe said, the example of Britain has convincingly shown that "manufactures, instead of impeding agriculture, . . . are actually its greatest and most certain support . . . indispensably necessary to the prosperity of the landed interest."[21] Coxe therefore vigorously and persistently urged that government action be taken to quicken the growth of manufactures. Both he and Hamilton called particular attention to the benefits that American grain growers would obtain from the domestic manufacture of malt liquors.[22] Not many writers showed comparable enthusiasm for manufactures. Until commercial difficulties compelled him to change his views, Jefferson opposed manufactures for social reasons, while George Logan, although he favored small-scale manufactures, warned his countrymen not to permit agriculture to become dependent on manufactures, citing as an object lesson the experience in France of Louis XIV, whose efforts "to render the agricultural interest subservient to his project of manufactures, occasioned the ruin and destruction of both."[23] But although there may have been disagreement about whether the agricultural interest should be primus or merely primus inter pares, there was apparently complete agreement that the government should protect and aid this very useful and socially beneficial interest. Agriculture ought to be kept flourishing and vigorous, zealously guarded against injury, and it should be especially protected against exploitation by commercial, financial, or foreign interests.

As to how agriculture could be kept vigorous, there were sharp differences of opinion. Thus Jefferson, even though he had lived in France and must have observed the disadvantages of *morcellement,* nevertheless said that "legislators cannot invent too many devices for subdividing property."[24] John Taylor, on the other hand, alleged that "by cutting up the landed interest into little farms," good managerial talent would drift away from agriculture, leaving the agricultural

19. *View of the United States,* p. 384 [1793].
20. Ibid., p. 297 [1792].
21. Ibid., p. 55 [1794].
22. Ibid., p. 38 [1787]; p. 319 [1792]; Hamilton, *Public Papers* (McKee), p. 38 [1790].
23. *Five Letters to the Yeomanry,* pp. 17–18 [1792].
24. *Writings of Thomas Jefferson,* ed. P. L. Ford (New York, 1899), VII, 35 [1785].

interest incapable of defending itself against "the whole family of legal, exclusive or aristocratical interests." He warned that the agricultural interest would atrophy economically and politically "unless a sound mind is lodged somewhere within it."[25] But Taylor took pains to point out that the American agricultural interest ought not fall into the "gross error" of "imagining itself to bear a resemblance to the English landlord interest." The American farmers, he said, more nearly corresponded to the British tenantry "being composed, generally, of cultivators."[26] The English landlords, in contrast, represented an exclusive, exploitative hierarchy that extracted wealth from a servile laboring class. In America, such a gulf between rich and poor, between a privileged landlord class and "an ignorant agricultural interest," could be prevented by a liberal land policy plus a system of universal education.[27] But fragmentation of landholdings ought to be avoided, lest, "as landed possessions are divided, the leisure and income of the proprietors" be diminished. Should this occur, the "weight of talents" would gravitate toward cities, thereby making it possible for mercantile and financial interests "to acquire an ascendant [sic] over the landed interest, gradually impoverished by division."[28]

National policies therefore should be carefully examined to ensure that no action "burdening or impeding agriculture" is taken inadvertently.[29] Commercial regulations devised for the benefit of merchants, which might injure agriculture, ought to be constantly guarded against.[30] Markets must be kept free and competitive, asserted George Logan. He warned Americans especially about the factorage system whereby British credit extension had "made the Farmer tributary to the Storekeeper; the Storekeeper, to the Merchant of Philadelphia; the Merchant of Philadelphia, to the Merchant of Great Britain."[31] An ardent if erstwhile disciple of Adam Smith, Logan strongly emphasized the dangers of governmental interference.[32] "The Yeomanry of America," he said, "only desire what they have a right to demand—a

25. *Principles and Policy,* p. 620 [1814].
26. Ibid., pp. 618–619.
27. Ibid., p. 618.
28. Ibid., pp. 262–263.
29. Tench Coxe, *View of the United States,* pp. 9, 13, 37–38 [1787].
30. See Hutcheson, *Tench Coxe,* p. 123.
31. *Letter to Citizens,* pp. 15–16 [1800]; see also Tench Coxe, *View of the United States,* p. 33.
32. He cited the discouraging effects on Greek agriculture which resulted from market restraints imposed upon farmers: "This unjust regulation served a temporary purpose of supplying the city with provisions, at a low price; but the Farmers, feeling themselves injured, converted so great a proportion of the country into olive yards, that in a short time provisions became dearer than ever." *Five Letters to the Yeomanry,* p. 13 [1792].

free unrestricted sale for the produce of their own industry."[33] Precisely how this "unrestricted" market could be created and maintained became a central question since it involved international as well as domestic policy. Boston merchants, led by James Bowdoin, argued that an American commercial policy modeled on the British navigation laws was necessary,[34] while advocates of manufactures insisted that the "precarious operations of foreign trade" would be eliminated if an adequate home market were developed.[35] Logan, however, advocated an open-market solution for the farm problem. By enacting commercial restrictions, he said, we will only "injure ourselves by preventing a sale for the surplus produce of our agriculture."[36] Instead of such a shortsighted policy, America should "adopt a genuine system of policy, founded on the Rights of Man"; it should declare "total freedom of commerce, within the United States." Moreover, if America imposes tariffs on imports from foreign nations, "can we expect that they will not retaliate, and in their turn obstruct the progress of our trade, by embarrassments particularly injurious to the agricultural interest?"[37]

How could the exploitation of the agricultural interest by other domestic interests or by foreign interests be prevented? It became a central argument of the Anti-Federalists that a domestic financial interest most seriously threatened the well-being of farmers. The great danger with which farmers are always confronted, asserted that redoubtably enemy of banks and high finance John Taylor, "lies in the legal depredations of the various parties actuated by exclusive interests . . . whose business it is to get what they can from the rest of the nation."[38] Condemning the whole Federalist program as such a "depredation," Taylor alleged that the funding act was designed to create "an enormous aristocracy or monied interest"[39] whose ill-gotten gains would be mostly derived from farmers and laborers. Likewise the profits of the Bank of the United States would constitute a subtraction from the incomes of agricultural workers.[40] George Logan sounded an even more portentous warning: the federal excise law, he charged,

33. Ibid., p. 28.
34. *Observations upon the Necessity and Importance of the American Navigation Act*, p. 47.
35. See Barton, *The True Interest of the United States, and Particularly of Pennsylvania Considered*, p. 26; Coxe, *View of the United States*, p. 21; Hamilton, *Report on Manufactures*, in *Public Papers* (McKee), pp. 196–200.
36. *Five Letters to the Yeomanry*, pp. 24–25 [1792].
37. Ibid.
38. *Principles and Policy*, pp. vii–viii [1814].
39. *Enquiry into Certain Public Measures*, p. 41 [1794].
40. Ibid., p. 10; *Principles and Policy*, p. 620.

"violates the domestic rights of the farmer," bank charters give a "rich monied interest" the power to trench into the property of farmers,[41] while Hamilton's *Report on Manufactures* is nothing but a scheme for granting "exclusive privileges, bounties and premiums, to a few monied men."[42] Since all this Federalist chicanery has been disguised "under a false pretence of serving the agricultural interest,"[43] many farmers have been grossly deceived. But unless the American yeomanry are protected against the financiers, they will presently find themselves reduced to "a miserable, dependent peasantry."[44] Yet despite the censorious remarks directed specifically at them, Hamilton and his associates were by no means the only politicians who justified proposed laws by emphasizing the putative benefits to be conferred upon the agricultural interest. A Pennsylvania law for erecting a loan office (April 11, 1793) alleged that such an institution "will be greatly beneficial to agriculture."[45] A Delaware (Newcastle) request for permission to raise money for harbor improvements by a lottery (February 7, 1794) was based on the argument that the project would "have a beneficial tendency in promoting the commercial and agricultural interests."[46] A New Jersey act (November 24, 1786) imposing license taxes on stages, ferries, and taverns was justified in the preamble as affording fiscal relief to landowners.[47] The charter of the Union Bank of Massachusetts (1792) stipulated that "one fifth part of the whole funds of this bank" should be "wholly and exclusively" devoted to making loans to "the agricultural interest."[48] Hamilton was therefore doing just about the same thing that other politicians did when he alleged that his funding scheme would make it easier for farmers to pay their debts and would raise the value of land.[49] That every shrewd politician would verbally patronize agriculture is understandable when one recalls that, in 1790, about

41. *Letters Addressed to the Yeomanry of the United States, Containing Some Observations on Funding and Bank Systems* (Philadelphia, 1792), pp. 8, 24.

42. Ibid., p. 26. By 1798, however, Logan took a less dogmatic position: "It is to the peculiar interest of the Farmers," he said to the Tammany Society, "that they should give every encouragement to the Mechanics and Manufacturers of the United States; by which they may procure a certain and steady market at their own doors, for the surplus produce of their industry." *Address before the Tammany Society,* p. 9.

43. *Five Letters to the Yeomanry,* p. 26 [1792].

44. Ibid., pp. 18–19.

45. *14 Pennsylvania Statutes at Large,* 481–482, ch. 1697, sec. 1–2.

46. *2 Delaware Laws,* 1189–1191, ch. 600.

47. *New Jersey Laws* (1786–1789), 377, XI ch. CLXXXVII.

48. *Massachusetts Laws* (1801), II, 549 (1792–1793), 16–17.

49. *Political Papers* (McKee), p. 9 [1790]. Pelatiah Webster, arguing in favor of high excise and customs duties on articles of luxury, also promised that his fiscal policy would raise the value of land. *Political Essays,* p. 239 [1783].

nine-tenths of the gainfully employed belonged to the agricultural interest.

Merchants, the Natural Negotiators of Wealth

"I wish," said Pelatiah Webster, "that Congress might have the benefit of that extensive and important information" which merchants possess.[50] For their business makes them "perfectly acquainted with the sources of our wealth"; moreover their activity is "more intimately and necessarily connected with the general prosperity of the country, than any other order of men."[51] If this lavish praise of merchants seems extravagant, it should be recalled that Webster was himself a merchant. But it was not only merchants who found merit in the mercantile interest. John Taylor, for example, admitted that next to the agricultural group "no separate interest would constitute a less exceptionable legislator than commerce, on account of its close connexion with agriculture and manufactures."[52] But whereas the mercantile interest, by virtue of its function, might conceivably serve as a suitable lawmaking group, Taylor warned that there are "complicated means" which the mercantile interest "could practise, to make other interests, and even those of agriculture subservient to hers."[53] Logically, however, the mercantile claim to some measure of political priority was sound, and Pelatiah Webster had made this abundantly clear. Because "negotiation is the business of their lives," merchants are better acquainted with a nation's surpluses and wants than any other occupational segment. They have, moreover, "a natural interest" in supplying a nation with scarce goods and in finding markets for its surpluses.[54] Tench Coxe found similar merit in the mercantile interest: it is, he said, ever "attentive to the general interests," since it comes "forward with offers to range through foreign climates, in search of those supplies" which a nation cannot itself provide at all or only at prohibitive cost.[55] "Trade is of such essential importance to our interests," Pelatiah Webster pointed out, that "the general benefit of the community" cannot be advanced without it.[56] Farmers "will not toil and sweat thro' the year to raise great plenty" unless there are merchants who stand ready to buy their produce. Conversely, agriculture provides most of the materials of commerce,[57]

50. *Political Essays*, p. 215 [1783].
51. Ibid.
52. *Principles and Policy*, p. 333 [1814].
53. Ibid.
54. *Political Essays*, p. 216 [1783].
55. *View of the United States*, p. 24 [1787].
56. *Political Essays*, p. 216 [1783].
57. Coxe, *View of the United States*, pp. 6–7 [1787].

since "a nation can only carry on a permanent commerce, upon the surplus produce of its labours," a surplus that must originate with either the agricultural or the manufacturing interest.[58] Agriculture and commerce are therefore mutually interdependent; hence the agricultural interest will be "too well convinced of the utility of commerce" to advocate "the entire exclusion [from government] of those who would best understand its interest."[59] Functionally there ought always to be "a due proportion between the commercial interest, the agricultural and the manufacturing interests,"[60] and, politically, representation should bear a close relation to the relative numerical importance of each interest.[61]

Pelatiah Webster, however, thought that since merchants were the "natural negotiators of the wealth of the country" whose activities largely determined the prosperity of agriculture and the progress of manufactures, the mercantile interest should be entitled to some special political consideration. He therefore proposed, in 1783, that the merchants in the several states should send delegates "to meet and attend the sittings of Congress." He further recommended that the merchant-delegates should "form a chamber of commerce," and he urged that the advice of this chamber ought to be "demanded and admitted concerning all bills before Congress" affecting trade.[62] Such a proposal, he argued, was eminently reasonable especially because "a very great part of our revenue must arise from imposts on merchandise."[63]

The close connection of commerce with other interests suggested the idea that the commercial interest was really composite. Thus Coxe said that importing, exporting, shipping, fishing, and manufacturing "may be properly considered as forming one interest."[64] He estimated that this aggregate of occupations employed about "one-eighth of the property and people occupied by agriculture." Hamilton also regarded the mercantile interest as something more than a trading group. When he recommended that Congress should consist primarily of landholders, merchants, and professional men, he was careful to explain that he expected the merchants to "cultivate, as

58. Logan, *Fourteen Agricultural Experiments*, pp. 40–41 [1797].
59. Hamilton, *The Federalist* (Lodge), LX, 377–378 [1788].
60. Noah Webster, *Collection of Essays*, pp. 119–120 [1785]. George Logan estimated that in 1798, one-twentieth of the gainfully employed were merchants or agents, one-twentieth mechanics and manufacturers, and the remaining eighteen-twentieths, farmers. *Address before the Tammany Society*, p. 8.
61. Hamilton, *The Federalist* (Lodge), LX, 376 [1788].
62. *Political Essays*, pp. 216–217 [1783].
63. Ibid., p. 218.
64. *View of the United States*, p. 7 [1787].

far as may be proper, the interests of the mechanic and manufacturing arts."[65] But Pelatiah Webster alleged that the mercantile interest deserved special governmental representation not because it was a compound interest but because the mercantile interest was qualitatively more competent than any other group to give advice to a legislature. Merchants, he argued, not only can give "the fullest and most important information" about economic affairs, but "are also the most likely to do it fairly and truly" since they would approve every measure calculated to benefit the nation's commerce and would oppose "any wild scheme" concocted by "an ignorant or arbitrary legislature."[66]

So the chorus of praise continued. Noah Webster found as much merit in "a regular commerce" as he did in agriculture or in the mechanic arts. Commerce kept men employed and preserved a nation's morals.[67] It was true, the schoolmaster admitted, that commerce "creates very great inequality of property." But here again, an essential distinction was emphasized: the inequality created by commerce does not beget a ruling class; instead a commercial fortune is constantly "revolving from person to person and entitles the possessor to no pre-eminence in legislation." Commerce therefore created an innocuous variety of inequality which was "not dangerous to the liberties of the rest of the state."[68]

Not all the social theorists of the 1780s and 1790s found the commercial interest so praiseworthy, patriotic, and blameless. John Taylor, who acknowledged that merchants could be suitable legislators, maintained that British merchants were exploiting British wage earners. In England, he said, "we must discern compulsion at the beginning, as well as at the end of her commerce. Her labour is compelled to sell low to her mercantile interest, and foreign nations or her colonies are compelled to purchase high of the same interest."[69] Like other social theorists who for thousands of years had inveighed against the age-old vice of merchants—buying cheap and selling dear —he signalized the dangers of certain types of mercantile activity. Merchants are "honorable and useful brokers," said Taylor, when they are engaged in supplying a nation's wants, but they are "pernicious and dangerous" whenever they become animated by "a spirit of monopoly"[70] and seek "exclusive privileges and prerogatives."[71]

65. *The Federalist* (Lodge), XXXV, 205–206 [1788].
66. *Political Essays*, p. 216 [1783].
67. *Collection of Essays*, p. 106 [1787].
68. *Sketches of American Policy*, p. 18 [1787].
69. *Principles and Policy*, p. 346 [1814].
70. Ibid.
71. *Enquiry into Certain Public Measures*, pp. 78–79 [1794].

George Logan inculpated the merchants on a different score. He accused them of what Eli Heckscher has called "an indifference toward goods."[72] Since merchants seek profits, they prefer an economic system wherein "every raw material and every manufactured article should pass through their hands."[73] They can therefore be expected to use their lobbying power to obstruct the development of domestic manufactures even though such a policy might be needed to ensure a nation's political independence. Merchants are wholly indifferent to a nation's harmonic economic development; they are more interested "in supporting the prosperity of the Foreign Manufacturers" than that of the domestic artisan. Their point of view is cosmopolitan, not national; "they should rather be considered as Citizens of the World, than Citizens of any particular Commonwealth."[74] Anticipating a concept which Henry C. Carey later developed in detail,[75] Logan pointed out the economic detriment that this lack of mercantile patriotism might have on a nation: "To send Clay to England to be returned made into Bricks, Limestone into Lime, and Wheat into Flour, would not be more absurd than the practice we have been in, for many years, of exporting our Flax-Seed, Iron and Furs to Europe, to be returned in a variety of Manufactured Articles, equally capable of being fabricated amongst ourselves."[76] Admittedly exporting raw materials and importing manufactures "would create a great quantity of shipping and would increase the business and wealth of the Merchants," but in spite of that "it would certainly add nothing to the actual wealth and independence of our Country."[77] Tench Coxe also acknowledged that mercantile motives might be inimical to sound national policy; if any manufactured commodity can be produced as cheaply at home as abroad, he said, its production "ought not by any means to be sacrificed to the interests of foreign trade."[78] As policy makers, therefore, merchants could not be depended on. They always try to buy cheap and sell dear; they are incurable monopolists; they are indifferent to what ought to be

72. *Mercantilism,* trans. Mendel Shapiro, 2 vols. (London, 1935), II, 80ff.
73. *Five Letters to the Yeomanry,* p. 22 [1792].
74. *Address before the Tammany Society,* pp. 8–9 [1798].
75. Carey drew a distinction between "trade," which merchants preferred, and "commerce" which was nationally beneficial. See *Principles of Social Science,* 3 vols. (Philadelphia, 1858), I, 199, 210, 213, 214, 217.
76. *Address before the Tammany Society,* p. 9 [1798]. Logan, who had in his earlier writings advocated Adam Smith's principle of an international division of labor, had by 1798 become an advocate of American manufacturing. This is not the only piece of evidence which indicates that the Republicans became the executors of the Federalist program.
77. Ibid.
78. *View of the United States,* p. 30 [1787].

a nation's rational economic development; they may even jeopardize a nation's independence.[79]

Nor was this the entire indictment levied against the mercantile interest. Taylor accused the merchants of joining forces with the financial interest in an attempt to monopolize the nation's money supply by means of the Bank of the United States.[80] Richard Henry Lee alleged that the Annapolis Convention represented a selfish political maneuver of the "commercial towns,"[81] designed to make it possible for northern merchants to exploit southern planters.[82] George Logan claimed that by doling out credit, merchants had farmers at their mercy, because "the credit thus given can at any time be withdrawn."[83] Nor did the withholding of credit constitute the only deleterious effect of a factorage system; overgenerous credit extension, Logan alleged, "has excited our Farmers to needless Expense, and involved them in difficulties for articles of mere luxury."[84] The implications were clear: commerce, although eminently natural and latently beneficial, was carried on by avaricious merchants whose activities might very readily become socially maleficent. If commerce is "moulded into a paper aristocracy," said John Taylor, it ceases to be a natural interest and becomes "false and factitious," enriching the merchants but injuring the agricultural or manufacturing interests.[85] Government must exercise constant surveillance, said Tench Coxe, to ensure that every mercantile stratagem is prevented "which injures agriculture, or benefits the merchant only, at great expense to the rest of the community."[86] No branch of commerce "should be so pursued, permitted, encouraged, or defended by the United States" which might "hazard the public liberty at home," or which "taxes the whole nation, nearly as great as, equal or superior to the exclusive profits of the mercantile body."[87]

How diligently the lawmakers obeyed these precepts is hard to know. Hundreds of laws were passed encouraging or restricting commercial practices. It should be observed here, however, that all

79. See Logan, *Address before the Tammany Society,* pp. 7–11 [1798].
80. *Principles and Policy,* p. 347 [1814].
81. *Observations of the System of Government,* p. 6 [1787].
82. Lee's "Letter to Governor Edmund Randolph" is quoted in Hutcheson's *Tench Coxe,* pp. 61–63.
83. *Letter to Citizens,* pp. 15–16 [1800]. This accusation was directed especially at British merchants. Coxe also pointed out the exploitation that had resulted from the British factorage system. *View of the United States,* p. 339 [1792].
84. *Letter to Citizens,* p. 16 [1800].
85. *Principles and Policy,* pp. 349–350 [1814].
86. See Hutcheson, *Tench Coxe,* p. 123 [1806].
87. Ibid., p. 121 [1806].

restricting legislation was not necessarily restraining; the great bulk of inspection laws, for example, were designed to widen markets by ensuring dependable quality of exported merchandise.[88] Merchants therefore often pressed for legislation that would outlaw practices deemed injurious, and manufacturers and "mechanics" sometimes joined forces with merchants in such demands.[89] The preambles to many laws represented proposed legislation as especially helpful to the mercantile interest,[90] but whether this was evidence of a sincere solicitude for that interest or merely a shrewd use of catchphrases for getting votes is difficult to ascertain. Obviously such things as harbor improvement legislation which would benefit merchants in particular towns may be considered as forthright government assistance to commerce.[91]

The apparent utility of domestic and foreign trade, the need of an essentially agricultural nation for markets, and the grievances of exporters of agricultural commodities who had been discomfited under the British factorage system—all these considerations led to legislative willingness to grant some governmental assistance to commerce. "Sound policy," wrote Tench Coxe in 1787, "requires our giving every encouragement to commerce and its connexions, which may be found consistent with a due regard to agriculture."[92] He proposed, for example, that special aid be given to the whaling and fishing industries because "this valuable branch of commerce" would greatly benefit the nation "without injuring our other essential interests."[93] Whether all branches of commerce should be encouraged, whether an American navigation act modeled on the British acts should be passed, or whether retaliatory commercial regulations should be imposed—on these questions great difference of opinion existed. Men like James Bowdoin[94] insisted that nothing less than complete confine-

88. Thus a Massachusetts act "to ascertain the quality of Pot and Pearl Ashes" was intended to ensure "our manufacturers of the highest market price for their Ashes." See David Townsend, *Principles and Observations Applied to the Manufacture and Inspection of Pot and Pearl Ashes* (Boston, 1793), p. 3.

89. See, for example, the petition of the Providence Association of Mechanics and Manufacturers "praying that a number of Articles exported from that Town may be subjected to Inspection." *Rhode Island Acts and Resolves, Oct., 1790, 14;* and *June, 1792, 21.*

90. A New Hampshire law authorizing the establishment of a bank (January 3, 1792) stated that the proposed bank "will be particularly beneficial to the trading part of the community." *New Hampshire Laws,* V, 833–834.

91. For example, the Delaware law authorizing the raising of twelve thousand dollars for the construction of piers at New Castle. *2 Delaware Laws,* 1189–1191, ch. 60c [February 7, 1794].

92. *View of the United States,* p. 9.

93. Ibid., p. 11.

94. *Observations upon the Necessity and Importance of the American Navigation Act* [1797].

ment of American commerce to American ships was called for in order to develop an adequate merchant marine, while, at the other extreme, former free traders like George Logan argued that commercial restraints always damaged the general welfare. Colbert, said Logan, "did infinite injury to France" when he subjected French commerce to governmental legislation.[95] He should, Logan contended, have listened to that "old experienced merchant" (Legendre?) who when Colbert asked what steps should be taken to encourage commerce, supposedly replied "Let us alone."[96] But Logan's advocacy of *laissez-faire* was not typical;[97] hence sentiment favoring the encouragement of commerce prevailed. Precisely what the new government began to do to encourage commerce will be explained in subsequent chapters.[98]

Mechanics and Manufacturers, Creators of Full Employment

Although it was estimated in 1798[99] that manufacturers and mechanics comprehended about five percent of the gainfully employed American citizens and that this "interest" was therefore approximately equal in numbers to the mercantile interest, almost no discussion of a mechanic or manufacturing interest as such is to be found in the political and economic literature of the 1790s. Noah Webster,[100] Tench Coxe,[101] John Taylor,[102] James Madison,[103] and Alexander Hamilton[104] (in *The Federalist*, not in the *Report on Manufactures*) seem to be the only writers who specifically referred to a mechanic or manufacturing "interest." In view of Hamilton's famous *Report* and the elaborate discussion of manufactures in the writings of Tench Coxe, this may appear rather odd. There seem to have been, however, justifiable reasons for this neglect or underemphasis. In the first place, some writers apparently doubted that mechanics and manufacturers constituted a separate, homogeneous "interest." Coxe, for example, re-

95. *Five Letters to the Yeomanry*, p. 23 [1792].
96. Ibid., p. 19.
97. Hamilton admitted that if a system of free trade existed in all nations, "there is room to suppose that it might have carried them faster to prosperity and greatness than they have attained by the pursuit of maxims too widely opposite." But since such a system does not prevail, it becomes necessary for any one nation to protect its interests by government action. *Public Papers* (McKee), pp. 179, 200–201 [1791].
98. See below, chaps. VIII and IX.
99. Logan, *Address before the Tammany Society*, p. 8 [1798].
100. *Collection of Essays*, p. 119 [1785].
101. *View of the United States*, p. 7 [1787].
102. *Enquiry into Certain Public Measures*, p. 10 [1794].
103. *The Federalist* (Lodge), X, 54 [1787].
104. Ibid., XXXV, 204 [1788].

ferred to manufacturers as a part of a composite commercial interest,[105] while Jefferson implied that certain mechanic arts were subdivisions of agriculture rather than a separate interest.[106] Both points of view are easily understandable. The processing of agricultural products—flour milling,[107] meat packing, and similar occupations—could be construed as a part of commercial activity; similarly many of the household crafts—spinning, weaving, or the making of tools and utensils—could as properly be regarded as belonging to agricultural enterprise. Moreover some artisans simply sold their skilled services by fabricating, or processing, materials owned by their customers; whereas others purchased materials, manufactured them, and sold finished goods. Between these branches of "manufacturing" there was normally more competition than cooperation.

At any rate, the manufacturing interest lacked cohesion. Its membership included itinerant artisans, craftsmen who worked in small shops, handworkers in households or on plantations, apprentices learning trades from master craftsmen, homeworkers employed by merchant-employers, and some few shop or foundry owners and their employees. Their ranks also included the owners of forges, blast furnaces, sawmills, chair factories, shot towers, brickyards, and dozens of other modest industrial establishments. In time, a division between industrialists and wage earners was to take place; in the 1790s, however, this motley assortment of artisans and entrepreneurs constituted the amorphous "mechanics and manufacturers interest." It was this shapelessness and lack of homogeneity that led Hamilton to say, in *The Federalist*, that "mechanics and manufacturers will always be inclined, with few exceptions, to give their votes to merchants in preference to persons of their own professions or trades." Because manufacturers "furnish the materials of mercantile enterprise," they find in the merchant "their natural patron and friend." Merchants should therefore be considered as the "natural representatives" of the mechanics and manufacturers.[108]

By 1791, Hamilton's views had apparently changed, although nowhere in the *Report on Manufactures* does he emphasize the separateness of the manufacturing interests that he so ably and persuasively

105. *View of the United States*, p. 7 [1787].

106. *Notes on Virginia*, p. 303 [1785].

107. This affiliation of processing with commerce is attested by contemporaneous terminology. Thus the big flour mills in the Wilmington area were called "merchant-mills." (See C. B. Kuhlman, *The Development of the Flour Milling Industry in the United States,* New York, 1929.) Merchant-tailor, merchant-sawyer, merchant-cobbler all suggest similar affiliation of manufacturing with commerce.

108. *The Federalist* (Lodge), XXXV, 204 [1788].

defended. The social utility of manufacturing, however, is depicted with consummate skill. Manufactures ought to be encouraged, stimulated, even subsidized, because their extension would promote the common good. In a later chapter the arguments for governmental aid to manufactures, as well as some examples of state and federal legislation enacted to facilitate industrial development, will be analyzed. Here it is only necessary to recapitulate briefly Hamilton's classic defense of the social benefits which manufactures would yield. Manufactures will augment "the produce and the revenue of society," said Hamilton, because they permit the division of labor, a productive technique that results in greater skill and dexterity, in an economy of time, and in an extended use of machinery. Since manufacturing can be mechanized to a much greater extent than agriculture, "an artificial force" comes to the aid of man. Moreover, manufactures create "extra employment" by providing tasks suitable for all members of society.[109] By increasing the national volume of employment, manufactures quicken immigration and furnish "greater scope for the diversity of talents," thus making it possible for each person to bring into activity "the whole vigor of his nature." Furthermore, manufactures multiply the number and the diversity of business enterprises, thereby creating an enlarged demand for labor and capital. Finally, manufactures have a beneficial effect upon agriculture by creating reliable, near, and constant domestic markets for foodstuffs and raw materials.[110]

This well-reasoned defense of the social benefits of manufactures should not, however, be interpreted as a vindication of an already existing manufacturing interest. It was, instead, a brief intended to justify the development of such an interest in the future. It does reflect Hamilton's convictions that a manufacturing interest would not only be socially useful but would form an indispensable part of America's harmonic economic development. Hamilton's critics, however, were of the opinion that the new manufacturing interest which his *Report* so ably justified would be a very different interest from the existing fellowship of mechanics and manufacturers. For this reason Logan vigorously condemned "that baneful system of European Management which dooms the human Faculties to be smothered" and converts man "into a machine."[111] In much the same spirit Jefferson, in 1785, had warned his countrymen that factories would corrupt the "manners and principles" of the American people and fill the cities with "mobs"

109. Hamilton said that children and farmers' wives would find supplemental employment in nearby factories.
110. *Political Papers* (McKee), pp. 190–199 [1791].
111. *Letter to Citizens,* p. 17 [1800].

who would "add just so much to the support of pure government, as sores do to the strength of the human body."[112] But whereas Jefferson feared the social consequences of all industrialization, Logan favored the workshop and condemned the factory. Farmers, he said in 1798, should "give every encouragement to the Mechanics and Manufacturers of the United States" because they create a home market for agricultural products,[113] but they should do everything in their power to keep America free from "that unfeeling plan of Manufacturing Policy, which has debilitated the Bodies, and debased the Minds, of so large a Class of People as the Manufacturers of Europe."[114]

The discussion of manufactures really centered on at least two different interests. And although it would seem from a casual examination of the literature that these two interests were "manufacturers" on the one hand and "mechanics" on the other, such is not the case. Actually the "interest" already in existence in the 1790s was a composite of manufacturers and mechanics; while the other, which Jefferson and his Republican associates described, was an "industrialist interest." Logan made this distinction perfectly clear: we do not want to see in America, he said, "a Manufacturing Capitalist . . . fill his Coffers by paring down the hard-earned wages of the laborious artists he employs."[115] Tench Coxe, on the other hand, welcomed the new interest when he advocated that encouragement be given to "judicious European capitalists" who would introduce laborsaving machinery and artificial power. Their example, he argued, would before long "bring some of our own capitalists into the business" of manufacturing.[116] He therefore recommended that "any inviting measures" that might "court the capitalists, manufacturers, and artizans, of the several countries of Europe"[117] should be employed by the government.

Although most historians either say or imply that Hamilton's *Report* led to no legislative results because Americans failed to appreciate the importance of manufactures, there seem to be better grounds for suspecting that the *Report* bore no legislative fruit because many members of Congress feared that the Hamiltonian policy of encouragement would create a very different manufacturing interest, one that would be both socially and economically undesirable. The

112. *Notes on Virginia*, pp. 303–304 [1785].
113. *Address before the Tammany Society*, p. 9 [1798].
114. *Letter to Citizens*, p. 17 [1800].
115. Ibid., pp. 17–18.
116. *View of the United States*, p. 166 [1791].
117. Ibid., pp. 192–193.

bitter attack on the Society for Establishing Useful Manufactures,[118] a project Tench Coxe conceived and Hamilton aided and advised, reflects this antagonism to incorporated, large-scale, manufacturing enterprise. Such projects, said Logan, based on "exclusive privileges" granted to "a few wealthy individuals," will "inevitably destroy the infant manufactures of our country, and consign the useful and respectable citizens [mechanics] personally engaged in them to contempt and ruin."[119] "Private manufacturers" were consequently advised by a writer who signed himself "Anti-Monopolist" to "consider what will become of their various trades" if they were faced with the competition of "this enormous political, speculating, manufacturing scheme."[120]

A decade of diplomatic difficulty over commercial privilege nevertheless gradually reconciled most Americans to the need for more domestic manufacturing. Even so, acrimonious disagreement developed over the kind of manufacturing interest that ought to be developed. Logan[121] and Taylor[122] advocated a natural, unsubsidized expansion of small-scale enterprise, thereby serving as protectors of an existing mechanic and manufacturing interest. It is "the undoubted duty of every Citizen," Logan insisted, "to give encouragement to the Mechanics, and Manufacturers of our Country" by using American manufactures in preference to foreign.[123] But any project favored or subsidized by government, which "proposes to interfere in the occupations of the mechanic and manufacturer," violates the rights of the people and destroys the liberty which the American system of government was designed to protect.[124]

The eclectic nature of American economic thought reveals itself in this controversy about the manufacturing interest. George Logan, for

118. For a detailed history of the S.U.M., see Joseph S. Davis, *Essays in the Earlier History of American Corporations,* I (Cambridge, Mass., 1917), 349–518; and Mitchell, *Alexander Hamilton,* II, 181–198.

119. *Five Letters to the Yeomanry,* p. 20 [1792].

120. See Davis, *American Corporations,* I, 432. The protest of the mechanics against the promoters of the S.U.M. who were accused of "planting a Birmingham and Manchester amongst us" is presented in detail in ibid., pp. 427–453.

121. "The success of American manufactures will not depend on financial calculations, or legislative interference, but on the patronage and encouragement they may receive from patriotic citizens." *Five Letters to the Yeomanry,* p. 22 [1792].

122. Taylor vigorously opposed the use of tariffs or bounties as means for quickening industrial development. "The policy of protecting duties to force manufacturing," he warned, "will produce the same consequences as that of enriching a noble interest, a church interest, or a paper interest; because bounties to capital are taxes upon industry, and a redistribution of property by law." *Principles and Policy,* p. 569 [1814].

123. Logan, *Address before the Tammany Society,* pp. 7–8 [1798].

124. *Five Letters to the Yeomanry,* p. 9 [1792].

90

example, was both a Smithian radical and a staunch conservative. In his opinion manufacturing no more deserved governmental subsidy or protection than commerce or agriculture did;[125] for each interest the rule should be: *"laissez nous faire."* The purpose of this occupational freedom, however, was to protect old employments, not to generate new ones. Logan's spirited attack on the S.U.M. clearly illustrates this defensive or conservative aspect of his economic policy. Such a project as the S.U.M., he contended, would monopolize raw materials, "draw off" workmen from "private manufacturers," and undersell competitors.[126] Since the S.U.M. had no legal monopoly,[127] the interference with *laissez-faire* that Logan attributed to this "dangerous scheme" came down to unfair competition. For should corporate manufacturing establishments be founded, said Logan, "no citizen will think of giving seven years of the prime of his life to acquire the knowledge of any profession in which he may be supplanted by a junto of monied men."[128] Against combinations of wealthy merchants, or prospective factory-type manufacturers, small businessmen ought to be protected; against all political importunity of capitalists, the legislatures should defend an atomistic economic society.[129] But no evidence was introduced to show that small-scale enterprise would be vigorous or efficient.

Who were the mechanics for whom the enemies of Hamilton sought protection? In a delightful "Lecture," Absalom Aimwell addresses himself, seriatim, to the various American crafts.[130] Here we meet tailors, masons, and carpenters; joiners and cabinet makers; smiths "black and white," as well as bakers, barbers, weavers, hatters, fullers, and tanners; also shoemakers, cobblers, painters, coopers, and "gentlemen dyers"; makers of clocks, coaches, and musical instruments; and, in addition, sculptors,[131] saddlers, sailmakers, and printers. To Absalom Aimwell, all these "mechanics" were guildsmen: men of skill, carefully trained and socially useful. This occupational aggregate obviously constituted some sort of an "interest" with really common ambitions, although certainly not a closely knit one. Hamilton said there was actually less "affinity" between the carpenter and the blacksmith or between the linen manufacturer and the

125. Ibid., pp. 17–18, 19, 23; *Letters to the Yeomanry on Funding and Bank Systems*, pp. 12, 23.
126. *Five Letters to the Yeomanry*, p. 27.
127. Davis, *American Corporations*, I, 450.
128. *Five Letters to the Yeomanry*, p. 20 [1792].
129. Ibid., pp. 8, 10, 26; *Letters to the Yeomanry on Funding and Bank Systems*, p. 22 [1793]. See also John Taylor, *Principles and Policy*, p. 349.
130. *A Lecture Containing a Short History of Mechanics*.
131. Of figureheads perhaps.

stocking weaver "than between the merchant and either of them."[132] "Rivalship between the different branches of the mechanic and manufacturing arts," he argued, was "notorious," and hence no true interest existed. But although Hamilton was no doubt correct in emphasizing the competition and jealousies between artisans, it is nevertheless true that on a few national and local issues artisans joined forces for lobbying strength.[133] In Virginia, for example, they were apparently able to limit the use of slaves as boatmen and stevedores,[134] while in Rhode Island, they succeeded in persuading the legislature to pass inspection laws.[135]

Very seldom, however, did a majority of artisans engage in concerted action. Master workmen in particular trades might attempt to maintain a monopoly of local business. Workers in licensed trades sometimes took joint action to obtain higher fees. Indentured servants occasionally engaged in strikes or uprisings to compel redress of grievances. White workers combined their efforts to resist encroachments on their occupations by Negroes.[136] For the most part, except for some joint political action during the Revolutionary War, there was little concerted action in which all "mechanics" or "manufacturers" took part. The reasons for this fragmentation were historical and circumstantial. In the beginning of settlement, particularly in New England, efforts had been made to establish guilds patterned after English models. But none of the chartered organizations, such as those composed of shipbuilders, shoemakers, or coopers, long survived. The demand for ships, shoes, or barrels was so great that buyers were not much concerned about who made urgently needed things. Only in a few cities, and only in a very limited number of occupations, did guilds or "companies" succeed.[137] Meantime a growing variety of "mechanics," "manufacturers," and artisans were competing as distinct groups.

Interlopers steadily undermined the attempted monopolies of duly apprenticed master workmen. Despite laws that forbade shoemakers to tan hides, country cobblers invaded the tanners' business. In the

132. *The Federalist* (Lodge), XXXVI, 208 [1788].
133. For an excellent detailed documentation, see chap. III in Morris, *Government and Labor in Early America.*
134. Under a law of 1786, not more than half the men on bay and river boats could be slaves. *12 Hening* 3120–3123, 1786 ch. 42.
135. *Rhode Island Acts and Resolves,* Act 1790, 14; June 1792, p. 21.
136. Morris, *Government and Labor in Early America,* p. 136.
137. The Philadelphia Carpenters Company is an example. It was formed in 1724 and only carpenters who had been master workmen for six years were admitted to membership. Similar companies of carpenters were formed in other cities. For details see ibid., pp. 142–143.

building trades interlopers offered to do the work of master brick-layers at lower wages, and hence the efforts of the skilled craftsmen to enforce their "book of prices" became increasingly difficult. In the South the craft guilds had never taken root, and, as slavery expanded, many manufacturing tasks—brewing, brickmaking, weaving—were carried on by unfree labor. Meantime in the North some manufacturing, shoemaking for example, came to be organized on a "putting out" basis by Boston merchants who supplied leather and other materials to country cobblers who were paid "piecework" wages. Because of these divisive tendencies, it is understandable why so little artisan unity existed and why there was no single "mechanics interest."

Only as consumers of food and raw materials did all the mechanics and manufacturers promise to become a recognizable economic group. "The nearer the number of tradesmen, mechanics, artists, and all that description of people who usually inhabit towns, approaches that of the farmers," said William Barton, the less will the United States be dependent on foreign trade.[138] That was in 1786, a year of severe depression in trade and in men's spirits. From then onward, the role that mechanics and manufacturers could play as consumers was repeatedly emphasized. Moreover, both the advocates of capitalistic manufactures and the defenders of small-scale enterprise employed the home market argument, so that Coxe[139] and Hamilton[140] on this point found in their severest critics warm allies.[141] Meantime at least two state legislatures had made efforts to increase the domestic market for grain by granting tax exemptions to the brewers of malt beverages.[142]

But although the manufacturing interest may have lacked homogeneity and centripetency, it nevertheless had rather strong influences on legislation. State legislatures had to take careful account of the wishes of particular mechanics and manufacturers. To be sure no Pandoran swarm of manufacturers as yet hounded the members of Congress in and out of office; but even though no formidable lobbies existed, Congress could not disregard the manufacturers and processors. Nor did government officials seek to ignore the manufacturers; on

138. *The True Interest of the United States*, p. 26.
139. *View of the United States*, pp. 13, 38, 52, 55, 319, 384.
140. *Political Papers* (McKee), pp. 38, 196–200.
141. By giving encouragement to manufactures, said Logan, American farmers may provide themselves with "a certain and steady market at their own door." *Address before the Tammany Society*, p. 9 [1798].
142. *Massachusetts Laws* 1788–1789, 403–404 [June 22, 1789]; *New Hampshire Laws* VI, 75–76 [December 22, 1792]. Both Coxe and Hamilton had especially recommended that encouragement be given to brewers. See Coxe, *View of the United States*, pp. 38, 319; Hamilton, *Political Papers* (McKee), p. 38.

the contrary, Hamilton solicited information and advice from the manufacturing interest before he prepared his *Report*.[143]

It seems very probable that Hamilton, who had been called upon to supply Congress with information about the extent and adequacy[144] of American manufactures, sent a circular letter of inquiry to the local agents and representatives of the Treasury Department asking them to ascertain the state of manufacturing within their communities. At any rate, Hamilton's inquiries, however made, elicited a great deal of information about American manufacturing. The letters which have survived give a vivid account of the extent and variety of manufactures, the scale of industrial operations, and the difficulties with which American manufactures were confronted.[145] They reveal also what businessmen thought should be done to stimulate industrial development, proposals ranging all the way from lotteries to outright prohibition of competing foreign goods. But although the correspondence which Hamilton's inquiries called forth provides the richest source of information about American manufacturing in the 1790s, it throws but little light on the "manufacturing interest." Indeed the letters betray virtually no awareness that manufacturing constituted a separate interest. Nor do they mirror the controversy between Logan and Hamilton about small-scale versus capitalistic manufacturing. A Connecticut correspondence did say that "persons concerned in seting up new Manufactures have every obsticle to surmount which can arrise from clashing Interests,"[146] but precisely what he meant is not clear; businessmen, then as now, were more factual-minded than philosophical. There is one letter, however, which suggests that the manufacturing interest was construed as something distinct from the mechanics interest. Joseph Dana, a clergyman, had apparently been asked by George Cabot, a Beverly merchant, to give information about what manufacturing was being carried on in Ipswich, Massa-

143. See Arthur H. Cole, *Industrial and Commercial Correspondence of Alexander Hamilton* (Chicago, 1928).

144. "Adequate" in a political sense. Specifically, Hamilton was asked to ascertain whether American manufacturers were sufficiently well established "to render the United States independent of foreign nations for military and other essential supplies"; if not, he was expected to make recommendations about appropriate means for their development. See Arthur H. Cole, *Hamilton Correspondence*, p. xv.

145. Letters directly concerned with manufactures came from eight states: twenty-five letters from Connecticut, one from Delaware, six from Massachusetts, two from New Jersey, one from New York, two from Rhode Island, three from South Carolina, and eight from Virginia. They have been carefully edited by Arthur H. Cole, and their relation to Hamilton's *Report* has been explained in Cole's introduction to the *Hamilton Correspondence*.

146. "A Succinct Account of the Manufactures Carried on in the State of Connecticut," in Cole, *Hamilton Correspondence*, p. 4.

chusetts. Only lace and cordage, Dana replied, "unless we number the common mechanical arts, which, I conceive, is not the intention."[147]

Among Hamilton's papers, however, there was found a newspaper clipping from the *American Museum* that had apparently been sent to Hamilton by the author, William Barton. This essay contains a carefully documented descriptive and statistical account of American manufacturing; it shows, as Cole has said, "the results of considerable research."[148] Here we have an objective view of manufacturing, written by a scholarly person,[149] who very definitely regarded manufacturing as one of the important American interests. In his concluding paragraph Barton argued that the growth of manufacturing would benefit not only farmers but merchants as well. He therefore proposed that protective duties or bounties be employed to stimulate manufacturing and that a uniform system of commercial regulations be instituted to assist the development of domestic commerce. Judicious governmental policies, he promised, would energize agriculture, manufacturing, and commerce: and only "when all these interests are properly combined, . . . will many of the yet dormant resources of this great country be brought forward and its means of wealth be rendered efficient."[150] Thus Barton, like Noah Webster,[151] saw in proper harmony among interests the foundation of national prosperity.

Learned Men, the Impartial Arbiters

Practically without comment, the social theorists of the 1790s recognized the existence of a professional interest. Richard Henry Lee proposed that professional men be accorded legislative representation,[152] so that they might be able to guard their economic status. He admitted that they could be expected to act selfishly,[153] but in that regard they would not differ from any other interest. Hamilton, in contrast, had a higher opinion of professional men; "the learned professions," he said very confidently, "form no distinct interest in

147. *Hamilton Correspondence*, p. 54.
148. *Hamilton Correspondence*, p. xxiv.
149. Among other things Barton wrote a biography of David Rittenhouse. Mention has already been made of his *True Interest of the United States.*
150. Barton's essay is reprinted in Cole, *Hamilton Correspondence*, pp. 113–125.
151. *Collection of Essays*, pp. 119–120 [1785].
152. "A fair representation, therefore, should . . . allow professional men, merchants, traders, farmers, mechanics etc. to bring a just proportion of their best informed men respectively into the legislature." *Observations of the System of Government*, p. 10 [1787].
153. "Men who live by fees and salaries endeavor to raise them." *An Additional Number of Letters* (New York, 1788), p. 61.

society."[154] What he really meant was that they could be expected to take a fair, unbiased, objective view of legislative problems, and for that reason they would be "the objects of the confidence and choice of each other, and of other parts of the community." Hence in the conflict of interests that would surely emerge in Congress, the "learned man" would prove to be "an impartial arbiter."[155]

No one else went that far. John Taylor gave the "professional interest" a clean bill of health, finding it innocent of aristocratic tendencies[156] and nonpredatory. Indeed he was of the opinion that professional men had been as badly duped by the financial interest as farmers and mechanics had been;[157] but that, he went on to say, was quite understandable. Like the other "natural interests" the professional men had been "too busily engaged in a variety of useful occupations to hunt out ministerial secrets" concocted for the purpose "of erecting an enormous aristocracy of monied interest."[158] Only Noah Webster had any fears or suspicions about learned men, and being one himself he ought to be heard. His indictment against professional people was simply their unproductiveness; since "they do not increase the property of the State, but live on the property acquired by others," their numbers "should be as few as possible."[159] Similar proposals had been made by the seventeenth-century British political arithmeticians whose zeal for production led them to advocate a drastic limitation of clergymen and lawyers.[160] Like Nehemian Grew who said that fewer lawyers would be needed if the common law were codified,[161] Webster asserted that "an artful Legislature will take away some of the causes of litigation, and thus curtail the number of lawyers."[162] But although Webster may have doubted the social utility of some professional men, he recognized, as his contemporaries did, the existence of a "professional interest."

The Natural Interests and the Consumers

The Founding Fathers and their fellow citizens were not really consumer-minded. The impressive series of laws specifying the quality of merchandise, the elaborate regulations governing "searching and

154. *The Federalist* (Lodge), XXXV, 204 [1788].
155. Ibid., p. 206.
156. *Principles and Policy*, p. 118.
157. *Enquiry into Certain Public Measures*, p. 10 [1794].
158. Ibid., p. 41.
159. *Collection of Essays*, p. 117 [1787].
160. For details see my *Predecessors of Adam Smith*, pp. 99, 255–256.
161. Ibid., p. 135.
162. *Collection of Essays*, p. 117 [1787].

sealing," and the complex system of inspection had little to do with protecting the welfare of American consumers. Most of the inspected articles were intended for export, and the majority of regulations governing quality were therefore designed to preserve or to increase foreign markets for American products. Such regulations ensured quality control and constituted a variety of legislative product differentiation.[163]

Laws that can definitely be identified as consumer protection were few and infrequent; moreover legislative concern about the interest of consumers seems to have been restricted to a very limited number of commodities. The medieval crust had come to be pretty well broken up by the 1790s; consumers either did not need or did not demand the degree of consumer protection which had been traditional in medieval England and which had been copied rather extensively in the British colonies during the seventeenth century. The social theorists made only occasional, indirect references to consumers; none of them seem to have used the term *consumers' interest*. Only inferentially, then, can one refer to the consumers' interest as one that was definitely recognized.

An awareness of the stake that consumers have in economic policy is discernible, however, and a few illustrations will make this clear. Manufacturers are judicious and patriotic people, said Tench Coxe; they will be satisfied with moderate protective duties of about twenty-five percent because they will realize that "a further addition of duties would not promote the general [consumers'] interest."[164] Pelatiah Webster attributed comparable solicitude for consumers to merchants; they are always, he said, engaged in making goods abundant; indeed they have every incentive to make the supply of goods "as convenient to their customers as possible."[165] Coxe agreed. Merchants are ever "attentive to the general interest"; they "range through foreign climates" in search of goods which cannot be economically produced at home or "which Nature has not given us."[166]

Should the government do anything in behalf of consumers or merely trust to the alleged benevolence of manufacturers and mer-

163. Hamilton in his *Report on Manufacturing* proposed that "judicious regulations for the inspection of manufactured commodities" be instituted by the federal government. Such a policy, he said, would not only protect domestic consumers, but, by improving and preserving the quality of American manufacturers, would "aid the expeditious and advantageous sale of them, and . . . serve as a guard against successful competition from other quarters." *Political Papers* (McKee), pp. 244–245 [1791].
164. *View of the United States*, p. 19 [1787].
165. *Political Essays*, p. 216 [1783].
166. *View of the United States*, p. 24 [1787].

chants? It should do nothing whatever, said James Logan, and in support of his contention he pointed out the ill effects of ingratiating legislation, designed to mollify consumers, that demagogues employed in Athens, Rome, and Marseilles.[167] In each case, said Logan, governmental attempts to institute "a society of Plenty" had damaging effects upon agriculture or commerce. In Greece, grain farmers abandoned cereal cultivation when Solon forbade the sale of grain to non-Athenian buyers; in Rome precisely the same thing happened when "distant provinces were oppressed, in order to supply the city with bread"; while in Marseilles, when the government set low prices on provisions, "vessels avoided the port, and provision became dearer than before." Logan's recommendation, therefore, was that government should protect the producer rather than the consumer. This policy, he pointed out, had international as well as domestic application; by the exploitation of labor in British factories or on plantations in India, "by such horrid outrages, against the rights of millions of our fellow citizens," is the United States furnished with some of its commodities "at so cheap a price."[168] He therefore urged his countrymen to purchase domestic commodities even though the cost might be higher than that of imports made by sweated labor. But whereas Logan advocated administrative nihilism, Hamilton, in contrast, thought government should do something to protect consumers. He recommended that a federal system of inspection be instituted to assure the maintenance of quality in manufactured goods and thus "prevent frauds upon consumers."[169]

An intricate maze of inspection laws was on the statute books of the several states. Although most of these laws were intended to certify the quality of exports and were thereby designed to protect the reputation of American exports in foreign markets, a few of them were clearly intended to protect consumers. When Maryland, for example, threatened to punish by "fine, prison or pillory" all those "evilly disposed persons" who "from motives of avarice and filthy lucre" had been selling "diseased, corrupted, contagious or unwholesome provisions,"[170] the purpose was unmistakable. With equal concern for consumers, the Maryland legislature declared "that so necessary an article of consumption as Bread should be so far regulated that the citizens of this Commonwealth might not be exposed to fraud."[171] Maryland had in fact been protecting consumers for a

167. *Five Letters to the Yeomanry*, pp. 13–14 [1792].
168. *Address before the Tammany Society*, pp. 10–11 [1798].
169. *Political Papers* (McKee), p. 244 [1797].
170. *Maryland Laws 1801*, I, 224–225, 1784–1785, p. 133 [March 8, 1785].
171. Ibid., II, 850–851, 1798–1799, pp. 91–92 [February 26, 1799].

long time; back in 1711 the legislature passed an act regulating the composition and the size of bricks because "the firmness of building very much depends on the goodness of the material."[172] Such legislation was still prevalent in 1800 when an act was passed requiring all manufacturers of boots, shoes, pumps, sandals, slippers, or galoshes to stamp their products, thereby certifying "that the article stamped is merchantable, being made of good material and well manufactured."[173]

The Connecticut legislators also took a skeptical view of the benevolence of manufacturers toward consumers. For some reason tanning and the manufacture of leather seemed to warrant special governmental surveillance. But the leather legislation went beyond the "preventing of Deceits and abuses by Tanners, Curriers, Dressers and Workers up of Leather."[174] Butchers who gashed hides were liable to penalties; only skilled tanners were authorized to erect vats; improperly tanned leather was subject to seizure; finally, for enforcing the law, each town was required to choose "honest men skilled in leather" to search and seal every "dicker" of leather.[175] Some branches of the Connecticut iron industry were also regulated. An act of 1795 specified the weight and length of all nails exposed for sale,[176] thus further extending the regulations that had been imposed the year before on all manufacturers of bar iron.[177] The Maryland and the Connecticut laws indicate, however imperfectly, the existence of a consumers' interest. They reveal that legislators were as yet unwilling to rely upon the natural justice of a competitive economy. For these laws circumscribed the activities of one of the avowedly natural interests. Farmer-legislators needed little persuasion to convince them that manufacturers "are disposed to contend for monopolies"[178] and that only suitable compulsion would "prevent frauds upon consumers."[179]

Despite the vagueness of the political tracts and the paucity of legislation that can be unequivocally classified as consumer protection, the state governments did recognize a responsibility to consumers. But since the great bulk of consumers were engaged in agriculture, since a very small percentage of the population lived in cities, and

172. Ibid., II, 993–994, chapter XXIX.
173. Ibid., II, 903, 1798–1799, pp. 449–450 [February 27, 1800].
174. *Connecticut A. Laws,* 1784, p. 125; also 1796 Code, p. 270.
175. *Connecticut A. Laws,* 1784, p. 126; 1796 Code, pp. 271–272. A "dicker" was a "half-score," namely ten hides.
176. *Connecticut S. Laws,* 496–498 [May 1795].
177. Ibid., 478 [May 1794].
178. Lee, *An Additional Number of Letters,* p. 61 [1787].
179. Hamilton, *Political Papers* (McKee), p. 244 [1791].

since the urban wage-earning class was extremely small, consumers qua consumers could obviously make few demands for legislation. The regulations imposed upon manufacturers, therefore, did not indicate the strength of an articulate consumers' interest; they more nearly reflected the dominant legislative power of the agricultural and commercial interests.

IV

*The Attack
on the
Artificial Interests*

When . . . chicane, cunning, deceit, and
fraud, are adopted as the ordinary means
of making a good bargain, the men, who
practice in this way . . . are contemptible and dangerous in society.

James Sullivan

Wealth accumulated without industry, is
more likely to become the nidus of vice
and monarchy, than of virtue and republicanism.

John Taylor

The Contemptible Cunning of Financiers

HAMILTON'S financial program, involving as it did the funding of the national debt, the assumption of the debts of the states, the chartering of the Bank of the United States, and the imposition of excise taxes, precipitated a violent attack on the financial or "monied" interest. The most vitriolic controversy centered on the national debt. Hamilton and his Federalist associates maintained that the funding of all government debt at par would not only establish the credit of the new national government but would increase the nation's money supply, thus overcoming a chronic difficulty originating in the American balance of payment. Moreover, Hamilton asserted that since funded debt would answer "most of the purposes of money," trade would be energized; agriculture and manufacturing would be stimulated; interest rates would decline, thus lightening the burden of debtors; and land values would rise. All in all, funding the debt seemed to fulfill every requirement of good public policy: it promised to benefit each of the nation's natural interests and to advance the public interest.[1] To Hamilton's critics the situation was quite different. Funding the public securities at par, they said, meant cheating the "original creditors" of the government since the majority of original creditors had sold their securities at a discount. It meant a harvest for the speculators who had bought securities in the expectation of a liberal refunding program. Worst of all, it created a financial interest that was "factitious," "unnatural," and "illegitimate." This new interest, nurtured by governmental favoritism, was allegedly in the process of becoming a ruling class; and

1. See Hamilton's *First Report on the Public Credit* [January 9, 1790], which is most accessible in the *Political Papers*, ed. Samuel McKee, especially pp. 3–15. See also Coxe, *View of the United States*, p. 363 [1792].

102

this new "aristocracy of paper and patronage,"[2] it was charged, would corrupt the government, exploit all other interests, and weaken the productive efficiency of the entire nation. Out of this denunciation of the Hamiltonian financial program there emerges a picture of the financial interest that is scarcely objective. The caricature is nevertheless important. To the agrarian mind, financiers are always obnoxious. The alleged vices of the "monied interest" must therefore be depicted in the vivid language of Hamilton's enemies.

The arts of finance, James Sullivan declared, are not necessarily harmful to a nation. If the purchase and sale of public or private securities "is conducted with truth, sincerity, and fairness, it may be considered as reputable and honorable"; but if deceit is involved, "the men, who practice in this way . . . are contemptible and dangerous in society."[3] In Europe, stockjobbing had long been carried on by unscrupulous brokers who "rob the unwary and necessitous part of the community"; these sharp practices, Sullivan claimed, were now being transferred to the United States.[4] That private citizens would seize any opportunity to make money was to be expected,[5] but that members of Congress should engage in stockjobbing John Taylor branded as scandalous, since it meant that "an illegitimate interest is operating on the national legislature,"[6] seducing representatives away from the natural interest they were elected to represent. Moreover by forming alliances with a foreign monied interest, some speculating Congressmen were betraying the nation by permitting "our late most malignant and inveterate enemy" to obtain "an influence on our national councils."[7] Such treasonable action, however, might have been expected because "the paper interest is transitory. It is a bird of passage . . . incapable of national feelings or of national attachment."[8] As occasion demands, "it may connect itself . . . with French, Spanish, Dutch or English politics." Rapacious and usurious, the financial interest "is an inexorable creditor" ready to employ any means for its own enrichment. Its "sly tricks and legislative contrivance," always for its own purposes, make it "the most unnatural guardian" of the public good.[9]

The financial interest, said John Taylor, is made up "of gamesters,

2. Taylor, *Principles and Policy,* p. 29 [1814].
3. *Path to Riches,* p. 18 [1792].
4. Ibid., pp. 18–19.
5. Ibid., p. 43.
6. Taylor, *Enquiry into Certain Public Measures,* p. 24 [1794].
7. Ibid.
8. Ibid., pp. 60–61.
9. Ibid.

who play deep with each other whilst the public stakes the wager on both sides."[10] As an example of such financial legerdemain James Sullivan cited the founders of the Massachusetts Bank, who first inflated the currency, thereby raising the prices of public securities and of commodities, and then, by refusing to loan, they "sunk the price of the same articles," profiting in both boom and depression.[11] Such manipulation is not only unjust but unnatural, since currency and credit, which are "social rights," have by fraud been "bestowed by governments"[12] on the "monied few," thereby violating all the principles of "free governments." Thus, said Hamilton's critics, by the stratagem of an exclusive national bank charter, a "paper interest, computed at 5,000 [persons]" has enslaved "the nation, consisting of near 5,000,000."[13]

The enemies of Hamilton charged that speculation in public securities and in bank stock had deleterious effects upon a nation's economic efficiency. In a good society, cupidity must not be allowed to dominate men's minds;[14] if wealth can be accumulated not by industry but by "sudden variations in value," every incentive will be provided "for the exercise of ingenuity" in taking advantage of price fluctuations.[15] As a result, public morality will decline; for although a speculator "may begin with honest intentions," in a society which countenances sharp practices, competition will lead all stockjobbers to take "advantage of ignorance and necessity." Moreover, "when a few men . . . accumulate fortunes, and live in unequalled splendor, it corrupts the taste of the other part of the community."[16] A spirit of envy will pervade the entire nation, and the dignity of manual labor will be lost. Furthermore, "if we tempt men's desire, by hopes of boundless acquisition, the constant incitements of private interest, will leave no interval of time or reflection, to be appropriated to the public good."[17] Acquisitiveness will become the ruling passion of men's lives, while civic virtue will decline. Worst of all, wealth, acquired without productive effort, is more likely to become "the nidus of vice and monarchy, than of virtue and republicanism."[18]

10. Ibid., pp. 11–12.
11. *Path to Riches*, p. 47 [1792].
12. Taylor, *Principles and Policy*, p. 364 [1814].
13. Taylor, *Definition of Parties*, p. 4 [1794].
14. Taylor, *Enquiry into Certain Public Measures*, p. 61 [1794].
15. Noah Webster, *Collection of Essays*, p. 106 [1787].
16. Sullivan, *Path to Riches*, p. 40 [1792].
17. Taylor, *Enquiry into Certain Public Measures*, p. 61 [1794].
18. Taylor, *Definition of Parties*, p. 9 [1792]. "Speculation is pernicious to morals," said Noah Webster, "in proportion as its effects are extensive." *Collection of Essays*, p. 106 [1787].

The financial interest is least qualified to govern, said John Taylor, since it has no organic connection with agriculture, commerce, or manufacturing.[19] It is a "false and factitious" interest,[20] at "enmity with the common good."[21] National prosperity and wholesome economic development depend upon vigorous natural interests, not on a "system of paper and patronage" calculated to transfer property "to one interest at the expense of another."[22] The Hamiltonian program was not necessary for advancing the prosperity of the United States; it was only "necessary," said William Findley, "to increase the number and influence of the speculating order by cementing them more closely together in a common [single] interest."[23] It represented the "contemptible cunning of Financiers, who seldom possess any real intention to promote the general welfare."[24]

The Untitled Aristocracy of Paper and Patronage

It will be recalled that John Taylor formulated a theory of history which postulated that since time immemorial mankind has been ruled by a succession of minorities. An ancient aristocracy "supported by superstition," he alleged, was succeeded by another whose power stemmed from control over land, a feudal aristocracy which, in turn, was being superseded by an "aristocracy of paper and patronage."[25] Taylor pointed out that the power of any minority depends on control over resources and over people. The similitude between a financial and a feudal aristocracy, he said, is perfect: "money is made the basis of political power in one; land in the other."[26] Since land is indispensable to existence in an agricultural society, control over land involves control over persons. Money being equally indispensable in an exchange economy, control over a nation's money supply gives a financial aristocracy comparable power over the lives and goods of plain and ordinary people. The Federalist policies, said Taylor, had allowed the "monied interest" to usurp control, the financiers having literally "bought the nation"[27] by monopolizing public securities and bank stock. Nor was the power thereby acquired confined

19. *Principles and Policy*, p. 333 [1814].
20. Ibid., p. 349.
21. *Definition of Parties*, p. 11 [1794].
22. *Principles and Policy*, p. 135 [1814].
23. *Review of the Revenue System*, p. 77 [1794].
24. Logan, *Five Letters to the Yeomanry*, p. 23 [1792].
25. *Principles and Policy*, pp. 20–21 [1814].
26. Ibid., p. 335.
27. Ibid., p. 62.

to power over the federal government; it involved a command over state governments as well: "Only 100 people in Virginia, and 1000 in Massachusetts," Taylor asserted, "have really any political existence."[28]

Since this was not the kind of government that Americans had hoped to establish, the American people must either repudiate this new aristocracy or "sell their birthright for a mess of paper."[29] For a government dominated by a financial interest cannot achieve its selfish purposes without injuring "the great mass of the nation."[30] It will "create unnecessary offices," transfer the earnings of others to itself by taxes or bank profits,[31] and then lend these ill-gotten spoils back to the nation at high interest rates.[32] The new aristocracy, said Taylor, does not pretend to have "a monopoly of virtue, renown and abilities"; it represents merely a "monopoly of wealth."[33] Its sole principle is "an inordinate love of money." Does history, he inquired, "record the benefits which such a political principle hath procured for mankind"? Has any author, he asked even more caustically, "celebrated this new species of government—this money-cracy"?[34]

The fact that the new aristocracy "is not a titled order" does not make it less dangerous; indeed "a separate interest is more dangerous if it can create, sustain and enrich itself without being designated" an aristocracy.[35] This has been proven in England, where an "untitled paper interest" has "made prisoners of the two titled orders."[36] A titled aristocracy accepts certain social duties and responsibilities; a de facto ruling class, having none, can devote itself unreservedly to "corruption, charters, patronage, pensions," and speculation;[37] it can concern itself exclusively with "transferring to itself, the property of others."[38] As contrasted with a feudal aristocracy, which was attached to land, "an aristocracy supported by the public revenue," said William Findley "is not attached to any [natural] interest."[39] More-

28. *Definition of Parties,* p. 6 [1794].
29. "Into which they are themselves cooked; but of which they can never taste." Ibid.
30. *Principles and Policy,* p. 40 [1814].
31. Ibid., p. 391. "In America, the banking interest taxes, raises or diminishes these taxes, and publicly divides its collections, of about five million annually, under charters for long terms."
32. Ibid., p. 40.
33. Ibid., p. 29.
34. *Enquiry into Certain Public Measures,* p. 28 [1794].
35. *Principles and Policy,* pp. 316–317.
36. Ibid.
37. Ibid., pp. 117–118.
38. *Definition of Parties,* p. 6 [1794].
39. Findley, *Review of the Revenue System,* pp. 52–53 [1794].

over, since such a new ruling class is not "engaged in the pursuit of active industry," it will "have leisure for intrigue and both time, means, and inclination to influence the measures of government"; for "where avarice is the ruling principle," though there may be pride, "there can be no true honour."[40]

Like every other aristocracy, the paper interest had shrewd leaders. William Findley asserted that as soon as the preparations for speculation had been made, and as soon as Hamilton had combined "a sufficient number of local and speculating interests in support of his plans,"[41] William Duer "withdrew from the secretary's office, and put himself at the head of the speculating order."[42] By keeping the financial plan of the government secret "from those whose interests were not provided for," said Findley, the speculators were able to buy up public securities and lay the foundations for their control over the nation. All this chicanery, according to John Taylor, could take place because "the commercial, the agricultural, mechanical and professional interests" were "too busily engaged in a variety of useful occupations, to hunt out ministerial secrets."[43] Hence the "pecuniary interest" was unchecked by any "coequal power,"[44] and hence there came into being "the most oppressive" species of aristocratic government. For by "a second revolution" the new aristocracy took away from Americans their "domestic rights, liberty and equality."[45]

The Political Formula of the Monied Interest

John Taylor pointed out that every ruling class must justify its political authority. "All separate factitious interests," he claimed, "pretend that they benefit nations in some mode, too intricate to be investigated by the mass of mankind."[46] But the political formula of the monied interest surpasses any other in sophistry and deception; it "gravely tells nations that it enriches them by taking their money." Actually, by alleging that the funded debt will serve the functions of money,[47]

40. Ibid.
41. Ibid., p. 49.
42. Ibid., p. 17. For a detailed account of Duer's career, see Davis, *American Corporations*, I, 111–338; see also Mitchell, *Alexander Hamilton*, II, 8, 9, 27, 32, 136, 137, 155–157, 160–171.
43. *Enquiry into Certain Public Measures*, p. 41 [1794].
44. *Principles and Policy*, p. 612 [1814]. See also *Enquiry into Certain Public Measures*, p. 39 [1794].
45. Logan, *Letters to the Yeomanry on Funding and Bank Systems*, p. 24 [1793].
46. *Principles and Policy*, p. 338 [1814].
47. See Hamilton, *Political Papers* (McKee), pp. 7–9 [1790].

and by confounding ordinary people about the mysteries of banking, the financiers have provided themselves with "a handle, stronger than that of superstition, with which to manage nations."[48] Since the great majority of Americans are farmers, the proposals of the financial interest, said George Logan, are brought forward "under a false pretext of serving the agricultural interest."[49] Strip the facade away from the Hamiltonian financial scheme and what does one find? Nothing but the same deceitful "panegyrics" that have been used before by European "banking, money-changing, and stock-broking writers" to conceal their selfish purposes;[50] and in this spirit of skepticism and distrust, the Virginia Assembly remonstrated against the funding legislation: "In an agricultural country like this," asserted a Virginia memorial to Congress, a plan "to erect, and concentrate, and perpetuate a large monied interest" is a measure which instead of benefiting agriculture will lead to its "prostration."[51]

To expose the true purposes of the so-called monied interest, however, proved to be a difficult task. Political rationalization very often is designed to obscure intent, and since the lawmaking process represents an interplay of interests, the art of justifying means becomes one of the most important and subtle techniques of politics. An examination of a few acts of state legislatures will make this abundantly clear. Here, for example, is a Pennsylvania act incorporating an insurance company. What benefits would allegedly result? The insurance company, we read in the preamble, will keep "large sums of money" in the state that would otherwise be drawn away by "premiums and commissions to foreign correspondents." The new venture, it was promised, would not only help individuals, by insuring them against risk, but it would benefit "the community in general" by augmenting capital supply, and in doing so help "the mercantile interest in particular."[52] Nothing is said of the expected benefits to the stockholders; no mention whatever is made of the financial interest.

Another Pennsylvania act—one authorizing a marine insurance company—is even more interesting. One hundred and twenty-nine persons as well as twenty-nine business firms had subscribed to shares of stock. Yet the justification for the act of incorporation was stated to be that it "appears to the legislature" that chartering the

48. Taylor, *Principles and Policy,* p. 358 [1814].

49. *Five Letters to the Yeomanry,* p. 26 [1792].

50. *Letters to the Yeomanry on Funding and Bank Systems,* p. 19 [1793]. Here Logan apparently is quoting from Arthur Young.

51. "Address of Virginia Assembly," *13 Hening,* p. 237 [December 23, 1790].

52. *15 Pennsylvania Statutes at Large,* 41–42, ch. 1740 preamble [April 14, 1794].

insurance company would "be conducive to the interest of the state, as well . . . to the commerce as the agriculture thereof."[53] How much of this statement was fact and how much was window dressing? There is no way of knowing. No doubt some part represented an effort to devise a suitable "political formula," and the art of phrasing such formulas calls for a certain pious vagueness which will turn attention away from the more specific purposes of the interests that really are sponsoring the new legislation. Thus it was asserted that a new Pennsylvania bank (1793) would "be productive of great benefit to trade and industry in general,"[54] just as an earlier one had been chartered because it was going to be "useful to the commerce and agriculture of the state."[55] A Massachusetts bank, it was said, would be "particularly beneficial to the trading part of the community";[56] yet this same bank was later charged with manipulating the price level to the great disadvantage of the mercantile class.[57] The preamble to a Maryland bank incorporation act postulated that "the experience of commercial nations" had shown the "utility" of banks,[58] an argument used two years later by the framers of a Virginia law[59] for establishing a bank in Alexandria. Not to be outdone, a group of Richmond entrepreneurs petitioned for authority to establish a bank there, one that would "tend greatly to the advantage of agriculture, commerce and manufactures."[60]

The foregoing illustrations indicate clearly that Hamilton and his Federalist friends had no monopoly on the fine art of political rationalization. From Massachusetts to Virginia the practice of formulating persuasive phrases designed to show the public utility of financial institutions was followed. In line with this tradition, Hamilton in his several reports employed his argumentative skill to prove the utilitarian purposes of his financial policies. To his enemies, however, Hamilton's defense of his program was something insidious and stealthy; it was what Mosca later called a "political formula"[61] intended to justify the de facto political power of a minority group of monied men.

53. Ibid., 69–71, ch. 1747 preamble [April 18, 1794].
54. *14 Pennsylvania Statutes at Large,* 365, ch. 1667 preamble [March 30, 1793].
55. *12 Pennsylvania Statutes at Large,* 412–416, ch. 1278 [March 17, 1787].
56. *Massachusetts Laws* 1801, I, 115–117 [February 7, 1784].
57. Sullivan, *Path to Riches,* p. 47 [1792].
58. *Maryland Laws* (Kilty), 1790, ch. 5 [December 14, 1790].
59. *13 Hening* 592, 1792, ch. 76 preamble [November 23, 1792].
60. *13 Hening* 599, 1792, ch. 77 preamble [December 23, 1792].
61. *The Ruling Class,* p. 70.

The Perversion of Republican Government

Only a republican form of government, William Findley averred, can protect the "native dignity" and the equal rights of citizens.[62] But these essentials of a good society have been jeopardized by combinations of financial interests. This well-organized minority, said John Taylor, has followed the example of British stockjobbers who had "moulded the government . . . into a form most suitable to itself."[63] A true "republican policy" would never have suggested a funding system,[64] and certainly not one which had produced "the most detestable and enormous frauds" and had led to "a depravity of morals and a great decline of republican virtue."[65] The Constitution, George Logan alleged, "owed its existence to the influence and artifice of a few men"[66] who took advantage of the nation's distress so that they might speculate in public securities. It was not a mere coincidence that immediately after the adoption of the Constitution, government debt "assumed all the properties of a rising credit," and as appreciation took place, the "apparent success" of speculators "increased the number engaged in that kind of traffic."[67] On the heels of this initial speculative frenzy came the funding act which enabled the "monied men" to "defraud the great bulk of the community," by transferring wealth "from those who earned it to those who pilfered it."[68] Like their feudal predecessors, the financial aristocracy apparently hoped to create a new relation of "landlord and tenant," because the funding system is a device for subjecting all the land of the nation to a perpetual rent charge "payable to a few persons."[69] Whereas feudal lords had jurisdiction over particular parcels of land, the new "government of paper" has usurped the power of regulating the entire domestic economy and to "extract from it all the profit it can yield."[70]

Government, said Hamilton's critics, had therefore been converted "into a scheme of finance"; it had become "a credit shop" rather than an agency for dispensing public welfare.[71] Nor had the con-

62. Findley, *Review of the Revenue System*, p. 128 [1794].
63. *Principles and Policy*, p. 635 [1814].
64. "Address of Virginia Assembly," *13 Hening*, p. 237 [December 23, 1790].
65. Findley, *Review of the Revenue System*, p. 52 [1794].
66. *Letters to the Yeomanry on Funding and Bank Systems*, p. 3 [1793].
67. Sullivan, *Path to Riches*, p. 44 [1792].
68. Taylor, *Enquiry into Certain Public Measures*, p. 42 [1794].
69. *Definition of Parties*, p. 7 [1794].
70. Ibid., pp. 5–7.
71. Ibid., p. 7.

tamination been confined to the federal government; the "new monied interest" brought about political changes "favorable to aristocracy" in states "which were once the most republican."[72] As a consequence, people have lost confidence in their governments and are reluctant to support them by taxation; "free, moderate, and honest forms of government" are being destroyed[73] in the several states. Meantime the federal government, instead of "cementing the union of the states," has undermined national confidence and harmony by making it possible for the citizens of some states to obtain possession of the public securities of the citizens of other states "at a small part of their value."[74] Moreover, since the interest on the national debt will be mostly paid out of customs revenues, states without manufactures will perforce be compelled to pay the highest toll to the financial interest. How then, asked William Findley, can it be argued that the Hamiltonian program is a "national blessing"? Are "princely estates" accumulated by speculators a national blessing? Can discontent or friction between northern and southern states be called a blessing? Is the enriching of a few and the impoverishment of the many a national blessing? Is the corruption of government, the "filling both Houses of Congress with bank directors or stockholders, a national blessing?"[75]

Political power, said John Taylor, has been transferred "from the nation of the paper fabrick"[76] not by the people, not by the Constitution, but by a "spurious" government. A vicious "species of misrule" has been instituted;[77] indeed no form of government "can be more fraudulent, expensive and complicated than one which distributes wealth and consequently power by the act of the government itself."[78] Yet this is what the "government of paper" has done. It began by swindling the "original creditors" of the government;[79] it has subsequently entrenched itself behind a scheme of taxation and a system of banking which have given it control over the lives and the property of the entire nation. Throughout all these machinations it has been pretended that the Hamiltonian program could benefit the rank and

72. Findley, *Review of the Revenue System*, p. 125 [1794].
73. Taylor, *Principles and Policy*, p. 583 [1814].
74. Findley, *Review of the Revenue System*, p. 38 [1794].
75. Ibid., p. 40.
76. *Definition of Parties*, pp. 5–6.
77. *Principles and Policies*, p. 583 [1814].
78. Ibid., pp. 244, 366.
79. Logan, *Letters to the Yeomanry on Funding and Bank Systems*, pp. 3–4 [1793]. See also Pelatiah Webster, *Political Essays*, p. 277 [1785], and James Madison, *Writings*, ed. G. Hunt, I, 507.

file of the American people, whereas in reality the "paper contrivances" are "siren notes of wealth and cunning, designed to fascinate labour, whilst its fruits are devoured."[80]

The Exploitation of Other Interests

The charge that the financial interest intended to exploit all natural interests was as dogmatic as it was intemperate. The allegation was that every ruling class seeks to exploit plain and ordinary people and therefore adopts means to accomplish its ends; hence although the means adopted by the "paper aristocracy" were modern, their effect would be virtually equivalent to the establishment of chattel slavery because the ultimate incidence of taxation and bank profits must be on human labor. The argument may be most easily traced in the writings of John Taylor, but by incorporating the specific charges of other critics into his argument, he made the blanket indictment of the monied interest even more damning.

Exploitation was an old game, said Taylor. A ruling "faction" always enacts laws calculated to "bestow exorbitant wealth upon one class, and perpetual poverty upon the other."[81] To this end, a debtor-creditor relation has long been employed;[82] in Rome, for example, debtors were delivered bodily to their creditors. But the iron fetters of antiquity had now been superseded by "the stronger fetters of legislation,"[83] particularly legislation which has created a huge national debt, thereby making the great majority of the American people the debtors of a creditor minority. Unknown to the ancient world, this new technique, according to George Logan, "has become a general expedient with modern statesmen."[84] For not only does this device give the ruling clique command over living persons but perpetual control over "the property and labour of posterity."[85] In funding the debt and in creating the National Bank, the United States was actually imitating those "most ruinous parts" of British policy which had almost annihilated the British yeomanry;[86] and although the per caput burden of debt was greater in Britain than in the

---

80. Taylor, *Definition of Parties*, p. 9 [1794].
81. Ibid., pp. 6–7.
82. *Principles and Policy*, pp. 264–265 [1814].
83. *Definition of Parties*, p. 6 [1794].
84. *Letters to the Yeomanry on Funding and Bank Systems*, p. 8 [1793].
85. Ibid.
86. Ibid., pp. 18–19.

United States,[87] the American financial interest could be expected to seize every opportunity to increase the national debt because its exploitative power would thereby be augmented.

Rejecting all of Hamilton's judicious arguments in favor of a funded national debt,[88] Taylor asserted that every dollar delivered by means of taxation to the public creditors represented a corresponding diminution of the incomes of "the mass of the people" since "public creditors subsist upon the national labour."[89] He estimated that the annual interest on the public debt in Britain "would require twelve millions of slaves to discharge at eighty pounds sterling each."[90] Here then was a vivid measurement of the debt burden imposed by the British monied interest. In Taylor's opinion, the inevitable consequence of a public debt must be "a perpetual increase of taxes," and heavy taxation in time of peace he branded as "unexceptionable political slavery."[91] Logan took an equally dogmatic position; the pledge "pawned for the security of those [public] debts," he charged, must of necessity be "the land, the trade, and the personal industry of the people."[92] The whole matter, as he saw it, came down to simple arithmetic: whatever the public creditors received, the members of the several natural interests lost.[93]

Banking was merely another exploitative device. The "speculating order," said William Findley, by impounding seven and a half million dollars worth of public securities in the Bank of the United States had two objects in view: to appreciate the value of public securities by taking a large quantity "out of the market," and to derive banking profits from the identical securities on which they were already receiving six percent interest.[94] Taylor's indictment of the Bank was even harsher: since the charter authorized the deposit of public money in the Bank, "the higher the taxes are the more of this money is therein deposited." For this reason the Bank could be expected to exert all its influence to increase taxation since the larger the public

87. "The floating paper of America, may be computed," said Taylor, "at 120,000,000 dollars—that of Britain at 1,000,000,000. About 5,000,000 of people are mortgaged for the former, and 20,000,000 . . . for the latter." But Taylor pointed out that "the debt of Britain was incurred in one hundred years; that of the United States in fifteen." *Definition of Parties*, p. 7 [1794].
88. See below, pp. 130–136.
89. *Definition of Parties*, p. 8 [1794].
90. *Principles and Policy*, pp. 38–39 [1814].
91. Ibid., p. 285.
92. *Letters to the Yeomanry on Funding and Bank Systems*, p. 12 [1783].
93. Ibid. See also Taylor, *Principles and Policy*, p. 352 [1814].
94. *Review of the Revenue System*, p. 79. See also Sullivan, *Path to Riches*, pp. 38–39.

deposits, the larger the number of notes "the bank can circulate on Congress who were stockholders of the Bank would "have a private interest in the accumulation of public burthens."⁹⁵

A metallic money, said Taylor, cannot be increased at will, "an artificial currency" can; hence a banking system "possesses an unlimited power of enslaving nations."⁹⁶ Only the "rich class of citizens" can be stockholders of the Bank of the United States, whereas "labour supports it."⁹⁷ The chartering of the Bank really meant that a huge "annuity" had been "conjured up by law" payable exclusively to the rich.⁹⁸ He estimated the profits of all banks in the United States to be over five million dollars annually, a sum equal to "the annual labor of forty-six thousand five hundred working men" or to the "subsistence of two hundred and twenty-five thousand people."⁹⁹ This, in Taylor's opinion, was the social cost of the American banking system. For if a nation "bestows a pecuniary income" on bankers, "it conveys so much of its [labour] services to this order as the money represents"; moreover, the bankers receive "a title to every species of service from the multitude"¹⁰⁰ that they may elect to demand. In contrast with a feudal aristocracy, which laid specific labor services upon its serfs, the financial interest had made all members of society its slaves. Upon "the whole agricultural, mechanical, professional and mercantile interests . . . upon this aggregate must fall the gains so regularly collected"¹⁰¹ in taxes or in the profits of monopolized banking.

In the process of enriching itself, said Taylor, the financial interest weakens a nation in its international dealings, fosters undesirable luxury, and promotes indolence and dishonesty. Hamilton, it will be recalled, had argued that funding the debt would increase the nation's money supply because funded debt would be acceptable as money and its circulation would obviate the demand for specie. Taylor refused to be persuaded, insisting that a paper circulation, whether of public securities or of bank notes, would inevitably lead to the "expulsion of specie."¹⁰² He further argued that it was only

95. *Enquiry into Certain Public Measures*, pp. 25–26, 36–37 [1794].
96. *Principles and Policy*, p. 292 [1814].
97. "Money and credit, or the equivalent of them, were to be deposited as the only mode of acquiring bank stock. The poor had neither to deposit, the rich possessed both." *Enquiry into Certain Public Measures*, p. 15 [1794].
98. Ibid.
99. *Principles and Policy*, p. 309 [1814].
100. Ibid., pp. 291–292.
101. *Enquiry into Certain Public Measures*, p. 10 [1794].
102. *Principles and Policy*, p. 355 [1814].

by making specie scarce that the financial interest had been able to "create a necessity for some [monetary] substitute."[103] Having done so, however, the new aristocracy proceeded to monopolize the supply of the monetary substitute, regulating the amount available to the public and supplying "the needed currency upon the terms, and in the quantities it pleases."[104]

If the real purpose of the Bank had been to benefit the public, asserted Taylor, then Congress should have established a publicly owned bank. Had this been done, the interest paid on loans would have increased public revenues and decreased taxes.[105] But instead of such a rational arrangement whereby individuals would contribute to the public, there has come into existence a system whereby the public contributes to the wealth, and hence to the idleness and the luxury of "a separate interest."[106] How can such a situation contribute to a nation's strength?[107] How can a system which taxes "the active and industrious citizen" in order to "maintain the indolent and idle creditor" increase a nation's well-being?[108] Could anything be worse than laws "which tend to draw people from the honest and painful methods of earning fortunes"?[109] When it became known that the public debt would be funded, said Noah Webster, "not less than 20,000 men in America left honest callings, and applied themselves to this knavish traffic" of speculating in public securities. How can it be said that this "host of jockies"[110] benefited the nation?

Such was the indictment made against the financial interest. The gains of public creditors and Bank stockholders, said the critics, could not possibly correspond with the public good.[111] The income of the paper aristocracy represented a corresponding diminution of the incomes of the natural interests.[112] Meantime the existence of an unnatural interest perverted natural interests from their true functions,[113] increased the

103. Ibid., p. 298.
104. Ibid.
105. Ibid., pp. 305–306. Sullivan in his attack on the Massachusetts Bank had used the same argument. *Path to Riches*, p. 55 [1792].
106. *Principles and Policy*, pp. 305–306 [1814].
107. Ibid., p. 43.
108. Logan, *Letters to the Yeomanry on Funding and Bank Systems*, p. 12 [1793].
109. Pelatiah Webster, *Political Essays*, p. 290 [1785].
110. *Collection of Essays*, p. 105 [1787].
111. Taylor, *Enquiry into Certain Public Measures*, p. 35 [1794].
112. Logan, *Letters to the Yeomanry on Funding and Bank Systems*, p. 12 [1793]; Taylor, *Definition of Parties*, p. 8 [1784].
113. "Agriculture . . . guided by a false interest" becomes "infinitely less beneficial to commerce" while "commerce, moulded into a paper aristocracy," becomes "less beneficial to agriculture." Taylor, *Principles and Policy*, pp. 349–350.

unproductive members of society, and threatened the welfare of labor which is "the thermometer of good government."[114]

The Danger of Perpetual Oppression

A financial interest, circumstantially united, could conceivably be overwhelmed by an aroused public will. But if the new aristocracy were allowed to consolidate its power and to have its usurpation confirmed by acts of incorporation, a nation might easily become permanently enslaved. This was the argument that Taylor employed in his vigorous attack against the Bank of the United States, an argument Sullivan also used in his bitter condemnation of the Massachusetts Bank. Individuals, said Taylor, "can never defend themselves against associations,"[115] much less against corporations. For corporations "neither live nor die naturally";[116] they are created by law, and once established they perpetuate themselves by acquiring "legislative weight, without election."[117] Their unique strength originates in their successional nature, which justifies policies inappropriate to mortal persons. Hence all corporations find it to their interest to acquire political power[118] in order to further their long-range programs. And it is this inevitable usurpation of political power which makes a corporate financial interest so destructive of liberty.[119] Initial privileges conferred by law will be enlarged as the "successional body," for its own "self-preservation," succeeds in "seducing the representatives . . . from their natural allegiance."[120] Once a financial corporation has come into existence, it can be expected to use every weapon "to defend [its] legal or chartered privileges, to advance [its] private interest, and to annoy the publick."[121] Such accumulated power, said George Logan, will be a "perpetual source of oppression."[122] The chartering of the Bank of the United States "and the incorporating decrees of the state legislatures," he claimed, were "alarming exertions" of the power which the corporate interests had already acquired.[123]

The Massachusetts Bank, said Sullivan, had shown the real in-

114. *Definition of Parties*, p. 9 [1794].
115. *Principles and Policy*, p. 388 [1814].
116. Ibid., pp. 259–260.
117. *Definition of Parties*, p. 16 [1794].
118. Fobes, *A Sermon*, p. 23 [1795].
119. Taylor, *Principles and Policy*, p. 582.
120. *Enquiry into Certain Public Measures*, p. 37 [1794].
121. *Principles and Policy*, p. 613 [1814]. For a defense of a vested banking interest, see Pelatiah Webster, *Political Essays*, pp. 456–457 [1786].
122. *Five Letters to the Yeomanry*, p. 11 [1792].
123. *Letters to the Yeomanry on Funding and Bank Systems*, p. 24 [1793].

116

tentions of the corporate interests. Its founders "led the government into the disreputable idea of giving a corporation authority to act as private bankers, without their private estates being liable for their debts."[124] On a capital of $200,000, Sullivan asserted that the Massachusetts Bank had issued nearly a million dollars in bank notes, thus giving the stockholders a return "of thirty per cent upon their real money."[125] But the excessive rate of return was not the greatest evil; the really dangerous thing was the vast power a few men had over the money supply. These few men, said Sullivan, "will be able to command the markets, monopolize . . . what articles they please," and, by making money scarce or abundant, "fix a capricious estimate upon everything." By virtue of this tremendous power, they will be able "unduly to influence all the measures of the government."[126]

To John Taylor the Bank of the United States was the very center of "a phalanx of privileged orders."[127] Its power to issue bank notes, he said, really signified that "national currency is suppressed, and corporation currency interpolated."[128] Not only did the transfer of this sovereign power mean a conveyance of wealth "from the nation to the corporation," but it also meant that a perpetual control over the nation's entire economic life had been vested in the Bank; for the vast power which springs from discretionary control over a nation's money supply is equivalent to endowing a corporation "with the right of coinage without check or control."[129] The Bank, as Taylor saw it, had acquired even greater power because although a "coining corporation can only fleece the nation by putting in the alloy," the Bank "can fleece it by taking out as well as putting in the alloy."[130] By this power of "deranging" the value of money, the Bank "pares, clips, or sweats property at every contract, by making its measure contract or dilate" whichever is more profitable.[131]

The power that has been entrusted to the Bank, said Taylor, is actually the power of unlimited taxation—authority the people were unwilling to grant to the Senate.[132] And so the United States, after

124. *Path to Riches*, p. 51 [1792].
125. Ibid., p. 49.
126. Ibid., p. 55. Sullivan favored a state-owned bank. Such an institution, he said, would allow a government to borrow in anticipation of taxes, would permit people with loanable funds "to loan their money with more ease," would prevent overbanking, and would socialize banking profits. Ibid., pp. 54, 60, 71.
127. *Definition of Parties*, p. 16 [1794].
128. *Principles and Policy*, p. 369 [1814].
129. Ibid., pp. 368, 370.
130. Ibid., p. 386.
131. Ibid., pp. 369–370, 386.
132. *Enquiry into Certain Public Measures*, p. 23 [1794].

defending its property against Great Britain, has been "cheated of it by private fraud," and in the process the Bank of the United States "has found means to occupy the station precisely, which Great Britain was striving to fill."[133] For surely when currency is "measured out to a nation by corporations," the purpose will be to "enrich and strengthen the measuring interest."[134] It will do this, moreover, without "a single circumstance tending toward public happiness." For the Bank will actually be less beneficial than it would have been if it had been granted a monopoly of specie money, because, in that case, it might "by a prudent use of such a monopoly" enrich itself "at the expense of the world."[135]

The despotic power of the Bank, said Taylor, has been acquired by "debauching" the members of Congress. Insidiously the Bank has thereby acquired representation, while states have progressively been deprived of all or part of their representation. A member of Congress who serves the Bank "ceases to be a citizen of the Union, or an inhabitant of the state which chooses him"; indeed, since the Bank is in league with financial interests abroad, a "Bank member" of Congress "is more under the influence of foreigners than of those who elected him."[136] It would have been better, said Taylor, to have allowed the Bank direct representation "than to permit it to plunder the states of their several quotas." But since the Constitution made no provision for corporate representation, the Bank has obtained enough clandestine legislative power that "it is moderate to assert that it will be better represented than any state."[137] Thus in his indictment of the Bank, Taylor acknowledged that the very kernel of the whole problem of government and business was to be found in the theory of interests. The adoption of a territorial basis of representation had failed to cope with the interests; it had simply forced certain interests to obtain representation by extralegal means.

For Taylor, formal pluralism offered no solution to the problems of government and enterprise. The financial interest, he argued, would never be satisfied with an aliquot share of representation. Its sole motive was to acquire that degree of despotic control which every preceding aristocracy had sought. Hence there could be no compromise. If republican government was really intended by the Constitutional Convention, he said in 1794, "the end can only be attained by the

133. Ibid., p. 22.
134. *Principles and Policy,* p. 347 [1814].
135. Ibid.
136. *Enquiry into Certain Public Measures,* p. 37 [1794].
137. Ibid.

exclusion of the paper faction from the legislature."[138] Steps should therefore be taken to expel "the stock-jobbing paper interest," and to vest all legislative power exclusively in the "natural interests." Yet as he cogitated about the problem of the interests, he began to realize that legislative bodies could not be so easily and so quickly purged of all the men who represented unnatural interests; and as his political and social theory matured, he laid more and more emphasis on civic and moral forces. The ultimate solution of the problem of interests, said Taylor in 1814, must be found in the transcendence of group egoism. Genuine republican government can only be possible when a solicitude for the common good takes precedence over fidelity to one's own interest.

138. *Definition of Parties*, pp. 7, 15 [1794]; *Enquiry into Certain Public Measures*, p. 58 [1794].

V

The Counterclaim
of the
Financial Interest

A government ought to contain in itself
every power requisite to the full accomplishment of the objects committed to its
care, and to the complete execution of the
trusts for which it is responsible, free
from any other control but a regard to
the public good.

Alexander Hamilton

The Urgent Need for Economic Stabilization

THE ATTACK on the financial interest was something more than a condemnation of a group of conspirators against the guileless "natural interests"; it represented violent opposition to Federalist financial policies. Conversely the defense of these policies constituted a counterclaim for the so-called financial interests; and the person who did most to formulate the defense, as everyone knows, was Alexander Hamilton. Although by no means the only contemporary defender of the art of finance, he was certainly the most articulate, the most logical, and the most prolific protagonist of that group of Americans the Republicans branded collectively as a "monied interest." For this reason the arguments used to justify not merely Federalist finance but the tactics of financiers can be built around Hamilton's three most important public papers.[1] In order to do this, the essence of the Hamiltonian argument must be distilled out of the several reports.

The bold and consistent financial policies that Hamilton conceived and instituted had at least four major purposes: to restore public credit, stabilize business, ameliorate the adverseness of the trade balance, and energize the entire economy, thereby creating profit-generating opportunities for entrepreneurs. If these ends were to be achieved, however, he insisted that the appropriate institutions had to be created and certain concessions had to be made to "capitalists" both here and abroad. As we shall see, Hamilton was convinced that without these institutions, and without these concessions to the financial interest, there could be no prosperity for any of the natural interests and but few profit opportunities for the monied group.

1. The two reports on public credit (1790 and 1795, respectively) and the report on the Bank (1790).

121

By 1785 the need for commercial, fiscal, and monetary stability had become insistent. Massachusetts found itself in the throes of an incipient civil war. Business depression threatened merchants in many commercial cities and towns throughout the country, while scarcity of money, low prices, unpaid taxes, and mounting interest arrears harried many farmers. Government securities sold in a sluggish but highly speculative market at huge discounts. No part of the entire economy could be called really vigorous. Worst of all, there seemed little chance that agreement could be reached about any plan for forceful remedial action. Between the paper money men and the hard money men there seemed to be no possibility of compromise; unless new paper money is issued at once, said a contributor to a Worcester, Massachusetts, newspaper, "we shall be Slaves to the Subjects of Great Britain,"[2] a thesis widely held and strongly asserted, although other people felt just as certain that the nation's unhappy situation stemmed directly from "the pestilent effects of paper money."[3] So at the same time that the followers of Daniel Shays petitioned for new issues of paper money, anti-inflationist writers argued that paper money would certainly bring back "those scenes of want and misery experienced but a few years since."[4] Paper money, the conservatives argued, destroys not only confidence "between man and man," but trust in government.[5] There can be no stability, said Noah Webster, no "private confidence and public content" until all depreciated currency is "annihilated," until "Legislatures learn to revere justice."[6] Some comprehensive commercial, fiscal, and financial program would have to be devised to restore economic health, of that the schoolmaster was convinced, although he was not certain whether the whole public debt should be refunded or whether financial stability could be achieved by a less drastic method.[7]

But although there was rather general agreement that the entire country needed some "system and arrangement"[8] which would restore confidence in government, appreciate the value of public securities, and generate business prosperity, it seems equally clear that very few people understood the underlying causes for America's commercial and financial distress.[9] Alexander Hamilton did; hence when the Consti-

2. *Massachusetts Spy*, September 15, 1785.
3. Madison, *The Federalist* (Lodge), XLIV, 278 [1788].
4. *Massachusetts Spy*, February 16, 1786.
5. Madison, *The Federalist* (Lodge), XLIV, 278 [1788].
6. Noah Webster, *Collection of Essays*, p. 134 [1786].
7. Ibid., p. 110 [1787].
8. *Worcester Magazine*, July 2, 1786.
9. An article contributed to the *Massachusetts Spy*, November 25, 1785, by "Americanus" is one of the few really penetrating analyses of the interrelations between monetary, fiscal, and commercial factors antedating Hamilton's reports.

tution had been adopted and when he had been selected as secretary of the treasury, he promptly was able to make concrete recommendations for stabilizing and energizing the American economy.

All his proposals—for funding the debt, assuming the state debts, establishing the Bank, or stimulating manufactures—stemmed from a body of theory which can quite properly be called "political economy." For in the Hamiltonian economic program, government played a central part; as a consequence, Hamilton's basic doctrines were much more closely related to those of Malachy Postlethwayt and Sir James Steuart than they were to the atomistic theory of Adam Smith.[10] Like Postlethwayt, Hamilton was convinced that national economic vitality demanded planning on the part of businessmen, and like Steuart, he felt certain that such planning could not be systematic and truly purposeful unless it was coordinated by statesmen.

The Balance of Payments Problem

If the economic malaise had originated wholly in the unbalanced budgets, which the Revolutionary War had occasioned, the problem would have been relatively simple; it would merely have called for an appropriate fiscal remedy. But the roots of the disorder were much deeper; actually the wartime financial problem had aggravated a persistent, almost chronic, economic difficulty. The root cause of the economic maladjustments, which had disorganized foreign trade, demoralized governmental revenues, and precipitated Shays's Rebellion, was to be found in the American balance of payments. Hamilton was one of the few men of his time who really understood this.[11] For he was almost the only statesman of his generation who perceived how the investment process in a frontier region tends constantly to trench on money supply. To Hamilton, therefore, it was not a question of paper money versus specie, much less a question of whether taxes on luxuries should replace property taxes.[12] Rather, the problem involved the task of working out a program that would maximize the nation's existing money supply, augment that money supply by capital imports, generate confidence in credit (private and governmental), and channelize investment in ways which would ultimately correct a chronically adverse

10. Hamilton's scheme for using the public debt as a means of increasing the nation's capital stems apparently from ideas advanced by David Hume and Sir Matthew Decker. See below p. 131.

11. Tench Coxe and James Bowdoin also recognized the central importance of the balance of payments. So did an unidentified number of the Massachusetts legislature whose address before the General Court was printed in the *Worcester Magazine,* July 2, 1786.

12. As Pelatiah Webster argued so stubbornly and so confidently.

trade balance. This elaborate, interlocked agenda required the support of the "monied interest," of men ready and able to assume risks in anticipation of generous compensation.

The settlement of new regions, said Hamilton, "has a natural tendency to occasion an unfavorable balance of trade" because land speculation and the investment of savings in clearing and improving frontier farms necessarily diminish "the active wealth of the country."[13] Frontier investment "not only draws off a part of the circulating money, and places it in a more passive state,"[14] but it also "diverts" productive factors away from industries which could produce goods for export. Exports will therefore tend to decline relatively, and the net result of the investment process will be to keep the trade balance of new countries adverse. Admittedly a frontier nation is indemnified in the long run by the increase in national capital "which flows from the conversion of waste into improved lands."[15] The short-run disadvantage, however, may be utterly devastating: the nation may be gutted of cash,[16] with all manner of unhappy results. Improved property, for example, may be hard to sell, tax money troublesome to acquire, new enterprises difficult to launch. Hence both government and enterprises may be discomfited, and a general lack of confidence may undermine the stability of the entire economy. Meantime the business of importing foreign goods will become increasingly dependent upon foreign credits,[17] thereby threatening the solvency of importers.

Dangers such as these constantly threaten young countries. Yet the vigor of enterprise in newly settled areas depends upon the rate of investment, which in turn depends upon the prospects for recouping investments by the sale of improved land or the products thereof. Hence, the soundness of the entire process must rely upon the facilities making for liquidity. Because Hamilton understood this, he insisted that credit was more necessary in a new than in an old country,[18] for credit was "not only one of the main pillars of the public safety" but one of the "principal engines of useful enterprise and internal im-

13. *Report on Manufactures*, in *Political Papers* (McKee), p. 227 [1791]. The same point is made in the *Report on a National Bank*, in *Political Papers*, pp. 68, 71 [1790]. Although the contemporary references are consistently to the "balance of trade," internal evidence makes it perfectly clear that it was not simply the merchandise balance of trade but the entire balance of payments that writers like Hamilton and Coxe had in mind.

14. *Report on the National Bank*, in *Political Papers*, p. 71.

15. *Report on Manufactures*, in ibid., p. 227.

16. Ibid., p. 71.

17. Coxe, *View of the United States*, p. 503 [1793].

18. *Second Report on Public Credit*, in *Political Papers* (McKee), p. 170 [1790].

provement."[19] Properly provided, whether by the government, banks, or foreign capitalists, credit can vitalize the whole economy of a new country. But credit must be understood as something entire, something public and private, something foreign and domestic. In this aggregative sense, credit "might be emphatically called the invigorating principle."[20]

Only a few of Hamilton's contemporaries had any appreciation of the actual context of the whole economic problem which confronted the nation. Noah Webster and others quite properly emphasized that the several states, acting independently, could not cope with the trade balance problem.[21] For the most part, however, the integrality of public policy was not realized. Indeed, except for Tench Coxe,[22] only Hamilton seems to have understood clearly how fiscal and monetary factors were interrelated with foreign trade and the balance of payments. This interrelation made Hamilton's task much harder, especially since all manner of panaceas were currently being urged: paper money, taxes on luxury, or navigation acts. Hamilton's duty was to demonstrate that greater productive efficiency of the entire economy could be generated only by a wise integration of private and governmental activity and that only increased efficiency could overcome the "inconvenience" to which new countries are normally subject.[23]

The central problem had to do with the nation's supply of capital. The process of converting forest land into fields, lumber into buildings, the products of quarries and mines into milldams or iron furnaces—this variegated process of capital formation constantly interfered with the production of exports with which to pay for imports. Meantime the lack of liquidity resulting from fixed investments seriously limited the ability of the government to collect taxes whereby to reduce public indebtedness. To Hamilton it was clear that any policy which tended to stimulate capital imports would be nationally beneficial. That is what he meant when he said that "in a country situated like the United States, with an infinite fund of resources yet to be unfolded, every farthing of foreign capital which is laid out in internal meliorations, and in industrial establishments, of a permanent nature, is a precious acquisition."[24] Foreign capital ought to be courted, not

19. Ibid., p. 171.
20. Ibid., p. 169.
21. *Collection of Essays,* p. 135 [1786].
22. Evidence may be found in his *View of the United States,* pp. 193–194, 367–368, 503, where the putative effect of banks and public debt upon foreign trade is analyzed.
23. This entire argument is never succinctly stated. The best statement is found in the *Report on a National Bank,* in *Political Papers* (McKee).
24. *Report on Manufactures,* in *Political Papers* (McKee), p. 213.

feared. A foreign financial interest should not be regarded as a rival; instead, foreign capital "ought to be considered as a most valuable auxilliary," an engine for putting in motion "a greater quantity of productive labor, and a greater portion of useful enterprise, than could exist without it."[25]

The Hamiltonian program was therefore designed to facilitate capital imports. Tench Coxe, who was closely associated with Hamilton during the first few years of the new government, made this abundantly clear. The "redundant . . . private wealth in several foreign nations," he wrote in 1791, can become "an addition to our active capital" if "we preserve the honest spirit with which the reforms of the general and state governments have been lately made, and the wisdom with which they have been administered."[26] If public credit is strengthened and maintained, said Coxe, American governmental debt might easily be used as security for "a loan of as much coin from some foreign nation." The prudent investment of such capital imports might provide America with "cotton-mills, wool-mills, flax and hemp-mills, and other valuable branches of machine manufacturing"[27] which would obviate the necessity of many varieties of manufactured imports and thereby solve the balance of payments problem.

Unlike George Logan, John Taylor, and the other bitter critics of foreign financial interests, Hamilton and Coxe had no misgivings about the purchase of American public securities by European investors. The immediate benefit of foreign purchases of government debt, Coxe contended, will be to appreciate the value of these securities. The longtime consequence, he predicted, would be to stimulate the immigration into the United States "of the families of those foreigners, who have made large investments."[28] Similarly Hamilton argued that the purchase of shares in the Bank of the United States by foreigners was not only beneficial in the short run but would probably "prove an incentive . . . to emigration" and thereby facilitate still more capital imports.[29]

The Whole Fabric of Hamilton's Economic Policy

Because fiscal exigencies made it necessary for Hamilton to inaugurate his reform program by funding the debt, it has been assumed that his

25. Ibid., p. 212.
26. *View of the United States*, p. 239 [1791].
27. Ibid., p. 166.
28. Ibid., pp. 365–366.
29. *Report on a National Bank*, in *Political Papers* (McKee), p. 63.

plan for a national bank and his recommendations that manufactures be promoted were ancillary to his central concern with public credit. This interpretation, which one encounters in almost every political history, is superficial and inaccurate. For it could as easily be argued that Hamilton's major concern was with banking and manufacturing, and that public credit represented the subsidiary factor. Again and again Hamilton asserted that a funded debt would enlarge the nation's supply of capital, that funding was necessary to relieve the inconvenience caused by the scarcity of money. But it is really quite fruitless to attempt to assign a logical priority to any single part of Hamilton's program. The several parts formed integrant segments of a cohesive plan.

The "whole fabric"[30] of Hamilton's policy comprehended "the means by which national exigencies are to be provided for, national inconveniences obviated, national prosperity promoted";[31] it was precisely because these objectives could not be achieved singly that Hamilton advocated a loose interpretation of the Constitution.[32] The issue of interpretation came to the forefront when the constitutionality of the proposed Bank of the United States was questioned by both Thomas Jefferson and Edmund Randolph. Hamilton's almost belligerent defense of the legality of the Bank indicates that he regarded the Bank as an indispensable part of his entire program. In much the same spirit that Pelatiah Webster had justified the incorporation of the Bank of North America as "an act of finance" designed to promote "the general interest, the liberties, and general welfare of the States,"[33] Hamilton impatiently rejected the legalistic objections of Jefferson and Randolph. The "abstract question" of whether Congress had the power to erect a corporation was not of essence;[34] the whole matter centered on the right of the government to employ a banking corporation as an appropriate "quality, capacity, or means"[35] for the advancement of national prosperity. What Hamilton defended, in his letter to Washington about the constitutionality of the Bank, was the right of

30. This phrase appears in Sullivan's *Path to Riches.*
31. *Constitutionality of the Bank,* in *Political Papers* (McKee), p. 108 [1791].
32. "A government," said Hamilton, "ought to contain in itself every power requisite to the full accomplishment of the objects committed to its care, and to the complete execution of the trusts for which it is responsible, free from any other control but a regard to the public good." *The Federalist* (Lodge), XXXI, 182 [1788].
33. *Political Essays,* p. 451 [1786].
34. *Constitutionality of the Bank,* in *Political Papers* (McKee), p. 102.
35. Ibid., p. 105. For a carefully researched account of the controversy over the constitutionality of the Bank, see Mitchell, *Alexander Hamilton,* II, 86–108, chap. 5.

the secretary of the treasury to a "great latitude of discretion in the selection of those means" which promised to promote "national prosperity."[36]

That the Bank occupied a pivotal place in Hamilton's economic policy, and that his fiscal program was interlocked with his plan for increasing the nation's money supply, was admitted by some of his most censorious critics. "The game he has played," said James Sullivan, "is very deep, as well as very splendid"; but "the whole fabric he has raised with so much éclat, may be at once overthrown by a run upon the bank." For in Sullivan's opinion it was the intricate interrelations of Hamilton's financial policies that constituted their weakness. Should the Bank be compelled by governmental exigencies to issue credit greatly in excess of its capital, Sullivan predicted that Hamilton might have to "follow Mr. Law to Venice . . . to find an asylum from the public resentment."[37] Moreover he feared the delicately equipoised financial mechanism might be disarranged when Hamilton was no longer secretary of the treasury. But Sullivan made it perfectly clear that Hamilton's financial system had neatly interlocked private and governmental credit, and had intermeshed public finance and banking.[38]

Public Credit and National Prosperity

On the "maintenance of public credit," said Hamilton in the first of his remarkable public documents, "depends . . . the individual and aggregate prosperity of the citizens of the United States."[39] For not only does sound public credit stabilize the affairs of a government, but it also increases the transactional activity within a nation and facilitates the importation of capital, thereby permitting the development of a country's economic resources. Hence it is wholly specious to assume that private credit, which energizes business, is something independent of public credit; actually "public and private credit are closely allied, if not inseparable."[40] One cannot flourish while the other is faltering, because "credit is an entire thing; . . . wound one limb, and the whole tree shrinks and decays."[41]

Private credit allows people to take up land, cultivate it, and pay for

36. *Constitutionality of the Bank,* in *Political Papers* (McKee), p. 108.
37. *Path to Riches,* p. 45 [1792].
38. Ibid., p. 46.
39. *First Report on Public Credit,* in *Political Papers* (McKee), p. 4 [1790].
40. *Second Report on Public Credit,* in *Political Papers* (McKee), p. 171 [1790].
41. Ibid., p. 172.

their farms out of the joint product of land and labor; it permits other persons with business ability but lacking capital to carry on trade; it makes it possible for artisans who possess skill, but have no money, to buy tools and materials and thereby set up as manufacturers.[42] Private credit is therefore indisputably "among the principal engines of useful enterprise and internal improvement"; it is a "substitute for capital"[43] which is "little less useful than gold or silver" in extending the scale of operations of the natural interests. Of all this, contended Hamilton, no proof is necessary, since credit has so obviously permitted the extension of American agriculture, commerce, manufacturing, and mechanic arts. What did call for explanation was the interrelation of private and public credit.

Public credit, said Hamilton, confers a double benefit upon a nation's natural interests. In the first place it protects the investments which have already been made, thus providing scope for the beneficent action of private credit; in the second place it activates and enlarges a nation's total credit, thus maximizing the productivity of all the natural interests. Hamilton wasted few words in demonstrating that public credit was useful in safeguarding the investments of farmers, merchants, and manufacturers. Governmental expenditure, he pointed out, had not only made possible the defense of the frontiers but had protected American businessmen "against the enterprises of other nations."[44] But to obtain such benefits, a nation must, if necessary, be able to borrow against the security of its future enrichment. For a young nation possessed of but limited capital and inconvenienced by an adverse balance of payments, this "faculty to borrow . . . considerable sums on moderate terms" was more necessary than for older, occupationally differentiated, and capital-rich countries.

The second benefit which public credit could confer upon a nation's natural interests required much more elaboration since it involved a demonstration of how public credit could overcome the capital deficiency that resulted from the adverse balance of payments with which new countries were unavoidably confronted. Consequently, the analysis involved an examination of the economic effects of public debts upon the enterprise system. Although Hamilton did say that "the

42. Ibid., p. 171.
43. Modern monetary theory, by reason of its incisive analysis of the savings-investment process, has blunted the criticism which neoclassical economists levied against Hamilton's contention that wise fiscal policy could increase a nation's capital. In their zealous effort to prove that Hamilton confused money and capital, his nineteenth-century critics failed to recognize that an increase of loanable funds may permit investment to precede savings.
44. *Second Report on Public Credit,* in *Political Papers* (McKee), p. 170.

proper funding of the present debt will render it a national blessing,"[45] he did not accept the simplistic view that the size of the public debt was a matter of indifference. His funding program, therefore, did not rest on the "one big family" doctrine which asserted that "no state can be ruined, bankrupted, or indeed much endangered, by any debt due to itself alone."[46] On the contrary Hamilton stated quite unambiguously that "the creation of debt should always be accompanied with the means of extinguishment" since only by such foresight can public credit be rendered "immortal."[47] What he did vigorously assert was that if a nation had been compelled to contract a large public debt, this claim upon future governmental revenues could be administered in such a way that the very existence of the debt could generate a larger volume of business activity and thereby, over time, create a repayment capacity. This argument, which lies at the very core of Hamilton's fiscal, monetary, and international trade theory, must be explained in more detail.

The argument rested on two primary assumptions. In the first place, it posited the existence of a "monied interest" ready and willing to purchase and hold government securities provided adequate tax measures were instituted so that interest payments could regularly be made. In the second place, it presumed that the debt would not all be held internally, thus postulating that the transference of some of the debt to a foreign rentier class would temporarily ameliorate the adverseness of the balance of payments. But government debt would not be purchased by either domestic or foreign rentiers unless it had "acquired an adequate and stable value." The purpose of the funding act was to confer this "adequate and stable value" on what had previously been a "mere commodity" subject to "occasional and particular speculation."[48] It was designed to guarantee to every holder of public securities that the government, having consolidated the total debt, would punctually perform all the provisions of the contracts it had entered into with its creditors. Such an assurance, Hamilton predicted, would make it possible for the funded debt to serve as a substitute for money. For as soon as public securities had been stabilized in value,

45. *First Report on Public Credit,* in *Political Papers* (McKee), p. 45. For this remark Hamilton was excoriated. See, as an example, William Findley's *Review of the Revenue System,* p. 38.
46. Pelatiah Webster, *Political Essays,* pp. 1–2 [1776]. It should be noted that although Webster stated this doctrine succinctly, he was a bitter enemy of deficit financing during and after the Revolutionary War.
47. *First Report on Public Credit,* in *Political Papers* (McKee), p. 46. *Second Report on Public Credit,* in ibid., p. 153.
48. *First Report on Public Credit,* in *Political Papers* (McKee), p. 8.

they would become the objects of "established confidence"[49] and would pass current as readily as money in large transactions and would ensure liquidity of certain assets.[50] When this had occurred, the net effect upon the entire economy, said Hamilton, would be the equivalent of a net increase in the nation's money supply. Merchants would be able to carry on more trade, the value of lands would rise, agriculture would be extended, and new manufacturing enterprises could be established, provided an adequate measure of protection against foreign competition was afforded.

Nor, said Hamilton, was this merely a theory unsupported by experience. "The force of moneyed capital which has been displayed in Great Britain, and the height to which every species of industry has grown up under it"[51] supplied demonstrable proof that public securities can and do answer the purposes of capital. Moreover Hamilton argued that the post-Constitutional upturn in American business was attributable to the improvement in public credit which the funding act had produced. Industry, he said, "seems to have been re-animated," commerce has increased, navigation has experienced "considerable spring," and finally "there appears to be . . . a command of capital which till lately, since the Revolution at least, was unknown."[52] Tench

49. Ibid., pp. 5, 7.
50. See below, p. 133.
51. *Report on Manufactures*, in *Political Papers* (McKee), pp. 214, 218. The industrial development in Britain, said Hamilton, cannot be explained in terms of "the quantity of coin which that kingdom has ever possessed." Since the vitalization of enterprise has been "coeval with its funding system," he asserted that it was the "prevailing opinion of men of business, and of the generality of the most sagacious theorists of that country that the operation of the public funds, as capital, has contributed to the effect in question." No doubt one of these "sagacious theorists" to whom Hamilton referred was David Hume who asserted that "public securities are with us become a kind of money, and pass as readily at the current price as gold or silver." See Hume, *Political Discourses* (Edinburgh, 1752), "Discourse VIII. Of Public Credit," p. 128. The argument that funded debt would perform the functions of money had been advanced eight years earlier by Sir Matthew Decker in his *Essay on the Causes of the Decline of the Foreign Trade* (London, 1744). His fifth proposal for the restoration of Britain's prosperity, "to pay off our debts by public bonds," is the clearest anticipation of Hamilton's funding act. The funded debt, Decker predicted, would constitute "a currency more valuable than our coin," and the resulting enlargement of purchasing power would stimulate trade (by reducing interest rates), increase employment, raise the value of land, and by these several things augment Britain's wealth and increase its population. Decker's proposals for funding the British debt were contained in the article "Funds" in Malachy Postlethwayt, *Universal Dictionary of Trade and Commerce* (London, 1751), which went through several editions, and this may have been the channel through which Decker's ideas were transmitted to Hamilton. For Decker's proposal, see *An Essay on the Causes of the Decline of the Foreign Trade*, pp. 220–228.
52. *Report on Manufactures*, in *Political Papers* (McKee), p. 218.

Coxe made even stronger claims, ascribing the whole course of business revival to the funding of the public debt. "There is in every walk of life or business," he wrote in 1792, "a greater proportion of money than was observable two years ago." He pointed to the increase in "public works and buildings," to the volume of "private building, of equal variety, and comparative value," to the rise in the price of land, and to the greater abundance and the higher prices of raw materials; all of which he interpreted as evidence that funding had vitalized the entire economy.[53] He asserted that the "re-animation" of the public debt, whose total value was "ten times larger than the amount of all the specie ordinarily circulating in the country," had stimulated business enterprise everywhere, contending that "there was never applied . . . so great an aggregate of money as is employed directly or indirectly at the present time."[54]

The Liquidity of Artificial Capital

That the adoption of the Constitution and the enactment of the funding act had stimulated business could scarcely be denied.[55] But whether this was merely a psychological response to the prospects of a stronger central government and had little or nothing to do with the putative capacity of funded debt to perform the functions of money was less clear. It was therefore incumbent upon the advocates of funding to show why business revival could be causally related to the appreciation of public securities. The best statement of this argument is to be found in the writings of Hamilton and, before him, in those of Samuel Gale.

"Whosoever will reflect a single moment," wrote Gale, "must be convinced, that publick credit is neither more nor less, than a publick machine for bringing capitals into action. The actual capitals that shall thereby be brought into actions, may indeed be applied to one use or to another; to a good one, or to a bad one. But this had nothing to do with the machine."[56] Yet Gale did not show how

53. *View of the United States*, pp. 364–365 [1792].

54. Ibid., preface, p. 11 [1794]. In support of this assertion, Coxe lists a series of projects which have been undertaken: the building of dams, canals, roads, etc.

55. Hamilton's critics contended that the kind of business activity that had been generated was unwholesome and inequitable. Thus James Sullivan, although he admitted that previous to the adoption of the Constitution public securities had been "a dead, inactive kind of property," and although he agreed that the funding act had "furnished a large, and active capital for commerce" which "answers as extensive a purpose . . . as would be answered by real money," nevertheless claimed that the Hamiltonian policy was "a great grievance and burden to the people" because it increased the wealth of the financial interest at the expense of other classes of people. *Path to Riches*, pp. 16, 44 [1792].

56. *Essay II: On the Nature and Principles of Publick Credit* (St. Augustine, 1784), p. 22.

132

"capitals" were "brought into action" any more than did James Bowdoin, who stated that the funding of the federal debt and the assumption of state debts had led to "the introduction of near eighty millions of dollars into circulation," which, in turn, had "extended" the "means of industry" and "greatly enlarged"[57] the value of land and other property. Fortunately Hamilton was a little more specific: "Public funds answer the purpose of capital, from the estimation in which they are usually held by moneyed men; and consequently, from the ease and dispatch with which they can be turned into money. This capacity for prompt convertibility into money causes a transfer to stock to be, in a number of cases, equivalent to a payment in coin."[58] For this reason, Hamilton declared that "in a sound and settled state of the public funds, a man possessed of a sum in them, can embrace any scheme of business"[59] which might promise to be profitable.

It should now be clear why Hamilton was so uncompromisingly insistent that the public debt must be funded at face value. For if government securities could become high-grade investments, three chief benefits would result. Monied men would be able to hold their idle balances in government securities. By virtue of the liquidity of their funds (which could be achieved by transferring securities to rentiers or to other businessmen whose cash balances were increasing) entrepreneurs would be in a position to seize quickly opportunities that promised profit. In the second place, the chance to make a safe and semiliquid investment in government securities would permit entrepreneurs to take greater risks with a portion of their funds, especially since they were receiving interest on their idle balances. Funding the debt, therefore, promised to release a larger amount of "adventure capital" than would otherwise have been available. In the third place, government securities might actually be used as money in large trans-

57. *Observations upon the Necessity and Importance of the American Navigation Act,* p. 30, [1797].
58. *Report on Manufactures,* in *Political Papers* (McKee), p. 214.
59. Hume had been fully as explicit: "Whenever any profitable undertaking offers itself, however expensive, there are [where public securities pass current as money] never wanting hands enow to embrace it; nor need a trader, who has sums in the public stocks, fear to launch out into the most extensive trade; since he is possset of funds, which will answer the most sudden demand that can be made upon him. . . . In short, our national debts furnish merchants with a species of money, that is continually multiplying in their hands, and produces sure gain [interest], beside the profits of their commerce. This must enable them to trade upon less profit." *Political Discourses,* p. 128. Decker had made substantially the same point. A funded debt, he said, will increase trade "by creating a currency more valuable than our coin: money lying by, brings in nothing but all these bonds pay something for keeping, and I presume that no persons (much less the Bank or the Bankers) would keep money by them lying dead, when they could have current bonds that bore only a half per cent interest." *An Essay on the Causes of the Decline of the Foreign Trade,* pp. 222–223.

actions,[60] and here Hamilton simply asserted that more purchasing power brings greater business activity.[61]

The foregoing advantages would emerge if the entire debt was held domestically. Even greater national advantages would result if the funding of the debt led to the purchase of public securities by foreign rentiers. For, in this case, the total capital resources of the nation would be positively enlarged not merely in the short run by the amount of foreign exchange transferred by the foreign rentiers to the American sellers of securities, but in the long run, since the capital supplied by foreigners "laid out in this country upon our agriculture, commerce, and manufactures, will produce much more to us than the income they [foreign rentiers] will receive from it."[62]

Hamilton admitted quite readily that a funded debt did not create "an absolute increase of capital," but he did contend that "by serving as a new power in the operations of industry" the debt would have "a tendency to increase the real wealth of a community."[63] Fair-minded critics such as James Sullivan granted this contention; the funded securities, he admitted, did perform money work both within the nation and

60. Much of the criticism levied against Hamilton centered on this last and probably least important point. Thus William Findley claimed that public securities had "not supplied the place of money in promoting purchase of land, the payment of debts or any of the common dealings of the country." *Review of the Revenue System,* p. 37 [1794].

61. But none of these benefits could emerge, said Hamilton, unless the public debt is funded, since an unstabilized floating debt will lead to haphazard speculation which will make money scarce and business activity fitful and uncertain.

62. *First Report on Public Credit,* in *Political Papers* (McKee), p. 48. The same argument was used to justify the purchase of shares in the Bank of the United States by foreigners. The dividends paid to foreign rentiers, Hamilton claimed, would be "more than replaced by the profits" arising from the employment of the borrowed capital. *Report on a National Bank,* in *Political Papers* (McKee), p. 63.

63. *Report on Manufacturers,* in *Political Papers* (McKee), p. 219. Samuel Gale had pointed out that whereas a public debt mobilized capital, it did so at a debt-service cost, and hence he advocated the use of a sinking fund so that a government could avail itself of a fall in interest rates by retiring high interest-bearing securities. Hamilton, although he advocated the use of a sinking fund, argued that the debt-service cost of the "artificial capital" does not constitute a "destruction of capital" if the debt is internally held since the interest received by the public creditors does not constitute a subtraction from money in circulation. And as far as foreign security holders are concerned, if 6 percent interest and 2 percent amortization is the cost of $100 of new capital, then $92 will be the net addition of new capital at the end of the first year, $84 at the end of the second, and so on, plus the productivity of the capital resulting from its employment by an entrepreneur. See Gale, *Essay II: On the Nature of Publick Credit,* pp. 24–25; and Hamilton *Report on Manufactures,* in *Political Papers* (McKee), pp. 215–217. Sullivan contended, however, that the debt-service cost of the new capital was an "involuntary contribution," which deprived people "of a great share of their profit in trade." *Path to Riches,* pp. 16–17 [1792].

in international transactions.[64] What Sullivan condemned was the inequity of compelling taxpayers to pay toll to the financial interest.[65] Hamilton conceded that there were certain latent dangers involved: it does not follow, he carefully pointed out, that because funded government debt can perform money work, the greater the public debt, the greater the social benefit. There can be too much "artificial capital." An excessive amount may lead to oppressive taxation and hence constitute a social evil. But "where this critical point is," said Hamilton, with becoming candor, "cannot be pronounced; but it is impossible to believe that there is not such a point."[66]

Within certain limits experimentally discoverable, however, Hamilton was convinced that "artificial capital" could be genuinely beneficent. It would enlarge the working capital of merchants, farmers, and manufacturers, tending thereby to intensify competition and reduce the rate of profits;[67] it would lower interest rates; and it would raise the value of lands particularly by obviating the necessity of forced sales.[68] Here then was the "invigorating principle,"[69] which could ensure the growth of the United States; here the means which would expedite foreign loans at low interest rates.[70] Moreover, the resulting business activity would be the best insurance against agrarian discontent[71] and against maladjustments in the value-ratios of real and personal property.[72]

That public creditors would benefit from his funding program Hamilton admitted quite frankly.[73] But the gains from the apprecia-

64. *Path to Riches*, p. 16 [1792].
65. "When nations have been pressed with expensive wars, or other intolerable calamities, they have had recourse to their public credit; in the support of which, every member of the civil community has been in some measure interested. But the idea of giving a few men a corporate capacity [e.g., by means of the Bank of the United States] to issue, regulate, and control the medium of commerce among a great trading people, was before unprecedented." Ibid., p. 47.
66. *Report on Manufactures*, in *Political Papers* (McKee), p. 220.
67. The lowered rate of profits could be attributed partly to the interest which entrepreneurs would receive on idle balances, which could promptly be rendered income yielding by purchasing government securities in the open market.
68. *First Report on Public Credit*, in *Political Papers* (McKee), pp. 7–9. The "decrease in the value of lands ought, in a great measure, to be attributed to the scarcity of money; consequently, whatever produces an augmentation of the moneyed capital of the country must have a proportional effect in raising that value. The beneficial tendency of a funded debt, in this respect, has been manifested by the most decisive experience in Great Britain."
69. *Second Report on Public Credit*, in *Political Papers* (McKee), p. 169.
70. Coxe, *View of the United States*, pp. 363–364 [1792].
71. Ibid., p. 365.
72. Bowdoin, *Opinions respecting Commercial Intercourse*, p. 30 [1797].
73. *First Report on Public Credit*, in *Political Papers* (McKee), p. 6; *Report on a National Bank*, ibid., p. 92.

tion, as will presently be shown, were conceived to be a legitimate reward for risk-taking. Moreover, the funding program was conceived as a remedial measure designed to strengthen public credit. Once the integrity of the government had been established, the costs of public borrowing would decline, and this reduction would inure to the advantage of all taxpayers. Thus Hamilton betrayed far more optimism than Gale did in 1784 when he declared that "the grand practical principle of funding, consists in preserving such a balance or equilibrium, in the circulation of money . . . that the rate of interest shall not continually rise higher and higher . . . in consequence of new loans."[74] With characteristic self-confidence, Hamilton thought in terms of positive fiscal reforms, not merely of fiscal amelioration.

The Voice of Policy and the Voice of Humanity

Hamilton's proposal that the public securities be paid in full to whomsoever held them, regardless of whether he was an "original creditor" or a transferee, raised a furious storm of protest. Although this literature of dissent is large, one central argument pervades it, one that Pelatiah Webster stated as succinctly as any of his contemporaries. "Appreciating the securities, and redeeming them at full value," he wrote, five years before Hamilton's funding scheme was adopted, "gives not the least remedy to the sufferers by the depreciation, but is an additional injury to them."[75] For inasmuch as the securities, at the time of redemption, "will not be in the same hands in which they depreciated . . . the sufferers will find themselves taxed to make up the money, which they lost by the depreciation, that it may be paid to the present holders of the securities, who never lost anything." Here then, he charged, was a double injury. The "original creditors" had accepted securities for military supplies, for army pay, or had purchased them. Was it not unfair that these public creditors who, because of adversity had been compelled to sell their securities, let us say, for three shillings,[76] should see speculators redeem them at twenty shillings? And was it not grotesquely unfair that such "original creditors" should be compelled to pay taxes to make redemption at par possible?

Yet although there can be no denying that from 1789 onward "the

74. Samuel Gale, *Essay II: On the Nature of Publick Credit,* p. 35 [1784].
75. *Political Essays,* pp. 296–297 [1785].
76. For the actual movement in public security prices, see Davis, *American Corporations,* I, 187. For a vivid account of the conflict over funding, see Mitchell, *Alexander Hamilton,* II, 57–85.

Rage of the Day" was the speculative purchase of government securities,[77] it does not necessarily follow that all the profits of the speculators were made at the expense of the "original holders." In the first place, some of the "original holders" hung on to their securities and benefited from the appreciation that Hamilton's policies engineered. In the second place, the rise in the price of securities was not an uninterrupted trend. Less courageous speculators sold to more daring speculators. Nor were all buyers of securities necessarily speculators; "many were investors pure and simple."[78] None of these qualifications, however, can erase the historical fact that many "original holders" had disposed of their securities in the 1780s for two, three, four, or five shillings, nor do they alter the fact that on August 4, 1790, state and federal debts were funded at face value into new securities which reached par value less than a year later. Some people gained a huge windfall,[79] and to a very large extent this windfall must be attributed to Hamilton's decision to make no distinction between the "original holders" and the "present possessors."

He made the decision in the face of fierce opposition. If it was, as Pelatiah Webster said, "a matter of public notoriety and general belief, that almost the whole of the widows, orphans, soldiers, and other distressed public creditors"[80] who had sold their securities had done so at great discounts, was it not just and proper that speculators be reimbursed merely for the actual amount they had paid and that only "original creditors" who had been able to keep their securities should be rewarded by payment in full?[81] For, aside from the fairness of this proposal, was it not also a lesson of history that "men of overgrown riches, especially of sudden acquirement, are dangerous to any community," simply because "human nature cannot bear, without corruption, such sudden leaps into the heights of greatness, prosperity, wealth, and influence"?[82] And was it not inevitable, asked Richard Henry Lee, that funding all the debt at face value would create a

77. *Craigie Papers*, II, 124, quoted in Davis, *American Corporations*, I, 188.
78. Davis, *American Corporations*, I, 182.
79. Beard thought the gain was at least forty million dollars (*Economic Interpretation of the Constitution*, p. 35), and Davis does not challenge this estimate although he does suggest that part of the appreciation ought to be attributed to "improved business conditions for which the governmental improvements were by no means wholly responsible" (*American Corporations*, I, 195n).
80. *Political Essays*, p. 277 [1785].
81. The most radical proposal was that in the refunding program the government should pay to each "primitive possessor" the difference between what he had received when he sold his securities and full value. See *First Report on Public Credit*, in *Political Papers* (McKee), p. 10.
82. *Political Essays*, pp. 76–77.

"monied interest" that would "forever be warring against the landed interest"?[83]

And why should Hamilton, who later scorned the legalistic arguments of Jefferson and Randolph against the constitutionality of the Bank, be such a stickler for a legalistic interpretation of the claims of the public creditors? The issue, said Noah Webster, although admittedly a legal one, was first and foremost an ethical question. It is true, the schoolmaster explained, that if a man sells a promissory note for half its value to a transferee who subsequently collects in full, the seller "has no remedy at law." And even though inequity is here involved, the laws protecting transferees should not be changed, because they are designed to cover general cases not particular ones.[84] But "when such particular losses become general, the principle loses its force. Sufferings, multiplied to a certain number . . . require the interference of the legislature."[85] Webster argued that although "contracts are sacred things," and although normally "legislatures have no right to interfere with them," there are circumstances which alter this general rule. For "it is the business of justice to fulfill the intention of parties in contracts, not to defeat them."[86] Webster thus concluded that whenever gross injustice would result from strict adherence to contracts, equity should dictate the necessity of deviation.

All these arguments in favor of discrimination between "original holders" and "present possessors" of public securities Hamilton rejected, not summarily but "after the most mature reflection."[87] The whole idea of discrimination he branded "unjust and impolitic," since it would be "injurious even to the original holders" and "ruinous to public credit."[88] For even if some scheme of discrimination could be devised which would be equally fair to those original creditors who had disposed of their securities and to those who had not (which he asserted could not be done), Hamilton contended that such a policy would be unwise. In his opinion the whole matter turned on the consequences of discrimination for the entire economy, and viewing the problem in this light, he concluded that "if the voice of humanity pleads more loudly in favor of some than of others, the voice of policy, no less than justice, pleads in favor of all."[89]

83. See Davis, *American Corporations*, I, 195.
84. The inference is that violent injustice will not normally result from the sale of negotiable instruments.
85. *Collection of Essays*, pp. 282–283 [1787].
86. Ibid., p. 130 [1786]. In this context the arguments for a deviation from contractual responsibility had reference to "tender laws."
87. *First Report on Public Credit*, in *Political Papers* (McKee), p. 10.
88. Ibid., pp. 10–11.
89. Ibid., p. 15.

For solving the interrelated problems of government and business, the voice of policy demanded that public credit be made infallible, that the nation's money supply be augmented, and that business enterprise be stimulated. If the funding of the debt was to contribute to making public credit unimpeachable, the government would have to stand ready to pay each and every holder in full. If funded debt was to serve as a substitute for money, the transferability of public securities must be facilitated. Finally, if public debt was to augment the working capital of businessmen, every effort would have to be made to ensure that public securities would be easily assignable without danger of depreciation. Hamilton therefore built his whole case for payment in full on the doctrine of the sanctity of contract. None of the essential ends of public policy could be attained unless every buyer of public securities "stands exactly in the place of the seller," unless he has the "same right with him to the identical sum" expressed in the contract.[90]

Whosoever has acquired this right "by fair purchase," said Hamilton, ought therefore be protected. That such a purchaser happened to have bought public securities at a discount should in no way alter the obligation of the government. The discount resulted from the failure of the government to make proper provision for servicing its debts; "the buyer had no agency in it, and therefore ought not to suffer."[91] He bought the securities at the market price, and in doing so he "took the risks of reimbursement upon himself." If an improvement of public credit has raised the value of public securities, the purchaser, asserted Hamilton, "ought to reap the benefit of his hazard—a hazard which was far from inconsiderable, and which, perhaps, turned on little less than a revolution in government."[92] As for the persons who had alienated their securities, they constituted two categories: those who sold because of pecuniary distress, and those who disposed of their securities because they lacked confidence in the government. Those original holders who were compelled to sell entered into an act of assignment, forswearing their claims upon the government in exchange for needed cash; moreover, since they knew that the public was obligated to pay the security owners, they tacitly agreed to contribute taxes for the servicing and ultimate redemption of the public debt. Those original holders who sold from lack of faith actually sought to shift their claims upon the government to the purchasers of their securities; they did this either because they thought their securities

90. Ibid., p. 11.
91. Ibid.
92. Ibid.

would soon be worthless or because they preferred liquidity in order to make more profitable investments. Since there could be no way of assessing the motives which had prompted alienation, discrimination would be impossible even if it were desirable.[93] But even if it were possible, it could only be achieved by a breach of contract, thus prejudicing the very ends which funding was designed to accomplish.

Whether this chain of reasoning can be construed as proof that Hamilton actually gave aid and comfort to the speculators is still a moot question. No evidence has been uncovered to prove that Hamilton tipped off his wealthy friends that the government would pay in full. That he welcomed the appreciation of security prices, which speculation caused, and that he purchased securities on government account[94] in the open market, after the funding act was passed, for the avowed purpose of raising the market value of funded debt—all this is perfectly clear. Moreover such action was entirely consistent with his arguments for full payment and for complete security of transfer based upon "the voice of policy." Unless security of transfer is guaranteed, he said, public securities cannot serve as money, and hence interest rates will be higher, enterprise will stagnate, and public credit will falter. And so it came to pass that Hamilton, if we can take him at his word, acted solely in the interests of the nation's economic efficiency when he fulfilled the precepts of a Connecticut preacher who charged rulers with the responsibility for treating a nation's creditors "with the scrupulous fairness of mercantile punctuality."[95]

The Utility of Banks and Especially of a National Bank

The storm and fury which the funding legislation precipitated became even more bitter when Hamilton proposed, on December 18, 1790, that the United States establish a national bank. By the enemies of high finance this was interpreted to mean that the financial interest sought to devise still another instrument of exploitation. It was therefore incumbent upon Hamilton to show that a central bank was "not a mere matter of private property, but a political machine of the greatest importance to the State,"[96] one capable of benefiting all members of society and of strengthening the public credit of the nation. And it becomes quite clear, if one reads the *Report on a*

93. Ibid., pp. 11–12.
94. For the sinking fund.
95. Timothy Dwight, *Virtuous Rulers a National Blessing*, p. 17.
96. *Report on a National Bank*, in *Political Papers* (McKee), p. 80.

140

National Bank carefully, that Hamilton hoped to knit together and to expedite his entire financial program by means of the Bank. For this reason, he vigorously opposed the objections that Thomas Jefferson and Edmund Randolph raised about the constitutionality of the proposed institution.[97]

Recognizing that there existed strong opposition not only to a federally chartered bank but to all banks, Hamilton devoted more than half of the *Report on a National Bank* to an incisive exposition of the social utility of commercial banking institutions. Part of this defense was a paraphrase of arguments that Gouverneur Morris had employed several years earlier,[98] a fact which might be construed to indicate that Hamilton could have been a spokesman for a financial interest. But the *Report* went far beyond a partisan defense of banks and bankers; it attempted to show the indispensability of banks for any vigorous economic development and to demonstrate particularly the imperative necessity of a national bank if the United States was to overcome the normal disadvantages of new countries. For Hamilton implied that without the aid of such an institution, the full advantages of funding could not be realized. The Bank of the United States was therefore to be the instrument for expediting and magnifying the benefits of "artificial capital."

Although the utility of banks had been recognized in all the "most enlightened commercial nations,"[99] in America, said Hamilton, "doubts have been entertained," and "jealousies and prejudices have circulated."[100] It has been alleged, he remarked, that banks increase usury, prevent private lending, stimulate "overtrading," encourage speculation by unskillful people, enable unscrupulous businessmen to carry on fraudulent activities, and worst of all, tend to expel specie.[101] All these charges, argued Hamilton, are untrue.

In the first place, banks tend to "abridge rather than to promote usury." It is true that banks demand punctual repayment, and by doing so they may compel businessmen who have overextended themselves to borrow from usurers. But this will be only a temporary condition; by insisting on punctuality, banks help to correct bad business

97. In his long letter to Washington of February 21, 1891. Printed in *Political Papers* (McKee), pp. 100–137.

98. See "An Address to the Assembly of Pennsylvania on the Abolition of Banks," in Jared Sparks, *Life of Gouverneur Morris* (Boston, 1832).

99. *Report on a National Bank*, in *Political Papers* (McKee), p. 53.

100. In view of the fierce attack which the defenders of the "natural interests" had made on the "financial interest" (see above, chap. IV), this remark must be interpreted as a diplomatic understatement.

101. *Report on a National Bank*, in *Political Papers* (McKee), p. 59.

habits, forcing businessmen to calculate their expectations more carefully. Indeed, by refusing to lend to tardy or unreliable borrowers,
banks favor the "wary and industrious" entrepreneurs and "discredit
the rash and unthrifty," thereby discountenancing "both usurious
lenders and usurious borrowers." Moreover, by augmenting a nation's
money supply, banks "counteract the progress of usury."[102]

Nor is it true, said Hamilton, that banks interfere with private
lending. The charge that banks will monopolize all lending operations
ignores the fact that bank assets must be kept liquid, a requirement
which prevents commercial banks from making longtime loans on
mortgages. Furthermore, the increased business activity that banks
always generate will augment the current streams of new savings; and
since charter limitations on the capital of banks will prevent the investment of these savings in bank stock, a larger amount of loanable
funds will perforce be made available to private lenders. And to the
extent that foreign capitalists purchase American bank stocks, "a positive increase of the gold and silver of the country" results. Profitably
employed, this additional specie will increase domestic savings still
further and thereby increase private lending operations.[103]

The charge that banks "furnish temptations to overtrading" Hamilton countered by two arguments. In the first place, he asserted that
bank credit would not stimulate overtrading any more than enlarged
stocks of specie money would. "The abuses of a beneficial thing," he
cautioned, must not be the basis for its condemnation. Against the
"overtrading of a few individuals" should be placed the offsetting advantages of banks as well as "the new and increased energies" that
enterprise derives from bank credit.[104] Rather than stimulating reckless
business ventures, banks restrain and penalize incompetent entrepreneurs. For if a bank lends to "ignorant adventurers," not only will it
suffer a direct loss but it will discover that the blunders of unskillful
customers may upset business confidence and undermine the value of
the entire portfolio of loans and discounts. Bank directors, therefore,
will zealously strive to seek out competent businessmen and to discriminate against the inefficient. In effect banks will apportion credit
on a merit basis, withholding credit from reckless and fraudulent entrepreneurs. Conversely they will "enable honest and industrious men
. . . to undertake and prosecute business with advantage to themselves and to the community." They will therefore promote the full

102. Ibid., pp. 60–61.
103. Ibid., pp. 62–63.
104. Ibid., pp. 63–64.

employment of the factors of production, protect deserving entrepreneurs against "fortuitous and unforeseen shocks," and maximize the volume of sound and sagacious business activity.[105]

Having shown that banks do not increase usury, prevent private lending, stimulate overtrading, or aid incompetent or fraudulent businessmen, Hamilton addressed himself to the "heaviest charge" levied against banks—the allegation that they cause gold and silver to be exported. He admitted that anything which tended to diminish a nation's specie supply ought to be avoided because the precious metals always constitute "the most effective wealth" since they can be used to meet any external demands that may confront a nation. But inasmuch as "a nation that has no mines of its own must derive the precious metals from others," by exporting the products of land and labor, "the quantity it will possess will . . . be regulated by the favorable or unfavorable balance of its trade." Whether that balance be favorable or unfavorable will depend on "the state of its agriculture and manufactures, the quantity and quality of its labor and industry." If it can be shown, said Hamilton, that banks augment "the active capital of a country" and that this, in turn, "generates employment," then it follows that banks will tend to induce a favorable balance of trade "by furnishing more materials for exportation." He therefore rested his defense of banks on a theory of factoral employment, insisting that the "vivification of industry," which banks generate, would not only increase domestic business activity but would ensure an adequate supply of gold and silver.[106]

After demonstrating the benefits that a nation derives from private banking institutions, Hamilton next went on to show the particular advantages of a national or "public" bank; and here his justification of banks coalesces into the "whole fabric" of his economic policy. A national bank, as Hamilton conceived it, should be an agency for maintaining public credit and for increasing a nation's supply of "artificial capital." Although these two functions of a "public bank" are closely interrelated, they are partially distinct. Public banks, said Hamilton, are "of the greatest utility in the operations connected with the support of public credit."[107] They expedite the payment of taxes, thus ensuring the servicing of the public securities which are usable as "artificial capital." They facilitate loans to taxpayers, thus assuring punctuality in the payment of taxes. More important, however, is their capacity of increasing the circulating medium and quickening its

105. Ibid., pp. 64–65.
106. Ibid., pp. 65–68.
107. Ibid., p. 53.

velocity.[108] By obviating the shipment of specie, banks decrease "trouble, delay, expense and risk" and increase the speed with which payments can be made. Meantime the uncovered issue constitutes a net addition to a nation's currency supply. This positive increase, when coupled with the swifter velocity, produces "what, in a practical sense . . . may be called greater plenty of money," enabling all people to pay their taxes and thereby help maintain public credit.[109]

A national bank will also strengthen public credit by making it possible for the government to borrow funds for meeting "sudden emergencies." For a central, public bank actually pools "the capitals of a great number of individuals": moreover, "the mass formed by this union" is "magnified" by virtue of the ability of the bank to issue credit in excess of its actual capital.[110] Because a public bank can be so patently serviceable in maintaining public credit, said Hamilton in his "Opinion" on the constitutionality of the Bank, it would be foolish to forbid the government "to make use of that instrument."[111] A public bank, he argued, was designed to serve the general interest;[112] it would enable the government to collect taxes and to borrow when necessary. It would also expedite the payment of the nation's foreign creditors.[113] And since such a public bank, "if rightly constituted," would from time to time have to apply for a recharter, it could be expected to perform these several services for the government faithfully and competently.[114]

It was not on the foregoing ancillary functions, however, that Hamilton built his main justification of public banks. Since the chief utility of any bank stemmed from its power to augment and to animate capital, the greatest service of a national bank would be its capacity to coordinate this beneficent process. To make this argument clear, Hamilton took great pains to show just how this could be achieved. Gold and silver, when used merely "as the instruments of exchange and alienation," he explained, may quite properly be denominated "dead stock."[115] They "acquire life" only when deposited in banks, since here they may "become the basis of a paper circulation" much

108. Ibid., p. 58.
109. Ibid., p. 59.
110. Ibid., p. 57.
111. *Constitutionality of the Bank,* in *Political Papers* (McKee), p. 135.
112. Ibid., p. 131.
113. *Report on a National Bank,* in *Political Papers* (McKee), p. 69.
114. Ibid., p. 84. Unlike Pelatiah Webster, Hamilton did not emphasize the usefulness of a central bank as a depository for public funds. See Webster, *Political Essays,* p. 440n [1786].
115. *Report on a National Bank,* in *Political Papers* (McKee), p. 54.

larger than their "actual quantum."[116] The uncovered issue is tantamount to a net addition to a nation's money supply, permitting a larger volume of business activity and hence a more complete employment of the factors of production. This alchemic power of banks is made possible by inter-customer clearance of debts, since "experience proves" that money "much oftener changes proprietors than place."[117] For many creditors of a bank, a transfer of credit on the bank's books constitutes entirely satisfactory payment, and, as a result, a bank soon discovers the proper safe ratio that must exist between its note-issue liabilities and its specie reserve. As confidence in a bank's ability to meet its liabilities in specie becomes known, this reserve ratio widens, because "a great proportion of the notes . . . pass current as cash" and tend to remain "indefinitely suspended in circulation."[118] Concurrently the reputation of the bank will induce the possessors of gold and silver to deposit their specie for safekeeping, thus augmenting the bank's reserves and permitting further issues of bank notes. This "effective fund" of specie contributed by depositors, coupled with the capital of the stockholders, enables a bank to extend loans to two or three times its capital stock.[119] It is for these reasons, said Hamilton, that "the introduction of banks . . . has a powerful tendency to extend the active capital of a country," and thereby to "add new energies" to all business operations.[120]

There was nothing abstract about Hamilton's reference to "capital." He simply meant funds available for entrepreneurs. Thus he pointed out that if a merchant keeps his idle money in a chest, waiting for a favorable business opportunity, neither he nor society gains. The funds are sterile and unemployed. But if a merchant deposits his idle money in a bank, or if he buys bank stock with it, both he and the business community will benefit. As depositor or stockholder, said Hamilton, the merchant will be assured complete liquidity of his funds.[121] Meantime, however, the merchant's deposits (or share of the bank's capital) "is a fund" against which loans can be made to other deserving, punctual, and competent entrepreneurs. Thus "the money

116. Ibid., p. 55.
117. Ibid., p. 56.
118. Ibid., p. 55.
119. Ibid., p. 56.
120. *Report on Manufactures,* in *Political Papers* (McKee), p. 211.
121. "When any advantageous speculation offers, in order to be able to embrace it, he has only to withdraw his money, if a depositor, or, if a proprietor, to obtain a loan from the bank, or to dispose of his stock—an alternative seldom or never attended with difficulty." *Report on a National Bank,* in *Political Papers* (McKee), p. 55.

of one individual, while he is waiting for an opportunity to employ it . . . is in a condition to administer to the wants of others" even though it is not "put out of his own reach when occasion presents." In this way, Hamilton claimed, banks "increase the active capital of a country," and by enlarging "the mass of industrious and commercial enterprise" they "become nurseries of national wealth."[122]

Public benefit rather than private profit ought to be the object of a national bank. For a new country, harassed by an unfavorable balance of payments, a national bank could exert all its credit-creating power to overcome this "inconvenience." The funding act, Hamilton predicted, would provide the United States with a large amount of "artificial capital." But if a national bank, whose capital was composed of 25 percent specie and 75 percent public debt, was authorized, the expansion of the nation's artificial capital could be much greater; for by virtue of the bank's capacity to circulate an uncovered bank-note issue, the artificial capital created by the funding act could be multiplied two or three fold. Yet this credit expansion, said Hamilton, would involve none of the dangers of paper money. Because bank notes would be redeemable in specie on demand, the monetary standard would not vary, since it would always be a fixed amount of specie. Moreover, the amount of bank notes extant would never be an arbitrary amount. Any overissue, asserted Hamilton, would always lead to a demand for conversion; hence "there is a limitation in the nature of the thing" which would adjust total issues to the total demand created by the volume of business activity.[123]

The bank Hamilton proposed that Congress should establish was therefore intended to maximize the nation's supply of "artificial capital," and yet, at the same time, to provide the right amount of credit accommodation, as indicated by entrepreneurial activity. But this correct amount would itself be a resultant of the stimulus which artificial capital would impart to business enterprise and would be related experiencially to specie reserves. Purchase of public debt, or of bank shares, by foreigners would increase the nation's specie supply; so would a more favorable balance of trade resulting from greater production of exports. Either circumstance would allow the national bank to extend still more bank credit and hence to carry the process of enterprise stimulation forward cumulatively.

Since the chief function of a national bank ought to be to animate the

122. Ibid., p. 57.
123. Here it will be observed that Hamilton's theory is similar to that of the "banking school" which was to figure so prominently in the monetary controversy of the British "Bank Restriction" period.

business enterprise of the whole nation, the government should determine the capital, "fixing bounds which are deemed safe and convenient," leaving "no discretion" in the stockholders to "stop short" of these bounds or "to overpass them."[124] Because Hamilton was convinced that the entire capital should be placed under one responsible management, he vigorously opposed "a plurality of branches."[125] To ensure that the management would be responsible to the public, he advocated a system of rotation for the directing officers, arguing that such rotation would prevent the national bank from becoming "subservient to party views," or to a "particular set of men,"[126] or to foreign stockholders who would not be concerned with advancing national well-being and general prosperity.[127]

But although the government should make certain that a national bank served the entire nation, the direction of the bank ought not be entrusted to government officials. A weak or incompetent government, said Hamilton, would threaten the solvency of the bank, destroy confidence in the institution, and thereby prevent it from performing the socially beneficial functions for which it had been created.[128] The only way to guarantee "a careful and prudent administration," argued Hamilton, would be to place the national bank "under the guidance of individual interest," because "the keen, steady, and, as it were, magnetic sense of their own interest" would lead the proprietors of the bank to administer it with such scrupulous care that public confidence would be maintained.

The public responsibility of a national bank, however, must not be allowed to become secondary.[129] For that reason Hamilton recommended that the government should reserve the right to inspect the affairs of the bank to ascertain that "so delicate a trust" as that of creating bank credit "is executed with fidelity and care."[130] He also proposed that the government ought to be a minor stockholder and

124. Because the constitution of the Bank of North America allowed the stockholders to decide whether the capital should or should not be increased, Hamilton argued that the Bank of North America could not be relied upon to perform central banking functions properly. Stockholders might be deterred from increasing the capital from fear of a diminution of profits even though national well-being might indicate the desirability of an enlarged capital. Ibid., p. 76.

125. On this score he was overruled. See James O. Wettereau, "The Branches of the First Bank of the United States," *The Tasks of Economic History*, supplemental issue of *The Journal of Economic History* (December 1942).

126. *Report on a National Bank*, in *Political Papers* (McKee), p. 78.

127. Ibid., pp. 80, 88.

128. Ibid., p. 83. Similarly Pelatiah Webster had contended that a state-owned bank would lead to tyranny in government. *Political Essays*, p. 440 [1786].

129. *Report on a National Bank*, in *Political Papers* (McKee), p. 76.

130. Ibid., p. 85.

147

hence a sharer in the bank's profits, a provision that was included primarily "to enlarge the specie fund of the bank, and to enable it to give a more early extension to its operations."[131] No formal partnership between the government and the financial interest was contemplated except insofar as the government established "bounds" to private banking activity.[132] Within the bounds stipulated in the charter,[133] the private stockholders would be free to operate. Hamilton's plan for a national bank, like his funding program, therefore placed primary reliance on the wisdom and integrity of the financial interest.

The Social Justification of the Financial Interest

That reliance on the monied group was a preconception of Hamilton's political economy becomes quite clear when the several parts of the "whole fabric" of his economic policy are examined. "Those who are most commonly creditors of a nation" (and by this Hamilton certainly meant the rentier class) he described as "enlightened men."[134] That many of these "enlightened friends of good government"[135] had engaged in extensive speculation in public securities elicited no criticism. They took "the risks of reimbursement," said Hamilton, "a hazard which was far from inconsiderable"; and once the funding act had been passed, each security holder deserved "to reap the benefit of his hazard."[136] In Hamilton's opinion, the bullish activity of the risk takers had benefited all security holders who had been compelled to sell. Moreover, the speculators had shown exemplary confidence in the American government, which contrasted strikingly with the "want of confidence"[137] of many security holders who disposed of their securi-

131. Under Hamilton's plan this addition of specie would not be immediate since the government would actually borrow its contribution from the bank. In repaying this loan, however, it would incrementally increase the specie holdings of the bank. Ibid., p. 94.
132. Pelatiah Webster had argued that a privately owned and operated bank could "be deemed public" if state revenues were paid into it and disbursed from it. *Political Essays,* pp. 438, 440 [1786].
133. For example, fixation of the capital stock, limitations on holding real estate, restriction of debts, maximum interest rate, limitation of loans to the government, rules governing the selection of officers, provisions for the payment of dividends, and a requirement for governmental inspection. See *Report on a National Bank,* in *Political Papers* (McKee), pp. 86–90.
134. *First Report on Public Credit,* in *Political Papers* (McKee), p. 5.
135. Ibid., p. 7.
136. Ibid., p. 11.
137. Ibid., p. 12. For a similar view see Tench Coxe, *View of the United States,* p. 363.

ties because they were fearful that their paper property would depreciate.

The foresight, the willingness to assume risks, and the resources of the financial interest were called for if public credit was to be strengthened. And only if public credit were made unimpeachable could public securities perform money work and thereby serve as "artificial capital." When the domestic risk takers, by their optimistic activity, had raised the value of the public debt "to its true standard," said Hamilton, foreign speculators would begin to purchase securities, and, when that happened, foreign capital would flow into the country to the advantage of American agriculture, commerce, and manufacture.[138] Thus the speculative pursuits of the monied group would indirectly help the nation to overcome an unfavorable balance of payments and compensate for the scarcity of capital. Formation of a national bank would carry this beneficent process still further. The profit-making opportunities of the bank would lead foreign capitalists to become shareholders, and their purchase of shares would lead to a "positive increase of the gold and silver of the country."[139] Since these capital imports, as bank reserves, would permit a two or three fold issue of bank notes, the business activity generated by each dollar of imported capital would be several times the dividend paid to the foreign stockholders.

Cooperation of domestic and foreign capitalists was therefore needed to strengthen public credit, to establish a national bank, and, by these agencies, to increase the nation's supply of specie and of artificial capital. Hamilton insisted that the government should under no circumstances tax government securities, since if it did "solid capitalists" would not be willing "to adventure their money upon so precarious a footing."[140] For the same reason, the government ought to renounce expressly any intention of sequestrating the property of foreign capitalists.[141] Hamilton even went so far as to suggest that foreign capitalists ought not be regarded as the citizens of particular foreign countries, arguing that when a government entered into a contract with a foreign capitalist, it should regard him as "an individual in a state of nature" rather than as a citizen of a particular state.[142] Neither diplomatic tension nor even a state of war should be allowed to alter in any way the relations between the government and foreign capitalists.

The government ought to be equally solicitous of American

138. *First Report on Public Credit,* in *Political Papers* (McKee), p. 48.
139. *Report on a National Bank,* in *Political Papers* (McKee), p. 63.
140. *Second Report on Public Credit,* in *Political Papers* (McKee), p. 165.
141. Ibid., p. 174.
142. Ibid., p. 167.

capitalists. For that reason Hamilton proposed that all security holders share in the benefits of funding without discrimination[143] and urged that the Bank be constituted in such a way as to afford monied men "competent motives" to operate it.[144] Only by allowing the directors of the Bank to follow "their own interest" could the Bank be assured of "a careful and prudent administration," since only then would borrowers be compelled to repay their loans punctually.[145] He warned Congress that monied men could not be expected to share this control with the landed interest. Land is an illiquid asset, and therefore an "unfit fund" for a bank-note issue. If landholders were admitted to partnership in a national bank, they would share in profits which originated in the money funds of the capitalists. To such an arrangement, said Hamilton with complete confidence, monied men would not consent.

In all his far-reaching proposals, Hamilton took great care not to alienate the financial interest. Thus, although he argued in his *First Report on Public Credit* that the trend of interest rates would probably be downward,[146] he nevertheless proposed that security holders should be given the option of funding their securities into 6 percent bonds, and in the *Report on a National Bank* he rather grudgingly approved a 6 percent maximum interest rate because the opinion of "the mass of moneyed man" was a "powerful argument" against an experiment with a 5 percent rate.[147] The financial interest had stubbornly insisted on 6 percent[148] and, in the face of this intransigence, Hamilton had to concede a rate high enough to attract capital. For not only had the members of the financial interest supplied the capital which had raised the market value of public securities; they had also provided the capital for a national bank in whose profits the government was to share.[149] There was admittedly a great deal of truth in James Sullivan's

143. *First Report on Public Credit,* in *Political Papers* (McKee), pp. 10–15.
144. *Report on a National Bank,* in *Political Papers* (McKee), p. 76. Although Hamilton had taken pains to emphasize the benefits which would result from investments by foreign capitalists in public securities and in stock of the National Bank, he looked with disfavor upon any arrangements which would permit foreigners to obtain control of the Bank. Such foreign control, obviously, could frustrate the capacity of the Bank to energize American enterprise. See Ibid., p. 80.
145. Ibid., pp. 83, 60.
146. *Political Papers,* p. 26.
147. Ibid., p. 94.
148. For an indictment of this attitude, see J. T. Callendar, *Sedgwick & Co., or a Key to the Six Percent Cabinet* (Philadelphia, 1798).
149. Thus, said Tench Coxe, the United States will "draw a share of the profits of the bank without furnishing any of the capital." *View of the United States,* p. 363 [1792].

admission that the American public debt had obtained "motion only from the sagacity of a few."[150] Indeed it was on this "sagacity" that Hamilton attempted to construct an economic policy which would ensure permanent national prosperity.

It should now be quite clear that it is highly superficial to allege that Hamilton sought merely to align the rich and wellborn behind the new government; nor is it a fair judgment to assert that he was primarily concerned with advancing the opportunities of capitalists. He recognized that a monied interest existed, and he actively sought the support of its members. He did favor the financial group, but he did so because they held the keys to America's central economic problems: the burden of debt which the Revolutionary War had created, the adverse balance of payments which inescapably confronted any new country, and the unemployed natural resources which could be productively utilized if investment could be stimulated. Thus, in the Hamiltonian political economy, the ultimate social justification of the financial interest was its ability and its readiness to assume entrepreneurial risks which had macro-economic benefits. For performing this most useful function, Hamilton believed a generous reward ought to be provided.

150. *Path to Riches*, p. 44 [1794].

VI

Attitudes toward Commercial, Occupational, and Entrepreneurial Freedom

All men are not philosophers, but they
are generally good judges of their own
profit.

John Witherspoon

For a government to interfere in the
occupations or in the private actions of
citizens is not only injust and impolitic
but is highly dangerous to the liberties of
the People.

George Logan

Four Meanings of Economic Freedom

THE concept of *laissez-faire* as a hypothesis of the proper relation between government and enterprise is a misunderstood chapter in the history of American culture. In both Britain and France, formal theories of economic liberty were propounded in the eighteenth century, with Adam Smith and the physiocrats serving respectively as exponent and advocates. In the United States, even though the reality of economic freedom became in many ways more ubiquitous and more complete than in either Britain or France, it is difficult to find any thoroughgoing, eighteenth-century proponents of *laissez-faire*,[1] and even harder to find much explicit evidence of legislative acceptance of a theory of economic freedom.

Nevertheless a body of *laissez-faire* doctrine emerged, and in a variety of ways this politico-economic concept did have a subtle effect on legislation. But the American free-trade theorists formed neither a school of thought nor a political party. Moreover, the American current of *laissez-faire* thought seems to have originated in specific domestic difficulties and was only to a very limited extent inspired by European libertarian philosophy; indeed, only a few of the pamphleteers in the 1790s drew on British or French *laissez-faire* theory, and some of those who did sharply criticized their European teachers. For example, John Taylor of Caroline, although he persistently upheld freedom of enterprise, asserted that Adam Smith had been "corrupted" by a "wealthy and powerful aristocracy."[2] Nor was the meaning of economic freedom rigorously defined; in some contexts "free

1. Although Thomas Jefferson and John Taylor are generally regarded as advocates of *laissez-faire*, it should be pointed out that Jefferson's views were altered after 1807 and that Taylor frankly espoused governmental intervention on behalf of the agricultural interest.
2. *Principles and Policy*, p. 547 [1814].

FOUNDATIONS OF AMERICAN ECONOMIC FREEDOM

trade" refers to international policy, in others to domestic. Moreover, the severest critics of certain types of governmental intervention were sometimes the most ardent defenders of various kinds of state interference with business freedom.

Some of the reasons for the anomalous nature of American *laissez-faire* thought originated no doubt in the linkage between the idea of economic freedom and the theory of interests. The defenders of the agricultural interest, for instance, sang the praises of a free-trade commercial policy, arguing that only by such an arrangement could farmers and planters be assured of adequate markets.[3] But the commercial policy supported by the agricultural interest cannot be interpreted as something revolutionary or novel; actually it called for a virtual return to the scheme of things which had existed before the Revolution. It reflected a belief that the United States should continue to be a producer of foodstuffs and raw materials and that the essentially colonial nature of the American economy ought not be altered even though political independence had been won. This strand of *laissez-faire* thought may therefore be designated as essentially conservative if not actually reactionary.

Representatives of the mercantile interest, in contrast, had little to say about international free trade, although they had a great deal of criticism to levy against all the price-fixing laws which had restricted mercantile operations during and after the Revolution. Hence Pelatiah Webster became the most vigorous and persuasive advocate of a mercantile brand of "freedom of trade" and a spirited defender of "a free, open market" as the most efficient way of providing a nation with the largest possible supply of high quality goods. This mercantile concept of economic freedom represents a protest against governmental intervention with the price system; it is the American counterpart of the traditional "*laissez-nous faire*" which has been ascribed, rightly or wrongly, to a seventeenth-century French merchant.[4]

Because manufacturers and mechanics were far less articulate than gentlemen farmers, merchants, and economists, we do not know

3. See, for example, John Taylor, *Tyranny Unmasked* (Washington City, 1822), p. 35; *Annals of Congress*, XLI (May 4, 1824), 678–680; Thomas Jefferson, *Works* (Washington), V, 440; VIII, 405; VII, 646; Logan, *Five Letters to the Yeomanry*, p. 25.

4. See August Oncken, *Die Maxime laissez faire et laissez passer, ihr Uhrsprung, ihr Werden. Ein Beitrag zur Geschichte der Freihandelslehre* (Bern, 1886). For a criticism of this ascription of "*laissez-faire*" to a merchant named Legendre, see Hazel Van Dyke Roberts, *Boisguilbert, Economist of the Reign of Louis XIV* (New York, 1936), pp. 339–360.

whether the manufacturing interest played an important role in formulating the American doctrine of *laissez-faire*. But those few writers who reflected a solicitude for the mechanics and small-scale manufacturers most certainly did insist that freedom to choose an occupation ought not be prejudiced by governmental favors to an industrial or "capitalist interest."[5] Legislative interference with the free choice of occupations, it was asserted, brings only mischief and oppression;[6] hence the only justifiable policy is to allow each individual to decide for himself,[7] since only then can the best distribution of workers among the various occupations be achieved.[8] The sanction for an individual's right to choose his calling was found in the doctrine of natural rights, and with the passage of time the mechanics found justification in natural rights for the demands they were to make collectively upon both employers and state legislatures. The court of Nature did not merely confirm the sacred right of choosing one's occupation;[9] it presumably compelled adherence to an immutable "natural order," thus frustrating all the foolish efforts of legislators who attempted to "warp employment against its natural bent."[10] But notwithstanding the assurance that "the laws of nature will continue to operate, in spite of the feeble opposition of human powers,"[11] the history of the nineteenth-century American labor movement shows quite clearly that the artisans were not content to await the natural justice vouchsafed for them by social theorists.

The financial interest, no less than the agricultural, commercial, or manufacturing interests, also championed economic freedom. Private ownership and direction of banks or other corporations were con-

5. See above, chap. IV. In 1793, the Virginia legislature resolved "that the senators of this state, in the Congress of the United States, be instructed to use their utmost exertions, to have a clause inserted into the Constitution of the United States, tending to prohibit any director of the bank of the United States from being a member of either house of Congress." *Session Laws* (Shepherd), 284 [December 11, 1793].

6. See, for example, Logan, *Five Letters to the Yeomanry*, pp. 13, 17, 19 [1792].

7. See Taylor, *Arator; Being a Series of Agricultural Essays, Practical and Political* (Georgetown, 1813), p. 34; also his *Tyranny Unmasked*, p. 106 [1822]; also his remarks, *Annals of Congress*, XL (April 22, 1824), 565.

8. Madison, *Works*, VI, 96; V, 342 [1789]; see also Jefferson, *Works* (Washington), VIII, 13 [1801]; and Bordley, *Essays on Husbandry*. Tench Coxe must also be included as a staunch defender of the mechanic's right to choose his occupation. See his *View of the United States*, pp. 66–67 [1790].

9. See for example an oration by Dr. S. L. Mitchell before the Agricultural Society of New York (January 10, 1792) in the *Transactions of the New York Society for the Promotion of Agriculture, Arts, and Manufactures*, I, 4 [1792].

10. Bordley, *Essays on Husbandry*, p. 378 [1794].

11. Noah Webster, *Collection of Essays*, p. 310 [1789].

sidered to be consistently more sagacious, and hence more beneficial to the community at large, than governmentally controlled ventures. Unregulated speculation in both private securities and government debt found a host of defenders, particularly when the ranks of speculators increased on the eve of the Hamiltonian funding operations.[12] Freedom to invest, and freedom to assume risks, came to have not merely a Lockean sanction but presumed utilitarian justification. Provided monied men were given ample opportunity to organize banks, establish corporations, or purchase securities, said Hamilton, and provided the government established a proper legislative framework within which financial activities could be conducted, the entire nation would benefit,[13] not only from the increased volume of domestic business activity which would result, but from the economic autonomy which would offer a means of escape from the colonial status that an unfavorable balance of payments and a want of manufacturing establishments had hitherto imposed upon the American nation.

The disagreement between the natural interests and the financial interests must not be construed, therefore, as a bona fide struggle between advocates of *laissez-faire* on the one hand and upholders of intervention on the other. The controversy really centered on the question of which interest ought to have the larger measure of freedom, as well as on the social consequences that might result from the exercise of a larger measure of freedom by one interest rather than another. Each major interest defended that type of economic liberty which promised to advance the well-being of its constituents. The agricultural interest placed chief emphasis upon international free trade, upon that part of *laissez-faire* theory more properly designated as *laissez-passer*.[14] The commercial interest upheld freedom from interference with the price mechanism, with the organization of production, and with the distributive machinery of the marketplace; hence, the merchants came to be the defenders of a *laissez-faire*[15] policy in the more literal sense. The manufacturers and mechanics, although they were by no means the only advocates of occupational freedom, had an especial interest in seeing to it that they might engage in whatever employment seemed most profitable; they sought a policy which could well be called *laissez-travailler*.[16] And finally the financial interest championed

12. See Davis, *American Corporations,* II, passim.
13. See above, chap. V.
14. Let goods move without the restraint of tariffs or prohibitions.
15. More precisely, *laissez-nous faire*: let us alone.
16. New terminology is always unwelcome but the entire content of *laissez-faire* thought calls for at least four, not one or two, terms.

the freedom to buy and sell not physical goods but the legal representation of wealth—a type of freedom that might be called *laissez-placer*.[17]

These four freedoms, however, did not form the entire content of the American concept of *laissez-faire*. Like one of the early currents of British economic liberalism which assailed the business monopolies granted by the Stuarts,[18] American agrarian *laissez-faire* thought waged bitter and relentless war on Federalist financial policies, charging that these policies represented an attempt by an aristocratic faction to monopolize the nation's money system. All monopolies are "odious," the framers of the Maryland Constitution had declared in 1776; they are "contrary to the spirit of a free government" and to "the principles of commerce," and "ought not to be suffered." The framers of the New Hampshire Constitution were of the same mind: "free and fair competition" in all trades and industries, they said in 1784, "is an inherent and essential right of the people," one that "should be protected against all monopolies and conspiracies which tend to hinder or destroy it."[19]

It is largely because the Republicans stigmatized their opponents as monopolists that *laissez-faire* thought has come to be associated with the followers of Jefferson. But it is superficial if not actually erroneous to conclude that the Republicans were the sole standard-bearers of American economic liberalism. In reality, none of the eighteenth-century politicians or pamphleteers can be called simon-pure non-interventionists, although, as the tariff issue became more controversial, the southern agrarians gradually became the defenders of a broader program of *laissez-faire* than their fellow citizens in the Middle States and in New England. But the entire fabric of American economic liberalism was destined to go far beyond the free-trade and anti-monopoly sentiment of the southern agrarians; indeed the main elements of American *laissez-faire* thought came to be the freedom to choose an occupation, to establish a business, to participate in speculative ventures, and to compete within a domestic market protected by a formidable tariff. It is this composite *laissez-faire* movement which is of basic importance, rather than the differences between agrarian and capitalist interpretations of economic liberty. For it was economic freedom in this broader, institutional sense that imparted vigor to American economic life.

17. Freedom to invest.
18. See Hecksher, *Mercantilism*, I, 269–294.
19. On the opposition to monopolies, see below pp. 187–189. See also Shaw Livermore, *Early American Land Companies* (New York, 1939), pp. 67–69.

The Psychological and Philosophical Justification
of Economic Freedom

The driving force that animates an economy, said the contemporaries of Washington, is self-interest. The explanation for this, according to John Witherspoon, was very simple: ordinary people are generally good judges of their interests.[20] Every economic activity is induced and directed by an instinctive self-love, and this "spring of all action" must be regarded as "the most necessary principle in creation."[21] No governmental coercive power can take the place of this "immediate, apparent, and sensible personal interest,"[22] nor will any altruistic solicitude for the public good supplant it; "if a man's regard to his own character, fortune and family is not a sufficient inducement to make him careful, industrious, and thrifty," said Pelatiah Webster, "it is not to be presumed, that any regard he may have to the public can make him so."[23] In the same way that Adam Smith based his concept of enterprise on egoism, the American social theorists rested theirs on self-love, "the strongest of all passions and motives."[24]

Certain ethical qualifications, however, pervade the American discussion of self-interest. The acquisition of property, it was said, must ever be "guided by good moral principles";[25] it must represent the "earnings of labour, the reward of merit"; and only if it does, can it become "the almoner of age, and the soul of civilization."[26] Vigor of enterprise may indeed seem to require that self-seeking should be "both uncontrouled and encouraged,"[27] but public welfare, on the other hand, cannot be ensured by giving selfishness free rein or by tempting man's immorality "by hopes of boundless acquisition."[28] The object of public policy should be to restrain the deleterious consequences of unbridled cupidity, while retaining the force and vitality that originates

20. *Essay on Money as a Medium of Commerce* (Philadelphia, 1786), p. 56.
21. Noah Webster, *Collection of Essays*, p. 382 [1787]. See also his *Sketches of American Policy*, p. 24n [1785], and Logan, *Letter to Citizens*, p. 5 [1800].
22. Witherspoon, *Essay on Money*, p. 56 [1786].
23. *Political Essays*, p. 69 [1780].
24. Ibid. See also Noah Webster, *Sketches of American Policy*, p. 3 [1785]. A likely linkage between the Scottish and the American emphasis on self-interest would be through John Witherspoon who came to New Jersey in 1768. In Scotland, an individualistic theory of enterprise was well entrenched long before Adam Smith formulated his systematic theory. See, for example, Sir James Steuart's views, in my *Predecessors of Adam Smith*, pp. 214–216.
25. Taylor, *Principles and Policy*, p. 561 [1814].
26. Ibid., p. 279.
27. Taylor, *Definition of Parties*, p. 9 [1794].
28. Taylor, *Enquiry into Certain Public Measures*, p. 61 [1794].

in a reasonable self-interest.[29] Norms of legitimate or permissible self-interest must therefore be established by law,[30] or by a self-imposed morality,[31] if the well-being of the entire community is to be safeguarded.[32] For self-interest is both personally and socially beneficial only when it enables people to improve their status without trespassing on the rights, privileges, and opportunities of other individuals.[33]

Aside from establishing suitable boundaries within which self-interest should operate, statute law should do nothing to hinder the exercise of individual initiative. For the right to seek one's own well-being was declared to be one of the most hallowed natural rights, one which individuals do not relinquish on becoming members of civil society.[34] Within civil society all persons, to be sure, are expected to promote the welfare of the entire society; but they "are not bound," said a New Hampshire preacher, "to sacrifice all private views, and to act wholly from public motives." Indeed inasmuch as self-preservation "is the first law of nature," a concern with individual happiness is entirely legitimate. Every member of civil society should therefore be free to promote his own well-being "when it is not attended with injury to the community."[35]

The appeal to natural rights and to natural law was designed to show that the exercise of self-interest is an inalienable right, that natural law brooks no interference, that the natural order is essentially self-regulating and thus does not need the intrusion of statute law, and that adoption of an enterprise system consistent with natural law will provide society with a more efficient and a more just scheme of things than any invention of the mind of man. All governmental policy must recognize the force of natural law; moreover "whether society be tacit or conventional" its object should be to protect the individual in the "exercise of his primitive and natural faculties of labour and free will."[36] Only those human propensities which jeopardize the natu-

29. Taylor, *Principles and Policy*, p. 167 [1814]; *Definition of Parties*, p. 515 [1794].
30. Noah Webster, *Sketches of American Policy*, p. 6 [1785].
31. Adams, *Defense of the Constitutions*, pp. 111–112 [1787].
32. Noah Webster, *Sketches of American Policy*, p. 48 [1785]; *Collection of Essays*, pp. 83, 84, 382 [1787]; Sullivan, *Path to Riches*, p. 18 [1792]; Pelatiah Webster, *Political Essays*, p. 290 [1785]; Taylor, *Enquiry into Certain Public Measures*, p. 5 [1794].
33. See Eugene Tenbroeck Mudge, *The Social Philosophy of John Taylor of Caroline* (New York, 1939), p. 15.
34. Logan, *Letters to the Yeomanry on Funding and Bank Systems*, p. 5 [1793].
35. Robert Gray, *A Sermon*, pp. 13–14 [1798].
36. Taylor, *Construction Construed, and Constitutions Vindicated*, p. 206.

ral rights of other persons should be curbed, and on these grounds Taylor demanded the imposition of restraints on the "paper aristocracy" that had, in his opinion, so egregiously violated the natural rights of the American farmers and mechanics.[37]

The argument of the Republicans, for whom John Taylor and George Logan served as self-appointed spokesmen, was that Hamilton's policies had perverted government from its true function. Whatever prevents people "from making all that they can" or from "employing their stock and industry in the way that they judge advantageous to themselves," said Logan, citing Adam Smith as his authority, "is a manifest violation of the most sacred rights of mankind."[38] Since all natural rights are individual rights, it becomes the duty of government to safeguard the freedom of individuals to provide for their own wants "in their own way"; indeed, only by guaranteeing this measure of individual liberty does any government prove that it is "founded in reason and justice, and not in error and fraud."[39] The range of the presumed individual natural rights was indicated by more precise suggestions: thus Jefferson said that Europeans had a natural right to emigrate to America in order to better their status;[40] Dr. S. L. Mitchell declared that the abrogation of laws of entail and primogeniture would restore "the natural right of every man to a certain part of the earth's surface";[41] and George Logan asserted that one generation has no natural right to impose a burden of national debt on a future generation.[42]

The argument based on natural law, emphasized particularly by the Republicans, maintained that an economic system arranged in conformity with "the wonderful regularity of all Nature" could alone

37. This demand is reiterated in Taylor's writings. See, for example, *Tyranny Unmasked*, p. 130 [1822]; *Principles and Policy*, pp. 414–415 [1814]; *American Farmer*, III (July 20, 1821), 131; *Enquiry into Certain Public Measures*, p. 61 [1794].

38. *Five Letters to the Yeomanry*, p. 10 [1792].

39. John Taylor, *Annals of Congress*, XL (April 22, 1824), 565; *Tyranny Unmasked*, p. 106 [1822].

40. *Works* (Ford), VIII, 458. Madison implied the same thing. *Works*, VI, 65–66.

41. *Transactions of New York Agricultural Society*, I, 4 [1792].

42. *Letters to the Yeomanry on Funding and Bank Systems*, pp. 9–10 [1793]. If all the members of one generation were born on the same day, if all lived for sixty-five years, and if they all died the same day, then, by natural rights, they should receive the earth debt free when they came of age and they would hold it for thirty-four years, having meantime a right to contract only such debts as could be repaid during their lifetime. Basing his analysis of an atomistic renewal of population structure on the actuarial studies of Comte de Buffon, Logan concluded that a government has no "natural right" to contract debts which cannot be repaid within nineteen years.

ensure "order, proportion, fitness and congruity."[43] Nor could the dictates of Nature long be ignored: "great natural principles" will establish themselves despite man's stupidity, because "any departure from them will be checked and reformed by dear experience."[44] Proper employment of a nation's labor and capital must be determined not by arbitrary governmental decisions but by patient observation of the natural capacity of a nation to engage in particular types of production. Wise legislators, said John Beale Bordley, will not attempt to change the pattern of occupations which natural factors have fostered;[45] at best they can but "gently incline" or modify a nation's economic development. Monopolies, or the granting of undue preferences, said the enemies of Hamilton, not only infringe the natural rights of persons but violate the law of nature which is "ordained to regulate men in society,"[46] and which "has an equal authority with municipal law" and hence must be equally respected.[47]

The natural order was said to be self-regulating.[48] It punishes the slothful by poverty[49] and provides a nation with the right employments and with a proper supply of money.[50] It is as hostile to monopolies designed to promote the advantage of the few[51] as it is to schemes to equalize property by law.[52] Moreover, the benefits of economic policies sanctioned by natural law, said John Taylor, had already been abundantly demonstrated in the colonial period;[53] this experience with a naturalistic development, rather than an uncharted program of industrial subvention, ought to be the guide to America's future policy. The true function of government is to secure to each individual the fruits of his own industry;[54] any attempt to use governmental power to distribute property for the benefit of a minority is not only immoral,[55] but the harbinger of "confusion and distress"[56] for the great majority

43. Logan, *Address before the Tammany Society,* pp. 1–7 [1798].

44. Pelatiah Webster, *Political Essays,* p. 96 [1780].

45. *Essays on Husbandry,* p. 378 [1794].

46. Logan, *Letters to the Yeomanry on Funding and Bank Systems,* pp. 22–23 [1793].

47. Ibid., p. 5. See also his *Address before the Tammany Society,* pp. 7–11 [1798]; and Noah Webster, *Collection of Essays,* p. 310 [1789].

48. Taylor, *Principles and Policy,* p. 356 [1814].

49. Noah Webster, *Collection of Essays,* p. 313 [1789]; Sullivan, *Path to Riches,* p. 43 [1792].

50. Taylor, *Principles and Policy,* p. 356 [1814].

51. Bordley, *Essays on Husbandry,* p. 378 [1794].

52. See Mudge, *Social Philosophy of John Taylor,* p. 163.

53. Ibid., p. 44.

54. Taylor, *Arator,* p. 193 [1813].

55. Taylor, *Construction Construed,* p. 15 [1820].

56. Logan, *Address before the Tammany Society,* p. 11 [1798].

of people whose natural rights have been violated. No European state has ever adequately safeguarded its subjects' natural rights,[57] and largely for that reason emigrants have come to America[58] where a larger measure of economic freedom exists. The amplitude of opportunity which the United States has afforded, said the natural law theorists, is convincing proof of the superiority of economic policy formulated in obedience to the laws of the natural order.

The Jeffersonian agrarians found in natural law convenient and useful weapons for their attack on the economic policies of Hamilton. The funding act, the bank charter, and the attempt to foster manufactures by bounties or protective duties were described either as violations of natural rights or as senseless efforts to fly in the face of immutable natural law. Meantime, even though merchants and financiers did not seek sanctions for their *laissez-faire* theory in natural law, they tried to ground their policy proposals on the innermost nature of man. Merchants described price-fixing laws as "abridgements of natural liberty,"[59] and even Alexander Hamilton, although he carefully avoided such terms as natural law or natural rights, nevertheless based his argument for private ownership of the Bank of the United States upon a theory of individualism that was definitely tinctured with a Lockean concept of natural rights.[60]

The Persistence of Demands for Intervention

The multitude of state laws prescribing specific varieties of governmental intervention with business activity, together with the much smaller body of federal legislation restricting entrepreneurial freedom, indicate clearly that the American enterprise system in the Age of Washington did not operate under a system of *laissez-faire.* Commerce was restricted by state tariff laws before the adoption of the Constitution and by a federal tariff system after the new government came into operation. Moreover, certain branches of commerce, both before and after the Constitution, were regulated by state inspection laws. Nor was domestic industry exempt from regulation: some branches of manufacture were subject to governmental surveillance designed to maintain the quality of the goods offered for sale, while other types of industry were circumscribed by price restrictions. Except for chattel slaves, choice of an occupation, however, was essen-

57. Taylor, *Tyranny Unmasked,* p. 307 [1822].
58. Logan, *Address before the Tammany Society,* p. 7 [1798].
59. Pelatiah Webster, *Political Essays,* p. 24 [1789].
60. See Paschal Larkin, *Property in the Eighteenth Century, with Special Reference to England and Locke* (Cork, 1930), chap. V.

tially free, although a number of unpleasant limitations upon servants and freed slaves persisted.[61]

Neither in state legislatures nor in Congress did there appear to be any disposition on the part of lawmakers to entrust the entire regulation of enterprise to the invisible hand of self-interest. The annual crop of state laws regulating enterprise showed no sign of decreasing; if anything the number of business restrictions tended to increase after the Revolution, while after 1787 the federal government, within its delegated areas of jurisdiction, embarked upon quite a comprehensive program of legislative interference. Moreover, the appropriateness of governmental assistance to the major segments of the American economy seems to have been willingly endorsed by the Founding Fathers. That there was no disposition on the part of George Washington to follow a noninterventionist program is attested by his first annual message.[62] "The advancement of agriculture, commerce, and manufactures by all proper means will not, I trust," said the president, "need recommendation"; to this part of the message the Senate politely replied that since agriculture, commerce, and manufactures formed "the basis of the wealth and strength" of the republic, they "must be the frequent subject of our deliberation" and would "be advanced by all proper means in our power."[63] The reply of the House was equally cordial to the president's suggestion: "We concur with you in the sentiment that agriculture, commerce, and manufactures are entitled to legislative protection."[64]

Yet, despite the proliferation of regulatory legislation by the states and the federal government, and despite the apparent congressional agreement that the government should assist the development of "commerce, agriculture, fisheries, arts, and manufactures,"[65] a sizable amount of argument favoring a *laissez-faire* program is nevertheless discernible in the contemporaneous literature. The discussion centers on the four aspects of economic liberty already mentioned: freedom to import and export, freedom to organize production and to compete in an open market, freedom to choose an occupation, and freedom to invest. Synthetically viewed, this fragmentary discussion constitutes a crude doctrine of the presumed societal benefits that would result

61. See Richard B. Morris, *Labor and Government in Early America*, pp. 390–512.
62. January 8, 1791. For the text see James D. Richardson, *A Compilation of the Messages and Papers of the Presidents* (New York, 1897), I, 57–59.
63. January 11, 1791. Ibid., I, 60.
64. January 12, 1791. Ibid., I, 61.
65. See President John Adams's first annual message, ibid., I, 241 (November 22, 1797).

from a system of commercial, occupational, and entrepreneurial freedom.

The Case for Freedom to Export and Import

Except for a few words of approval by Benjamin Franklin, John Witherspoon, and John Adams, the policy of free trade was advocated primarily by Thomas Jefferson, George Logan, and John Taylor. Jefferson found corroboration for his free-trade views in Adam Smith,[66] whereas Taylor seems to have been more influenced by Malthus.[67] In his earlier writings Jefferson agreed with Taylor who recommended a return to the type of commercial arrangements that had preceded the Revolutionary War, arguing that the United States ought to remain what it had been and still was: an essentially agricultural nation. Since America had a surplus of agricultural commodities and Britain a surplus of manufactured goods, an international exchange on a free-trade basis, said Taylor, must of necessity be to the advantage of both nations. The United States was particularly well fitted by nature to be an agricultural nation, and for that reason ought not attempt to develop manufactures by the aid of tariffs or bounties.[68] In his *Notes on Virginia* Jefferson agreed, even though later his views changed. Since he thought it "impossible that manufactures should succeed in America" because of the high wages "occasioned by the great demand for labor in agriculture,"[69] Jefferson, in 1788, advised his countrymen to "let our workshops remain in Europe."[70] In much the same way, George Logan in his earlier tracts had also advocated com-

66. "In political economy," said Jefferson, "I think Smith's Wealth of Nations the best book extant." *Works* (Washington), III, 145 [1790]. An American edition of Smith's work was published in 1789. Jefferson owned two English editions, one published in 1784. See Joseph J. Spengler, "The Political Economy of Jefferson, Madison, and Adams," reprinted from *American Studies in Honor of W. K. Boyd* (Durham, 1940), p. 5. Jefferson also referred to the "excellent books of theory written by Turgot and the economists of France."

67. "Malthus is the only authority cited by Taylor in support of his agrarian economy and free-trade program. Adam Smith is dismissed because Taylor believed he had been misled by the banking aristocracy which ruled in England." Mudge, *Social Philosophy of John Taylor,* p. 28. "There is no specific mention of any of the French Physiocratic doctrines, with the general assumptions of which Taylor is in agreement." Ibid., p. 153.

68. See Mudge, *Social Philosophy of John Taylor,* pp. 186–187.

69. *Works* (Washington), II, 412 [1788].

70. Ibid., VIII, 405 [1782]. This argument was partly economic, partly sociological. He feared the contagion which industrialization and urbanization might bring. "It is better to carry provisions and materials to workmen there [Europe], than bring them to the provisions and materials, and with them their manners and principles. The loss by the transportation of commodities across the Atlantic will be made up in the happiness and permanence of government." Ibid.

pletely unrestricted international trade, pointing out the benefits that free trade had conferred upon Holland[71] and arguing that experience had abundantly proven that a "perfectly free commerce" would facilitate the marketing of America's agricultural surpluses and thereby "ensure the prosperity of our country."[72]

The proposals of the Jeffersonian Republicans had the blessing of Benjamin Franklin (who had advocated free trade a decade before the Revolution)[73] and the cautious endorsement of John Adams, who in 1780 expressed an opinion that America would for a very long time continue to be a producer of raw materials and food, drawing most of its manufactured goods from Europe.[74] John Witherspoon dealt only tangentially with commercial policy, but in his condemnation of paper money he showed how domestic inflation would alter the terms of trade to America's disadvantage and thereby decrease the European market for American exports.[75] Although Boston or Philadelphia produced no enthusiastic supporters of international free trade, in Virginia, by contrast, the whole climate of opinion was more favorable, inasmuch as southern staples, for a century and a half, had found their best markets in Europe. The southern sentiment, so vividly expressed by John Taylor, to a very considerable extent represented an acquiescence in an economic arrangement which was to remain essentially colonial long after the signing of the Declaration of Independence.

Jefferson's fears about the feasibility of a republican form of government in an industrialized nation had much to do with his advocacy of free trade; moreover, in 1785 he could be counted among those disillusioned Americans who had earlier envisaged an independent America able to carry on trade with all parts of the world under advantageous commercial treaties. Instead of this, American ships were excluded from the West Indian trade and were subject to onerous restrictions in the ports of France and Spain.[76] Hence when Jefferson, in 1785, said that America should "throw open the doors of commerce" and allow foreigners to bring whatever products they chose to American ports,[77] he carefully stipulated that such concessions should be

71. *Five Letters to the Yeomanry,* p. 14 [1792].
72. Ibid., p. 25.
73. "I find myself inclined to adopt that modern view," wrote Franklin in 1767, "which supposes it best for every country to leave its trade entirely free from all incumbrances." The more free commerce is, he added, "the more it flourishes, and the happier are all the nations concerned in it." See M. R. Eiselen, *The Rise of Pennsylvania Protection* (New York, 1932, rev. ed., 1969), p. 10.
74. *Works,* VII, 255 [1780].
75. *Essay on Money,* pp. 43–44n [1786].
76. Channing, *History of the United States,* III, 408–409.
77. *Notes on Virginia,* p. 318 [1785].

made on the condition that other nations would grant reciprocal freedom to American ships. For the effect of free trade, Jefferson argued, would always be to satisfy "mutual wants" by means of "mutual surpluses" and to ensure that "the greatest mass possible would then be produced," thereby permitting not only an increase in population but a betterment of "human life and human happiness."[78] Even after he had been compelled by circumstances to abandon his attempt to institute a regime of free trade, he still insisted that maximum world production and optimum happiness could be achieved only by allowing each nation to employ its resources in producing those commodities for which it was especially fitted.[79]

Up until the rupture of diplomatic relations that persuaded him to recommend the Embargo Act, Jefferson adhered to his theory of free trade and his justification of a passive foreign trade. But that policy, as Spengler has shown,[80] was premised on the maintenance of international peace, a condition which no longer obtained when Britain and France began to jeopardize neutral commerce by far-flung and systematic policies that we now call "economic warfare." And although Jefferson, "always a practical man, adjusted his views on trade and manufactures to meet the new conditions," his advocacy of domestic manufacturing did not really constitute a recantation of his earlier opinions. He merely admitted that "an equilibrium of agriculture, manufactures, and commerce" had become "essential to our independence" and that a degree of circumstantial autarky was now called for. He therefore recommended that America should strive to provide itself with "manufactures, sufficient for our own consumption, of what we raise the raw material (and no more)" and "commerce sufficient to carry the surplus produce of agriculture, beyond our consumption to a market for exchanging it for articles we cannot raise (and no more)."[81]

Because Jefferson and Taylor favored free trade, it should not be assumed that they necessarily eschewed each and every form of governmental intervention. In his second annual message, Jefferson proposed that the American fisheries ought to be developed "as nurseries of navigation" and that all manufactures "adapted to our circumstances" should be protected;[82] in his sixth annual message, he recommended the continuation of certain import duties lest an advantage be

78. *Works* (Washington), VII, 646 [1793].
79. Ibid., V, 315 [1808].
80. *Political Economy of Jefferson, Madison, and Adams,* p. 14.
81. *Works* (Washington), V, 440 [1809].
82. December 15, 1802. See Richardson, *Messages and Papers of the Presidents,* I, 334.

given "to foreign over domestic manufacturers."[83] Likewise Taylor, although more consistently libertarian than his fellow Virginian, departed occasionally from a strict noninterventionist program. Complete freedom to produce exportable staples, he said, had led to serious soil exhaustion which could only be rectified by some governmental interference with the complete freedom of enterprise.[84] Yet despite the exceptions they found it necessary to admit, both Jefferson and Taylor were as strongly prejudiced in favor of uncontrolled domestic enterprise as they were convinced of the beneficence of unrestricted foreign trade. Even so they contributed very little to the doctrine of *laissez-faire* as a regulator of production. The best analysis of the free market came instead from the pen of Pelatiah Webster, that very able preacher, merchant, and publicist.

The Theory of the Automatic Market

Webster's methodical defense of a free market was a protest against the complicated price-fixing schemes employed during and after the Revolutionary War. Because his theory was developed with great nicety, Webster became the darling of the nineteenth-century exponents of *laissez-faire*. But modern experience with rationing and price-ceilings has done much to dissipate the unwarranted Victorian criticism of the eighteenth-century legislators who faced a problem of war economics realistically and who recognized that free markets may be quite unsatisfactory regulators of production and arbiters of distribution in periods of wartime dislocation.[85]

To Webster, however, the whole price-fixing apparatus represented a foolish and futile attempt to defy the laws of nature. In his opinion, "the price that any article of trade will bring in a free, open market, is the only measure of the value of that article." If this competitively determined price "is warped from the truth, by any artifices of the merchant, or force of power, it cannot hold." "The error," he said, "will soon discover itself, and the correction of it will be compelled by the irresistible force of natural principles." Because of this self-correcting mechanism, "it is not possible for merchants to raise goods too high, or the force of power to keep them too low."[86] Hence neither artificially high prices nor artificially low prices "can last long."

83. December 2, 1806. Ibid., I, 397.
84. *Arator*, VI [1813].
85. See J. M. Clark, "Profits and the Entrepreneur, Relations of History and Theory," *The Tasks of Economic History*, supplemental issue of *The Journal of Economic History* (December 1942), pp. 141–142.
86. *Political Essays*, p. 15 [1779].

Attempts to control prices are, therefore, as unwise as they are futile, simply because "trade if let alone, will ever make its own way best." Business, Webster claimed, is "like an irresistible river"; it "will ever run safest, do least mischief and most good, when suffered to run without obstruction in its own natural channel."[87] An uncontrolled price mechanism will maximize production,[88] improve the quality of the goods brought to market,[89] and tend constantly to supply markets with the scarcest kind of goods.[90] Moreover, since all buyers and sellers have equal opportunity to buy or sell at the prevailing market price, a free market is not only more efficient but more just than any scheme of regulation.[91] Such a market will adjust supply to demand, automatically increasing supply when necessity demands a larger quantity of commodities;[92] in addition, freely determined prices will provide a barometer of the relative scarcity of particular goods, thereby compelling all buyers to economize on high priced goods. As a consequence, a free market provides society with rationing machinery which prevents the improper use of scarce commodities in times of national emergency.[93] Furthermore, inasmuch as high market prices act as magnets attracting the largest possible supply of goods to markets,[94] they give every producer an incentive to maximize production. Yet

87. Ibid., p. 66 [1780].
88. "Every industrious man will procure all the goods he can for sale; this is the way to get most money; and gain is the soul of industry." Ibid., p. 9 [1779].
89. "Every man will make his goods for market of the best quality he can, because they will bring more money and quicker sale than goods of mean quality." Ibid.
90. "Every man will endeavor to carry to market the most scarce goods because there is the greatest demand and the best price for them." Ibid.
91. "Every man will go to market and return in good humor and full satisfaction, even though he may be disappointed of [his failure to obtain] the high price he expected, because he has the full chance of the market and can blame nobody." Ibid., p. 10.
92. "In times of danger distress and difficulty, every man will use strong endeavor to get his goods to market, in proportion to the necessity and great demand for them; because they will bring the best price." Ibid.
93. "When things grow scarce and dear, every man will use them with the best economy and make the stock in hand go as far and last as long as possible; or if he is destitute, will buy as little as will ever serve his necessity. This naturally preserves the stock on hand from needless profusion and waste, and converts it to the best and most prudent use for the benefit of the community, and naturally tends to ward off high distress or total want till the high price and great demand, by their natural operation, will bring further supplies to market." Ibid.
94. "In times of scarcity, every man will have strong inducements to bring all he can spare to market, because it will then bring the highest price he can ever expect, and consequently the community will have the benefit of all that exists among them, in a much surer manner than any degree of force can extort it." Ibid.

they accomplish this desirable end without any coercion whatever, relying instead solely upon individual self-interest.[95] Finally, a free market is the only agency that can reveal whether or not there is an actual scarcity of particular commodities. Fear of scarcity will raise prices; higher prices, however, will increase the market supply. If no actual scarcity exists, the increased quantities of goods offered for sale will, in turn, lead to a fall in prices. From his analysis of the market mechanism, Webster concluded that "freedom of trade . . . is absolutely necessary to the prosperity of every community, and to the happiness of all individuals who compose it."[96]

Although Webster's admiration for an unregulated domestic market system may well have been shared by many of his contemporaries, only comparatively few writers declared their endorsement of *laissez-nous faire,* and most of those who did admitted the necessity and the desirability of some degree of intervention. Tench Coxe, for example, although he strongly favored protection for new manufacturing enterprises, approved of an "open market," pointing out that if producers were protected from unfair competition, the judgment and enterprise of entrepreneurs would tend to supply a community with the right kind, and with an adequate supply, of merchandise.[97] James Madison, although he also admitted exceptions to *laissez-faire* policy, can be counted among the sincere advocates of an open-market economic system: "If industry and labor are left to take their own courses," he wrote in 1789, "they will generally be directed to those objects which are the most productive." He felt confident that entrepreneurial wisdom would allocate the factors of production more satisfactorily than any arbitrary decisions "of the most enlightened legislators." Neither the national interest nor that of individuals, in his opinion, could be "promoted by legislative interference."[98]

In his first annual message to Congress, Jefferson made it clear that

95. "For no principle can draw into the market, all the supplies which are attainable, so effectually, as the cheerful good-will and interest of the owners." Ibid., p. 11.

96. "In times of scarcity, when all the goods that are to be had, are exposed to sale, it is not possible the prices should exceed the degree of scarcity, for when the prices rise too high, they will soon determine whether the scarcity is real or not, for if not real the high price will bring such quantity to market as will soon lower the price." Ibid.

97. *View of the United States,* pp. 164–165 [1791].

98. *Works,* V, 342 [1789]. Madison had a fairly wide acquaintance with European economic literature, especially those writers who favored a system of economic liberty. He refers to Hume, Smith, Malthus, Montesquieu, Raynal, Condorcet, Turgot, Necker, Godwin, and De Tracy. See Spengler, *Political Economy of Jefferson, Madison, and Adams,* p. 9. For a discussion of the exceptions to *laissez-faire* policy that Madison admitted, see ibid., pp. 15, 16, 17.

he favored an open market as a regulator of production: "Agriculture, manufactures, commerce, and navigation, the four pillars of our prosperity, are . . . most thriving when left most free to individual enterprise."[99] He did not say "completely free," however; indeed, he admitted that "protection from casual embarrassments" might require some governmental intervention.[100] This readiness to qualify is in fact typical of most of the American advocates of entrepreneurial freedom. George Logan was perhaps the most doctrinaire proponent of governmental nihilism in the economic sphere. The prosperity of new countries, he said, quoting Adam Smith, depends upon the abundance of land and upon people's liberty "to manage their own affairs, their own way."[101] It was he also who called attention to Legendre's alleged reply to Colbert, "Let us alone," a reply that Logan thought the "citizens of the United States engaged in agriculture, in manufactures, in mechanics, and even in the Cod-fishery" should give to the American Congress.[102] And although Logan thought that American manufacturing should be encouraged, he doubted the wisdom of governmental assistance. Like Bordley,[103] he feared the indirect consequences of governmental intervention, and for that reason he urged his countrymen to buy American-made manufactures as an act of patriotism, even though better foreign-made commodities might be available at lower prices.[104] Whereas Coxe, Hamilton, Bowdoin, and other protectionists would restrict the supply of foreign goods entering the free and open domestic markets, Logan would restrict the demand for foreign goods, thus achieving the same end without the interposition of any governmental powers.

Because *laissez-nous faire* is a concept separable from *laissez-passer,* both the advocates of international free trade and the protectionists could find virtue in an unrestricted domestic market mechanism, and herein is found one of the keys to the vitality of the American belief in economic freedom. For although international free trade did not

99. December 8, 1801. For the text see Richardson, *Messages and Papers of the Presidents,* I, 318.
100. On the relation of Jefferson's economic ideas to previous and contemporaneous European economic thought, see Spengler, *Political Economy of Jefferson, Madison, and Adams,* pp. 5–9.
101. *Five Letters to the Yeomanry,* p. 26 [1792].
102. Ibid., p. 19.
103. "It is a principle of sound prudence that whenever in matters of government, law, and commerce, any material alteration is proposed, we should beware of latent consequences, and look forward and consider, however flattering appearances are, what may be the mischievous tendency of such innovation when adopted. . . . It is not easy to determine upon theory the success of political innovations." *Essays on Husbandry,* pp. 301–302.
104. *Address before the Tammany Society,* pp. 7–8 [1798].

become a part of the American way of life, the free and open market which Webster eulogized was realized perhaps more completely in America than in any other country. What Americans came to believe in, almost devoutly, was the beneficence of domestic competition as a regulator of production and prices and as a device for allocating labor and capital, a state of affairs that was to a high degree made possible by the constitutional prohibition of trade barriers between the American states.

Competition, said Pelatiah Webster, prevents the exploitation of consumers.[105] Laws that attempt to limit the number of transactions so that there "should be but one step between the importer and the consumer," wrote John Witherspoon, are not only absurd but actually disadvantageous to the community. For it may be "safely affirmed that the more merchants the cheaper [the] goods,"[106] because there is "no distribution so equal or so plentiful" as that provided by a competitive profit-making system. Competition among sellers will protect consumers, while competition among buyers will ensure that farmers and other producers can "always obtain the best prices, which circumstances will justify."[107] Best of all, competition is an automatic process that "brings everything to its proper level of price and quality."[108]

What effect this praise of competition had on legislation is rather difficult to say. Laws against forestalling or engrossing were still on the statute books in several states,[109] and in Maryland, at least, legislation against engrossers was reenacted after the adoption of the Constitution.[110] There is little positive evidence of legislative reliance upon competition. Pennsylvania, it is true, did enact a law "in aid of the Callowhill Market" which declared in the preamble that "the holding of open market" where "buyer and seller may . . . meet together" will be "beneficial to both."[111] But there was nothing novel in this; many such market laws were to be found. Moreover, the text makes it perfectly clear that the purpose of aiding the Callowhill Market was to reduce the competition which street hawkers were giving provisioners who hired stalls there. Of more significance, perhaps, was a New

105. "All experience teaches, that the more hands the goods in market are held by, the cheaper they will be, and the more difficult to raise the price." *Political Essays*, p. 17 [1779].
106. *Essay on Money*, p. 34 [1786].
107. Coxe, *View of the United States*, pp. 292–293 [1792].
108. Thomas Jefferson, "Special Message to the Senate and the House" (February 2, 1802), in Richardson, *Messages and Papers of the Presidents*, I, 323.
109. For example, 1 *Delaware Laws*, 183, 249ff; *Pennsylvania Laws*, 225–226, ch. 1398.
110. *Maryland Laws* (Kilty), May 1788, ch. 17; 1793, ch. 59.
111. 13 *Pennsylvania Statutes at Large*, 225–226, ch. 1398 [March 18, 1789].

York act which abolished rights of purveyance, stipulating that every citizen should be free to "sell his goods to any other person."[112] It is possible that greater market freedom was emerging, and that a belief in the beneficence of competition was challenging the typical colonial legislative emphasis on surveillance. But in some departments of the American economy, competition was apparently creating new difficulties. In a special message to Congress in 1803, Jefferson called attention to the problems that had arisen as a result of unregulated trade with the Indians. Because private traders not only aroused the cupidity of the Indians, but often provided them with undesirable commodities, Jefferson proposed that the government should increase the number of government trading posts and drive the private traders out of business by underselling them.[113] But even this instance indicates the trend of thought: the private traders were to be driven out of business not by force but by the power of governmentally subsidized competition.

The best evidence of declining governmental intervention in the marketplace is to be found in a Pennsylvania law of 1793 which suspended the assize of bread.[114] The traditional practice had been for the legislature to establish a scale of weights for the four-penny loaf, a scale which was related inversely to a series of flour prices; thus when flour prices rose, the bakers were permitted to decrease the weight of the four-penny loaf. The entire system had been designed to protect consumers by the administratively awkward scheme of adjusting the weight of a loaf of bread to the variable price of flour. In 1793, however, the Pennsylvania legislature admitted that a question had arisen whether the bread assize did not "infringe the equality of rights established by the State Constitution."[115] The bread assize was therefore suspended. The new scheme of things simply required bakers to make loaves of certain avoirdupois weight, each loaf to be

112. *New York Laws,* II, 346–347, ch. 2 [January 26, 1787].

113. Richardson, *Messages and Papers of the Presidents,* I, 340–342.

114. 14 *Pennsylvania Statutes at Large,* 510–511, ch. 1702 [September 4, 1792].

115. Article V in the 1776 Pennsylvania Constitution which had denounced "the particular emolument . . . of any . . . set of men" was discarded when the Constitution was rewritten in 1790. This article, therefore, could not be the one referred to by the framers of the 1793 law suspending the bread assize. When the legislature spoke of the "equality of rights established by the constitution," it evidently referred to the more abstract "equality" mentioned in the Declaration of Independence that had been incorporated (in more definitely Lockean phraseology) both in the 1776 Pennsylvania Constitution and that of 1790. The really significant thing is that the legislature construed "equality of rights" as having an economic rather than a political meaning. For the text of the constitutions, see Ben Perley Poore, ed., *The Federal and State Constitutions* (Washington, 1878), II, 1541, 1554.

marked according to its weight (in figures at least an inch high) so that all buyers might "be fully informed of the weight or quantity of the bread they are about to purchase." Aside from this certification, the protection of the consumer against exploitation was left to the competition of the free and open market.

The Merits of Occupational Choice

Although the theory of a free and open market tacitly assumed that businessmen ought to be free to choose their occupations, the arguments advanced in favor of occupational freedom went beyond these purely entrepreneurial considerations. Actually the history of occupational freedom is intertwined inseparably with the course of American democratic thought and with the heroic attempt of American social theory to reject completely the traditional European idea of classes. As a result, even in the 1790s, long before democracy in the Jacksonian sense had taken root, the doctrine of occupational freedom is seldom confined to purely economic considerations; it is overlaid, indeed often suffused, with social, ethical, or political factors. Only by a rigid exclusion of all arguments advanced in favor of a more democratic social structure can one find a discussion of the economic benefits attributed to a greater freedom of occupational choice; when such refinements are made, the theory of occupational liberty that remains turns out to be a little anemic. For the most part it merely reasserts the putative social benefits stemming from self-interest and stresses the greater degree of industry and application which free choice of occupation generates.

But there is one really emphatic note that pervades the economic discussion of occupational freedom: an insistence that freedom to choose an occupation helps ensure full employment and maximum production. The "best" distribution of workers among occupations, said Madison, is one that promotes the "health, virtue, intelligence, and competency" of the greatest number of citizens.[116] Complete "free choice of occupations" might "gradually" create such a society; coercion never could, simply because unwilling labor is inefficient labor. The best policy, therefore, is to let each individual "employ his talents in his own way."[117] But Madison hoped, as Jefferson did,[118] that the majority of Americans would elect to be farmers, arguing that the larger the farmer-owner class, "the more free, the more independent,

116. *Works,* VI, 96–99.
117. Ibid., V, 342 [1789].
118. *Works* (Washington), VIII, 405 [1782]; I, 403 [1785].

and the more happy must be the society itself."[119] Tench Coxe, in contrast, did not share this preference for agrarian occupations; yet he was equally convinced that occupational freedom provided the best recipe for full employment. Since Pennsylvania imposed virtually no restraints on occupational choice, he said, there are very few individuals "who live without some business, profession, occupation or trade."[120] As a result, "all capital stock is kept in action," leading to the maximum production of goods.[121]

In addition to stimulating full utilization of a nation's labor supply, freedom to choose an occupation was considered a stimulator of immigration,[122] thereby further increasing the nation's total productive capacity. If immigrants are allowed to choose their occupations, said Coxe, many artisans will be attracted to the United States, and their industry and skill will hasten American industrial development. Nor will the benefits be entirely unilateral: because European countries are relatively overpopulated, a transference of their excess population to the United States would ameliorate economic conditions both here and abroad.[123] Actually, asserted Coxe, European countries were unwittingly stimulating emigration by injudicious regulations, aiding the "supreme law of necessity" by challenging people to migrate to regions where cheaper food, better wages, and greater occupational opportunities exist.[124] Freedom to migrate, said Madison, always promotes happiness by transferring people "from places where living is more difficult to places where it is less difficult."[125] But such an increase of happiness is not a mere consequence of migration: it can only be achieved if the migrating persons have the right to select whatever employments best suit their abilities.

The test of the wisdom of occupational freedom was therefore to be found in its effect upon total production and upon the distribution of wealth. In addition to these materialistic criteria, however, certain psychological effects of occupational freedom were also emphasized. Only when every man can make his own decisions, contended Pelatiah Webster, only when every man can "taste and enjoy the sweets of that liberty of person and property," will social contentment be maximized.[126] A good civil society, according to James Sullivan, exists when

119. *Works*, VI, 99.
120. *View of the United States*, p. 441 [1793].
121. Ibid., p. 143 [1791].
122. Ibid., p. 165.
123. Ibid., pp. 239–240.
124. Ibid., p. 227.
125. *Works*, VI, 65–66.
126. *Political Essays*, p. 24 [1789].

every member "has a clear right to gain all the property which vigilance and industry . . . can bestow upon him."[127] John Taylor of Caroline was equally certain that sound public policy should give scope and range for personal occupational preferences.[128] Because workers should be given every opportunity to advance public prosperity, he recommended complete occupational freedom,[129] insisting "that it is both wise and just, to leave the distribution of property to industry and talents."[130] Oddly enough, John Adams, whom Taylor so mercilessly attacked for his aristocratic prejudices, seems to have endorsed occupational freedom, on one occasion at least, with equal cordiality.[131]

Freedom to Invest, Speculate, and Lend Money

The great controversy in the Age of Washington concerned the fourth aspect of American *laissez-faire* theory—the right of individuals to invest, to speculate, and to lend money. Yet the literature of this dispute is, in all likelihood, a poor barometer of the currents of opinion inasmuch as the critics of speculation were so much more articulate than the defenders. Republican opposition to Federalist policies, antagonism between debtor and creditor groups, and enmity of inland farmers toward seaboard merchants tended to confuse and to obscure the issue under debate. Consequently, for all its bitterness, the criticism of the financial interest ought not be construed as a denial of the right to invest or even of the right to speculate. It represented a criticism of certain types of investment and certain kinds of speculation. The right to make shrewd investments and the right to hold property in the hope of an appreciation of its value were not only sanctioned but respected: "The true profit of America," said John Adams, "is the continual augmentation of the price and value of land."[132] On this score, there was surely no disagreement between Adams and Taylor, especially since Taylor's fortune can be partly attributed to his successful investment in agricultural land.

It was generally recognized, moreover, that the investment process required a favorable political environment. An "unstable government," said the authors of *The Federalist*, "damps every useful under-

127. *Path to Riches*, pp. 5, 6 [1792].
128. *Enquiry into Certain Public Measures*, p. 21 [1794]; *Principles and Policy*, p. 366 [1814]; *Construction Construed*, p. 248 [1820].
129. *Arator*, p. 34 [1813].
130. *Principles and Policy*, p. 282 [1814].
131. See *Works*, VI, 530 [1808].
132. *Works*, VIII, 294 [1780].

taking" by deterring investment. "What prudent merchant," it was asked, "will hazard his fortune in any new branch of commerce . . . ? What farmer or manufacturer will lay himself out" financially unless some assurance is given that investments will be protected?[133] The reiterated demand that government should defend property represented a popular sanction of private investments. Business cannot flourish in despotic countries, claimed Pelatiah Webster, because despotism threatens not only the security of property but the freedom of individuals to invest their capital as they choose.[134] The vigor of enterprise, it was repeatedly asserted, depends upon entrepreneurial liberty, simply because self-interest "is the mainspring in the dealings of men of business."[135]

But whereas the right of individuals to buy farms or to launch mercantile or manufacturing enterprises went unchallenged, the establishment of chartered corporate ventures[136] and speculation in public securities encountered vigorous opposition. The enemies of the "monied interest" alleged that the activities of promoters, and more especially of speculators, not only created inequality in wealth but tended to undermine a republican form of government. Repeated proposals were accordingly made that the government ought to distinguish between those business activities which should be entirely free and speculative ventures which should be forbidden or at least restrained. To such proposals Robert Morris had replied, in 1782, "that it is much beneath the dignity of Government to intermeddle in such considerations." Moreover, beyond being undignified, said Morris, interference is actually disadvantageous to the public welfare, since "speculators always do least mischief when they are left most at liberty." Competition, which regulates other branches of business, is equally effective among speculators; leave them alone, Morris advised, and they will "invariably counteract each other." Moreover, even if it were possible to outlaw speculation, this is "precisely the thing which ought not be prevented."[137] Like Hamilton, Morris emphasized that speculation created a market for intangible property, thus facilitating the liquidity of idle business capital. An enterprise system

133. *The Federalist* (Lodge), LXII (Hamilton or Madison), 390–391 [1788]. See also Beard, *Economic Interpretation of the Constitution*, p. 53.

134. *Political Essays*, p. 439 [1786].

135. See the remarks of William Bingham in Davis, *American Corporations*, I, 429.

136. On the meaning of corporate activity in the late eighteenth century, see Livermore, *Early American Land Companies*, chap. III.

137. *Journals of the Continental Congress*, XXII, 435. The individual businessman, said Morris, is "able to judge better of business and situation than the Government can." Ibid.

must be ready to seize business opportunities whenever they emerge; hence every agency that makes it possible for businessmen to provide themselves with funds promptly must benefit the entire economy. The resiliency of enterprise, so went the argument, depends not only upon freedom to invest, but upon an adequate number of speculators—in short on the existence of a capital market.

The defenders of speculation denied categorically that the extensive purchase and sale of public securities had resulted in deleterious effects. Those merchants, farmers, manufacturers, and artisans who had the good judgment to hold their stock "until it rose to par," said "A Citizen," were able to pay off their debts "and are now prosecuting business on their own capitals."[138] Only those public creditors who lacked confidence in the government or who preferred liquidity, it was alleged, had sold at large discounts.[139] To be sure, prospects of satisfactory servicing and ultimate redemption of the public debt influenced the value of securities, but, here again, freedom to speculate proved its utility. For the greater the number of speculators and the better organized the market, the more accurately would these prospects be reflected in the value of securities. Conversely, where speculators were few and where market facilities were wanting, "the ignorant became the dupes of those who were better informed" and it became more difficult "to come at the true state of the market."[140] Even bitter critics of stock speculation admitted that stockjobbing was not inherently evil: when "this business is conducted with truth, sincerity and fairness," said James Sullivan, "it may be considered as reputable and honourable."[141]

In much the same way that Hamilton's funding and assumption program had precipitated violent criticism of speculation in public securities, the launching of the Bank of the United States and the establishment of the Society for Establishing Useful Manufactures crystallized a latent fear of corporate enterprises.[142] In defense of corporate projects, advocates of entrepreneurial freedom argued that groups of investors should have unrestricted liberty to pool funds for enterprises

138. In the *Columbian Centinel*. See Davis, *American Corporations*, I, 181 [1792].

139. Hamilton, *Political Papers* (McKee), pp. 11–12 [1790]. The same argument was used by Coxe, *View of the United States*, p. 363 [1792].

140. See the discussion precipitated by a Pennsylvania bill designed to tax auction sales of public and private securities. Davis, *American Corporations*, I, 198.

141. *Path to Riches*, pp. 10–11. [1792].

142. On the distrust of corporate ventures, see Livermore, *Early American Land Companies*, pp. 61, 67.

too large or too venturesome for individual businessmen. A "union of many individuals," it was pointed out, not only amasses adequate capital for large-scale ventures, but distributes the risk among a number of persons, no one of whom could have borne it alone.[143] In addition, corporate enterprise can more easily enlist the financial aid of foreign capitalists,[144] thereby attracting much needed capital. And although the untutored mind might suppose that investments by foreigners militate against the welfare of Americans, this was branded a superficial, indeed an erroneous, judgment, since foreigners who supply capital for American business ventures actually "contribute considerably to our advancement."[145]

The channels of investment ought therefore to be kept entirely free from governmental interference. No distinction should be made between investment (in the purchase-to-use sense) and speculation (purchase-to-resell). Nor should any limitation be placed upon group investment, provided such joint enterprise did not constitute a monopoly disadvantageous to other investors and to the public.[146] Opposition to favoritism was voiced in many of the conventions that ratified the Constitution; the Hancock-Adams resolutions in the Massachusetts convention, for example, proposed an amendment to the federal Constitution forbidding Congress to erect companies of merchants "with exclusive advantages of commerce."[147] The fact that five conventions made similar recommendations indicates that antimonopoly sentiment was widespread and persistent. But this strand of *laissez-faire* thought ought not be considered peculiarly American; indeed one of the earliest British uses of the term *free trade* represented a protest against Jacobean monopolies and screened an effort on the part of interlopers, and would-be interlopers, to participate in hitherto restricted enterprises.

The clearest arguments in favor of freedom to invest are contained in Noah Webster's spirited attack on the usury laws.[148] With a logic that reminds one of Bentham's criticism of Adam Smith, Webster attempts to show that dealings in money ought to conform to a general open-market policy, and that only by means of a thoroughgoing system

143. See excerpts from the *Gazette of the United States,* in Davis, *American Corporations,* I, 446.

144. As Hamilton pointed out. Ibid., I, 365.

145. Francis Adrien van der Kemp, *Speech . . . at a Meeting . . . at Whitestown, for the Institution of a Society of Agriculture* (Whitestown, 1795), p. 8. See also Hamilton, *Political Papers* (McKee), pp. 48, 63, 70, 172, 212–213.

146. See Livermore, *Early American Land Companies,* pp. 5, 8, 12, 20, 36, 38, 62.

147. Ibid., p. 67.

of economic freedom can the capital resources of a nation be distributed equitably and efficiently. Money, said the schoolmaster, is "a species of commercial property" in which a person has "complete ownership." By virtue of this "complete ownership," the possessor of money has "the same natural right" as the owner of any other form of property: he may sell, loan, or exchange it "to any advantage" provided only that no fraud is involved and provided "the minds of the parties meet in the contracts."[149]

Government has no right, asserted Webster, "to interfere with private contracts," to limit mercantile profits, or to restrict rents. Equal freedom should be accorded to moneylenders, unless it can be proven that dealers in money cause "some great public inconvenience" which warrants governmental interference.[150] The contention that, unless interest rates are limited, the "monied men" will take advantage of the "poor and needy" Webster rejects as untenable because "the restraint is no remedy for the evil." For, although usury laws can forbid interest rates from exceeding 6 percent, it does not follow that the "poor and needy" will be able to borrow at 6 percent or less. Indeed it may mean that impoverished people will not be able to borrow any money whatsoever, inasmuch as moneylenders "have the right of withholding" their funds or of "employing" their money in more profitable investments. As a consequence, debtors faced with the necessity of raising money immediately may be obliged to make forced sales, "to sacrifice twenty, perhaps fifty or a hundred percent."[151] Had they been allowed to borrow, said Webster, "at ten, fifteen, or even twenty per cent," they might have been able to extricate themselves from their financial difficulties, and, indeed, to have profited from the use of borrowed funds. Instead of helping the "poor and needy," the usury laws play into the hands of the "monied interest." Skillful businessmen "will not loan money at legal interest" for the simple reason that "they can do better with it"; and one way of doing

148. The usury laws which Webster assailed were almost identical in the several states. Contracts calling for interest rates higher than a legal maximum were to be void except contracts covering the "letting of cattle" and certain maritime contracts concerned with "bottomry, insurance, or course of exchange." Legal maximums for "scriveners, brokers, solicitors or drivers of bargains" were also included in some of the usury laws. For representative statutes, see *New Jersey Laws* (Allinson), 110–111; *Massachusetts Laws*, 1801, I, 166–167; *Connecticut Statutes at Large*, 1784, 260–261; *Rhode Island Laws*, 474–477; *Vermont Session Laws*, 1787, 170–171; *New Hampshire Laws*, V, 683–684; *New York Laws*, II, 365–367; 1 *Delaware Laws*, 97–98; *Virginia Laws*, 12 (Hening), 337–338; *Maryland Laws* (Kilty), 704, ch. 69.

149. *Collection of Essays*, p. 304 [1789].

150. Ibid., pp. 304–305.

151. Ibid., p. 306.

better with it is to buy up the property of debtors who have been forced to sell their farms or houses at sacrifice prices because of their inability to borrow.[152]

The cause for this anomalous situation, claimed Webster, is to be found in the foolish unwillingness of legislators to grant complete freedom to the possessors of money to invest or lend it in any way they may think best. He relates a conversation he once had with Benjamin Franklin "on this subject." Apparently Webster and Franklin found themselves in perfect agreement, for Franklin pointed out that if a man with £1000 could invest in real estate and receive 15 percent return, he most assuredly would not lend his money for 6 percent.[153] Why should one form of investment be free and the other restricted? Why should a man have "an unrestrained right to take any sum he can get" for the use of a house, and yet have his right to a competitive return upon a loan "abridged by law"? Laws limiting interest, in Webster's opinion, are as absurd as laws against witchcraft; they originated "in ages of monkish bigotry"[154] and are not only "illiberal" but positively harmful to economic society.

The distinction between trade in goods and trade in money, said Webster, is entirely specious. Besides, "if legislators have a right to fix the profit on money," they have an equal warrant to restrict the profits on "every commodity in market."[155] To Webster it was clear that either effort represented an infringement of natural rights and that each was equally ineffectual.[156] The value of money, he argued, depends "on the quantity in circulation and the demand"; its price, like that of any other commodity, can be determined only by the free interplay of market forces. Like his Philadelphia namesake, the lexicographer insisted that any interference with the automatic market, however benevolent in intention, always makes commodities "scarce and dear."[157] In the case of money, efforts to limit interest rates lead to an efflux of specie,[158] because the entire commercial world is subject to

152. To save their property from foreclosure, debtors will try to borrow from the bootleg market. But since violating the usury laws "exposes the lender to a loss of the money, and a fine or forfeiture besides," the black market interest rates will be "in proportion to that risk." Hence, once again, the usury laws will benefit the rich rather than the poor. Ibid., pp. 310–311.

153. Ibid., p. 305n.

154. Ibid., p. 334 [1790].

155. Ibid., p. 308 [1789].

156. "The legislatures of several states during the late war were rash enough to make the attempt [to fix commodity prices]; and the success of the scheme was just equal to the wisdom that planned it." Ibid., p. 311.

157. Ibid., p. 310.

158. Ibid., pp. 309, 310.

the same natural forces; "money and commodities will always flow to the country, where they are most wanted and will command the most profit."[159] If interest rates were unrestricted, if money were left "to command its own price in market," loanable funds would flow into the country and decrease domestic interest rates.[160] The foolish interference of the usury laws, however, had caused moneylenders to export specie, thus diminishing the supply of loanable funds and raising the rate of interest. All of which, said Webster, is understandable enough; "let the price of wheat be fixed at half a dollar a bushel, and in two years we should not have a bushel in market. It is the same case with money."[161]

Thus Noah Webster built his argument in favor of freedom to invest on the theory of the automatic market. The entire price mechanism, he insisted, should be unrestricted. Proper allocation of loanable funds can be achieved only if complete freedom to lend or to invest is permitted. "To make a law that a man shall not take but six per cent for the use of money . . . is a daring violation of private rights, an injury often to both parties, and productive of innumerable embarrassments to commerce."[162] Legislation designed to outlaw a voluntary contract between a lender and a borrower stipulating interest at 8 percent, a contract "which each deems favorable for himself," is tyrannical enough "to be placed on the catalogue of papal bulls."[163] The true function of government should be to prevent fraud and to determine an equitable rate of interest "where the parties have not determined it by agreement."[164] All other matters can be safely entrusted to self-interest and the automatic market.

Government as a Protector of Economic Freedom

What general rules of economic policy did American ideas about *laissez-faire* indicate? How should government proceed to institute a greater measure of economic freedom? Since the concept of *laissez-faire* was composite, since it reflected the demands of several "interests," and since no genuine libertarian program can be identified with any one political party, the answer to these questions cannot be

159. Ibid., p. 308.
160. Ibid., p. 310. "Had been permitted to bear its own price according to the demand for it in America since the war, it would have been kept in the country, or introduced until the rate of interest had fallen, even below the legal standard."
161. Ibid.
162. Ibid., p. 313.
163. Ibid., p. 334.
164. Ibid., p. 313.

found by the simple expedient of contrasting Hamiltonian with Jeffersonian economic policy or by attempting to identify intervention with one political party and *laissez-faire* with another. As so frequently happens, political history here reveals itself an untrustworthy guide to a study of economic development. For the American belief in economic liberty transcended party loyalty; in one meaning or another, it was becoming a part of a general climate of opinion. The problem, therefore, is to discover some of the major trends in public opinion about the proper role of government and enterprise. Viewing the task in this light, we can see that American *laissez-faire* thought centers on a preference for a naturalistic economic development, a persistent demand for democratic economic policies assuring equality of opportunity, a deep-rooted opposition to monopoly, an antagonism toward price-fixing, and a reiterated demand that the rewards of industry should not be jeopardized by any violation of the rights of property. Each of these currents need to be analyzed and documented.

From the writings of Benjamin Franklin stems a branch of thought that asserts that governmental intervention with business enterprise is always mischievous. History, said George Logan, "does not furnish a single instance of Legislators interfering, and directing the occupations of citizens, but with injury," and in support of this thesis he cites the ill effects of governmental intervention in Greece, Rome, Spain, and France.[165] Legislators should recognize these lessons of history and confine their activities to the formulation of laws consistent with the natural order; it is impossible, for example, to equalize property by law or to eliminate the poverty of the indolent.[166] The advocates of intervention, said John Witherspoon, are misguided; they pass "tender laws" and other legislation "directly contrary to the first principles of commerce" not necessarily for any selfish reasons but more often "from pure ignorance."[167] John Taylor was not equally charitable: he branded the Hamiltonian monetary and fiscal policies as a conspiracy of the "financial interest" to monopolize the money system

165. *Five Letters to the Yeomanry*, pp. 13–14, 17–18, 23 [1792]; *Fourteen Agricultural Experiments*, pp. 38–39 [1797]. Solon's interference with the automatic market, said Logan, succeeded only in making provisions scarce. It was imitated by Rome and had similar effects. Regalian control over Spanish trade doomed the vigor of enterprise in that country, even as Colbert's efforts to hasten French industrial development led to the "ruin" of both French industry and agriculture.

166. See Taylor, *Principles and Policy*, p. 634 [1814]; Sullivan, *Path to Riches*, p. 7 [1792].

167. *Essay on Money*, pp. 34–35 [1786]. Laws against forestalling and regrating, said Witherspoon, "have the most powerful tendency to prevent, instead of promoting full and reasonable markets."

and thereby levy toll on the agricultural and mechanic interests.[168] The regulation of money and credit by a single bank he considered the worst kind of governmental intervention, because it involved interference with the entire price mechanism. He warned that such wholesale "interposition with all prices" would do incalculable harm, especially when it could be shown that governmental interference with single industries "has invariably terminated in mischief." The best policy, said Jefferson, is to "let things take their natural course without help or impediment."[169] Accordingly he rejected a proposal for federal participation in the New Orleans Canal Company, arguing that it ought to be the policy of the government not to embark upon enterprises "better managed by individuals."[170] His views were shared by his fellow Republicans,[171] who contrasted the egalitarian nature of an economy based on free private enterprise with the favoritism that must inevitably result[172] from projects such as the Bank of the United States or the Society for Establishing Useful Manufactures.

The most specific recommendation of the believers in naturalistic economic development was that the government should allow industries to develop without the aid of tariffs, bounties, or any other form of subvention. Thus the Germantown Society for Promoting Domestic Manufactures, acting on a conviction that "every manufacture . . . should be supported by its intrinsic value," resolved that it would "never use its influence with government" to prevent the importation of foreign manufactured goods, but would "exert itself to promote a free unlimited commerce," since that policy alone can advance "the true interest of every country."[173] In this declaration, the influence of Franklin is clearly evident, who, despite the high wages which retarded manufacturing activity in the colonial period, had repudiated the use

168. *Principles and Policy*, p. 356 [1814]. For the entire Taylorian indictment of the financial interest, see above, chap. IV.

169. *Works* (Washington), II, 413.

170. Ibid., V, 319. As president, however, Jefferson followed a more pragmatic policy. He replaced private trading with the Indians by a factorage system, approved of the building of the National Road by the federal government, and recommended the passage of the Embargo Act.

171. "For a government to interfere in the occupations or in the private actions of citizens," said Logan, "is not only unjust and impolitic, but is highly dangerous to the liberties of the People." *Five Letters to the Yeomanry*, p. 19 [1792].

172. See especially Taylor, *Tyranny Unmasked*, pp. 54, 88, 92 [1822], who describes in caustic language how a "little, smiling, fat group" of capitalists were transferring self-government "from a nation to a combination between governing and capitalist sects."

173. *The Constitution of the Germantown Society for Promoting Domestic Manufactures* (Philadelphia, 1790), p. 6.

of subventions, arguing that manufactures must grow naturally.[174] George Logan, one of Franklin's staunchest disciples, vigorously objected to subsidized industries: "We ought not desire the establishment of any kind of manufacture in our country," he said, "which cannot support itself, without Government granting to its agents bounties, premiums, and a variety of exclusive privileges."[175] Subsidized industries, he charged, are always less efficient than private enterprises that must make their own way.[176] The only proper way to help American manufactures, Logan claimed, is to build up sentiment in favor of buying American-made products,[177] by impressing upon American citizens that they should maximize the business opportunities of their fellow citizens.[178]

The Republican condemnation of tariffs was essentially different from contemporaneous European free-trade (laissez-passer) thought, especially because it reflected a widely held preference for a naturalistic type of economic development in a new country. Manufacturing enterprises, said the American libertarians, will gradually be established in the United States as soon as skilled artisans migrate,[179] and when a sound credit system is instituted by a multiple bank system capable of lending money "to those who are likely to make a proper use of it."[180] But tariffs should be scrupulously avoided not merely because they invite retaliation,[181] but because they impose a tax upon all consumers,[182] decrease the current supply of manufactured goods,[183] and frustrate the harmonious economic development which can occur only when all businessmen have equal opportunity to employ their capital and their talents as they choose. The first aspect of economic policy—a preference for naturalistic economic development— therefore merges with a second not quite so libertarian goal, a demand for democratic arrangements designed to ensure equality of opportunity.

"Vast inequality of fortunes," said Noah Webster, not only is inconsistent with republic government,[184] but militates against general welfare and weakens national strength. Land policy must therefore have as

174. See Eiselen, *Rise of Pennsylvania Protectionism*, pp. 9–10.
175. *Five Letters to the Yeomanry*, p. 23 [1792].
176. Ibid., p. 16. See also Coxe's opinion, Hutcheson, *Tench Coxe*, p. 31.
177. *Address before the Tammany Society*, pp. 7, 8, 10 [1798].
178. *Five Letters to the Yeomanry*, p. 22 [1792].
179. Bordley, *Essays on Husbandry*, passim [1794].
180. Witherspoon, *Essay on Money*, p. 48.
181. See Mudge, *The Social Philosophy of John Taylor*, p. 190.
182. Taylor, *Arator*, p. 20 [1813].
183. See Mudge, *The Social Philosophy of John Taylor*, p. 188.
184. *Collection of Essays*, pp. 331–332 [1790].

184

its object a wide distribution of property rather than the creation of "great estates." Indeed "the basis of a democratic and a republican form of government" must be "a fundamental law, favoring an equal or rather a general distribution of property."[185] To this end, laws should require an equal division of the estates of intestates. Jefferson would go even further; he favored the equal division of all inheritances as the "best corrective" to "overgrown wealth"[186] which would otherwise be "dangerous to the State."[187] The purpose of such legislation should not be to equalize fortunes, for that is impossible,[188] but to set in motion "constant revolutions of property," thereby stimulating "vigilance and industry" by "giving every citizen an equal chance of being rich and respectable."[189]

But economic policy ought to do more than that; it should help people to become property owners. Here John Adams shows himself to be far less the aristocrat than John Taylor has described him. The only way to preserve a republican form of government, he said, was by making "the acquisition of land easy to every member of society." Like Jefferson,[190] Adams recommended a policy designed to divide land into small holdings "so that the multitude may be possessed of landed estates."[191] Madison favored such a plan, because he thought unequal distribution of property the most common and persistent cause of social disharmony.[192] The misery of the lower classes, he said, can be ameliorated only when greater economic freedom is provided by laws favoring a "subdivision of property."[193] Again and again John Taylor affirmed his faith in a land policy designed to populate America with a landowning yeomanry. The engrossing of property in Europe, he asserted, has "enslaved" the great mass of people, and this should be an object lesson to American legislators

---

185. Ibid., p. 327.
186. "Equal partition of all inheritances is the best of all agrarian laws." *Works*, I, 69 [1821].
187. *Works* (Washington), VI, 575 [1816].
188. Logan, *Five Letters to the Yeomanry*, p. 12 [1792]; Backus, *Absalom's Conspiracy*, pp. 24–25 [1798]; Noah Webster, *Collection of Essays*, p. 327 [1790].
189. Webster, *Collection of Essays*, p. 327.
190. "Legislators cannot invent too many devices for subdividing property." *Works* (Ford), VII [1785].
191. *Works*, IX, 376–377.
192. *The Federalist*, X (Lodge), 54 [1787]. "Those who hold and those who are without property," Madison went on to say, "have ever formed distinct interests in society." For similar views, Logan, *Five Letters to the Yeomanry*, pp. 12, 21 [1792]; Sullivan, *Path to Riches*, p. 7 [1792]; Noah Webster, *Collection of Essays*, p. 82 [1787].
193. *Works*, II, 247 [1786].

who should always remember that "a division of wealth by industry and talents, never enslaved any nation."[194]

But the democratization of economic policy should not be restricted to laws governing inheritance or land policy; it ought to pervade all legislation. Even Hamilton, who doubted the capacity of ordinary people, conceded that "the door ought to be equally open to all," so that the more vigorous and energetic persons might "rise superior to the disadvantages of situation."[195] Tench Coxe, far more sanguine about the potentialities of plain and ordinary people, commended the American policy of granting "great opportunities of comfort and prosperity" to the "industrious and honest poor."[196] Freedom to engage in any occupation, liberal apprenticeship arrangements, and "public promotion of useful knowledge," said Coxe, enable the poor to improve their condition.[197] Nor should these opportunities be confined to citizens: it had long been the policy of Pennsylvania, Coxe pointed out, "to receive all sober emigrants with open arms, and to give them immediately the free exercise of their trades, and occupations."[198] More than that, an immigrant who desires to become a citizen "may buy a farm, a house, merchandise, or raw-materials; he may open a workshop, a countinghouse, an office, or any other place of business." Best of all, he may pursue his calling "without any hindrances from corporation rules or monopolizing companies."[199] Other states could point with equal pride to their liberal naturalization laws and to the absence of restrictions on the purchase of property by foreigners.

Not all writers were as satisfied, as Coxe seemed to be, that American economic policy was adequately democratic. Logan asked that more opportunities be given "the weakest and most miserable fellow-citizen";[200] James Swan demanded the abandonment of the "inconsistent and cruel" faculty tax and the substitution of luxury taxes.[201] Good policy should always avoid taxing "the artificer's subsistence," said George Logan,[202] an opinion shared by Pelatiah Webster, who proposed that both land taxes and poll taxes be replaced by high luxury

194. *Principles and Policy*, p. 621 [1814].
195. *The Federalist*, XXXV (Lodge), 207–208 [1788].
196. *View of the United States*, p. 442 [1793].
197. Ibid., p. 159 [1791]; p. 68 [1790].
198. Ibid., p. 74 [1790].
199. Ibid., pp. 66–67 [1790]; p. 214 [1791].
200. *Five Letters to the Yeomanry*, p. 22 [1792].
201. *National Arithmetick*, p. 60 [1786].
202. *Letters to the Yeomanry on Funding and Bank Systems*, p. 12 [1793]. He pointed out that the British tax system had had damaging effects upon small landowners. *Five Letters to the Yeomanry*, pp. 18–19 [1792].

taxes. The whole tenor of the demand for democratic economic policies was epitomized by Madison when he argued that the primary object of legislation should be to "reduce extreme wealth toward a state of mediocrity, and to raise extreme indigence toward a state of comfort."[203] Such a program called for "withholding . . . opportunities from a few," and hence the second goal of American libertarian policy blends with the third, the repudiation of monopoly.

In Massachusetts and Pennsylvania, the chartering of such institutions as the Massachusetts Bank and the Bank of North America precipitated a bitter denunciation of political favoritism. Within a decade, the controversy became even more acrimonious; the chartering of the Bank of the United States by the federal government was described by Republicans as the shameless creation of "a monopoly; which affects the equal rights of every citizen."[204] Then came the incorporation (in New Jersey) of the Society for Establishing Useful Manufactures, which elicited still another tirade against monopoly. As a consequence, the discussion of the monopoly problem is so hopelessly snarled up with party conflict that it is almost impossible to appraise the antimonopoly sentiment in its relation to *laissez-faire* thought. Since grants of monopoly had been regarded as an invasion of traditional British liberties,[205] the Republicans put their opponents at a very great disadvantage by stigmatizing them as advocates of a system of political favoritism.

John Taylor, for example, in his vitriolic attack on the Bank of the United States, used every argument he could summon to demonstrate that the Bank would levy toll on the entire nation for the benefit of its privileged stockholders.[206] The first duty of government to citizens should be to protect them against exploitation by minorities. Not only had the Federalists failed to do this, said Taylor, but they themselves had actually created agencies to despoil the laboring classes of the en-

203. *Works,* VI, 86.
204. Madison, *Works,* VI, 103. See also ibid., pp. 33, 37, 77 [1791].
205. See C. M. Andrews, "Conservative Factors in Early Colonial History," *Authority and the Individual* (Cambridge, 1937), pp. 154–169; Heckscher, *Mercantilism,* I, 269–293.
206. The purpose of every monopolist, said Taylor, is to obtain a higher rate of return than could be obtained under conditions of competition. The differential thus obtained constitutes a tax upon all persons who are compelled to purchase the monopolized commodity. It follows that the more indispensable a monopolized commodity is, the greater the injury to the public, and since money (or credit) is absolutely indispensable, a monopoly of banking is "more diffuse in its operations" than any other form of monopoly. It places in the hands of a few persons despotic power over every business activity. *Enquiry into Certain Public Measures,* pp. 11, 12, 18, 19–20, 74–75, 81 [1794]; *Principles and Policy,* p. 112 [1814].

tire nation, skillfully concealing their true purposes by pious declarations.[207] Honest public policy should be "founded on the idea, that it is both wise and just, to leave the distribution of property to industry and talents," permitting every citizen to keep all that he earns except his aliquot share of the cost of government. It should protect every member of society from the depredations of monopoly and exclusive privilege,[208] from the "insatiable lust" of the financial interest.[209] Legislators must therefore be eternally vigilant lest any individual or any group of men acquire "a superior privilege";[210] for that reason, corporations ought not be chartered unless it could be shown that they would benefit society as a whole.[211] On this score a violent attack was made on the Society for Establishing Useful Manufactures which, it was alleged, would undermine small-scale manufacturing establishments and render valueless personal skills acquired by long and expensive apprenticeship.[212]

That antimonopoly sentiment was widespread and insistent is attested by the efforts made in constitutional conventions to forestall monopolies. Power to grant corporate charters, said William Findley, that doughty ringleader of the Whiskey Rebellion, "was repeatedly moved for in the Federal Convention . . . but always rejected by a great majority."[213] In the state conventions, the antimonopoly challenge was even more vigorous, and many constitutions manifested "the strongest disapproval of monopolies."[214] Thus the Maryland Constitution declared monopolies "contrary to the spirit of a free government," while the New Hampshire Constitution proclaimed competition to be "an inherent and essential right of the people." These efforts, however, did not satisfy the American libertarians, and Jefferson bitterly criticized the failure of the Constitutional Convention to provide "clearly, and without the aid of sophisms for . . . restriction of monopolies."[215] Economic policy, said the believers in a democracy based

---

207. *Principles and Policy*, p. 112.
208. Ibid., pp. 282, 350, 422, 582.
209. *Enquiry into Certain Public Measures*, p. 13 [1794].
210. Sullivan, *Path to Riches*, pp. 6–7 [1792].
211. Madison, *Works*, VI, 37 [1791].
212. Logan, *Five Letters to the Yeomanry*, pp. 20–21 [1792]. For a résumé of the criticism directed against the S.U.M., see Davis *American Corporations*, I, 427–453.
213. *Review of the Revenue System*, pp. 72–73 [1794].
214. Logan, *Five Letters to the Yeomanry*, p. 20 [1792]. The Massachusetts Constitution, said James Sullivan, contained "a solemn compact" forbidding the legislature to grant "any legal exclusive right or privilege" to any person or group of persons. *Path to Riches*, p. 73 [1792].
215. *Works* (Washington), II, 329 [1787].

on economic freedom, should counteract monopoly in every form,[216] thereby preventing all "unreasonable and injurious encroachments upon the liberty of every individual citizen."[217]

There was still another evil against which citizens should be protected. Whereas monopolies represented the despotism of minorities, price-fixing was an unjust interference with private enterprise by the government itself, and while monopolies could be suppressed by the force of government, price-fixing could be avoided only by legislative forbearance. As a consequence, the defenders of an automatic market did their utmost to demonstrate the futility, the injustice, and the folly of price regulation. The "unhappy expedient" of regulating prices during the Revolution, said Pelatiah Webster, had disastrous effects upon business enterprise.[218] Few goods were brought to market, and those which were offered for sale were of poor quality. Tremendous resentment was created: against sellers and against the government. Hoarding increased, especially of scarce commodities. Houses and shops were searched, goods were seized, thus infringing personal liberty and violating property rights.[219] All these results, said Webster, might have been foreseen by anyone familiar with economic process: "prices must rise and fall with their causes"; hence every attempt to fix prices "necessarily implies injustice."[220] Moreover, price regulations have always "produced an effect directly contrary to what was expected of them."[221] Instead of providing low prices and an abundance of goods, they have led to "dearness and scarcity." For it is not possible to regulate the price of commodities without regulating the price of the factors of production. Any effective system of price control would therefore destroy all economic freedom by regulating not merely the price of goods but wages, rents, and profits as well.[222] Such

216. Pelatiah Webster recommended that all "metallic ores, minerals, and all other valuable fossils" in the public domain should be "reserved and sequestered for public use" so that "those vast sources of wealth" would not be "engrossed and monopolized." *Political Essays*, p. 498 [1781].

217. Robert Bell, *Bell's Address to Every Free-man but Especially to the Free Citizens of Pennsylvania, Concerning, a Tyrannical Embargo, Now Laid upon the Free Sale of Books by Auction* (Philadelphia, 1784), p. 8.

218. Merchants refused to sell at the governmentally established prices; stores were forced open "by committees &c"; in spite of penalties, illegal dealing in goods occurred, and "pains were taken to load the merchants with scandal and obloquy for combinations to raise the price of goods, depreciate the currency, &c. They were called Tories, Speculators, and many other hard names." *Political Essays*, p. 11n [1779].

219. Ibid., pp. 11–14.

220. Ibid., p. 13.

221. John Witherspoon, *Essay on Money*, p. 32 [1786].

222. Ibid., p. 33.

complete regulation would bring "a large train of evils": it would check the circulation of money "than which nothing can be more dangerous," and it would lead to business stagnation, lack of business confidence, and a depreciation of the value of money.[223]

The fact that stagecoach tickets and ferry tolls are regulated "with good effects," said Witherspoon, cannot be construed as evidence that general price-fixing laws will be equally successful; indeed "these instances have not the least connexion with laws regulating prices in voluntary commerce." Since each public service enterprise requires a franchise, and since the proprietors have entered into "voluntary engagements to ask no higher prices" than the stipulated rates, no violation of "free contract" is involved.[224] Conversely, because the "essential condition" of every lawful contract is that it be "free and mutual," fixing the market price of commodities destroys the contractual basis of the enterprise system.[225] But beyond being impracticable[226] and unjust, price-fixing attempts to "apply authority to that which is not its proper object, and to extend it beyond its natural bounds."[227]

The vigor of business enterprise "must be the effect of industry, inclination, hope, and interest." Only "very imperfectly" can industry be induced by authority, while inclination, hope, and interest cannot be directed at all by the force of government. It is wholly proper for the government to demand taxes from each citizen for the common expenses of the state; and it is legitimate, in times of national emergency, for the government to commandeer military supplies and provisions. But if the government decrees that citizens must sell commodities at certain prices, the fundamental distinction between freedom and authority has been violated, since property owners have been divested of their property unjustly and unnecessarily.[228] And so, in the final analysis, the opposition to price-fixing reduced itself to a demand for the protection of property.

Property, said Tench Coxe, may be called "the palladium of communities,"[229] for there can be no safety, no peace, no systematic provision for the wants of society when property rights are invaded.

223. Pelatiah Webster, *Political Essays*, pp. 15–16 [1779].
224. Witherspoon, *Essay on Money*, p. 33 [1786].
225. Ibid., p. 31.
226. The assize of bread, asserted Noah Webster, must always be related to the price of wheat, or else "the baker must be ruined, and the poor be destitute of bread"; all of which proves, he said, that "such laws rather follow the state of the market, than regulate it." Webster therefore concluded that municipal dwellers would be better supplied with bread if all regulations were abolished. *Collection of Essays*, p. 308 [1789].
227. Witherspoon, *Essay on Money*, p. 32 [1786].
228. Ibid., pp. 31–32.
229. *View of the United States*, p. 262 [1792].

Public policy must therefore facilitate the acquisition of property and must protect the property which each citizen has accumulated. Aside from an equitable tax contribution, no private property should ever be taken by the government "against the consent of the owners, without the most manifest necessity."[230] Nor should government enact any legislation that jeopardizes private property or alters the rights of individuals to receive property at some future time. Legislators should remember that "contracts are sacred things" and that government has no authority to interfere with them; "it is the business of justice to fulfil the intention" of contracting persons, "not to defeat them."[231]

This insistence upon the sanctity of contract and the inviolability of property pervades contemporaneous election sermons,[232] political tracts,[233] and economic literature.[234] Federalists and Republicans alike regarded private property as an indispensable stimulus to production and as an incentive to industry and thrift.[235] What Federalists and Republicans disagreed about was the direction from which an attack upon property might come. The Federalists believed that the threat to property originated with debtors and Shaysites and demanded a stronger government in order to resist this danger. The Republicans feared that small property owners would be defrauded of their property by the financial machinations of an economic aristocracy, and consequently they waged bitter war against any legislation that savored of special privilege. The disagreement centered on the distribution of property,[236] not on the merits of property as an incentive or on the appropriateness of property as a reward for manual or entrepreneurial exertion.[237] Good government, the Republicans in-

230. Pelatiah Webster, *Political Essays*, p. 66 [1780].

231. Noah Webster, *Collection of Essays*, p. 130 [1786].

232. See, for example, *The Republic of the Israelites: An Example to the American People* (Exeter, 1788), p. 11; Nathan Strong, *A Sermon*, p. 19; Daniel Foster, *A Sermon*, pp. 13–14; Samuel Parker, *A Sermon*, p. 15.

233. See Beard, *An Economic Interpretation of the Constitution*, pp. 156, 164.

234. See especially Coxe, *View of the United States*, and Pelatiah Webster, *Political Essays*.

235. "Property alone can stimulate to labor," George Logan, *Five Letters to the Yeomanry*, p. 11 [1792]. "The true sanction of private property, consists in its effect to stimulate men to industry," John Taylor, *Principles and Policy*, p. 364 [1814]. "There is a good reason to believe that, where the laws are wise and well executed, and the inviolability of property and contracts maintained, the economy of a people will . . . correspond with its means." Alexander Hamilton, *Political Papers* (McKee), p. 67 [1790].

236. An improper distribution of property, said George Logan, "is the great malady of civil society." *Five Letters to the Yeomanry*, p. 11 [1792].

237. "The fruit of labour or industry," said John Taylor, "is an unequivocal species of private property." *Principles and Policy*, p. 561 [1814].

sisted, should "protect and defend" the property "of every one of its members"[238] against any invader.[239] It must ensure above all that legislators do not use the instruments of authority to increase the property of minorities at the expense of the rank and file of citizens.[240] The Federalists, on their side, alleged that the decade which produced Shays's Rebellion represented an attack upon the rights of property, one that threatened the very foundations of the enterprise system.

Property rights and economic freedom were regarded as definitely complementary. The prosperity of commerce, the productivity of agriculture, or the full employment of capital, said Tench Coxe, cannot be assured unless a nation maintains "with sincerity and vigilance, the freedom of its citizens, and with energy and firmness, the rights of property."[241] The right to acquire "money, lands, or other property" by any chosen trade or employment, and the right to keep the rewards of industry "without hindrance or molestation"[242] he considered the real hallmarks of a republican government.

238. Logan, *Five Letters to the Yeomanry*, p. 7 [1792].
239. "There are two modes of invading private property," said John Taylor: "the first, by which the poor plunder the rich, is sudden and violent; the second, by which the rich plunder the poor, slow and legal." Both "impair the national prosperity and happiness, inevitably flowing from the correct and honest principle of private property." *Principles and Policy*, p. 280 [1814]. See also Richard Henry Lee, *Observations on the System of Government*, p. 43 [1788].
240. John Taylor, *Principles and Policy*, p. 656 [1814].
241. Tench Coxe, *View of the United States*, pp. 4, 256 [1787].
242. Ibid., pp. 102–103.

VII

The Legitimacy of Intervention

Howsoever wise the theory may be
which leaves to the segacity and interest
of individuals the application of industry and resources . . . there are
exceptions to the general rule.

James Madison

[Government should aid and encourage]
that industry, those occupations, and
kinds of business, which most enrich,
strengthen and happify a nation.

Pelatiah Webster

The Responsibilities of Legislators

THE American belief in economic freedom was seldom doctrinaire. Indeed the essentially pragmatic character of American thought is revealed by the willingness of some of the very same individuals who justified a large measure of entrepreneurial freedom to signalize certain areas wherein governmental intervention appeared to be not only desirable but quite necessary. This attitude is well illustrated by James Madison who went so far as to say that a dogmatic noninterventionist policy might frustrate a nation's economic development.[1] No general or invariable theory could take proper cognizance of particular historical conditions; free trade (*laissez-passer*), for example, requires "a reciprocal adoption by other nations," a circumstance that had been vainly hoped for in 1783 but was not at all realized. Unilateral adoption of free trade, in Madison's opinion, was therefore imprudent.

The general view, discernible in contemporaneous literature, was that the responsibility of government should involve enough surveillance over the enterprise system to ensure the social usefulness of all economic activity. It is quite proper, said Bordley, for individuals to "choose for themselves" how they will apply their labor and their intelligence in production. But it does not follow from this that "legislators and men of influence" are freed from all responsibility for giving direction to the course of national economic development. They must, for instance, discountenance the production of unnecessary commodities of luxury when common sense indicates the need for food and other essentials.[2] Lawmakers can fulfill their functions

---

1. *Works*, VIII, 341–342.
2. *Essays on Husbandry*, p. 312; for a comparable view, see *Necessaries; Best Product of Land* (Philadelphia, 1776), p. 12. The colonial government of Pennsylvania revived an excise tax on distilled spirits in 1779 to prevent the dimi-

THE LEGITIMACY OF INTERVENTION

properly only when they "become benefactors to the publick";[3] in new countries they must safeguard agriculture and commerce, encourage immigration,[4] and promote manufactures.[5] Admittedly, liberty "is one of the most important blessings which men possess," but the idea that liberty is synonymous with complete freedom from restraint "is a most unwise, mistaken apprehension."[6] True liberty demands a system of legislation that will lead all members of a society "to unite their exertions" for the public welfare. It should therefore be the policy of government to aid and foster certain activities or kinds of business that strengthen a nation,[7] even as it should be the duty of government to repress "those fashions, habits, and practises, which tend to weaken, impoverish, and corrupt the people."[8] The art of government calls for an Aristotelian mean between complete liberty (which would be anarchy) and complete authority (which would be despotism), and hence the function of legislation should be "to unite and combine" public and private action so that they may "mutually support, feed, and quicken each other."[9] For history testifies that the happiness or wretchedness of nations not only depends upon the separate decisions of private individuals but rests to a great extent upon the wisdom of legislators.[10]

The Fostering Hand of Government

The forthrightness with which a lamination of interests was recognized often makes the vindication of intervention appear to be more a rationalization than an explanation. Intervention is justified, was the argument, only when it promises to subserve the general interest. National prosperity can be achieved when a nation possesses a proper

---

nution of the market supply of rye and wheat. The urgent need for army provisions made the distillation of whiskey an uneconomic use of grain supplies. See William Findley, *History of the Insurrection in the Four Western Counties of Pennsylvania* (Philadelphia, 1796), pp. 26–28.

3. Samuel Deane, *A Sermon,* pp. 30–31 [1794].
4. Ibid.
5. "Experiences teach," said Madison, "that so many circumstances must concur in introducing and maturing manufacturing establishments . . . that a country may long remain without them, although sufficiently advanced and in some respects even peculiarly fitted for carrying them on with success." *Works,* VIII, 342.
6. Timothy Stone, *A Sermon,* pp. 9–10 [1792].
7. Pelatiah Webster, *Political Essays,* pp. 239–240 [1783].
8. Ibid.
9. Ibid., p. 499 [1781].
10. Ibid., p. 500.

complement of employments, and when each of its occupations is efficiently organized. Where these goals can be attained by the invisible hand of self-interest, there is no need for intervention; where they cannot, it becomes both proper and prudent to employ "the fostering hand of government."[11] It was on these grounds that Tench Coxe recommended protection for American manufactures. He pointed out that although self-interest had led to the establishment of a number of industrial enterprises, some of which were carried on with diligence and skill, nevertheless manufacturing had not developed rapidly, primarily because American businessmen could not, for want of capital, avail themselves of the most efficient machinery. Liberty was therefore not enough; experience had shown that the assistance of the state was also needed. Advocates of *laissez-faire*, Jefferson, Taylor, and Logan, sharply disputed this need for governmental assistance for manufacturing,[12] insisting that a naturalistic economic development was preferable to the forcing box of protection.[13] In Congress, however, there is little evidence of this extreme attitude; there the question was rather one of how much legislative aid should be given to manufacturers. This became a moot question in the Age of Washington, one that was to remain unsettled decade after decade.

The disagreement as to whether special assistance should be given to manufacturing was only one illustration of a much larger political problem. The basic controversy involved the question of the proper areas of intervention, and, more particularly, the issue of which industries, or which occupations, should be regarded as essential to national safety and prosperity. At one extreme stood the advocates of American autarky[14] who urged the exclusion of all foreign goods that could possibly be replaced by domestic products. At the other extreme were arrayed the proponents of a "passive foreign trade," men like Jefferson, for example, who argued that "the difference of circumstance" made it unwise and inappropriate to transfer industrial tech-

11. This phrase occurs repeatedly in congressional debates and in contemporaneous literature. See in the *Annals of Congress* the remarks of Mr. Hartley (I, 114), Mr. Madison (I, 118), Mr. Fitzsimons (I, 150), Mr. Ames (I, 220); see also Tench Coxe, *View of the United States*, p. 357 [1792].

12. See above, chap. II, pp. 42–45.

13. See above, chap. VI, p. 155.

14. James Swan is a good example. Massachusetts, he said, could easily become self-sufficient in woolens and linens, indeed in all textiles as well as in leather products. Moreover, in the process of supplying themselves with manufactures, a fuller measure of employment would be attained for all American citizens. *National Arithmetick*, pp. 13–16 [1786]. See also *The Constitution of the Germantown Society for Promoting Domestic Manufactures* (Philadelphia, 1790), p. 3.

niques from Europe to America. In the opinion of the young Jefferson it was land monopoly that had compelled recourse to manufactures in Europe, a circumstance which did not obtain in the United States.[15] But neither militant autarky nor economic quietism represented the typical belief; the majority opinion lay somewhere between these extremes.

The majority view stressed the appropriateness and the wisdom of governmental aid to all basic interests—to all occupations that increased not only the supply of essential commodities but the volume of employment. And it could therefore be argued that because manufactures came within this general scheme of things, legislative aid seemed fitting and proper. "Might not several new manufactures be erected and fostered by the hand of government?" asked a Portland preacher;[16] would they not merit governmental aid if they could supply the people "with necessary things"? Manufactures will continue to be few, said Jeremy Belknap, as long as land is plentiful and cheap;[17] consequently if the state does nothing, manufactured commodities will have to be imported and a drain of specie abroad will persist. For this chronic problem, legislators must find a solution; for that reason Belknap recommended that "every species of home manufacture which can be carried on to advantage" ought to receive "all possible encouragement."[18] Coxe advocated a protectionist program because manufactures "will consume our native productions," "improve our agriculture," and "accelerate the improvement of our internal navigation," and because "dormant powers of nature" could then be utilized. Moreover, the resulting abundance of commodities would "give us real independence," thereby rescuing America from "the tyranny of foreign fashions and the destructive torrent of luxury."[19] Madison proposed a selective variety of "public patronage" and protection designed to supply America with an adequate supply of such goods as were frequently subject to "casual failures," especially commodities useful for public defense or for satisfying primary wants. He pointed out that "it will be an additional recommendation of particular manufactures" if their raw materials "are extensively

15. *Notes on Virginia*, pp. 302–304 [1785].
16. Samuel Deane, *A Sermon*, p. 25 [1794].
17. *An Election Sermon*, p. 27 [1785].
18. To Belknap, this was an urgent matter. Americans, he said, cannot "long maintain the character of an independent people, unless we cultivate industry and economy." *Election Sermon*, p. 27.
19. *View of the United States*, p. 53. Fear of luxury, allegedly stimulated by unrestricted imports, pervades the literature of the 1790s. Luxury, said Belknap, "has been the ruin of republican States in other parts of the world." *Election Sermon*, p. 27.

197

drawn from American sources,"[20] since industrial projects would then tend to generate secondary employment in forests, mines, and fields. This view was also held by Coxe and Hamilton.[21]

An example of the kind of industry that might appropriately deserve special governmental aid was shipbuilding. The personal skill of American shipwrights and the abundance of timber gave the nation a comparative advantage in ship construction, while the "commercial spirit" of American merchants fostered a demand for vessels. Moreover the nearness of fishing banks and the fact that most American agricultural products were sold in overseas markets also seemed to favor the growth of a merchant marine. Yet despite these propitious circumstances, there was no disposition to suppose that the maritime trades could be left to fend for themselves; fisheries, commerce, and shipbuilding, no less than manufactures, called for "due care and attention on the part of government."[22] Swan ranked "the labour of the cod-fisherman" next to that of the farmer "in point of utility" and urged that fishing and shipbuilding be given "every public encouragement,"[23] a view enthusiastically endorsed by Jeremy Belknap.[24] The Dutch, said Swan, had clearly demonstrated that fishing can contribute abundantly to national well-being and prosperity when vigorously assisted by the government.[25] Public policy, however, should never center on any single industry without considering the complementarity of occupations, for even though it is true that agriculture, fishing, and manufactures supply the "great staples" of the thirteen states, Pelatiah Webster said, it must be remembered that commerce is "the hand-maid of them all" and for that reason is equally deserving of governmental assistance.[26]

Although some branches of entrepreneurial activity in America had exhibited vigor and commendable enterprise,[27] others had not;

20. *Works*, VIII, 341–342.
21. Hamilton proposed a cohesive plan for the systematic development of manufactures, recommending bounties as the most effective kind of subvention. In much the same spirit, Coxe advocated "a rational and steady course of attention, private and public," rather than circumstantial or opportunistic protection. See Hamilton's *Political Papers* (McKee), p. xviii, and Coxe, *View of the United States*, pp. 55–56 [1794].
22. Coxe, *View of the United States*, pp. 99–100 [1790].
23. *National Arithmetick*, pp. 8–9 [1786].
24. *An Election Sermon*, p. 27 [1785].
25. *National Arithmetick*, p. 10 [1786].
26. We may consider agriculture, fishing, and manufactures, said Webster, "as the great sources of our wealth" and commerce "as the great conduit thro' which it flow." Hence "all these [employments] we ought in sound policy to guard, encourage, and increase as far as possible and load them with burdens and embarrassments as little as possible." *Political Essays*, p. 232 [1783].
27. "The merchants, navigators, fishermen, and shipbuilders of the United States may be safely affirmed to be four descriptions of our citizens, whose

one reason for this was that in foreign countries a "much stricter economy" and a correspondingly greater efficiency had emerged under governmental surveillance, a development which should serve as an object lesson for American legislators.[28] In the formulation of policy, international competition had to be kept in mind, inasmuch as it had profound effects upon American prosperity. If other countries gave assistance to particular industries, even great natural advantages would not permit American industries to compete internationally without some governmental aid. Moreover in all branches of enterprise, some planning was called for, and this should be undertaken with an appreciation of economic realities. Men like Coxe argued that any sound domestic economic development of the United States required very careful economic planning. Market towns should be deliberately located where enough water power would be available for manufacturing products ultimately needed by the agricultural hinterland, where fuel supplies would be adequate, and where transportation facilities would be ample.[29] In the majority of cases, the government would have to assume some responsibility for providing (or at least for maintaining) adequate transportation and communication facilities,[30] a task wholly appropriate to government since the benefits would presumably be shared in some degree by all members of society.

Specific functions of government would of necessity vary with time and circumstance. But the implications were that there could be no rational approach to particular problems unless agreement had been reached about the appropriateness of governmental intervention. In determining the proper areas of intervention, Webster, among others, repeatedly asserted that legislators should solicit the opinion of businessmen,[31] and this procedure was indeed followed by Alexander Hamilton when he sought information and advice from all parts of

---

industry is as uniformly energetic and well directed, as those of any country in the world." Coxe, *View of the United States,* pp. 356–357 [1792]. But in sharp contrast, agriculture was called the "most imperfectly conducted" occupation. Ibid., pp. 358, 359.

28. Ibid., p. 357.

29. Ibid., p. 401 [1793].

30. Belknap, *Election Sermon,* p. 26 [1785]; *The Federalist* (Lodge), XLII (Madison), 266–267 [1788].

31. Webster's reiterated contention that merchants should be consulted about all proposed legislation can be discounted somewhat when one recalls that Webster himself was a merchant. On the other hand, it reflects the dominant place of the commercial interest in a nonmanufacturing nation largely dependent on Europe for markets and for its supply of fabricated goods. See *Political Essays,* pp. 218, 219.

the country before writing his famous *Report on Manufactures.*[32] When Congress set about framing its first tariff law, it became clear that, as far as the theory underlying intervention was concerned, there was little dispute; general agreement had apparently been reached that one function of government should be to stimulate all nationally beneficial occupations and enterprises.[33] The great controversies in the Age of Washington arose from disagreements over which industries and occupations could properly be designated as nationally beneficial. Republicans denied that bankers or financiers came within that category or that industrialists of the Arkwright type would be socially and economically desirable,[34] and the sophisticated defense of the financial interest that Hamilton formulated only served to heighten the suspicions of his agrarian critics. In the meantime reactionary preachers and political arithmeticians like James Swan kept insisting that the first responsibility of government should be to suppress luxury[35] by regulating commerce and consumption. A realistic Congress, however, took a much broader view of government and business.[36]

The Furtherance of Agriculture

The central importance of agriculture in the American economy and the predominance of farmers in the social structure made a substantial measure of agreement about the claims of the agricultural interest for governmental assistance almost inevitable. The keynote was sounded by Jeremy Belknap: every country, he said, is furnished with some distinctive natural advantages; "to understand what these are and how they are to be improved, is a part of the business of wise and faithful rulers." Since America's "advantages" consisted primarily in its great abundance of agricultural resources, the furtherance of agricultural production was consequently conceived to be "a principal object of the legislator's care."[37] But although the production of foods, fibers, and staple raw materials best suited to American soil and climate should be stimulated, grandiose proposals

32. See Cole, *Industrial and Commercial Correspondence of Alexander Hamilton,* pp. xv–xxviii.
33. "When the trade, agriculture and mechanic arts, those great sources of not the wealth only, but even morality, of a country, are properly encouraged, the government is good." Pelatiah Webster, *Political Essays,* p. 195 [1781].
34. See above, chap. IV.
35. See Swan, *National Arithmetick,* pp. 21–22, 61–62; and Chandler Robbins, *A Sermon* (Boston, 1791), p. 31.
36. See below, chap. VIII.
37. *Election Sermon,* pp. 24–25 [1785].

for schemes to produce silk or wine should not be allowed to beguile farmers into squandering their labor or capital.[38] Among a welter of suggestions five varieties of governmental aid to agriculture had popular support: the improvement of agricultural techniques, the adoption of a proper program of land alienation, the enactment of commercial policies designed to help farmers, the provision of adequate agricultural credit, and the stimulation of domestic manufacturing with a view to increasing the market for agricultural products. A few words should be said about each of these respective policies.

The wasteful type of American agriculture which ultimately resulted in serious land erosion and soil exhaustion had already by 1790 become a matter of deep concern to many American citizens. Jefferson was particularly disturbed by the long-run consequences of the soil-exhausting tobacco cultivation, and he recommended cereal growing and animal husbandry as proper correctives.[39] Yet he apparently thought that example, rather than governmental direction, could be relied upon to restrain tobacco cultivation and to promote mixed farming. He attributed the "indifferent state" of American agriculture primarily to the abundance of land which tended, at least in the short run, to make soil-conserving techniques unprofitable.[40] Tench Coxe, in contrast, was far less willing to excuse the shortcomings of American farmers; in his opinion, the inefficiency of American agriculture had its origin in poor entrepreneurial direction. Soil exhaustion, inattention to fertilization, improper crop rotation, and unsatisfactory seeds—all these things he ascribed to the inertia and the stupidity of the farmers themselves,[41] regretfully concluding that the occupation which is "most precious in free governments" was "the least economically and attentively pursued."[42]

How could the government ameliorate this unhappy situation? Coxe, the Philadelphia businessman, argued that the development of manufactures would solve the problem by augmenting the domestic demand for farm products and, concurrently, by increasing the nation's supply of skillful entrepreneurs. A closer integration of industry and agriculture would result, and new norms of better business management would presently be extended to agriculture.[43] On the

38. *Necessaries; Best Product of Land*, p. 12.

39. *Notes on Virginia*, pp. 304–310 [1785]. See also, *Necessaries; Best Product of Land*, pp. 21, 13n [1776].

40. "In Europe the object is to make most of their land, labour being abundant: here it is to make the most of our labour, land being abundant." *Notes on Virginia*, p. 158.

41. *View of the United States*, p. 358 [1792].

42. Ibid., p. 359.

43. Ibid., pp. 13, 38, 301.

other hand, practical estate farmers like George Logan and John Beale Bordley believed that agricultural education held more certain promise. Bordley recommended the establishment of "pattern farms" to demonstrate better farming methods; he also proposed that "ingenious persons" be sent to Europe to observe the more advanced agricultural techniques practiced there, alert people who could, on their return, engage in an educational program designed to improve American farm practices.[44] Indirect aid to agriculture, such as for road building or for the encouragement of manufactures, would not, in his opinion, improve faulty methods of farming. But Bordley found to his dismay that most farmers did not share his enthusiasm for scientific agriculture, and he confessed that his plan for a state-supported agricultural society was rejected by the farmer legislators —"by husbandmen who were principally to be benefitted."[45]

Logan considered the minuscule size of American farms to be one of the causes for the wasteful and inefficient agricultural methods that prevailed. Farms ought to be no smaller than two hundred acres, he maintained, if progressive methods were to be employed.[46] Farming can never be systematic, he argued, if it is conducted by a "poor tenantry" or by farmer-owners who lack capital.[47] As contrasted with Jefferson, who favored subdivision of land so that the great majority of people could become landowners,[48] Logan advocated a system of

44. *Essays on Husbandry*, pp. 444, 445, 447 [1794]. These proposals ought not, perhaps, be ascribed wholly to Bordley. They were contained in a 1794 petition to the Pennsylvania legislature praying that a state-supported agricultural society be established. The petition came from the Philadelphia Agricultural Society and was prepared by George Clymer, Richard Peters, Timothy Pickering, and John Beale Bordley, although it seems likely that Bordley was the most active member of the group. The "broad and permanent" state society which was proposed should, in the opinion of the petitioners, endow professorships at the University of Pennsylvania and at the College of Carlisle, organize branch societies, establish "pattern farms," and finance representatives to be sent abroad to study European agricultural techniques. See Olive Moore Gambrill, "John Beale Bordley and the Early Years of the Philadelphia Agricultural Society," *Pennsylvania Magazine of History and Biography*, LXVI (October 1942), 410–439. For another proposal for governmental assistance for agricultural education, see the *Transactions of the New York Society for the Promotion of Agriculture, Arts, and Manufactures* (New York, 1794), pt. II, pp. xxxiii–xxxiv. In response to this proposal, the New York legislature, on April 12, 1792, appropriated £750 to be used for the payment of the salary of a professor of natural history, chemistry, and agriculture in Columbia College.

45. *Essays on Husbandry*, p. 449.

46. *Fourteen Agricultural Experiments*, p. 33 [1797]. "It is on the *larger*, not on the *smaller* farms we find a spirit of improvement, and a superiority of management to prevail."

47. Ibid., pp. 36–37. "The purses of the yeomanry are too weak, to carry on agriculture to their own profit, or to the advantage of the country." Ibid., p. 33.

48. *Works*, VII (Ford), 35 [1785].

commercial agriculture, dominated by businessmen "cultivating their own estates."[49] Such an agricultural system could be prudently and rationally coordinated by the government.[50] John Taylor of Caroline apparently shared this view: unlimited freedom for small farmers, sharecroppers, and plantation overseers, in his opinion, was mainly responsible for soil exhaustion. But without the aid of government this unfortunate situation could never be remedied,[51] and for that reason he urged his fellow-farmers to imitate the "maritime capitalists"[52] by forming a legislative lobby for "explaining respectfully to Congress" the proper kind of governmental aid that American agriculture needed.[53] George Washington advocated the establishment of a national agricultural society, and in a letter to Sir John Sinclair he made it perfectly clear that when the time was ripe for such an organization it ought to be given congressional aid.[54]

A second type of governmental intervention on behalf of agriculture had to do with land policy. Once land had been improperly farmed, almost irreparable injury resulted. The best way to guard against this, said the critics of American agriculture, would be to devise land policies that would promote efficient agriculture. To this end, land alienation should be supervised to keep the agricultural population near markets so that crops could be sold for cash, thereby allowing farmers to obtain enough capital to engage in soil-conserving agriculture. Freedom for the lumbering industry to leave its cutover lands in wretched condition generally meant that such lands would be withheld from agriculture, compelling farmers to go farther afield. Farmers who set about to make arable fields out of cutover land would have as much or more work to do as they would have had in clearing standing timber. But in cutover lands, there would be no compensation from timber or potash. Swan therefore proposed that cutover land be taxed into immediate agricultural use.[55] Pelatiah Webster recommended a solid, tier by tier, frontier settlement to prevent "speculators' islands" from pushing pioneer farmers farther inland.[56] His famous namesake condemned the indifference of legislators toward the fragmentation of land holdings,

49. *Fourteen Agricultural Experiments*, pp. 36–37 [1797].
50. Ibid., p. 41.
51. *Arator*, chap. VI [1813].
52. *Tyranny Unmasked*, p. 130 [1822].
53. *Arator*, p. 47 [1813].
54. *Letters from His Excellency George Washington President of the United States of America to Sir John Sinclair, Bart. M.P. on Agriculture, and Other Interesting Topics* (London, 1800), p. 30 [July 20, 1794].
55. *National Arithmetick*, pp. 18–19 [1786].
56. *Political Essays*, p. 494 [1781].

which was reducing the size of seaboard farms and forcing many farmers into a variety of subsistence agriculture incapable of providing them with enough revenues to maintain an efficient type of agriculture. This legislative shortsightedness, said Noah Webster, was driving hundreds of farmers, "poor and helpless, into an uncultivated wilderness."[57]

Since markets for most American farm products lay overseas, governmental assistance to agriculture called for the adoption of commercial policies designed to maximize the cash incomes of American farmers. The several states had attempted to meet this challenge by a complicated system of export regulations. But these laws, which sought primarily to maintain the goodwill of foreign buyers of American produce, were essentially defensive and protective; they did very little to increase the demand for American farm produce. A quest for more positive and aggressive policies divided American public opinion into two opposing camps. The advocates of *laissez-passer* alleged that complete freedom to import and export would maximize the foreign demand for American exports,[58] while the proponents of domestic manufactures urged that the old colonial custom of seeking overseas outlets for American farm products should be partially abandoned. Domestic industrial development, they argued, would provide a nearer, a more dependable, and, all in all, a more profitable outlet for a portion of American raw materials and foodstuffs.

That commercial policies should be designed to safeguard the prosperity of the predominant interest was too patent to be disputed,[59] but care obviously had to be exercised lest the enactment of commercial regulations would lead to retaliation by foreign countries which might have damaging effects upon American farm incomes. Jefferson believed that the best solution for this problem would be to make reciprocal arrangements with foreign nations,[60] and he therefore rejected as both dangerous and unwise the proposal of James Bowdoin that the United States should adopt a restrictive navigation law.[61] But whereas New England shipowners, operating in a region

57. *Collection of Essays*, pp. 329–330 [1790]. The seaboard objection to westward migration was not entirely impartial. The exodus of farmers into frontier regions often meant declining land values in marginal areas and decreasing real estate tax receipts for eastern towns, counties, and states.
58. See above, chap. VI, and George Logan, *Five Letters to the Yeomanry*, p. 28 [1792].
59. See, for example, Coxe, *View of the United States*, p. 8 [1789].
60. For an account of Jefferson's attempt to deal with this problem, see Hutcheson, *Tench Coxe*, p. 33.

which had few agricultural exports, lobbied for a drastic navigation policy designed to wrest the control of shipping out of British hands, merchants in the bread colonies realized that the commercial prosperity of New York, Philadelphia, and Baltimore was so intimately related to agriculture that commercial policies must perforce take primary cognizance of the agricultural interest.[62] The formulation of a satisfactory commercial policy, therefore, required some sort of a compromise that would be acceptable to farmers, shipowners, and merchants. How this was attempted legislatively will be explained in a subsequent chapter.[63]

Perhaps the most pressing problem of agriculture was the matter of agricultural credit. The persistence of primitive techniques, which Coxe condemned and Jefferson lamented, was to a very great degree the consequence of a scarcity of intermediate credit. This had long been a chronic problem, and the several colonial land-bank schemes had been abortive attempts to solve it. Following the traditional European banking customs, banks in Boston, Philadelphia, and New York restricted most of their lending to short-term commercial paper. They were neither willing nor able to make the longer term loans that farmers needed, and, as a result, farmer-legislators made persistent efforts to institute state-operated loan offices or other agencies capable of supplying farmers with much needed credit accommodations.

The best statement of the need for governmental provision of agricultural credit is found in the writings of William Barton.[64] His contention was that the fertility and extent of land had predestined agriculture to be the main source of wealth in the United States. But land can be productive only when labor-power is expended upon it. Since this expenditure of labor must be made before any return is available, a farmer must perforce depend upon "the instrumentality of credit" to "subsist him in the intermediate time."[65] More production, or more efficient production, necessarily requires a larger amount of credit, since it is only by an ability to "anticipate" the product of several years' labor that enlarged investments can judiciously be made in stock, tools, buildings, or any other kind of agricultural

61. *Observations upon the Necessity and Importance of the American Navigation Act.* For this history of the controversy in the Confederation Congress, see Edward C. Burnett, *The Continental Congress,* pp. 636ff.

62. See Pelatiah Webster, *Political Essays,* p. 216 [1783].

63. See below, chap. VIII.

64. *The True Interest of the United States and Particularly of Pennsylvania Considered.*

65. Ibid., p. 11.

capital.[66] Because commercial banks will not, or cannot, provide such intermediate credit,[67] the responsibility for providing it should be assumed by the government;[68] and it is very much to the advantage of the public that adequate credit facilities be made available to the agricultural classes. For unless farmers can expand their production, exports cannot increase, and hence the balance of trade will continue to be adverse, draining away the nation's precious money supply.[69] A system of public loan offices would not only obviate this difficulty, but would develop the nation's productive power and increase the incomes of farmers, thereby enabling the government to collect more taxes for other appropriate public functions.[70]

Barton was representative of a large group of persons that advocated governmental provision of agricultural credit. His idea was not a novel one; Franklin had enthusiastically endorsed such a scheme before the Revolution.[71] Moreover, loan offices had repeatedly been sponsored in the several state legislatures, and such an institution had actually been set up and operated with notable success in Pennsylvania. John Witherspoon, although conservative in most of his views, strongly urged the establishment of loan offices, pointing out, as Barton did, the inability of commercial banks to provide adequate long-term credit for farmers.[72] James Sullivan was equally insistent that the government ought to provide special borrowing facilities for farmers. He asserted that, except when land was appreciating, normal farming revenues were never large enough to permit farmers to pay the interest rates currently demanded by commercial banks.[73] Actually, because their paper did not suit the liquidity requirements of commercial banks, farmers seldom could borrow, and it was precisely for this reason that Sullivan supported a special system of credit at low interest rates. The history of American agriculture in the nineteenth and twentieth centuries has demonstrated that Sullivan was right.

66. Ibid., p. 12.
67. "The farmer, who is desirous of borrowing a little pecuniary capital toward enabling him to improve or cultivate his estate, cannot obtain a farthing from the Bank, on the security of his lands, be their value what they may: whilst the merchant, whose property is of the most precarious and delusive nature, may readily procure a fictitious capital to facilitate his importation of foreign merchandise." Ibid., p. 19.
68. Ibid., pp. 11, 12, 17–18.
69. Ibid., p. 19.
70. Ibid., pp. 17–18.
71. In his *Remarks on a Representation from the English Board of Trade to the King of Great Britain* [1764].
72. *Essay on Money*, pp. 46, 51, 52, 53 [1786].
73. *Path to Riches*, p. 66 [1792].

The discussion about the appropriateness of governmental intervention in behalf of agriculture centered therefore on such problems as soil exhaustion, land policy, commercial regulations, and agricultural credit. That the imposition of tariffs might constitute a form of agricultural assistance was only coyly, vaguely, and cautiously suggested. How much of this argument represented a dressing up of the protectionist program in order to forestall agrarian opposition cannot be known, but since agriculture was the predominant interest, the proponents of protection were necessarily compelled to represent their program as being beneficial to the farming group. Thus Hamilton in his *Report on Manufactures* contended that the establishment of manufactures would have "an immediate and direct relation to the prosperity of agriculture."[74] He predicted that domestic manufacturing plants would provide a steady market for raw materials such as hides, wool, or flax, and that meantime the expanding manufacturing population would simultaneously constitute a market for flour and meat.[75] Industrial development would also lead to the immigration of artisans, thus increasing the nonagricultural population[76] and widening the market for agricultural produce still more.

Hamilton promised, too, that manufactures would benefit farmers by eventually lowering the prices of manufactured goods, thereby helping to raise the real income of the agricultural classes by the joint influence of larger revenues and lower costs.[77] Home markets, moreover, would tend to reduce the fluctuations in prices which traditionally had characterized the export and import trades. Above all he insisted that any policy which would further the complementarity of occupations would tend to help all groups.[78] Full employment of every nonagricultural element within a nation's population, said Hamilton and Coxe, is the best recipe for the continued prosperity of farmers. Let adequate protection be afforded to manufactures, and the indirect advantages will make unnecessary any more specific assistance to agriculture. For a considerable part of the nineteenth century that became the belief not merely of industrialists but of a very sizable part of the American public.

74. *Political Papers* (McKee), p. 196 [1791].
75. Ibid., pp. 197, 198; see also Coxe, *View of the United States,* p. 301 [1792].
76. Ibid.
77. *Political Papers* (McKee), p. 226.
78. Ibid., p. 231; Coxe, *View of the United States,* pp. 13, 38 [1787]; William Findley, *Review of the Revenue System,* p. 61 [1794].

The Defense of an "Active" Foreign Trade

The essentially diplomatic unanimity of opinion about the appropriateness of governmental intervention on behalf of the agricultural
interest contrasts with the disagreement over governmental aid to
the commercial, the manufacturing, or the financial interests. This
diversity of views was vividly reflected in the discussion regarding the
kind of commercial policies that the new government should adopt.[79]
The formulation of commercial policy involved not only economic
but important political considerations; thus John Adams pointed
out that if the United States were to adopt a free-trade policy, it
would probably have "the most luxurious set of farmers that ever
existed" and yet would not be able to defend its seacoast "against
the insults of a pirate."[80] In his opinion the policy of the American
government should therefore be to develop a navy and a merchant
marine,[81] to "repel monopolies by monopolies," and to "answer prohibitions by prohibitions."[82] Hamilton admitted the theoretical benefits
of free trade, but took great pains to emphasize that the commercial
restrictions imposed on American goods by European governments
had seriously interfered with American commerce,[83] thereby making
manufactured goods scarce and expensive. Unless the government
intervened, the United States would continue to be a virtual colonial
adjunct of Britain, lacking the variety of occupations which national vigor and stability insistently demand. The basic issue, said
the proponents of commercial intervention, reduced itself to the
fundamental question of whether the new government should favor
an "active" foreign trade or resign itself to a "passive" variety of
commercial policy.

Throughout the annals of commerce, this was an old controversy.
In England, for example, much of the discussion of foreign trade
in the seventeenth and eighteenth centuries had centered on the
disadvantages to Britain resulting from a "passive" trade; indeed,
the chief purpose of the Navigation Laws had been to replace
"passive" foreign trade by an "active" one.[84] A nation with a "passive"
trade, it was alleged, is not truly independent: its access to markets

79. See below, chap. VIII.
80. *Works,* VIII, 380–381 [1786].
81. Ibid., VIII, 411.
82. Ibid., VIII, 383.
83. *Political Papers* (McKee), p. 201 [1791].
84. The best contemporaneous appraisal of this problem is to be found in
Malachy Postlethwayt's *Britain's Commercial Interest Explained and Improved*
(London, 1757), II, 381ff, and in Sir James Steuart's *Inquiry into the Principles*

is dependent on the shipping facilities of other nations. The prices
it receives for its exports are reduced by the factorage charged by
alien merchants; conversely its supply of imports, as well as the cost
of these imports, is externally regulated to maximize the revenues of
alien merchants, manufacturers, and shipowners, to say nothing of
foreign governments. Wise commercial policy must therefore replace
a "passive" foreign trade with an "active" one.

To a very large extent, the foreign trade of the American colonies
had been "passive," especially that of the tobacco and rice colonies.
British shipowners had dominated the trade of Virginia, Maryland,
and the Carolinas, and we have it on the authority of Jefferson that
by their control over the prices of exports and imports British merchants had succeeded in keeping southern planters bound down by
debts that "became hereditary from father to son for many generations," so that colonial planters "were a species of property annexed
to certain mercantile houses in London."[85] Although later on Jefferson
favored policies designed to replace a "passive" trade with an "active"
one, at the time of the Constitutional Convention he found the real
cause of the peonage of the southern planters in British credit extension. "I look forward," he wrote from Paris in 1787, "to the abolition
of all credit" as the "only remedy" for the adversities of the southern
planters.[86] Thus in the 1780s and 1790s Jefferson vigorously defended
a "passive" foreign trade, arguing that such a policy would permit
an essentially agrarian economic development and would ensure
that the United States would be populated by "cultivators of the
earth" whom he considered "the most virtuous and independent citizens."[87] Moreover, a "passive" foreign trade seemed to Jefferson the
best guarantee against embroilment in European wars. His support
of free trade, therefore, had as much political as economic inspira-

---

of Political Economy (London, 1767). Steuart's discussion of "active" versus
"passive" foreign trade can most readily be found in his collected Works (London, 1805), I, 247ff. For a critical account of a "passive" foreign trade, see
Heckscher, Mercantilism, II, 61ff. See also my Predecessors of Adam Smith,
pp. 203–204, 225–227.

85. Works (Federal Edition), V, 28 [1786]. British credit extension, said
George Logan, "has made the Farmer tributary to the Storekeeper, the Storekeeper to the Merchant of Philadelphia: the Merchant of Philadelphia to the
Merchant of Great Britain. The Credit thus given, can, at any time, be withdrawn; the Debts thus contracted, can, at any time, be demanded; and the
Peace and Comfort of a numerous Body of American Citizens are now, and
have long been, at the Mercy of the British Merchants." Letter to Citizens, pp.
15–16 [1800].

86. Works (Federal Edition), V, 308 [1786].

87. Notes on Virginia, p. 319 [1785].

tion; it was largely to facilitate a peaceful, agrarian development that he proposed that Americans should "leave to others to bring what we shall want, and to carry off what we can spare."[88]

Spokesmen for the mercantile and manufacturing interests, in sharp contrast, defended commercial policies that would make American foreign trade progressively "active." Thus, in *The Federalist,* Hamilton took great pains to explain how the commerce of a collection of disunited states would be harassed by foreign nations, and how certain "maritime nations," by confining America "to a passive commerce," would actually "prescribe the conditions of our political existence."[89] Were that to occur, Americans would then receive only "the first price" of their commodities and none of the profits of manufacture and trade; worse than that, the "unequaled spirit of enterprise, which signalizes the genius of the American merchants and navigators, and which is itself an inexhaustible mine of national wealth, would be stifled and lost."[90] James Bowdoin sounded an equally portentous warning: whenever a country allows its commerce to be carried on by foreigners, "its citizens become depressed and impoverished."[91] It was presumably to obviate such an eventuality that the "merchants and traders" of Portsmouth, New Hampshire, petitioned Congress that a law be enacted "for the establishment of the foreign trade of the United States upon principles of reciprocal benefit, becoming the dignity of a free and independent nation."[92]

The leading advocates of an American navigation policy designed to exclude foreigners from the American carrying trade were James Bowdoin, Jr., and Tench Coxe. Before the Constitutional Convention, when it seemed unlikely that the several states would ever be willing to delegate control over commerce to the Confederation Congress, Governor Bowdoin of Massachusetts had attempted to persuade the states, one by one, to institute navigation laws modeled on those of

88. Ibid.
89. *The Federalist,* XI (Lodge), 63–64 [1787].
90. Ibid., p. 64.
91. "Virginia, the two Carolinas, and Georgia, afford an example in point, where English and Scotch merchants and factors carry on the commerce, and retire to their native country, with the wealth which they thereby acquire, to the injury of those states." *Opinions respecting Commercial Intercourse,* p. 43 [1797]. That this view was shared by southerners is attested by the remarks of Aedanus Burke in Congress on February 3, 1790. He urged the exclusion of "European merchants and factors of merchants, who come with a view of remaining so long as will enable them to acquire a fortune, and then they leave the country, and carry off all their property with them. These people injure us more than they do us good. . . . I can compare them to nothing but leeches. They stick to us until they get their fill of our best blood, and then they fall off and leave us." *Annals of Congress,* 1st Cong., p. 1156.
92. Ibid., pp. 994–995 [March 26, 1790].

Great Britain. A decade later, his son urged the new government, which now had the power to regulate commerce, to adopt a restrictive navigation law, promising that such a policy would turn the trade balance in America's favor, increase employment in the seaboard states, stabilize mercantile profits, and make the United States economically as well as politically independent.[93] Tench Coxe was equally convinced of the desirability of confining all imports either to American ships or to the vessels of countries that produced the imported commodities. He supported the idea of a complete American monopoly of the coastwise trade, and he proposed that Congress should penalize, by discriminatory tonnage duties, all countries that restricted the free entry of American exports.[94] Only such retaliation, in his opinion, could break down the "charges, prohibitions, and exclusions" which shackled American commerce;[95] only such a policy could make possible the development of an "active" foreign trade.

Commerce is of such importance to a nation, said another Pennsylvanian,[96] that "on the right management of this great concern" depends not only the strength but the "respectability" of nations. Legislators must therefore "watch over its operations with an eagle eye"; above all, they must establish commercial policies that will benefit every major interest of the nation, not merely the merchants and traders.[97] Yet for all the praise of an active foreign trade, when more specific programs were called for, the spokesmen for the manufacturing interest indulged in poorly concealed special pleading. Thus Coxe, the ardent advocate of manufactures, proposed that imports should be progressively decreased until the amount imported from each foreign country had been equated with the amount exported to it.[98] This should not be done by "any precipitate or coercive means," but by the slow development of domestic manufacturing, since "it is a sound maxim of our political economy that so far as we cannot trade abroad, we shall certainly manufacture at home."[99] To nationalists like Coxe an "active" foreign trade was not enough;

93. *Opinions respecting the Commercial Intercourse between the United States of America, and the Dominions of Great Britain,* passim.

94. *View of the United States,* pp. 242–245; Hutcheson, *Tench Coxe,* pp. 33–34.

95. Ibid., pp. 240, 241, 249–250 [1791].

96. William Barton, *The True Interest of the United States,* p. 23.

97. Isaac Ledyard cautioned his countrymen to "look coldly on traders" since that part of the community "is already too numerous"; moreover, he alleged that merchants were primarily responsible for the unfavorable balance of trade. *Mentor's Reply to Phocion's Letter; with Some Observations on Trade* (New York, 1784), pp. 16–17.

98. *View of the United States,* p. 151 [1791].

99. *An Examination of the Conduct of Great Britain, respecting Neutrals* (Philadelphia, 1807).

public policy should be designed to foster manufacturing and thereby increase the demand not only for domestic raw materials but for capital and labor.

The Quest for Full Employment

The encouragement of manufactures could scarcely be defended as an appropriate public policy unless it could be shown that the domestic production of finished commodities would have beneficial effects on the community at large. The advocates of manufactures therefore concentrated their arguments on two main theses: that manufacturing would aid the agricultural interest by increasing the demand for raw materials and food, and that it would at the same time promote the prosperity of all other groups by ensuring the "full employment"[100] of the nation's population. It was primarily on these grounds that the architects of public policy recommended governmental action designed to encourage the launching of new manufacturing enterprises and to stimulate the development of manufactures already established.

The employment argument, which had played an influential part in British economic literature of the seventeenth and eighteenth centuries,[101] had been used in America before the Revolution by persons eager to justify new branches of enterprise. Jared Eliot, for example, promised that a domestic silk industry would be "of great advantage to the poor" because it would afford them employment. After the Revolution, when the exclusion of American ships from the West Indies had almost crippled the trade arrangements which had made it possible for the United States to finance the importation of manufactures, a strong protectionist sentiment, already nurtured by the wartime interruption of trade, produced a bewildering series of state protective laws. Advocates of domestic manufacturing seized the opportunity to bemoan the unemployment caused by importing foreign goods[102] and to assure their countrymen that only by the development of new industries under governmental patronage could an adequate volume of employment be maintained. Promoters of

100. This phrase, which was used by both Hamilton and Coxe, had reference to continuity of employment and to the utilization of the maximum number of persons in some kind of productive employment. It ought not be confused with the more precise meaning of "full employment" in Keynesian economic theory.

101. See Edgar S. Furniss, *The Position of the Laborer in a System of Nationalism* (Boston, 1920); Hecksher, *Mercantilism.*

102. "It is a shame," wrote James Swan, "that primers, spelling and other school books should be allowed to be imported from Great Britain, when so many of the printers in this State are forced to be idle." *National Arithmetick,* p. 20n [1786].

ambitious projects, like the S.M.U.,[103] made the most of this argument,[104] promising that a planned cluster of manufacturing enterprises would not only provide work for skilled artisans but would generate a far more important volume of secondary employment in commerce and agriculture.[105] In such semi-mechanized ventures, moreover, the effectiveness of human labor would be increased by utilizing "the potent elements of fire and water,"[106] thus bringing "an artificial force" to the aid of "the natural force of man."[107] This, in turn, would greatly increase and cheapen consumers' goods and greatly expand demand, thereby augmenting the need for more labor. Meantime, the employment argument was used by writers typified by James Swan whose ideals seem to have been complete autarky;[108] by the organizers of the early manufacturing societies, who favored the establishment of new industries so that all the people "may be honorably and usefully employed";[109] and by leaders of the early agricultural societies, who advocated the coordinated expansion of husbandry and domestic manufactures.[110]

More convincing than the rather obvious assertion that the establishment of manufacturing enterprises would create employment was the contention that manufacturing would provide work for persons hitherto unemployed, and that government subvention to new industries would therefore bring about the "full employment" of the nation's population. This thesis had been touched upon before 1791,[111]

103. For the history of this grandiose project, see Davis, *American Corporations,* I, 349–518, and Mitchell, *Alexander Hamilton,* II, 181–198.

104. See Coxe, *View of the United States,* p. 166 [1791].

105. Ibid., p. 166; Hamilton, *Political Papers* (McKee), pp. 188, 230 [1791].

106. Coxe, *View of the United States,* pp. 41–42 [1787].

107. Hamilton, *Political Papers* (McKee), p. 192 [1791].

108. *National Arithmetick,* passim [1786].

109. *The Constitution of the Germantown Society for Promoting Domestic Manufactures,* p. 5 [1790].

110. See the oration of Dr. S. L. Mitchell before the New York Society for the Promotion of Agriculture, Arts and Manufactures in the *Transactions,* I, 4 [1792]. See also Bordley, *Essays on Husbandry,* p. 374 [1794], and Logan, *Letter to Citizens,* p. 18 [1800].

111. Homemade cloth, said James Swan, can be made cheaper than factory-made cloth notwithstanding the economies of mass production simply because homemade cloth provides supplementary work for farm families "at seasons and hours, when nothing else would be done." *National Arithmetick,* p. 16 [1786]. The employment that new manufacturing enterprises will provide, said Tench Coxe, will prevent idleness, and thereby root out "vicious habits" and "wickedness" which are the inescapable concomitants of unemployment. *View of the United States,* p. 49 [1787]. Moreover, manufactures would make it possible for those persons "whom the decline of navigation has deprived of their usual occupations" to find remunerative work. Ibid., p. 37 [1787]. In contrast, Jefferson, after having made a study of American fisheries, concluded that the extension of maritime commerce offered the only practical solution of unemployment among fishermen. See Hutcheson, *Tench Coxe,* pp. 31–32.

213

but it was not until the appearance of Hamilton's *Report on Manufactures* that its full implications were demonstrated. Manufacturing enterprises, said the secretary of the treasury, "afford occasional and extra employment to industrious individuals and families, who are willing to devote the leisure resulting from the intermissions of their ordinary pursuits to collateral labors."[112] By means of handicraft manufactures, a farmer can augment his income "from the increased industry of his wife and daughters"; while in factories work would be provided by persons otherwise idle. Hamilton pointed out that four-sevenths of the employees in British cotton mills were women and children.[113] His erstwhile assistant Tench Coxe, who may well have had a hand in preparing the *Report on Manufactures,* also approved of child labor, arguing that factory employment would keep children from "rambling" and save them "from early temptations."[114] In addition to young people, "women, valetudinarians, and old men could be employed," and manufactures would furnish "greater scope for the diversity of talents and dispositions."[115] Every person would soon "find his proper element," and this circumstance would "call into activity the whole vigor of his nature." Labor in manufactures was said to have a double advantage over that expended in agriculture; not only was it "constant and regular" as contrasted with agricultural labor which was "periodical and occasional," but it provided workers with "a wider field to exertions of ingenuity."[116] By virtue of the premium that manufacturing placed on resourcefulness, Hamilton argued that labor used in manufacturing was actually more productive than that spent in agriculture; hence if public policy, as one of its goals, sought the maximization of output, governmental patronage to manufacturing enterprises had a further justification. The central thesis upon which Hamilton rested his case, however, was that the "establishment and diffusion of manufactures" would accomplish this end by the full employment of the nation's labor supply, since the effect of manufactures would be to make "the total mass of useful and productive labor, in a community, greater than it would otherwise be."[117]

The experience of Pennsylvania was cited as proof of the wisdom of giving encouragement to manufacturing enterprises. Coxe claimed that at least one-fourth of the adult male workers in Philadelphia

112. *Political Papers* (McKee), p. 193 [1791].
113. Ibid., p. 194.
114. *View of the United States,* p. 55 [1787].
115. Hamilton, *Political Papers* (McKee), p. 195 [1791].
116. Ibid., p. 183 [1791].
117. Ibid., p. 187 [1791].

were engaged in manufacturing[118] and that several inland towns in Pennsylvania had an even higher proportion "of manufacturers." He attributed the prosperity of Lancaster in particular to the employment which manufacturing had provided; for here was a community "fifty-six miles from a sea port and ten from any practised boat navigation" where 234 out of 700 families lived by manufacturing.[119] The progress of manufactures had been so rapid, said Coxe, that a labor shortage had already emerged, leading to the immigration of artisans from abroad and to the introduction of laborsaving machinery.[120] Four years earlier, James Swan had called the attention of Massachusetts citizens to the example that Pennsylvania had set, attributing the gains which that relatively young state had made in population growth to its foresight in encouraging manufactures.[121]

But the secondary employment that domestic manufactures would generate in agriculture, mining, or forestry was heralded as even more important than the actual work involved in fabricating finished goods. Distilling and brewing would increase the demand for grain,[122] since "ardent spirits and malt liquors are, next to flour, the two principal manufactures of grain";[123] for that reason the reservation of the home market for American brewers and distillers was recommended as both "practical and desirable." Likewise the prohibition of the importation of nails, edged tools, and builders' hardware was urged, because all the raw materials for their manufacture were available;[124] the same argument was employed to justify a proposed prohibition of the import of coarse woolen cloth.[125] The use of imported mahogany was condemned in view of the availability of walnut, maple, and birch lumber out of which to make furniture,[126] while the manufacturing of linseed oil, starch, leather, linen, rope, earthenware, and hats was defended in terms of the benefits which domestic processing would confer upon the raw material producers.[127] As the frontier moved further away from the seaboard, the advantages that manufactures would give to the primary industries would presumably increase, since the creation of localized markets for food and raw

118. *View of the United States,* p. 228 [1791].
119. Ibid., p. 312 [1792].
120. Ibid., pp. 63–64 [1790].
121. *National Arithmetick,* pp. 45–46 [1786].
122. See Coxe, *View of the United States,* p. 15 [1787], pp. 107–108 [1791].
123. Hamilton, *Political Papers* (McKee), p. 258 [1791].
124. Swan, *National Arithmetick,* p. 41 [1786]; see also Hamilton, *Political Papers* (McKee), p. 250 [1791].
125. Swan, *National Arithmetick,* p. 63 [1786].
126. Ibid., p. 64.
127. Coxe, *View of the United States,* p. 15 [1787].

materials[128] would make it unnecessary for frontiersmen "to draw raw materials through . . . bad roads" and to sacrifice half or two-thirds of their value for carting and transoceanic freight.[129] In contrast, the demand for domestic manufactures would result in higher prices for farm, forest, and mine products, thus stimulating greater output and a larger volume of employment. Far from diverting labor from agriculture, said the advocates of industrialization, the domestic production of manufactured goods would increase employment on farms by making farming more profitable,[130] even though, by stimulating immigration, manufactures might well increase the number of persons embarking upon agricultural pursuits.[131]

Inasmuch as the intensity of agriculture always depends on the adequacy of markets, Hamilton insisted that domestic manufactures must perforce benefit the agricultural interest. A home market would be more reliable since it would not be subject to closure either by war or by the political machinations of foreign powers.[132] Instead it would be a steady and permanent market, one that would grow in proportion to the "natural" rate of industrialization. This natural tendency toward industrialization, however, cannot assert itself in the face of "adventitious barriers" which interfere with "a successful competition." If foreign countries, either as a consequence of advantages arising from experience, skill, or momentum, or as a result of tactical advantages acquired by "artificial policy" should prevent the United States from experiencing this natural drift toward industrialization, it would become the proper function of government to help manufacturers to overcome the obstacles which were impeding industrialization. Because foreign nations were underselling American manufacturers and interfering with the "natural" and normal process of industrialization, Hamilton urged Congress to employ the machinery of government to counteract these untoward influences, confidently predicting that once manufactures were firmly rooted in the United States, they would become equal to or more efficient than their European counterparts.[133]

128. Ibid., p. 53.
129. Ibid., pp. 298, 380; see also Hamilton, *Political Papers* (McKee), p. 229.
130. Coxe, *View of the United States*, pp. 41–42 [1787].
131. Hamilton, *Political Papers* (McKee), p. 195 [1791].
132. Ibid., pp. 196–198, 202, 224–225.
133. Ibid., pp. 205–206, 210 [1791]. Five years earlier, James Swan had advanced the infant-industry argument as justification for his proposal that Massachusetts should prohibit the entry of farm tools, hinges, bolts, nails, pots, kettles, brass products, earthenware, pewter, furniture, candles, ships' gear, rope, and loaf sugar. If the importation of these commodities were forbidden, said Swan, "they would be furnished here, very soon, as cheap as they could be

The Safeguarding of Economic Independence

None of the proposals concerning agriculture, commerce, and industry can be divorced from a preconception that pervaded American political thought in the Age of Washington, a widespread belief that policy should be deliberately pointed toward nationalistic goals. The case for an "active" foreign trade, for example, was by no means argued exclusively in terms of the immediate benefits which an American merchant marine would confer upon American merchants, farmers, or consumers; it rested partly on a conviction that political independence should be paralleled by an appreciable degree of self-sufficiency. This instinctive urge in the direction of autarky was, of course, reinforced by the discomfiture that certain groups of people and certain regions had suffered not only under the British colonial system but in the Confederation Era. Planters deep in debt to British merchants or factors, for instance, sought to escape from their fiscal peonage, while American merchants or manufacturers, faced with persistent, indeed often crushing, British competition, hoped to overcome the disadvantages under which they operated. Nor should it be forgotten that a considerable degree of organic economic solidarity was recognized to be indispensable if the political unity of the new nation was to survive. Tench Coxe said such matters could not be left entirely to "the piety of American patriotism"; indeed nationalistic sentiment might prove to be evanescent unless it was propagated "by the interchange of raw materials, provisions, fuel, and manufactures."[134] Only by mutual interdependence of regions and interests could the union of the states be permanently cemented.

---

from Europe." *National Arithmetick*, pp. 19–20 [1786]. William Barton was equally confident that if restrictions were laid upon foreign manufactures and continued "until the [unfair] competition, occasioned by the disparity in prices in the foreign and domestic articles of the same kind, shall be destroyed," manufactures could develop in the United States despite the high American level of wages. *The True Interest of the United States*, pp. 27–28 [1786]. James Bowdoin, who favored prohibitions as enthusiastically as Swan did, seems to have ignored the question of whether American costs of production would ultimately be as low or lower than European costs. *Opinions respecting Commercial Intercourse*, p. 39 [1797]. In one of his essays, Coxe favored rather cautious experimentation, advocating governmental assistance to "one branch of manufacture at a time" so that the cost-reducing tendencies of industrial maturation could be tested. *View of the United States*, p. 222 [1791]. Elsewhere, however, Coxe recommended the establishment of a whole group of manufacturing enterprises, all to be protected by moderate duties. See his plan for a cluster of thirty-five industries in a unified market-manufacturing town. Ibid., pp. 388–392 [1793].

134. *View of the United States*, p. 320 [1792].

Advocates of an "active" foreign trade, of a home market for raw materials and food, or of agricultural and industrial self-sufficiency could appeal to the deep-seated resentment against foreign, especially British, business interests. Thus, even as late as 1800, George Logan complained that American cities were "filled with British Subjects, who conduct our trade; with British Agents, who drain our wealth; and with British Politics, British Interests, and British Influence."[135] One goal of public policy should therefore be to "lessen these enormous Evils" and "to render our Citizens . . . really as they ought to be, independent of Foreign Countries."[136] Noah Webster had said as much on the eve of the Constitutional Convention,[137] while, ten years later, James Bowdoin demanded that American citizens "be protected in their professions and callings, against foreign interference."[138] Madison's attitude can also be described as essentially nationalistic;[139] his legislative recommendations were designed to protect American farmers and businessmen from vassalage to foreign interests.[140] In much the same way, Bordley's economic philosophy was tinctured with nationalism; he warned his countrymen that Poland ought to be an object lesson to America, pointing out that countries which failed to develop manufactures ultimately became the satellites of foreign nations.[141]

Fear of foreign influence did not, however, bring agreement about public policy. Thus, although John Taylor of Caroline assailed foreign banking penetration,[142] charging that by this means Great Britain was able to tyrannize over the rank and file of American farmers,[143] he was nevertheless the bitter foe of nationalists like Coxe and Hamilton who insisted that America could escape from foreign eco-

135. *Letter to Citizens*, pp. 16–17 [1800]. See also his *Address before the Tammany Society*, pp. 7, 8–9 [1798].
136. *Letter to Citizens*, p. 17.
137. "Instead of a free commerce with all the world, our trade is everywhere fettered with restraints and impositions, dictated by foreign interest; and instead of pouring wealth into our country, its present tendency is to impoverish the merchant and the public." The remedy for this unhappy situation, in Webster's opinion, was a union of the states so that a legislative program dedicated to national welfare could be set in motion. *Collection of Essays*, pp. 82–83 [1787].
138. *Opinions respecting Commercial Intercourse*, p. 39 [1797].
139. See Spengler, *The Political Economy of Jefferson, Madison, and Adams*, pp. 16–17.
140. See, for example, *Works*, pp. 341–342.
141. *Essays on Husbandry*, pp. 373–374 [1794].
142. See Mudge, *The Social Philosophy of John Taylor*, p. 88.
143. "The degree of influence by British capital over American banks, cannot be estimated. Whatever it is, a corresponding degree of effect must follow. It can diminish the prices of our exports both here and in Britain, and increase the English profit in re-exportation." *Principles and Policy*, p. 384 [1814].

218

nomic dependency only by balancing agriculture and industry, and by establishing central financial institutions which could provide American entrepreneurs with adequate credit accommodations.[144] But Taylor's brand of agrarian nationalism proved hard to defend, especially when war between France and Britain contracted the sea lanes and made foreign commerce both expensive and hazardous. Economic independence, if it was ever to be realized, called for the encouragement of key industries, and Hamilton's realistic understanding of the nexus between politics and economics stands out fully as vividly here as in his financial policies. Because, under existing political circumstances, the United States could not trade with European countries on equal terms, he said, Americans would presently find themselves the "victims of a system"[145] unless the power of the federal government was used to safeguard the interests of American farmers, merchants, and manufacturers. Hamilton therefore declared himself in favor of policies that would diversify American enterprises, asserting that a nation which combines manufacturing and agriculture is both more prosperous[146] and more secure[147] than a country primarily agricultural. In his opinion, the central issue confronting the new government was not whether American energies should be divided between industry and agriculture; it was simply a question of selecting appropriate means whereby a reasonable degree of economic autonomy could be achieved.

The Choice of Means

Ever since the Revolution the problem of how the United States could achieve national economic independence had been under discussion, but no agreement had been reached as to whether this called for governmental restrictions on foreign goods or for positive governmental aids to American entrepreneurs. The means, therefore, seemed to have been reduced to two main categories: "duties on imported commodities [or] bounties on domestic manufactures."[148] In this context, "duties" comprehended all impositions on foreign goods whether prohibitive or merely protective, while "bounties" covered all

144. As early as 1792, Coxe declared that the United States had made notable progress in emancipating itself from dependence on British merchants and factors. *View of the United States*, p. 339.

145. *Political Papers* (McKee), p. 201 [1791].

146. Ibid., pp. 224, 226.

147. Ibid., p. 227. "Not only the wealth but the independence and security of a country appear to be materially connected with the prosperity of manufactures."

148. Barton, *The True Interest of the United States*, pp. 27–28 [1786].

grants of money, premiums, or tax exemptions. The pamphlet literature appears to favor "bounties," although the complex series of state tariffs would seem to indicate a definite legislative preference for "duties."[149]

Bounties had been employed time and again by the British government to foster new colonial enterprises, and this may explain the enthusiasm for them by pamphleteers in the Confederation and Constitutional eras. At any rate, Swan,[150] Ledyard,[151] Belknap,[152] and Barton[153] warmly recommended the use of bounties in the 1780s, as did Bordley,[154] Coxe,[155] Bowdoin,[156] and Hamilton[157] in the 1790s. It was understood that domestic producers might enjoy a preferential situation as a result of either import duties or the payment of "pecuniary bounties,"[158] and that it was possible to employ both means at the same time.[159] Either device would help American businessmen to overcome the disadvantages resulting from inexperience or from high wages; and it was asserted that England had achieved its industrial efficiency by the judicious use of import duties and bounties.[160]

Of all the means available for encouraging new enterprises, Hamilton thought bounties were the best and the "most efficacious."[161] They provided "positive and direct" encouragement to new ventures by "increasing the chances of profit, and diminishing the risks of loss." As contrasted with import duties, they would not raise the price of

149. A general view of the state tariffs is given in chap. VIII below.
150. Swan proposed that import duties on salt should be collected and the receipts used for paying bounties to domestic salt makers. He also recommended that bounties be paid for the production of nails, farming tools, iron, wool, linen, hemp, wine, cider, barilla, and duck. *National Arithmetick*, pp. 17, 31–32, 33–34, 44 [1786].
151. *Mentor's Reply to Phocion's Letter*, p. 16 [1784].
152. *An Election Sermon*, p. 25 [1785].
153. *The True Interest of the United States*, p. 28 [1786].
154. Bordley recommended bounties on "plain clothing and blankets, arms and ammunition," promising that such a policy "would soon cause those essentials to abound in the country." *Essays on Husbandry*, pp. 378–379 [1794].
155. See Hutcheson, *Tench Coxe*, pp. 100–101 [1791].
156. Bowdoin alleged that the Massachusetts bounty on whale oil had saved the whale fisheries "from total ruin" when Great Britain imposed such high duties on American whale oil that they were equivalent to a prohibition. *Opinions respecting Commercial Intercourse*, p. 24n [1797].
157. *Political Papers* (McKee), pp. 235–240 [1791].
158. See Ledyard, *Mentor's Reply*, p. 16; Barton, *True Interest*, p. 28; Hamilton, *Political Papers*, p. 129. "What are all the duties on imported articles," asked Hamilton, "but so many bounties?"
159. Barton, *The True Interest of the United States*, p. 28. Barton cited Sir James Steuart in support of his argument.
160. Belknap, *An Election Sermon*, p. 25; Swan; *National Arithmetick*, p. 32.
161. *Political Papers* (McKee), p. 235 [1791].

commodities to the disadvantage of consumers; indeed, bounties might lead to lower prices inasmuch as any imported commodities would have to be sold in competition with subsidized domestic goods. Consequently, whereas high import duties might easily make protected articles scarce, bounties would make goods abundant.[162] Furthermore, bounties could be used to stimulate not merely new industrial enterprises, but new agricultural ventures hitherto unprofitable; import duties, in contrast, could not benefit an agricultural nation which had an export surplus except indirectly. Bounties, on the other hand, might foster the production of new raw materials, thus providing domestic manufacturers with supplies near at hand.

The best policy, in Hamilton's opinion, would be to coordinate import duties and bounties by levying duties on fabricated materials and using the receipts from the customs to pay bounties on domestically produced raw materials. Manufacturers would then be able to launch business ventures without fear of ruinous competition, while farmers would be able to engage in new branches of agriculture with the assurance of a home market.[163] A double advance would thereby be made in the direction of national economic independence, while concurrently a larger volume of employment would be provided in both industry and agriculture. The major objection to bounties —that they involved "giving away the public money without an immediate consideration"—Hamilton described as untenable, since every subvention (and import duties were no exceptions) involved a "temporary expense."[164] The only issue was whether this "temporary expense" should be paid directly out of public funds or whether it should be indirectly collected from consumers by the increased cost of protected commodities.[165] Hamilton favored forthright and unconcealed subvention. "There is," he informed Congress in his *Report on*

162. Ibid., p. 236.
163. Ibid., pp. 237–238.
164. Ibid., pp. 238–239.
165. A third possibility—that private societies should pay bounties—had been suggested by Swan. In Massachusetts no state funds had been made available for the payment of bounties except those appropriated for bounties on whale oil and for a "clock-jack manufactory." In view of the unwillingness or the inability of the legislature to subsidize new industries, Swan proposed that a statewide "society" be established, with county branches, to collect funds throughout the Commonwealth for the payment of bounties. *National Arithmetick*, pp. 32–33 [1786]. When societies of this type were later organized, they soon realized their inability to embark upon any program calling for the payment of bounties, and confined their aid for new ventures to the awarding of premiums. They did, however, urge state legislatures to subsidize new enterprises by means of bounties. Thus, the New York Society for the Promotion of Agriculture, Arts, and Manufactures recommended that the New York legislature should pay bounties on maple sugar. See *Transactions*, II, vii [1794].

Manufactures, "no purpose to which public money can be more beneficially applied than to the acquisition of a new and useful branch of industry; no consideration more valuable than a permanent addition to the general stock of productive labor."[166] Nor can there be, continued Hamilton, any constitutional objection to the payment of bounties, since the Congress has the responsibility for providing for the general welfare; hence he concluded that "there seems to be no room for a doubt that whatever concerns the general interests of learning, of agriculture, of manufactures, and of commerce" is a legitimate object of congressional subvention.[167]

Duties on imports, which were destined to become the characteristic form of American protection to new industries, received scant attention in the eighteenth-century pamphlet or tract literature. Duties were, to be sure, often bracketed with bounties as appropriate means of encouragement, but, except for Hamilton's *Report on Manufactures,* there was apparently no searching analysis of their merits and shortcomings. This omission may have been due to the familiarity of most people with import duties. It is quite clear, from the maze of state tariffs, that state legislators had consistently favored the use of import duties. Hamilton made this point when he said that protective duties were "sanctioned by the laws of the United States," and he stressed that they were so validated because they had "the additional recommendation of being a source of revenue."[168] But in his appraisal of bounties, the kind of subsidy he preferred, Hamilton took pains to demonstrate the disadvantages of import duties, especially their tendency to raise prices and to distribute the cost of subvention unequally among consumers. He did commend the outright prohibition of imports, however, but only in those cases where an industry was mature enough and "in so many hands, as to insure a due competition, and an adequate supply on reasonable terms."[169] Nevertheless, he had misgivings about the use of export prohibitions on raw materials of manufactures. Resort to this device, he cautioned, ought to be made "with great circumspection," since such a policy might "keep down the price of the produce of some other branch of industry," generally of agriculture, thus compelling one interest to pay the cost of subsidizing another interest.[170]

166. *Political Papers* (McKee), p. 238 [1791].
167. Ibid., p. 240.
168. Ibid., p. 234.
169. Ibid.
170. Ibid., p. 235. He admitted that "those who are injured, in the first instance, may be, eventually, indemnified by the superior steadiness of an extensive domestic market." Nevertheless he considered the use of export prohibitions imprudent and recommended that they "be indulged with a sparing hand."

Minor means comprehended under the generic category of "bounties" included tax exemptions for new enterprises and premiums awarded for conspicuous technical or productive effort. Neither device could have any great influence, although they might encourage entrepreneurs to undertake new ventures or to persist in them. The most promising form of tax exemption, and the one which came into general use, was the placing of certain necessary raw materials on a free list. The wisdom of such a policy, said Hamilton, should be obvious, since "it can hardly ever be advisable to add the obstructions of fiscal burthens to the difficulties which naturally embarrass a new manufacture."[171] In analyzing this problem, however, Hamilton does not seem to have appreciated the difficulties that were to emerge; the efforts of manufacturers to have hemp placed on the free list, for example, led to bitter opposition of the agricultural interest,[172] as did the subsequent attempt to admit raw wool free of customs.[173] In the case of those raw materials which were not produced within the United States, no criticism arose over exempting them from customs duties. The federal government proceeded to follow the precedents established by the state tariffs,[174] and accordingly placed a number of essential raw materials on the free list.

Drawbacks constituted another form of immunity from import duties. Here the tax exemption was contingent upon the reexportation of the materials after they had been fabricated. The purpose of this device, which had been used by several states and which was to be employed by the federal government, was to permit American manufacturers to compete in foreign markets, thus increasing the scale of operations of American firms. But only to the extent that the tax remission succeeded in creating or widening foreign markets for American-manufactured goods could drawbacks encourage the development of new industries. Drawbacks must therefore be accounted a rather unimportant means for stimulating new enterprises.

The same thing may be said about premiums, even though there seems to have been great enthusiasm for them in the 1780s and 1790s. As contrasted with bounties (which would be paid for

171. Ibid., p. 241.
172. See below, pp. 241–242, 244–245.
173. See Frank W. Taussig, *Tariff History of the United States* (New York, 1923), pt. I.
174. Other varieties of tax exemption were also suggested as means of stimulating new branches of production. Swan proposed that imported sheep should be tax exempt in order to increase the supply of wool, and in a rather vague passage he recommended that all "profits" earned in those industries which the government sought to encourage should be tax exempt. See *National Arithmetick*, pp. 17, 44 [1786].

stipulated quantities of goods produced), premiums would be given as rewards for unusual output or for the production of commodities of noteworthy quality. Swan had proposed that Massachusetts award premiums to fishermen who returned with the first "full fare" of mackerel or the largest quantity of salmon in a season,[175] and to farmers who raised the greatest number of sheep or the largest amount of flax.[176] Robert Bell, although he objected strenuously to most forms of governmental intervention, declared that "experience had proven the wisdom of giving premiums to manufacturers in order to foster diligence and ingenuity";[177] while Andrew Lee thought every service to the nation should be "rewarded at the common expense," recommending premiums for all useful inventions and for important improvements in manufacture or husbandry.[178] Such rewards, said John Beale Bordley, ought to be in proportion to the usefulness of the services rendered;[179] accordingly he suggested that societies formed to promote agriculture or manufactures should advise legislators as to how a suitable premium policy should be framed.[180] Tench Coxe proposed that Congress reserve "a million acres of choice western lands" to be used "as the basis of a fund" out of which premiums could be paid,[181] while Swan recommended that "certain titles and offices of honor, might be conferred on those who should be found most industrious in promoting agriculture and manufactures."[182]

The main advantage of premiums lay in the double appeal they made to vanity and acquisitiveness, rendering them, as Hamilton pointed out, "a very economical means of exciting the enterprise of a whole community."[183] In such a program the cooperation of

175. Ibid., p. 9.
176. Ibid., p. 17. Although Swan called these rewards "bounties," they would actually have been premiums.
177. *Illuminations for Legislators and for Sentimentalists* (Philadelphia, 1784), p. 4. Proposals of this kind prepared the way for one of the very important innovations in governmental administrative policy adopted by the First Congress, namely the adoption of a patent system under the provisions of which inventors could be rewarded for their ingenious discoveries by a temporary monopoly, the assumption being that the monopoly gains from the sale, rental, or use of a new invention would be tantamount to a "premium." For the early history of this administrative innovation see Leonard D. White, *The Federalists: A Study in Administrative History* (New York, 1948), pp. 136–137.
178. *The Origin and Ends of Civil Government* (Hartford, 1795), p. 15.
179. *Essays on Husbandry,* p. 378n [1794].
180. Ibid., p. 439.
181. *View of the United States,* p. 48 [1787]; see also, Hutcheson, *Tench Coxe,* p. 101.
182. *National Arithmetick,* p. 45 [1786].
183. *Political Papers* (McKee), p. 241 [1791].

private societies could also be enlisted,[184] so that an even greater stimulus to innovation might be given by virtue of the interaction of "sound policy and public spirit."[185] The societies could be especially helpful in ascertaining the productive techniques employed in other countries and in familiarizing American producers with them.[186] But Hamilton doubted that private societies could ever be very influential because their funds would usually be too limited to sustain any continuous program. He therefore concluded that although private societies were probably useful, in the United States, where large fortunes were relatively few, "the public purse must supply the deficiency of private resource."[187]

When Hamilton presented his *Report on Manufactures,* Congress had already made its initial decision about the means it would employ to further agriculture, commerce, and industry. Main reliance had been placed not on bounties but on import duties,[188] and despite Hamilton's advice, tariffs became the typical means which the federal government was to utilize. Import duties did, to be sure, have the virtue of providing the government with much needed revenue. But against that must be set their chief disadvantages: the concealment of the cost of subvention, and the risk that a tariff system might make it possible for relatively inefficient producers to enjoy a measure of monopoly control inside a formidable customs barrier.

184. See Logan, *Letter to Citizens,* pp. 22–28 [1800].
185. Coxe, *View of the United States,* p. 36 [1787].
186. Ibid., pp. 47–48; see also *The Laws and Regulations of the Massachusetts Society for Promoting Agriculture* (Boston, 1793), p. iv.
187. *Political Papers* (McKee), p. 276 [1791].
188. See below, chap. VIII.

VIII

The First Congressional Definitions of the Role of Government

The Congress shall have Power To lay
and collect Taxes, Duties, Imposts and
Excises, to pay the Debts and provide for
the Common Defense and general welfare of the United States; but all Duties,
Imposts and Excises shall be uniform
throughout the United States.

Constitution of the United States

The Urgency of a Revenue-yielding Tariff

O N July 4, 1789, Congress passed the first of a long series of tariff acts, thereby establishing precedents that were to influence the American enterprise system profoundly. That the tariff act was passed on the anniversary of the Declaration of Independence was entirely accidental.[1] The heat of the summer and the weariness caused by three months of debate no doubt had more to do with fixing the date when compromises would be acceptable than did any patriotic impulses. But the fact remains that the first tariff was passed on July 4, thus giving generations of orators ample justification for tariff speeches on that hallowed day—the birthdate of two venerated American institutions.

From the time the First Congress convened until the act was finally passed, the tariff issue dominated almost every congressional debate. Petitions for patents or copyrights were laid on the table and neglected; discussions of western lands, of monopolies, and even of funding were cut short. But there was ample reason for this procedure: unless adequate revenue could be obtained promptly, the new government could not long survive. It should not be assumed, however, that fiscal considerations held exclusive sway, for despite Madison's praise of a system of liberty, the great majority of Congressmen favored some measure of protection. The major "interests" were ably represented in Congress: agriculture, commerce, manufacturing, and finance, as well as many subdivisions of each occupational or business segment. Distillers and brewers, candle makers, steel manu-

---

1. Although the 4th of July was celebrated in the 1780s, it was not a holiday. Probably the reverence we pay was not shared by the Founding Fathers; many of them no doubt recalled that the Declaration was actually signed, not on July 4, 1776, but on August 2. For the history of the signing of the Declaration, see Burnett, *The Continental Congress.*

facturers, and shipbuilders, to say nothing of specialized merchants, asserted their respective claims to protection or to other forms of governmental patronage.

The debates veered unpredictably day after day from a discussion of "duties on imports" to an examination of the need for "tonnage duties." The two legislative objectives were gradually separated, however, so that whereas the tariff act became law on July 4, the tonnage act was not finally passed until July 20. Both laws drew heavily upon precedents which legislation in the several states had established. This was especially true of the tariff act; indeed the last refuge of a harried proponent of a particular tariff rate was always an attempt to prove how beneficent a particular degree of protection had been to some "interest" or other in his state. Meantime the urgency of a revenue-yielding tariff also compelled Congress to borrow heavily from the states' experiences with tariffs. Therefore, the first tariff must be regarded partly as a synthesis of existing state tariffs and partly as a batch of compromises ultimately reached after weeks of bitter and rancorous debate. Nevertheless, it would be incorrect to conclude that the tariff and tonnage laws were devoid of underlying legislative theory; beneath the importunity of immediate problems can be found the interplay of the theory of interests, the theory of entrepreneurial freedom, and a philosophy of intervention.

Outwardly, the first American tariff seemed to be entirely forthright. Entitled "An Act for Laying a Duty on Goods, Wares, and Merchandise Imported into the United States," it asserted, in its preamble, that it was designed to collect revenue to support the government and to pay the debts of the United States, although it was also intended for "the encouragement and protection of manufactures."[2] Equally explicit were the duties to be imposed when the tariff became effective on August 1, 1789. But the real and peculiar quality of the tariff act, the one that was to project itself into the nineteenth and twentieth centuries, lay hidden in the admixture of specific and ad valorem duties; for here was an arrangement capable of infinite variation and of subtle revision, one that concealed immeasurable degrees of subvention to particular occupations, employments, and interests. The origin of this scheme of things can be attributed partly to state precedents, partly to the actual methods used in framing the first tariff, a process which the committee entrusted with drafting the law had hoped to speed up by providing the members of Congress with a list of articles appropriately dutiable. The members, presumably, had only to agree about the amounts

2. 1 *U.S. Laws*, 24–27, 1st Cong., 1st Sess., ch. 2 [July 4, 1789].

which should be filled in on the blank spaces opposite the articles. But there the debate began! Should Jamaica rum pay twenty cents or ten cents? Should porter pay thirty cents a dozen bottles or twenty cents? For articles less easy to measure or count, ad valorem duties had been proposed. Here questions arose over the justice of uniform rates for a miscellaneous group of articles, a problem ultimately solved by having five categories, paying 5, 7½, 10, 12½, and 15 percent respectively, and by designating still another group of articles as duty free. Finally there was the matter of drawbacks—provisions for the repayment of most of the duties on reexported commodities. And it was not long before the special provisions made for a drawback on salt, used for salting fish, led to a strong demand for the conversion of drawbacks into bounties.[3]

The Dead Hand of the State Tariffs

The general plan of the first tariff—the employment of specific and ad valorem duties, the imposition of higher rates of duty on luxuries, and the use of a free list—was borrowed from state experience. But a digest of state tariffs during the Confederation Era is very difficult to make; impost laws were frequently hidden away in general revenue acts covering taxes on lands, auctions, or tonnage. Moreover the distinction between imposts and excises was often vague and indefinite; liquor excise laws, for example, often included complicated discriminations against foreign-made beverages. The earliest state tariffs were primarily revenue measures; accordingly, the duties ranged from 1 to 3 percent on most imports, although a belief in the desirability of sumptuary legislation inspired higher duties on liquor, sugar, chocolate, tea, carriages, and other luxuries. South of Pennsylvania there is little evidence of protectionist objectives.[4] In contrast, the states north of Maryland, although they tended to regularize their tariffs around a basic 2½ percent duty, made numerous protectionist experiments, and the preambles to their impost laws contain frank avowals of intentions to stimulate certain industries. A particularly strong protectionist movement developed in the middle 1780s[5] in all the northern states except

3. See below, pp. 277–278.

4. Higher duties on cordage and hemp, as in the Virginia legislation of 1786, no doubt had protectionist intent, as did also the higher than average duties on rum from the northern states.

5. The rapidity with which this movement got underway is attested by the chronology of higher tariffs. Beginning with the Massachusetts law of July 1, 1784, there followed comparable legislation in New York on November 18, 1784, in Rhode Island in June of 1785, in Pennsylvania on September 20, 1785, and in New Hampshire on March 4, 1786.

Connecticut and New Jersey. As a consequence, detailed lists of specific duties appeared, presumed to be adequately protective to benefit certain domestic enterprises, while ad valorem duties rose to 15, 20, 22½, and 25 percent. The purpose of this legislative trend is well illustrated in the preamble to the Pennsylvania law of September 20, 1785, which was very honestly entitled "An Act to Encourage and Protect the Manufactures of This State by Laying Additional Duties on the Importation of Certain Manufactures Which Interfere with Them."[6] The Pennsylvania legislators asserted that when the war interrupted the importation of European goods, "divers useful and beneficial arts and manufactures" established themselves in Pennsylvania, and that the "artisans and mechanics" who undertook these new enterprises had helped to win the war. Partly out of gratitude to these artisans, and partly because "good policy" demanded the continuance of manufacturing, the legislators declared themselves in favor of duties high enough to ensure the well-being of domestic manufacturers, even though this might mean that domestic products would be more expensive than untaxed imported commodities.

Examples of how the federal lawmakers borrowed specific tariff arguments, rates, or categories of dutiable goods from the state impost laws will be shown when the debates in Congress are analyzed. The examples given here are intended only to indicate that the general scheme of the first federal tariff was to a large extent borrowed from state precedents. Specific or ad valorem duties were levied on seventy-four commodities,[7] while only thirteen kinds of imports were designated

6. 12 *Pennsylvania Statutes at Large,* 99–100, ch. 1187.

7. Of the seventy-four enumerated dutiable articles, forty-nine were assessed specific duties: distilled spirits (Jamaica proof), 10¢ per gal.; all other distilled spirits, 8¢ per gal.; molasses, 2½¢ per gal.; Madeira wine, 18¢ per gal.; other wine, 10¢ per gal.; beer, ale, or porter (in casks), 5¢ per gal.; cider or porter (in bottles), 20¢ per doz.; malt, 10¢ per bu.; brown sugars, 1¢ per lb.; loaf sugars, 3¢ per lb.; other sugars, 1½¢ per lb.; coffee, 2½¢ per lb.; cocoa, 1¢ per lb.; candles (tallow), 2¢ per lb.; candles (wax or spermaceti), 6¢ per lb.; cheese, 4¢ per lb.; soap, 2¢ per lb.; boots, 50¢ per pair; shoes, slippers, or galoshes (leather), 7¢ per pair; shoes or slippers (silk or stuff), 10¢ per pair; cables, 75¢ per cwt.; tarred cordage, 75¢ per cwt.; untarred cordage, 90¢ per cwt.; twine or packthread, $2.00 per cwt.; unwrought steel, 56¢ per cwt.; nails and spikes, 1¢ per lb.; salt, 6¢ per bu.; manufactured tobacco, 6¢ per lb.; snuff, 29¢ per lb.; indigo, 16¢ per lb.; wool and cotton cards, 50¢ per doz.; coal, 2¢ per bu.; pickled fish, 75¢ per bbl.; dried fish, 50¢ per quintal; playing cards, 10¢ per pack; hemp (after December 1, 1790), 60¢ per cwt.; cotton (after December 1, 1790), 3¢ per lb.; tea (imported direct from India or China in American-built or American-owned ships), Bohea, 6¢ per lb., Sonchong, 10¢, Hyson, 20¢, other green tea, 12¢; tea (imported from Europe in American ships), Bohea, 8¢, Sonchong, 13¢, Hyson, 26¢, other green tea, 16¢; tea (imported in any other manner), Bohea, 15¢, Sonchong, 22¢, Hyson, 45¢, other green, 27¢.

The highest ad valorem duties (15 percent) were imposed on coaches, chariots,

as exempt from the 5 percent ad valorem duties imposed on all commodities not specifically enumerated.

The tonnage act of July 20, 1789, no less than the first tariff, projected state policies into the federal sphere. As early as 1783, Maryland had imposed a tonnage duty of five shillings on British vessels.[8] On the heels of this came an attempt by the Confederation Congress to obtain power to regulate commerce, both domestic and foreign.[9] Nothing came of this effort, however, largely because the several states attached so many different limitations on the grant of power which the Congress requested.[10] When it became evident that no so-

---

chaises, and carriages; the next highest (12½ percent) on goods from India or China (other than tea) imported in foreign ships. Then came the 10 percent category, comprising looking glasses, window glass, and all other glass except ordinary bottles; china, stone, and earthenware; gun powder; paints ground in oil; shoe and knee buckles; gold and silver lace; gold and silver leaf. Dutiable at 7½ percent were black books; writing, printing or wrapping paper; paper hangings; pasteboard; cabinet wares; buttons; saddles; gloves (leather); hats of beaver, fur, or wool; ready-made millinery; iron castings; slit and rolled iron; tanned or tawed leather, and all manufactures of leather not "otherwise rated"; canes, walking sticks, and whips; ready-made clothing; brushes; gold, silver, or plated ware; jewelry and pastework; anchors, wrought tin, and pewter ware.

All nonenumerated commodities were dutiable at 5 percent ad valorem except those expressly exempt from duties. This free list included saltpeter; tin (in pigs or plate); lead; old pewter; brass; iron and brass ware; copper (in plates); wool; cotton (until December 1, 1790); dyeing woods or dyeing drugs; raw hides; beaver and other furs; deerskins.

Drawbacks were authorized of all duties (except those on distilled spirits) if the imported commodities were exported within twelve months. One percent of the duties, however, was to be withheld to pay the expenses of customs officers. Salt used in salting fish was covered by a special drawback provision, one that presently led to a vigorous demand for bounties on fish exports. Every quintal of dried fish exported was to be judged worthy of a 5¢ drawback, as was every barrel of pickled fish or salted provisions. A general discount of 10 percent on all duties was to be allowed on all imports imported in American vessels. 1 *U.S. Laws*, 24–27, 1st Cong., 1st Sess., ch. 2 [July 4, 1789].

Essentially the first tariff represents a synthesis of preceding state tariffs. No new principles are involved, none of the commodities taxed except coal were new on the import list. The rates were frequently borrowed from state tariffs although in other cases they were fixed upon after long and bitter debates.

8. *Maryland Laws (Hanson)*, 1783, ch. 29 [December 26, 1783].

9. Burnett, *The Continental Congress*, pp. 619, 633–636, 663, 665–668.

10. See *Maryland Laws (Kilty)*, 1784, ch. 67 [January 22, 1785]; *New Hampshire Laws*, V, 25 [November 5, 1784]; ibid., V, 81 [June 23, 1785]; ibid., V, 158 [June 19, 1786]; ibid., V, 203–204 [December 28, 1786]; *Massachusetts Session Laws*, May 1784, 158 [July 1, 1784]; *Rhode Island Acts and Resolves*, October 1785, p. 10; ibid., March 1786, p. 6; *Connecticut Statutes at Large*, 317 [May 1785]; ibid., 347 [October 1786]; *New York Laws*, II, 102, VIII, ch. 56 [April 4, 1785]; *New Jersey Laws*, 84–85, p. 125, IX, ch. 6 [November 4, 1784]; ibid., 85–86, 223–224, X, ch. CIX [November 26, 1785]; 11 *Pennsylvania Statutes at Large*, 391–392, 1119 [December 15, 1784]; 2 *Delaware Laws*, 831, ch. 126b [1786]; 11 *Virginia Laws (Hening)*, 388–389, May 1784, ch. 21; 24 *North Carolina S.K.*, 561, 1784, ch. 9 [June 2, 1784]; 4 *South Carolina Statutes at Large*, 596,

lutions for American commercial problems were to come from that quarter, a movement designed to obtain the passage of identical navigation acts in several states was begun. Since there were no prohibitions on British goods and but few tonnage restrictions on British ships, British merchants, factors, and shipowners were gradually regaining control over American trade. Indignant Boston merchants brought pressure on the Massachusetts legislature, and under the leadership of Governor Bowdoin, who had long favored a discriminatory navigation policy,[11] Massachusetts forbade the export of American produce in British-owned ships and imposed additional tonnage duties on foreign ships bringing in imports.[12] Apparently by previous agreement, New Hampshire passed a similar law,[13] and the two states strongly urged other states to do likewise.[14] Between September 1785 and January 1786, Rhode Island, Pennsylvania, Virginia, and North Carolina followed suit,[15] though the acts passed varied widely from the Massachusetts-New Hampshire legislation. Largely through the refusal of Connecticut to join the movement, the whole plan for concerted state action collapsed. By 1786 it had become obvious that neither a grant of power to the Confederation Congress nor a uniform state navigation policy could be agreed upon. One by one the states suspended or modified their navigation laws, although discriminatory tonnage duties were for the most part retained or new scales were imposed.[16] Preferential tonnage duties on the ships of those nations which had entered into commercial treaties with the United States had been introduced by Pennsylvania, a policy presently followed by similar legislation in Virginia and in North Carolina,[17] thus setting up precedents for such a proposal when the new Congress began its debates on the tonnage act of 1789.[18]

1208 [March 21, 1784]; ibid., 720, 1300 [March 11, 1786]; *Georgia Laws* (*Watkins*), 340, Watkins No. 346 [August 2, 1786].

11. See Burnett, *The Continental Congress*, p. 635.

12. *Massachusetts Session Laws*, May 1785, 289–290 [June 23, 1785].

13. *New Hampshire Laws*, 78ff [June 23, 1785].

14. Burnett, *The Continental Congress*, p. 636.

15. *Rhode Island Statutes at Large*, October 1785, 29f; 12 *Virginia Laws* (*Hening*), 32 [October 1785]; 24 *North Carolina S.R.*, 718–720, 1 Martin 392 [December 1785]; 12 *Pennsylvania Laws*, 99ff [September 20, 1785].

16. As in Virginia, 12 *Virginia Laws* (*Hening*), 289f [October 1786].

17. 12 *Pennsylvania Laws*, 99ff [September 20, 1785]; 12 *Pennsylvania Statutes at Large*, 233–235, ch. 1227 [April 8, 1786]; 24 *North Carolina S.R.*, 718–720, 1 Martin, 392 [December 1785]; 12 *Virginia Laws* (*Hening*), 290f [October 1786].

18. It was the failure to achieve any unified action that deepened the gloom precipitated by Shays's Rebellion in Massachusetts and by the Rhode Island paper money craze. The navigation act fiasco no doubt intensified the demand for constitutional revision, already begun by the Annapolis Convention.

It was therefore on a sizable body of state precedents that the first Congress devised its first tonnage act. Even so, the problem of enacting suitable tonnage legislation baffled and confused the members of Congress. Originally, it seems, the plan had been to include tonnage duties in the first tariff; little by little, however, the two problems were separated. And whereas the first tariff proved to be a complex and detailed document, the tonnage law was simple and brief. Tonnage duties were imposed "on all ships and vessels entering the United States," but a clear-cut distinction was made between three varieties of ships: American-owned vessels (which were to pay six cents a ton), American-built vessels wholly or partly owned by foreigners (which were to pay thirty cents a ton), and all other ships (which were to be charged fifty cents a ton).[19] Thus a discriminatory policy long advocated by merchants of Boston, New York, and Philadelphia had finally been adopted on a nationwide scale.

Despite the heritage which the Confederation Congress passed on to the new government, and despite the pervasive influence of state precedents, the new Congress made many important legislative innovations. The main purpose of the ensuing analysis is to appraise the legislative principles that underlay the debates in the House of Representatives,[20] to signalize the legislative demands that were made upon Congress, and to discover exactly what members of Congress thought the new government should do to restrain, aid, or improve the enterprise system. Since the tariff and the tonnage acts were the chief concern of Congress during the first session, the debates on these two laws will be examined in detail to test contemporary ideas about the appropriate functions of government in its relation to occupational or business groups. The development of emergent and broader concepts of the economic functions of government will be discussed in a subsequent chapter.[21]

Revenue and Protection: Liberty or Intervention

In opening the discussion of the tariff in the House, James Madison pointed out that two issues would need immediate attention: the fiscal problem of providing the new government with adequate revenue; and, the regulation of foreign trade for the purpose of aiding farmers, merchants, manufacturers, or shipowners.[22] He urged that revenue

19. *U.S. Laws*, 27–28, 1st Cong., 1st Sess., ch. 3 [July 20, 1789].
20. A similar analysis cannot be made of the Senate debates inasmuch as they were not reported.
21. See below, chap. IX.
22. *Annals of Congress*, 1st Congress, I, 107 [April 8, 1789].

considerations be kept uppermost, recommending a temporary tariff as a stopgap until the long-run objectives of Congress could be more carefully formulated. But his proposal was summarily rejected by two of the Pennsylvania representatives, Thomas Fitzsimons and Thomas Hartley, who advocated the immediate adoption of a more permanent tariff designed to assist American manufacturers. Fitzsimons argued that the tariff should be "calculated to encourage the productions of our country, and protect our infant industries," although he thought it should also operate as a "sumptuary restriction" upon articles of luxury.[23] Hartley said the first object of the tariff should be to impose such duties on imports as would "give the home manufacturers a considerable advantage"; he therefore stressed that it would be "politic and wise" to extend "the fostering hand of the General Government" to "all those manufactures which will tend to national utility."[24] It should always be the function of an "enlightened nation," contended Hartley, to give manufacturers enough encouragement so that new branches of production can be developed and perfected; but he was careful to point out that the sheltered industries ought not be allowed to oppress other parts of the national community.[25] Thomas T. Tucker of South Carolina apparently thought that the Pennsylvania representative was too exclusively concerned with the manufacturing interest. At any rate, he asserted that the tariff should "attend to the interests of every part of the Union"; indeed it should be so arranged that it would benefit agriculture and commerce as well as manufactures. He therefore recommended that the House should "collect the opinion" about the role of government from the members from all the states.[26]

At this juncture Madison, in a long speech, laid before the House his ideas about the legitimacy of governmental intervention with foreign trade. Ideally, he said, commerce ought to be "as free as the policy of nations [and he meant the family of nations] will permit." He declared himself to be the friend of "a very free system of commerce" because he was convinced that "commercial shackles are generally unjust, oppressive, and impolitic." He spoke of his conviction that "if industry and labor are left to take their own course, they will generally be directed to those objects which are the most productive," and that an unfettered enterprise system would achieve these ends "in a more certain and direct manner than the wisdom of the most enlightened legislature could point out." The national interest

23. Ibid., I, 110–111 [April 9, 1789].
24. Ibid., I, 114.
25. Ibid., I, 115.
26. Ibid.

is no more promoted by restrictions on trade, claimed Madison, than those of individuals are advanced by restraints upon the ways in which people choose to apply their industry and abilities. He based his theory of entrepreneurial freedom on the benefits which must inevitably arise from a division of labor among persons, regions, or countries.[27]

But despite the normal superiority of a libertarian scheme of things, Madison was of the opinion that Congress ought not hesitate to impose restrictions on foreign goods and ships. The task before Congress should be to discover justifiable exceptions to a system of *laissez-passer*. Of course, freedom of commerce, if subscribed to by all nations, would be the best arrangement; but since this plan had not been adopted by the family of nations, any unilateral adherence to it would mean that "one nation might suffer to benefit others."[28] Under existing circumstances, "if America were to leave her ports perfectly free and make no discriminations" between American and foreign ships, American vessels would presently find themselves excluded from all foreign ports, and thus every major economic interest of the United States would suffer. The tariff problem ought to be approached, therefore, not in terms of an ideal theory but realistically in terms of "national prudence"; the tariff should be considered as a political device for widening markets for American exports and for diversifying American industries.

The United States possesses, said Madison, a wide variety of raw materials. Some kinds of manufacturing had already developed without any government aid or encouragement; in other cases, however, protection had definitely stimulated certain useful industries. These beginnings ought not be sacrificed; moreover, "it is not possible for the hand of man to shift from one employment to another, without being injured by the change."[29] Thus the protection of investments, already made, constituted a first exception to Madison's libertarian

27. "We should find no advantage in saying, that every man should be obliged to furnish himself, by his own labor, with those accommodations which depend on the mechanic arts, instead of employing his neighbor, who could do it for him on better terms. It would be of no advantage to the shoemaker to make his own clothes, to save the expense of the tailor's bill, nor of the tailor to make his own shoes, to save the expense of procuring them from the shoemaker. It would be better policy to suffer each of them to employ his talents in his own way. The case is the same between the exercise of the arts and agriculture—between the city and the country—and between city and town; each capable of making particular articles in abundance to supply the other; thus all are benefited by exchange, and the less the exchange is cramped by the government, the greater are the proportions of benefit to each. The same argument holds good between nation and nation, and between parts of the same nation." Ibid., I, 116–117.

28. Ibid., I, 117.

29. Ibid., I, 117–118.

ideal. Nor was it only industries actually established that merited protection; other branches of production might ultimately become as efficient as similar ones abroad if the "fostering hand of government" were to sustain them in their years of adolescence. Congress ought to scrutinize all the productive possibilities of the new nation and assist those employments that promised ultimate success.

Madison found little virtue in restrictions on foreign trade that had sumptuary inspiration,[30] although admittedly they could be thought of as exceptions to a free-trade commercial policy. Embargoes in time of war constituted more justifiable intervention, as did protective duties designed to build up industries needed for national defense. Above all, the purely fiscal benefits of intervention ought to be considered. Duties on imports could be easily collected; they would be borne with reasonable equality; and they would probably fall to some extent upon foreigners. For these reasons, Madison was prepared to support the demands for protection which were being urged so insistently by the Pennsylvania members of the House. A month later, when the tonnage act was under debate, he summarized his views by saying that "it is an old maxim, that trade is best left to regulate itself; yet circumstances may and do occur to require legislative interference."[31]

After Madison's careful exposition of the legislative principles which he believed should underlie the tariff discussion, there seems to have been little disagreement about general objectives. The immediate task was to frame a revenue-yielding tariff which would at the same time stimulate American agriculture, protect American manufactures, and promote American foreign trade. In their eagerness to assist these basic interests, however, the members of the House often tended to neglect the urgent fiscal necessity that had made the tariff the first major business of Congress. Thus George Gale of Maryland reminded his colleagues that whereas a duty of nine cents a gallon on beer might greatly aid domestic brewers, it would "defeat the purpose of obtaining revenue."[32] The advocacy of moderate duties, however, was not always a disinterested concern with maximizing customs revenues; it is quite clear, for example, that the Massachusetts representatives Fisher Ames, Elbridge Gerry, and Benjamin Goodhue favored low duties on molasses so that the Boston and Medford distillers might have lower costs of production. But the danger of customs evasion argued in favor of moderate duties. Widespread smuggling, which had greatly troubled

30. "I acknowledge that I do not, in general, think any great national advantage arises from restrictions passed on this head." Ibid., I, 118.
31. Ibid., I, 255–256 [May 4, 1789].
32. Ibid., I, 151 [April 15, 1789].

the British officials before the Revolution, increased during the war and was no doubt stimulated by the complexity of the state tariff systems in the postwar era. High customs duties would augment the profits of smuggling, and grave doubts were expressed about whether the federal government would ever be able to police the entire Atlantic coast. "I am opposed to high duties," said Tucker of South Carolina, "because they will tend to introduce and establish a system of smuggling,"[33] a view eagerly seconded by Ames of Massachusetts who contended that unless the revenue law had popular approval smuggling would increase enormously.[34] Government, he maintained, must check these "unruly sallies of self-interest," a task that "requires an unwearied attention" under any circumstances and becomes virtually impossible when the latent gains of illicit trade are increased by high import duties.

Southern representatives, like Tucker of South Carolina and Theodorick Bland of Virginia, justified their opposition to high duties by arguing that high customs would yield less revenue than low ones, but what they were actually doing was resisting the pressure of manufacturers for vigorous protection. Tucker, for example, insisted that a blanket 5 percent tariff would raise an adequate revenue and would give "a sufficient encouragement to manufactures," especially since the cost of transport could be regarded as the equivalent amount of protection for American industries.[35] Bland of Virginia protested against specific duties, arguing that whereas Congress seemed willing to agree that the unenumerated commodities should be taxed by but 5 percent, the arbitrary specific duties on enumerated articles were often the equivalent of 50 percent. Congress was so determined to impose high duties, said Bland, that greater sums than the government will ever need will be collected.[36] Southern opponents of high duties found allies in members of the House who were anxious to prove that merchants would be greatly discomfited by high customs. "Mercantile capitals" are very limited, asserted Elias Boudinot of New Jersey, and high duties will mean that merchants will find a large proportion of

33. Ibid., I, 303 [May 8, 1789]. He also alleged that high duties would oppress "certain citizens and States, in order to promote the benefit of other States and other classes of citizens."

34. Ibid., I, 310 [May 9, 1789].

35. Ibid., I, 307. Tench Coxe estimated that the cost of transport gave American manufacturers a 25 percent advantage over European competitors. *View of the United States*, pp. 16–17 [1787].

36. *Annals*, 1st Cong., I, 315–316 [May 9, 1789]. He also asserted that "there will not be found specie enough within the United States to pay the duties."

their working capital tied up by the tariff.[37] According to Gerry of Massachusetts, American merchants formerly could trade on British credit; now when that possibility has ended, Congress proposes "to lop off another part of their capital."[38] What the advocates of high duties forget, claimed Gerry, is that American merchants were never less able to bear high duties; they, no less than manufacturers, stand in great need "of the fostering hand of government."[39] But despite the pressure for low duties from southern agrarians and New England merchants, Madison insisted on the imperative need for adequate revenue. "I pay great respect to the opinions of mercantile gentlemen, and I am willing to concede much to them," he said, but he admonished the House that unless revenues were forthcoming from customs duties, the new government would be compelled to resort to direct taxes.[40]

More than anyone else it was Madison who kept the tariff debates on an objective level. Yet despite all his tact and diplomacy, every so often sectional animosities would flare up. But when James Thatcher of Massachusetts asked southern representatives how they would like to have duties imposed on Negro slaves, it was Boudinot of New Jersey, rather than Madison, who poured out the healing oil. He said he regretted "to hear anything that sounds like an attachment to particular States"; as for himself, he assured the House that he considered himself "as much a representative of Massachusetts as of New Jersey,"[41] and he declared that nothing would induce him "to injure the one more than the other." The general interest, argued Boudinot, could only be safeguarded by following "the principle of mutual concessions"; indeed, he admitted it would be impossible to impose any duty which would not affect some region or some occupational group more than another. The best that could be hoped for would be a tariff which "endeavored to equalize the burthens as much as possible." Not all members of the House took an equally catholic view; in the interests of the distillers, the Massachusetts delegation put up a stubborn fight for high duties on distilled spirits and low duties on molasses. Ames even went so far as to warn the House that unless the molasses duties were kept low, Massachusetts would repudiate the new government.[42] Somewhat angered by this unbending attitude, Madison accused the Massachusetts members of trying to sacrifice the rights "of 3,000,000

37. Ibid., I, 325.
38. Ibid., I, 327.
39. Ibid., I, 328.
40. Ibid., I, 314.
41. Ibid., I, 225 [April 28, 1789].
42. Ibid., I, 230.

of our fellow citizens" for the benefit "of a few distilleries."[43] But neither sarcasm nor ridicule could weaken Fisher Ames's devotion to his constituents; he now argued that molasses was a necessary of life, that "no decent family" could do without it, that a tax on molasses would be as odious as a tax on bread, and that by imposing high duties on such essentials Congress would take away the greatest virtue of the United States, which had always been "the best country for the poor to live in."[44]

From the very outset, therefore, it became obvious that it would be extremely difficult for the members of Congress to disregard the legislative demands of particular regions and interests. Ames was right when he said, "If the hand of Government is stretched out to oppress the various interests" by unequal taxes, "we shall destroy the fond hopes entertained by our constituents, that this Government would ensure their rights."[45] His contention was that the individual states had already discovered which interests should be properly assisted, and that the general principle had already been established "that promoting the interests of particular States increases the general welfare."[46]

But apparently not all members of Congress were so certain that the general welfare could be left to the interplay of self-seeking groups. The proposal to impose duties on salt led to a long discussion of the regressive tendencies of such a tax;[47] in contrast, the appropriateness of duties on distilled spirits received general approval after the warning by a Philadelphia physician that liquor was deleterious to public health was considered. In general, however, the incidence of customs duties was given but little attention. Roger Sherman of Connecticut did say that Congress need not worry about the effect the tariff might have on merchants;[48] as for the duties, "the consumer pays them eventually, and they pay no more than they choose, because they have it in their power to determine the quantity of taxable articles they will use."[49] But when Josiah Parker of Virginia, just when the House debates were drawing to a close, proposed a ten-dollar duty on every Negro slave imported, a storm of protest immediately broke loose. James Jackson of Georgia alleged that Virginia "was an old settled state" which al-

43. Ibid., I, 229. He pointed out that the government need have no fear of liquor smuggling. The distilleries, he said "would exert themselves in aiding the Government to collect the duty on foreign rum" since imported spirits of any kind would compete with domestic rum. Ibid., I, 328 [May 9, 1789].

44. Ibid., I, 233 [April 28, 1789].

45. Ibid., I, 234.

46. Ibid., I, 231.

47. Ibid., I, 165–174 [April 17, 1789].

48. Ibid., I, 317 [May 9, 1789].

49. Ibid.

ready "had her complement of slaves," and he thought it grossly unfair to impose a high duty on slaves when there were new states that did not yet have enough of them.[50] But the discussion of duties on slaves had scarcely gotten under way when it became evident that this explosive subject might overturn all that the House had so painfully accomplished. Under pressure from both northerners and southerners, Parker withdrew his motion. Three days later, on May 16, the House passed the tariff bill. The Senate bill was not through its third reading until June 11. By June 27 the differences between the House and the Senate had been resolved; two days later the Senate approved the revised bill, and a week later, the tariff bill became law.

The Tariff and the "Great Staple"

When Theodorick Bland of Virginia looked over the list of articles which the House Committee proposed should be dutiable, he noticed quite a few "calculated to give encouragement to home manufactures." This, he said, might be "in some degree proper," but he reminded his colleagues that American manufactures "were only in their infancy" and were consequently unable to "answer the demands of the country." By making so many manufactured goods dutiable, Congress would "lay a tax upon the whole community, in order to put money in the pockets of the few."[51] More particularly, the tax would fall upon agriculture, which Madison had properly described as the "great staple" of the United States.[52] High tonnage duties, he alleged, would also "embarrass" agriculture, since America did not possess enough ships to transport its products to foreign markets.

Bland's proposal for a scaling down of duties evoked no congressional enthusiasm, since it was patently clear that the fiscal emergencies of the government dictated that duties on goods or ships must be high enough to provide an adequate federal revenue. But inasmuch as American agriculture was dependent on export markets, there was precious little that Congress could do by means of the tariff to help the farmer. The majority of Congressmen, no doubt, agreed with Jackson of Georgia that "the agricultural interest ought to be encouraged and protected" because it could properly be described as "the principal and

50. Ibid., I, 350 [May 13, 1789].
51. Ibid., I, 129 [April 14, 1789].
52. "In my opinion, it would be proper also . . . to consider the means of encouraging . . . agriculture; which I think may be justly styled the great staple of the United States, from the spontaneous productions which nature furnishes, and the manifest advantage it has over every other object of emolument in this country." Ibid., I, 117 [April 9, 1789].

leading interest of the United States."[53] But what could the government do? A duty on beef, as Thatcher of Massachusetts pointed out, would be of no importance, since practically every state in the Union exported beef products.[54] Duties on beer and porter had the approval of some members of the House, because they would perhaps increase the domestic market for grain and thus "advance the agricultural interest."[55] Nevertheless, they would have but modest effects upon the prosperity of American farmers. Efforts to strike steel from the list of dutiable commodities—because it was "essentially necessary for agricultural improvements" and because duties on it "would operate as an oppressive, though indirect tax upon agriculture"[56]—proved unsuccessful. Indeed, the advocates of duties on steel seemed to have had little difficulty in convincing the House that moderate duties on iron and steel "would affect the agricultural interest very little," and that even if they did, the disadvantage would be "overbalanced" by the national benefits arising from the establishment of "such an important manufacture."[57]

The one victory the farm bloc won was the duty of sixty cents per hundred weight to be levied on imports of hemp after December 1, 1790. The Virginia delegation had fought stubbornly for this particular impost; they asserted that the southern states were well suited to the cultivation of hemp, and they insisted that it was the duty of Congress "to pay as much respect to the encouragement and protection of husbandry (the most important of all the interests in the United States)

53. Ibid., I, 286 [May 6, 1789].
54. Ibid., I, 151–152 [April 15, 1789]. Massachusetts, New York, and Pennsylvania, however, had imposed duties on beef and pork. See Massachusetts A. & L., 1782–1783, 506ff; ibid., 1784–1785, 28ff, 453ff; ibid., 1786–1787, 117ff; 2 New York Laws, 11ff; ibid., 509ff; 12 Pennsylvania Laws, 99ff. All these states plus New Hampshire and Connecticut levied duties on cheese. See Connecticut S.L., October 1784, 309f; Rhode Island S.L., June 1785, 18ff.
55. See, for example, the remarks of Thomas Sinnickson of New Jersey. Annals, 1st Cong., I, 151 [April 15, 1789].
56. Ibid., I, 153.
57. See especially the remarks of Fitzsimons of Pennsylvania, ibid., I, 154. With regard to iron and steel, the state precedents were unusually convincing. Protective duties had been imposed by New Hampshire, Massachusetts, New York, New Jersey, and Pennsylvania. For the state tariffs on iron and steel see, 5 New Hampshire Laws, 146, 172; Massachusetts A. & L., 1782–1783, 92f, 506ff; ibid., 1784–1785, 453ff; ibid., 1786–1787, 117ff; Rhode Island S.L., 1786, 21; Connecticut S.L., May 1784, 279f; 2 New York Laws, 11ff, 509ff; New Jersey S.L., 1786–1787, 406ff; 10 Pennsylvania Laws, 252ff; 11 Pennsylvania Laws, 262ff; 12 Pennsylvania Laws, 99ff; Maryland Laws (Hanson), April 1782, ch. 50; Maryland Laws (Kilty), November 1783, ch. 36; Maryland Laws (Hanson), 1784, ch. 84; Maryland S.L., 1785, ch. 76; 11 Virginia Laws (Hening), 374f; 24 North Carolina S.R., 549ff; 4 South Carolina Laws, 576ff; 5 South Carolina Laws, 8ff.

as they did to manufactures."[58] They argued that if it was good policy to encourage the manufacture of cordage in the United States, it would be even wiser to stimulate the production of the raw materials, so that America could become independent of other countries for cordage. Finally they emphasized that it would be difficult "to persuade the farmer that his interest ought to be neglected" while "particular artisans" were being assisted.[59] Alexander White of Virginia reminded the House that the United States was primarily an agricultural country, and that Congress "therefore ought to attend to the encouragement of that interest," while Thomas Scott of Pennsylvania demanded that agriculture receive "its proportion" of governmental assistance.[60] He predicted that protective duties on hemp would have a salubrious effect on the farmers beyond the Alleghenies, who would thereby "be encouraged to draw forth the bounties of nature from a rich and fertile soil." Yet it was a long, hard battle to obtain agreement on a duty of sixty cents on hemp; spokesmen for New England shipowners, like George Partridge of Massachusetts, admitted "the propriety of encouraging agriculture," but contended that "it ought not be done at the expense of the ship-builders."[61]

The Demands of the "Merchants and Traders"

A long, acrimonious debate took place in the House on May 12, 1789, and the disputants were as sticky as the molasses they were discussing. Some time before, the House had agreed on a six-cent duty on every gallon of imported molasses, but the Massachusetts delegation had succeeded in reopening discussion on this article and was making a tremendous push for reducing the duty on this indispensable raw material of the New England rum distilleries. The Massachusetts representatives lost this first round, although before the tariff bill finally became law they succeeded, with the cooperation of the Senate, in paring down the molasses impost from six to two and one half cents a gallon. On May 12, however, when the House voted a duty of five cents, their gloom was undeniable. The next day Thatcher of Massachusetts presented a petition "from the merchants and traders of the town of Portland" stating that "the proposed [five-cent] duty on molasses will operate injuriously on New England," and praying "that the article may remain free from duty."[62] Why did this petition

58. *Annals*, 1st Cong., I, 156 [April 15, 1789].
59. Ibid., I, 158 [April 16, 1789].
60. Ibid., I, 160–161.
61. Ibid., I, 158–159.
62. Ibid., I, 347 [May 13, 1789].

arrive at such an opportune time? And why did the "merchants and traders" of Portland betray such solicitude for the New England distilleries? The answer, of course, was that molasses constituted the most important means which the Caribbean area had of paying for their huge imports of New England fish. Any contraction of the American market for molasses would mean a decline in the demand of the sugar islands for pickled, salted, and smoked fish; any diminution of the trade with the Caribbean region would mean a decline in American commerce and navigation. Merchants, as Heckscher has pointed out, tend ordinarily to regard goods "purely from the standpoint of exchange."[63] They are essentially "indifferent" about the abundance or the scarcity of goods within a nation; they are disinterested in all matters except the profits which arise from exchange transactions. The American evidence supports this interpretation. It is inaccurate to allege that American merchants always opposed protective duties; if certain duties promised to increase raw-material imports, and to augment, rather than to decrease, mercantile activity, the merchants favored them. In general, however, largely because of the variety and abundance of American raw materials, the commercial interest looked with disfavor on any duties that might give a stimulus to domestic manufactures.

The First Congress seems to have listened attentively to the "commercial interest." Because merchants could supply Congress with valuable information about the probable revenues which might be expected from various scales of duties, Boudinot of New Jersey and other members of Congress urged that mercantile opinion be solicited. For the merchants not only were well informed about the volume of imports, but they were "more immediately interested in the events of the proposed [tariff and tonnage] measures, than any other class of men."[64] Boudinot told his colleagues that "there are gentlemen on this floor well calculated to represent the mercantile interests of this country," but he also warned the House that it ought to remember that its responsibility was to "promote the general good," not to advance "the local interests of a few individuals."[65] What did the commercial interest seek? Why were they "more immediately interested" in the tariff than any other group? Aside from a deep concern with the tonnage act,[66] American merchants were apparently most anxious to see that duties were kept low on hemp and cordage, on molasses,

63. *Mercantilism*, II, 56–57.
64. *Annals*, 1st Cong., I, 122–123 [April 11, 1789].
65. Ibid., I, 124.
66. See below, p. 252.

and on tea. From the House debates, it is clear that these specific demands had reference, respectively, to the cost of rigging ships, to the preservation of trade with the sugar islands, and to the development of the Far-Eastern trade.

Low duties on hemp had the support of some Congressmen who could not by any standards be labeled spokesmen for the merchants and shipowners. Madison, for example, "questioned the propriety of raising the price of any article" that entered into the cost of vessels. At the same time, being a Virginian, he could not resist wondering whether it might not be "politic" to take a somewhat longer view of the problem and consider the advisability of developing a domestic hemp-growing industry.[67] There were some state legislative precedents for this cautious suggestion. Both Massachusetts and New York had imposed duties on foreign hemp and on cordage, and had earmarked these customs revenues for the payment of bounties on homegrown hemp.[68] Connecticut granted tax exemption to hemp growers[69] and levied high duties on foreign hemp or cordage. Rhode Island, in contrast, put hemp on the free list in 1785;[70] so did Pennsylvania,[71] although in its act the duties on "tarred cordage, white rope, long lines, and twine" were raised even higher than those of Connecticut. Since all three states had important maritime interests, it seems evident that no complete agreement existed about the most expedient way of ensuring an adequate supply of cordage for American ships. Nor is it clear whether the three-shilling duty on hemp in Virginia can be construed as protective,[72] even though Madison's remarks might lead one to suspect that it was probably intended to assist the hemp growers. In the congressional debates on hemp, however, it was the merchants' and shipowners' demands which were the most insistent. Ames of Massachusetts bitterly opposed a federal duty on hemp, arguing that while

67. *Annals,* 1st Cong., I, 155–156 [April 15, 1789].
68. In Massachusetts, duties on cordage were imposed in 1783, 1784, and 1785. Whether these laws were designed to encourage domestic hemp growing is not clear. But in 1786, a new law levied 10 percent duties on cordage and 1 percent on hemp for the express purposes of paying a bounty on homegrown hemp. See *Massachusetts A. & L.,* 1786–1787, 117ff. Two years earlier, New York, in an act framed "to encourage the raising of hemp and manufacture of cordage," levied duties of 4 shillings per cwt. on both cordage and hemp, stipulating that the receipts be used exclusively for paying the hemp bounty. 2 *New York Laws,* VIII, ch. 68, sec. 4 [April 12, 1785].
69. *Connecticut Statutes at Large,* 345 [May 1787].
70. *Rhode Island Statutes at Large,* October 1785, 42f.
71. 12 *Pennsylvania Laws,* 99ff [September 29, 1785].
72. 12 *Virginia Laws (Hening),* 289f [October 1786]. Virginia was apparently the only state producing sufficient hemp to warrant its inspection before export.

it might encourage farmers and cordage manufacturers, it would greatly discourage "the maritime interest," and in doing so it would "reflect back upon those interests it was intended to cherish."[73] Fitzsimons of Pennsylvania deemed it unwise to persuade farmers to raise hemp when their labor could be better employed in more profitable crops; he thought it unfair that "navigation and shipping" should be "bur-thened" for the benefit of farmers.[74] His colleague Hartley preferred giving an outright bounty to hemp growers; such a policy would not "cramp the growth of a fleet" and would permit the United States to become "what nature had destined her to be—a maritime nation."[75] The farm bloc stood its ground, however, and the sixty-cent duty on hemp, which was ultimately voted, could not be considered a victory for the merchants and shipowners.

Indeed, it was probably the failure to obtain lower duties on hemp and cordage that led spokesmen for the "maritime interests" to reopen the debates on the molasses duty. Here it could be argued that high duties on molasses would ruin the American fisheries; "we exchange for molasses," said Ames, "those fish that it is impossible to dispose of any where else."[76] As a result of the Revolution, the fisheries were undeniably in trouble; huge imperial markets had been lost, and com-mercial treaties with European powers had done little to create new outlets. Thus it could properly be argued that the fisheries in 1789 also looked to the "fostering care of Government."[77] "Unless some extraor-dinary measures are taken to support our fisheries," claimed Gerry of Massachusetts, "I do not see what is to prevent their inevitable ruin." He stressed that a third of the New England fishermen were un-employed because of the "chilling policy of foreign nations."[78] A high duty on molasses would be the last blow; "if instead of protection from the Government, we extend to them oppression, I shudder for the consequences." Goodhue of Massachusetts also put in his oar; how can America build up a navy, he asked, without seamen, and how can mariners be trained if Congress insists on destroying the fishing trade by imposing a tariff on molasses?[79]

That the eastern Massachusetts representatives had a triple al-legiance—to the merchants, the fishermen, and the distillers—is clear

---

73. *Annals,* 1st Cong., I, 156 [April 15, 1789].
74. Ibid., I, 157.
75. Ibid., I, 159–160.
76. Ibid., I, 139 [April 14, 1789].
77. This was the burden of Ames's remarks on April 28. Ibid., I, 230.
78. Ibid., I, 233 [April 28, 1789].
79. Ibid., I, 344 [May 12, 1789].

enough from the debates. "If we do not import molasses," maintained Gerry, "we cannot carry on our distilleries nor vend our fish."[80] He predicted that a six-cent duty on molasses would diminish imports by at least a third, and decrease the market for fish in proportion. Ames argued that a high molasses duty would be grossly inequitable because "distilleries are not distributed equally throughout the country"; at the same time it would ruin the fisheries, which he described as "one of the most valuable interests of the United States."[81] Gerry resorted to the lessons of experience, asserting that although the "landed interest" had always dominated Massachusetts politics, and although it had consistently imposed a disproportionate share of the "public burthen" on the commercial interest, it had always had the wisdom to understand that high duties on molasses "would have destroyed the fisheries and navigation of the State."[82] He therefore proposed a two-cent duty, and in doing so forecast fairly accurately what the ultimate decision of Congress was to be.

Whereas the New England merchants had fought stubbornly for low duties on hemp and molasses, the request that Congress should encourage the China trade came primarily from Philadelphia. Fitzsimons pointed out that the Revolution had deprived American merchants of many of their prewar branches of trade. Excluded from the West Indies, they were obliged to seek other channels of commerce; and of these new ventures, the direct trade with the Far East proved to be the most profitable, but the most risky. American merchants, said Fitzsimons, "have gone largely into it"; the Oriental trade promises to give employment to many thousands of seamen and to require tons

80. Ibid., I, 348.
81. Ibid., I, 341 [May 11, 1789].
82. Ibid., I, 347 [May 12, 1789]. The story of the molasses and rum duties in the state tariff acts is extremely complicated. Excise laws overlap impost laws; rates were arranged to favor domestic over foreign rum; in some states molasses was admitted free if unloaded from American ships. In general, however, the molasses duties were low, ranging from 2½ percent to 5 percent. See 5 *New Hampshire Laws*, 145ff [March 4, 1789]; *Massachusetts A. & L.*, 1782–1783, 506ff [July 10, 1783]; ibid., 1784–1785, 453ff [July 2, 1785]; ibid., 1786–1787, 117ff [November 17, 1786]; *Connecticut Statutes at Large*, May 1784, 271ff; ibid., 279ff; 2 *New York Laws*, 11ff [November 18, 1784]; ibid., 509ff [April 11, 1787]; 10 *Pennsylvania Laws*, 252ff [December 23, 1789]; ibid., 411ff [April 9, 1782]; 11 *Pennsylvania Laws*, 146ff [September 17, 1783]; ibid., 262ff [March 15, 1784]; 12 *Pennsylvania Laws*, 99ff [September 20, 1785]; ibid., 403ff [March 15, 1787]; *Maryland Laws (Kilty)*, November 1782, ch. 26 [January 15, 1783]; *Maryland Laws (Hanson)*, 1784, ch. 84 [January 22, 1785]; *Maryland Statutes at Large*, 1785, ch. 76 [March 11, 1786]; 11 *Virginia Laws (Hening)*, 374f [May 1784]; 12 *Virginia Laws (Hening)*, 304f [October 1786]; 24 *North Carolina S.R.*, 549ff [June 2, 1784]; 4 *South Carolina Laws*, 576ff [August 13, 1783]; ibid., 607ff [March 26, 1784].

of American shipping.[83] In the Second and Third congresses, the claims of merchants engaged in the China trade were to be discussed in considerable detail, largely as a result of a series of petitions from several groups of merchants. Fitzsimons's attempt in the First Congress to keep the duties low on tea brought directly from China in American ships was therefore only a forewarning of a much more formidable China-trade lobby which was presently to exert appreciable influence upon Congress.

Even in 1789, however, Congress made some rather important concessions to the merchants engaged in the Oriental trade. The duties on tea imported directly in American-built or American-owned ships were set at less than half the duties imposed on the same commodities when brought in foreign ships and at about three-fourths the duties imposed when tea was brought from Europe in American ships.[84] This principle of discrimination in favor of tea brought directly from the Orient was copied by Congress from the state tariffs of New York and Pennsylvania,[85] thus indicating that the merchants of New York and Philadelphia had already obtained the aid of their respective state governments in their effort to open up new branches of foreign trade. The New England merchants, to be sure, did not neglect the opportunities for profitable trade with the Orient. In the First Congress, however, they seemed to have concentrated their lobbying strength on the attempt to revive activity in the fish and molasses trade of the Atlantic.

83. *Annals*, 1st Cong., I, 147 [April 14, 1789]; 175–176 [April 18, 1789].

84. The preferential position of the American merchants engaged in direct trade with the Orient can be seen from the schedule below:

Kind of tea	Duty when brought direct in American ships	Duty when brought from Europe in American ships	Duty when brought in any other manner
Bohea	6¢ per lb.	8¢ per lb.	15¢ per lb.
Sonchong	10¢	13¢	22¢
Hyson	20¢	26¢	45¢
Other green tea . .	12¢	16¢	27¢

Bohea was the cheaper variety of black tea, Sonchong a superior black tea from young leaves, Hyson an excellent green tea from China. "Green tea" meant tea made from steamed dried leaves.

85. A New York law of April 11, 1787, imposed duties of 4d on Bohea tea and 8d on all other tea except when imported directly from Asia in New York-built or New York-owned ships (when the duties were to be: Bohea, 3d, other tea, 6d). 2 *New York Laws*, 509ff. Pennsylvania gave much greater encouragement to direct trade with the Far East. By legislation of March 15, 1787, Hyson tea was to be charged 6d, green or Sonchong 4d, and all other tea 2d. But all varieties of tea were to be admitted customs free if brought direct from China or from the Cape of Good Hope in American-built or American-owned ships. 12 *Pennsylvania Laws*, 403ff.

The Modesty of the Manufacturers

The debates on the first tariff occurred two and a half years before Alexander Hamilton communicated his cogent and scholarly *Report on Manufactures* to Congress. The brilliance of that document contrasts markedly with the halting and hesitant discussion of manufactures in the House debates in April and May of 1789. Yet, to some degree, these first attempts to formulate a national policy designed to assist American manufacturers laid the groundwork for Hamilton's *Report*; moreover, the actual stimulus which the first tariff gave to American manufacturing no doubt helped to develop a widespread belief among businessmen that much more assistance should be given by the federal government to manufacturing enterprises. At any rate, it is entirely unwarranted to compare the relatively mature discussion of manufactures in December 1791 with the House debates of the spring of 1789. By 1791, the opinion of manufacturers was reasonably articulate; in addition, Hamilton had actually invited businessmen to tell him precisely what they thought the government should do in their behalf.[86]

In 1789 the demands of the manufacturing interest were cautious and modest. Specific demands seem to have been made by only a handful of industries, although protectionist sentiment was unquestionably more ubiquitous than the debates suggest. Fully a score of the dutiable articles enumerated in the first tariff were manufactured in sizable quantities in the United States,[87] and it is not unreasonable to assume that all or most of the duties on such commodities were intended to be at least partly protective. But as far as the debates indicate, only the protection sought by the brewers, the distillers, the candle makers, and the steel manufacturers seems to have produced disagreement. To this list may perhaps be added the demands of the coal miners, inasmuch as Bland of Virginia assured the House that the miners of Virginia could supply "the whole of the United States" with coal if "some restraint was laid on the importation of foreign coal."[88] Although there were no state precedents for this issue, Congress did impose a duty of two cents a bushel on coal, but whether the

86. See Arthur H. Cole, *Industrial and Commercial Correspondence of Alexander Hamilton* (Chicago, 1928), introduction.

87. Beer, ale, and porter; loaf sugar; candles; cheese; soap; boots, shoes, and slippers; cordage of all kinds; nails; manufactured tobacco and snuff; wool and cotton cards; glass; earthenware; paints; paper; buttons; saddles; hats; slit and rolled iron; tanned and tawed leather; anchors; pewter.

88. *Annals,* 1st Cong., I, 177 [April 18, 1789].

motive was primarily fiscal or whether this represented a deliberate attempt to stimulate domestic coal mining can only be conjectured. The debates merely record Bland's argument in favor of a protective duty.

The brewers found a staunch defender in Fitzsimons of Pennsylvania, who spoke enthusiastically in favor of a nine-cent duty on beer and porter. He assured the House that protective duties would multiply the number of domestic breweries, thus creating a domestic market for grain and providing additional employment. That breweries would be established could be adduced from the experience of Pennsylvania, where impost duties,[89] he said, had ended the importation of malt liquors and had even made it possible for Philadelphia brewers to export beer, ale, and porter. But while Fitzsimons emphasized the great benefits that would result from government aid to the brewers, Gale of Maryland argued that nine cents a gallon would be unwise on three counts: it would give the brewers a monopoly, defeat the purpose of obtaining a revenue, and enhance the price to the consumer. In the end the brewers had to content themselves with five cents a gallon on beer, ale, and porter when imported in casks, and twenty cents a dozen for bottled cider and porter. Nevertheless, it seems evident that the malt beverage duties were intended to be protective.

A remark by Thatcher of Massachusetts proved that they were: "we have done something," he said, "to favor the brewers in the middle States," and this, he argued, was ample reason why something should be done for "our Eastern brethren" engaged in distilling.[90] Like Ames, Gerry, and Goodhue, he extolled the virtues of rum; like them also, he justified low duties on molasses and high duties on foreign rum on the assumption that protecting the New England distilleries meant assisting the American fisheries and the American carrying trade concurrently.[91] The Massachusetts delegation used every reasonably plausible argument in their persistent demand for protection to dis-

89. Pennsylvania, like most of the other states, enacted several laws intended to protect breweries. To a general duty of 1 percent [December 23, 1780] was added another 1 percent on April 9, 1782. The next year, specific duties on ale and beer of 2/6 (per doz. bottles) replaced the ad valorem duties [March 20, 1783], although six months later a return was made to a general 1 percent ad valorem duty [September 17, 1783]. This was soon increased to 2½ percent [March 15, 1784]. When specific duties were next imposed (6d per gal.; 4s per doz. bottles), they were in addition to the 2½ percent general ad valorem duties [September 20, 1785]. In the same act, a 5 percent duty was levied on malted barley, and this in turn was increased by superadding specific duties of 2/6 [March 29, 1788]. See 10 *Pennsylvania Laws*, 252ff, 411ff; 11 *Pennsylvania Laws*, 65ff, 146ff, 262ff; 12 *Pennsylvania Laws*, 99ff: 13 *Pennsylvania Laws*, 57. The preambles of all these laws are frankly protectionist.

90. *Annals*, 1st Cong., I, 223 [April 28, 1789].

91. Ibid., I, 230, 238, 346. See also p. 236 above.

tilleries. Goodhue admitted that rum distilling would not help New England farmers, but he explained that since "nature has denied us fertility," New England was compelled to engage in fishing and manufacture. Therefore he insisted that these occupations ought to "be entitled to equal encouragement."[92] Gerry's contention was that since Massachusetts imported more molasses than all the other states combined, its "interest stands alone"; its representatives must perforce demand adequate protection for the rum manufacturers because of the "ill effects" which any other policy would have on the prosperity of the state.[93] Despite ridicule and sarcasm, the foursome kept up their agitation; rum was described as a "necessary of life" which had been used for so long that it would "be little less than a revulsion in nature" to ask New Englanders to change to a less ardent drink. When an unsympathetic member of the House opined that such an argument seemed to justify low duties on foreign rum, another less vulnerable defense of the distillers had to be concocted. Not all members of Congress, however, were unsympathetic. Jeremiah Wadsworth of Connecticut asserted that at least a half million dollars had been invested in American distilleries and that the preservation of this specialized capital demanded low duties on molasses and high duties on imported spirits.[94] Boudinot of New Jersey suggested that high American rates on foreign rum might discourage the West Indian planters from converting their molasses into rum and make them more willing to sell their blackstrap molasses as raw materials to American distillers.[95] Meantime the distillers of Philadelphia petitioned the House to widen the spread between the duties on rum and molasses, ratifying in effect the proposals that had been advanced so persistently by the representatives from Boston.

Whereas protection for breweries and distilleries precipitated long and often unpleasant debates, some degree of protection was apparently granted to other branches of manufacturing without any argument whatsoever. Perhaps this testifies to the shrewdness of the committee that drafted the tariff bill, or perhaps it indicates general agreement over the propriety of moderately protective duties. At any rate, aside from those on beverages, only the duties on candles and on steel seem to have been challenged. Tucker of South Carolina, for example, moved that the duties on tallow candles be deleted from the tariff bill. But Fitzsimons of Pennsylvania pointed out that candle

92. Ibid., I, 238.
93. Ibid., I, 346.
94. Ibid., I, 222–223.
95. Ibid., I, 132 [April 14, 1789].

making was "an important manufacture," one "far advanced toward perfection," and one which would soon be able to supply the entire American demand.[96] The biggest candle manufacturing establishment in the United States, in all probability, was that of the Browns in Providence, but since Rhode Island had not yet subscribed to the new government, the spermaceti candle makers did not have the benefit of a spokesman from that state. Even so, Congress imposed duties of six cents per pound on wax, or spermaceti, candles, and two cents per pound on tallow candles.[97]

The protest against a duty on steel, like the objection to duties on candles, was also voiced by southern representatives. And whereas Fitzsimons had answered Tucker, another Pennsylvanian, George Clymer, took the responsibility for justifying the proposed duty on steel against the criticism of Henry Lee of Virginia. Clymer admitted that the manufacture of steel was "in its infancy" and that the American steelmakers could not satisfy the entire domestic demand. Yet because all the materials for steelmaking were available in the United States, and because the industry was not only fairly well established but had solved their basic technical problems, "he deemed it prudent" that Congress should make a forthright effort "to emancipate our country from the manacles" in which it was held "by foreign [steel] manufacturers."[98] Whether it was the vividness of the metaphor which brought congressional endorsement cannot be known; at any event, the duty on steel, as finally approved, was fifty-six cents per hundred weight.

The limited debate on duties (which were clearly designed to protect a score of American industries) indicates that the First Congress did not need to be persuaded about the merits of governmental assistance to the manufacturing interest. The new Constitution symbolized an intention to consolidate in the economic sphere the advances that had been made politically almost a decade before. At the very outset of the tariff debates, the Pennsylvania representatives had insisted that the issue of protection ought to be faced frankly and forthrightly. Madison, sensing the mood of the House, abandoned his original

96. Ibid., I, 152 [April 15, 1789].

97. In imposing duties on candles, Congress once again followed state precedents. Massachusetts levied duties of 2½ percent in 1783, raised the rate to 7½ percent in 1784, and then to 20 percent in 1785. The next year the entry of candles was prohibited. Rhode Island had duties of 10 percent on candles, New York 5 percent, while Pennsylvania collected 2½ percent ad valorem plus a specific duty of 1d per pound. See *Massachusetts A. & L.*, 1782–1783, 506ff; ibid., 1784–1785, 28ff, 453ff; ibid., 1786–1787, 117ff; *Rhode Island S.L.*, June 1785, 18ff; 2 *New York Laws*, 11ff, 509ff; 12 *Pennsylvania Laws*, 99ff.

98. *Annals*, 1st Cong., I, 153 [April 15, 1789].

plan of engineering the passage of a temporary revenue measure. From
that time onward, the theoretical issue of protection was not debated;
indeed Madison himself argued that, given adequate assistance, American manufacturers could before long supply the nation with most
finished commodities.[99] It was only when southerners felt they were
being called upon to make too many concessions that they interposed
objections to particular duties. The problem of the rum distilleries
posed a much larger issue—the question of whether Congress should
attempt to build up an American merchant marine so that the new
government could free itself from dependence on foreign and particularly on British shipping.

The Tariff on Ships

The House debates demonstrate that as far as the tariff was concerned
the mercantile interest made but three major demands on Congress:
low duties on hemp and cordage, on molasses, and on tea. Their really
formidable lobby, one in which they joined forces with the shipbuilders, was directed toward something beyond the tariff: it sought a
preferential and, if possible, a quasi-monopolistic situation for American ships. That is why tonnage duties were discussed concurrently with
the tariff and why Boudinot said that the mercantile interest was more
concerned than any other group with the action of Congress. Spokesmen for American merchants and shipbuilders kept up their agitation
throughout the spring of 1789; the gist of their argument was that
although a tariff would help manufacturers and farmers, it could do
little to encourage the shipping industry.[100] What was needed to encourage the American merchant marine was a tonnage law that would
impose much higher duties on foreign than on American ships. Such
an act, it was contended, would stimulate shipbuilding,[101] stabilize

99. Ibid., I, 248–249 [May 4, 1789].
100. Fitzsimons of Pennsylvania put it this way: "Some gentlemen have
seemed to suppose, that the duties we have imposed are favorable to commerce,
and that we have done a great deal to befriend those engaged in that pursuit;
but, Sir, it is not true that an impost is an encouragement to commerce, the direct contrary is the fact. Look at the revenue . . . which you are about to derive
from that interest, and say, if it does not require some degree of protection in
return. All that your merchants ask, or expect from the sacrifices they make for
the general good, is, that a preference be given to American shipping." *Annals*,
1st Cong., I, 286–287 [May 6, 1789].
101. See the remarks of Samuel Livermore of New Hampshire, ibid., I, 285;
and a petition from the shipwrights of Baltimore "praying the attention of Congress to the increase of American shipping" and urging "the passage of a suitable
navigation act for its encouragement." Ibid., I, 242 [May 4, 1789]. Fitzsimons of
Pennsylvania said that shipbuilding had declined from an annual 5000 tons be-

mercantile profits,[102] and increase the number of seamen, thus providing the country with trained naval personnel.[103] Moreover, it would relieve the new nation from dependence on Great Britain,[104] and by its discrimination against foreign vessels, it would compel foreign nations to relax their onerous restrictions upon American ships.[105]

Special legislative aid to American shipping, it was argued, had the sanction of public opinion; "the general expectation of the country is, that there shall be a discrimination," said Abraham Baldwin of Georgia, "because the voice of the people calls for it."[106] Madison acknowledged that if Congress failed to pass a tonnage act, it would "disappoint the expectations of the warmest friends and advocates of the Constitution";[107] and Ames declared that the encouragement of foreign trade by the federal government "is looked upon to be indispensably necessary."[108] Encouraging American shipping, the proponents of tonnage duties maintained, would benefit every "interest" in the United States.[109] Since discrimination in favor of American ships would encourage shipbuilders to increase the total number of vessels, more American produce could be carried to market and at lower costs;

fore the Revolution to 1300 tons in 1788 and that the industry urgently needed "fostering care and protection." Ibid., I, 295.

102. This point was emphasized when opponents of a high tonnage duty accused the shipowners of seeking a monopoly. Madison, who defended discriminatory tonnage duties, admitted that American shipowners would probably "put a considerable part of the difference in their pockets," but argued that this surplus profit "is a tax we must pay for national security." Ibid., I, 247 [May 4, 1789].

103. Encouraging merchant shipping, said Fitzsimons, means simultaneously training a navy, without which the United States might one day find itself at the mercy of "two or three British frigates." Ibid., I, 290 [May 6, 1789]. See also Madison's argument, ibid., I, 247 [May 4, 1789].

104. See the remarks of Madison, ibid., I, 193; Baldwin of Georgia, ibid., I, 193, 247; Ames of Massachusetts, ibid., I, 265.

105. "If other nations have restricted our navigation by regulations or charges," said Ames, "we must restrict them by a tonnage, or some other duty, so as to restore an equality." Ibid., I, 264–265 [May 5, 1789]. Madison told the House that the United States need have no fear about beginning "commercial hostilities." Britain's large investment in shipping engaged in trade with America, he pointed out, was especially vulnerable; hence he predicted that "if we were to say, that no article should be exported from America to the West Indies, but that went in our own bottoms, we should soon hear a different language" from Britain. Ibid., I, 248 [May 4, 1789].

106. Ibid., I, 195 [April 21, 1789].

107. Ibid., I, 247 [May 4, 1789].

108. Ibid., I, 265 [May 5, 1789].

109. The restrictions imposed upon American foreign trade, said Madison, have restrained it "to an artificial channel" and it is consequently not as "advantageous to America" as it should be; hence it is "the duty of those to whose care the public interest and welfare are committed, to turn the tide to a more favorable direction." Ibid., I, 193 [April 21, 1789], 247 [May 4, 1789].

"every gentleman," contended Fitzsimons, ought therefore to see "how the commercial and agricultural interests are blended in this case" and how the benefits conferred on the shipowners will be transmitted ultimately to the farmers.[110] Madison held the same view; he disputed the assertion of his fellow Virginian that the tonnage act would injure American agriculture,[111] and stressed the complementarity of farming and foreign trade. Ames of Massachusetts went even further: the mere fact that we have several interests, he said, does not mean that we have opposite or conflicting interests; actually the several interests "support each other." Nature has simply dictated that certain regions should engage in particular occupations; "if one end of the continent is employed in manufacture and commerce, the other is attentive to agriculture." Promoting the prosperity of each interest "is compatible with the general interest";[112] the maritime interest, he went on to explain, had been willing to concede whatever seemed necessary to advance agriculture and manufactures, and hence it was only fair that these interests should in turn be willing to grant governmental aid to the maritime interest.

The need for governmental assistance to shipping, the advocates of tonnage discrimination claimed, had been demonstrated by the efforts which the several state legislatures had made to combat the commercial restrictions of foreign countries, especially those of Great Britain. Everyone remembers, said Madison, that the policy of Parliament had been to "seize every advantage which our weak and unguarded position exposed"; as a result, Britain "bound us in commercial manacles, and very nearly defeated the object of our independence."[113] To prevent this calamity, the states began to impose discriminatory duties on foreign vessels. According to Baldwin of Georgia, it was because these laws proved entirely inadequate that the Annapolis Convention was organized.[114] The very fact that legislators in Pennsylvania, Maryland, Virginia, and South Carolina had considered discrimination against foreigners necessary, said Boudinot of New Jersey, supplies the "best evidence" that the federal government ought to

110. Ibid., I, 290 [May 6, 1789]. Fitzsimons estimated that in a single year, Pennsylvania exported 40,000 barrels of beef and 100 tons of butter. Does this not show, he asked, how dependent the agricultural interest is upon the commercial? And does not this indicate the wisdom of a policy designed to make more shipping available so that larger quantities of farm produce can be exported? Ibid., I, 295 [May 7, 1789].
111. Ibid., I, 292 [May 6, 1789].
112. Ibid., I, 264 [May 5, 1789].
113. Ibid., I, 247.
114. Ibid., I, 194 [April 21, 1789].

enact a tonnage law designed to benefit all American shipping.[115] Madison pointed out that inasmuch as the states, by adopting the Constitution, had relinquished their power to regulate commerce, they now necessarily looked to Congress to protect and encourage their merchants and shipowners; and since most of the states had had tonnage laws on their statute books, it could properly be assumed that a federal tonnage law would be "pleasing to them."[116]

Despite all the arguments demonstrating that a tonnage act had the sanction of public opinion, would benefit all interests, and was based on abundant state precedents, the proposal laid before Congress that foreign ships be taxed fifty cents a ton and American ships only six cents a ton ran into stormy weather. It was only after a tempestuous debate, of four days' duration, that the tonnage act was finally steered into port. Although opposition came mostly from southern representatives who feared that high tonnage duties on foreign vessels would increase the cost of sending their agricultural exports overseas, objections just as stubborn were raised by John Laurance of New York and Wadsworth of Connecticut. Indeed Laurance was the first member of the House to protest the idea that discrimination should be made not only between American and foreign ships but between the ships of those foreign nations which had entered into commercial treaties with the United States and those which had not. Every member of the House understood, of course, that the second type of discrimination was directed primarily at Great Britain. Laurance urged a policy of patience and moderation toward Britain, contending that higher duties on the ships of nontreaty nations would not only lead to retaliation, but would decrease the total number of ships clearing from American ports, thus injuring the agricultural interest.[117]

Madison took up this challenge gingerly.[118] Those gentlemen who argue against any discrimination whatsoever, he explained, say in substance that the United States has an insufficient number of ships in which to transport American exports. They maintain that American exporters ought to "employ those vessels that will do our business cheapest." Such a policy, although it has been applauded as the simplest and best, fails to consider that naval power is indispensable to

115. Ibid., I, 272–273 [May 5, 1789].
116. Ibid., I, 297 [May 7, 1789].
117. Ibid., I, 244–245 [May 4, 1789].
118. Until this moment, it had not been entirely clear to the House that two questions were under debate: whether discrimination should be made in tonnage duties between American and foreign ships; and whether a further discrimination should be made between the duties imposed on the ships of treaty nations as compared with those of nontreaty nations.

national survival. If a wide differential between the duties paid by denizens and those paid by aliens means larger profits for American shipowners, this indirect subsidy must be regarded as the cost of national security.[119]

Madison's nationalistic defense of a discriminatory tonnage law seemed to fall upon deaf ears. Wadsworth insisted that British ships were absolutely essential if markets were to be provided for American lumber, pearl ashes, naval stores, rice, and tobacco.[120] Jackson of Georgia predicted a disastrous decline in the price of rice if British ships were deterred from loading American goods because of excessive tonnage duties.[121] He agreed with Laurance of New York that Congress should "act with moderation," especially since all the states had not yet adhered to the new government; a high tonnage duty, he warned, might prevent North Carolina from entering the Union since its lumber exports required abundant shipping facilities.[122] Nor should it be forgotten, said Jackson, that the southern states employ "mostly foreign shipping" and that any diminution of the available cargo space would have ruinous consequences because of the perishability of most southern exports. He also pointed out that the prices of tobacco, indigo, and rice had fallen so low that these products could not bear the higher transport charges which would result from a fifty-cent tonnage duty on British ships.[123] Against these indictments, Ames of Massachusetts made but little headway. He argued that southern products would rise in price if more American ships were made available by vigorous governmental encouragement; moreover, in that event, the prosperity of the South would no longer depend "on the caprice or mercy of any foreign nation."[124] He claimed that the produce of Massachusetts would never have found markets if New Englanders had chosen to adopt a "passive" foreign trade; indeed foreign nations would long ago have destroyed the prosperity of that region had not Yankee shipowners sought markets abroad for whale oil and fish.[125]

Rather than convincing the opposition, Ames only precipitated still more southern antagonism when he described the putative advantages of an "active" foreign trade. Aedanus Burke of South Carolina tried to resolve the difficulty by proposing a deferment of the tonnage legislation. He stressed that the southern people were willing "to render

119. *Annals,* 1st Cong., I, 247 [May 4, 1789].
120. Ibid., I, 251.
121. Ibid., I, 253–254.
122. Ibid., I, 262 [May 5, 1789].
123. Ibid., I, 263.
124. Ibid., I, 265.
125. Ibid., I, 266.

any assistance to increase the maritime importance of the Eastern States, as soon as they are able."[126] Madison seized the opportunity to offer a compromise, proposing a duty of twenty-five cents on foreign ships until January 1, 1791, to be followed by a sixty-cent duty thereafter. He submitted figures to show that over 65 percent of the total tonnage of shipping employed in the United States was already American-owned, and asserted that the dependence of the South on foreign ships had been exaggerated. He assured the House that within a "very short period of time," it would be possible for American shipowners to supply "all the tonnage necessary for our own commerce."[127] The compromise proved unacceptable. William Smith of South Carolina denied the relevance of Madison's figures, pointing out that a very large proportion of American vessels confined their operations to coastwide trade, and hence did not provide the South with facilities for moving their exports to market. He brought up the moot question of the incidence of tonnage duties, contending that a high duty on foreign vessels would inevitably be shifted back upon the southern planters who would then receive ruinously low prices for their exports; it should be evident, he argued, that "a duty on navigation is against the interest of South Carolina and all the agricultural states."[128]

From this moment on, the debates over the proposed tonnage act became a battle between interests and between sections. "I think we have already shown sufficient attention to the manufacturing States, by the import duties which are agreed to," claimed Smith.[129] With complete frankness he told the House that although "the people of South Carolina are willing to make sacrifices to encourage the manufacturing and maritime interests," he hoped the advocates of high tonnage duties on foreign vessels "will not press the matter too far." For if the government prevents the southern planters from getting a fair return

126. Ibid., I, 267.
127.

State	American Ships	Foreign Ships
Massachusetts	76,857	8,794
New York	55,000	30,000
Pennsylvania	44,089	28,012
Maryland	35,671	26,061
Virginia	26,705	29,567
South Carolina	31,904	25,073
Georgia	6,500	13,500

Although Madison had no figures for New Hampshire, Connecticut, New Jersey, or Delaware, he was confident that in those states American-owned shipping exceeded foreign. Ibid., I, 269.

128. Ibid., I, 270–271.
129. Ibid., I, 271.

for their products, it "must be answerable for the consequences."[130] Just what these "consequences" might have been is not evident from the debates, but at this juncture Boudinot of New Jersey offered another compromise: to allow South Carolina planters to get out from under their burden of debt to British merchants, he proposed a tonnage duty of twenty-five cents on foreign ships.[131] Before that proposal could even be debated, Tucker of South Carolina made a plea for still lower tonnage duties. He was of the opinion that discriminatory duties would prevent British ships from engaging in American trade; as a result, the tonnage law, rather than bringing in revenue for the treasury, would merely raise freight rates and swell the profits of Yankee shipowners.[132]

Samuel Livermore of New Hampshire denied that the tonnage duties would operate as a tax upon the South; it would be "a tax upon foreigners," one which they would be able to pay and one which they would be willing to pay rather than forsake the profits of the American carrying trade.[133] He denied, moreover, that the benefits arising from the tonnage act would be enjoyed exclusively by northern shipowners and shipbuilders; "this encouragement," he said, "is not confined to the Northern States" because it will be "participated in by the middle and southern" states as well.[134] Bland of Virginia nevertheless felt that the commercial interest was making unreasonable demands. The most important task of Congress, he contended, was "to attend particularly to the agricultural part of the United States." He urged the adoption of a temporary arrangement so that Congress might have more time "to get information relative to the state of agriculture and commerce."[135] Fitzsimons of Pennsylvania, however, pressed for an immediate vote on the proposed tonnage law, arguing that it would provide a great deal of revenue which would actually be paid, not by American exporters, but by the European consumers of American produce.[136] Madison rose to say that it was not a question of penalizing the agricultural interest in order to benefit the maritime interest; both would benefit because "both interests are compatible and consistent with each other."[137]

At this stage in the House debates the relation of interests to legis-

130. Ibid., I, 272.
131. Ibid., I, 272–273.
132. Ibid., I, 275.
133. Ibid., I, 283 [May 6, 1789].
134. Ibid., I, 285.
135. Ibid.
136. Ibid., I, 287.
137. Ibid., I, 292.

lation was explained with complete candor. The states that adopted the Constitution, admitted Smith of South Carolina, did so because they expected that the new government would favor their several branches of enterprise: "the manufacturing States wished the encouragement of manufactures, the maritime States the encouragement of ship-building, and the agricultural States the encouragement of agriculture."[138] What progress had Congress made in meeting these expectations? For the manufacturing interest, said Smith, "we have laid heavy duties upon foreign goods, to encourage domestic manufactures"; for the maritime interest, "we are now about to lay a tonnage duty, for the encouragement of commerce." Only the agricultural interest has been neglected. Tucker, also of South Carolina, warmly endorsed this indictment; moreover, he took pains to point out that he thought it quite legitimate that he should do his utmost to ensure governmental assistance for southern farmers, inasmuch as each member of Congress "is bound to support . . . the interest he is well acquainted with."[139] Only by such vigilance would all the interests within the nation receive their share of governmental aid, and only by the resulting legislative equilibrium could the general welfare be advanced.

And so the long debate about the tonnage act finally ended. Despite the stubborn objection of the southern representatives, the House voted to impose a fifty-cent duty on the ships of nontreaty countries and a thirty-cent duty on those of treaty countries, as compared with nine cents on American-built ships and six cents on foreign-built ships owned by Americans. Disagreements between the House and the Senate were gradually resolved, but the final law differed only slightly from the House bill. On July 20, the tonnage act became law; under it American-owned vessels were to pay six cents, American-built ships wholly or partly owned by foreigners thirty cents, while all other vessels were to pay fifty cents. The much-disputed discrimination between treaty and nontreaty nations had been eliminated as a result of the strenuous objections of the Senate. But since the thirty- and fifty-cent rates on foreign ships remained unchanged, the maritime interest had scored a major legislative victory.

The Word and the Deed

Of the forty-eight members of the Lower House in the First Congress, only one, James Madison, had made any contribution to the basic theory underlying governmental responsibility to business enterprise,

138. Ibid., I, 298 [May 7, 1789].
139. Ibid., I, 301.

a subject analyzed in detail in chapters VI and VII. He must therefore be regarded as the exception that proves that practical politicians as a rule are not political theorists. Nor should it be left unsaid that Madison was the only member of the House who even mentioned the Smithian theory of administrative nihilism. While the debates of the Second and Third congresses contain scattered references to economists and to political theorists, the formal discussions of the First Congress, aside from Madison's rejection of a system of natural liberty in favor of a system of "national prudence," are almost barren of any discussion of *laissez-faire*. Indisputably, the sentiment of the First Congress was in favor of governmental intervention on behalf of the several interests; it is therefore the theory of interests rather than the theory of business freedom which dominates the House debates of the First Congress. Revenue considerations, of course, were necessarily uppermost, but from the moment when Fitzsimons of Pennsylvania rejected a temporary tariff as unacceptable, the prevailing legislative objective became one of merging fiscal considerations with meliorative governmental action. The legitimacy of intervention elicited no criticism; only when some particular interest or some particular section thought it was not receiving its share of governmental assistance did anything remotely resembling a philosophy of governmental function creep into the House debates.

This is an extremely important conclusion. Congress had apparently accepted the idea that government ought properly to lend its assistance to any occupational group large enough and important enough in the national economy to deserve congressional recognition. In the debates on the tariff and on the tonnage act the claimants on governmental assistance were all "natural interests";[140] hence there was no controversy over "illegitimate" or "factitious" interests. And the remarkable thing is that when the funding act was discussed later, the *Annals of Congress* gives only the faintest intimation of the bitter denunciation of the "illegitimate" interests of speculators and monied men which loomed so large in the contemporaneous pamphlet literature. Indeed, the book and pamphlet literature moves in a different channel from that of the congressional debates. Apparently, to practical politicians, then as now, the contrasts between good and bad, between justice and injustice, between right policy and wrong policy were by no means as sharp as they appeared to the eyes of contemporary theorists. Legislative procedure, as contrasted with economic or political theory, simply assumed that the machinery of government ought to be employed to aid importuning interests; and each interest, in its effort to obtain its share

140. See pp. 42–43 above.

of governmental patronage, seemingly stood ready to make any reasonable concession to other interests. To test the validity of this interpretation, it becomes necessary to scrutinize the *Annals of Congress* once again in order to discover the further interplay of interests and to ascertain whether any new claimants on governmental assistance were emerging. This can best be done by analyzing the petitions addressed to Congress by groups of businessmen and by examining the persistent efforts made to revise the tariff and tonnage acts. To this subject the next chapter will be devoted.

IX

The Emergence of a Broader Program of Governmental Intervention

Mr. Samuel Smith presented a petition from the tradesmen, manufacturers, and others of the town of Baltimore . . . setting forth that . . . they have observed with serious regret the manufacturing and trading interest of the country rapidly declining, and the attempts of the state Legislatures to remedy the evil failing of their object; that in the present melancholy state of our country, the number of poor increasing for want of employment, foreign debts accumulating, houses and lands depreciating in value, and trade and manufactures languishing and expiring, they look up to the Supreme Legislature of the United States as the guardians of the whole empire.

Annals of Congress, April 10, 1789

Petitions and Pressure Groups

SOON after the first tariff had gone into effect, a stream of petitions began to pour in upon Congress, some asking for higher duties, some for lower.[1] A majority of the petitions concerned with tariff revision came from manufacturers, quite a few from merchants, but none from farmers. Of forty-one tariff petitions addressed to the House during the First, Second, and Third congresses, one asked for a general revision of the tariff laws, twenty-four requested higher duties on particular articles, nine urged Congress to lower or repeal certain duties, six sought drawback provisions, while only one recommended the continuation of an existing duty. The petitions had reference to more than a score of articles, ranging from such basic commodities as iron and coal to such luxuries as chocolate or snuff. Some of the petitions came from individual businessmen, others from groups of manufacturers or merchants in the same town; in at least three instances the arrival of identical petitions in quick succession suggests concerted action by groups of petitioners in several towns or cities.

Partly in response to these petitions and partly in order to deal with old and new fiscal problems, Congress revised the tariff four times between 1789 and 1794,[2] either by amending existing tariff laws or by including import duties in excise legislation.[3] The extent to which Congress acceded to the wishes of petitioners will be indicated briefly by comparing the precise demands of the petitions with the duties

1. The first tariff became law on August 1, 1789; the first petition asking for a revision of duties was presented to Congress on March 16, 1790. Five petitions in the calendar year 1790 were followed by two in 1791, eight in 1792, five in 1793, fourteen in 1794, and seven in 1795.

2. 1 *U.S. Laws*, 180ff [August 10, 1790]; ibid., 199ff [March 3, 1791]; ibid., 259ff [May 2, 1792]; ibid., 390ff [June 7, 1794].

3. As was the case in 1791, ibid., 199ff.

subsequently enacted. The primary concern of this chapter, however, is not the tariff but the general legislative principles of intervention which begin to take form in Congress. Since the tariff was only partly responsible for the emergence of this broader theory of governmental functions, the inquiry must go far beyond the tariff debates. The excise laws, for example, brought another stream of petitions and had a profound effect upon congressional opinion on the relations of government and business; so did the stormy arguments over bounties to fishermen and over the embargo voted on March 26, 1794. There were also minor controversies that helped clarify the underlying issues; the debates on the census, for instance, throw a great deal of light on the attitude of Congress toward the major interests. Yet inasmuch as the tariff, more than anything else, first compelled Congress to recognize its responsibility to businessmen, it is appropriate to begin this exploration of the broader governmental program by analyzing the precise demands of the petitions for tariff revision and by demonstrating the extent of congressional compliance with the wishes of the petitioners.

The Demands of Businessmen for Tariff Revision

The largest number of petitions from any single industry came from the manufacturers of cordage. The first two petitions, from cordage makers in New York and Philadelphia respectively, asked for higher duties on foreign cordage and for lower duties on hemp.[4] Although the *Annals of Congress* supplies no evidence, Congress apparently took some cognizance of these requests, since they came from leading American ports. At any event, in the tariff act of 1790[5] the hemp duties were lowered from sixty cents to fifty-four cents per hundred weight, while the duties on cordage were increased about a third.[6] The proposed tariff revision of 1792 elicited no petitions from cordage manufacturers, but it did precipitate some congressional debate about hemp and cordage. Laurance of New York, speaking no doubt on behalf of the shipowners and cordage makers of New York City, opposed any increase in the duty on hemp "on account of its being a

4. The petition "from the importers of hemp and the manufacturers of cordage of New York" asked that hemp be put on the free list and that the importation of foreign cordage be prohibited. *Annals*, 1st Cong., II, 1500 [March 16, 1790]. The Philadelphia cordage manufacturers asked merely for higher duties on cordage. Ibid. II, 1602 [April 29, 1790].

5. 1 *U.S. Laws*, 180ff [August 10, 1790].

6. Cables were raised from 75¢ to $1.00, tarred cordage from 75¢ to $1.00, untarred cordage and yarn from 90¢ to $1.50, twine or pack thread from $2.00 to $3.00.

raw material, and a very essential one too, to the navigation and commerce of the United States";[7] whereas Hugh Williamson of North Carolina and White of Virginia, since they represented the leading hemp-growing states, very naturally favored higher duties on hemp.[8] White admitted the wisdom of increasing the cordage duties because they were "designed to encourage the manufactures of the United States," but he insisted that "equal attention should be paid to the agricultural interest."[9] Actually Congress did show more than "equal attention," for although the cordage duties were raised about 60 percent,[10] the hemp duties were almost doubled.[11] The increased protection to the hemp growers, however, did not greatly decrease the dependence of American cordage manufacturers on foreign-grown hemp. Proof of this was presently brought to the attention of Congress when the New England cordage manufacturers petitioned for drawback privileges on all the foreign hemp they had processed into rope, twine, or pack thread. The Providence manufacturers sent the first of these petitions in 1793,[12] but Congress, when it revised the tariff in 1794, ignored their request. This probably explains why identical petitions were presented, in the winter of 1795, by the cordage manufacturers of Boston,[13] Newport,[14] and Providence,[15] urging Congress to authorize drawbacks on all foreign hemp reexported in the form of cordage. Thus the first industry to importune Congress for tariff revision in 1790 had definitely begun to consolidate its lobbying strength by 1795.

Meantime, the three petitions submitted while the 1790 tariff was being drafted, all asking for higher duties, were setting the pattern for many subsequent requests. The manufacturers of mustard in Phila-

7. *Annals,* 2nd Cong., 560 [April 19, 1792].
8. Williamson said that "experiments have proved" that hemp could be raised profitably "if duly encouraged"; and that, if it were adequately stimulated, hemp growing would "conduce to rooting out the cultivation to tobacco, which impoverishes the soil." Ibid.
9. "An interest as important as any other, at least." Ibid.
10. Cables and tarred cordage from $1.00 to $1.80, untarred cordage and yarn from $1.50 to $2.25, twine or pack thread from $3.00 to $4.00. 1 *U.S. Laws,* 259ff [May 2, 1792].
11. From 54¢ to $1.00. Ibid.
12. *Annals,* 2nd Cong., 834 [January 22, 1793]. Drawback procedures had been explicitly defined in the excise law of 1791. 1 *U.S. Laws* 199, sec. 57, March 3, 1791. For details see Leonard D. White, *The Federalists,* pp. 297–298.
13. "A memorial of sundry manufacturers of hemp . . . praying that the drawback of the duty imposed by law on the importation of foreign hemp, may be allowed on the same, when manufactured into cordage within the United States." *Annals,* 3rd Cong., 1131 [January 26, 1795].
14. Ibid., 1159 [January 30, 1795].
15. Ibid., 1162 [February 2, 1795].

delphia were successful,[16] as were the "sundry inhabitants" of Morris County, New Jersey, who wanted higher duties on copperas, vitriol, Spanish brown, Venetian red, and yellow ocher.[17] But the "manufacturers of Tobacco and Snuff in the town of Baltimore"[18] apparently had no influence on Congress; at any rate, the tariff of 1790 left these duties unchanged. Congress might have feared that higher duties on tobacco and snuff would decrease customs receipts—an assumption which seems reasonable in view of the predominantly fiscal nature of the tariff of 1790. Indeed that law was entitled "An Act making further provision for the payment of the debts of the United States,"[19] and its preamble declared it necessary to increase import duties for fiscal reasons. Accordingly higher duties were levied on commodities that could not be produced advantageously within the United States: on wines, spirits, molasses, tea, coffee, sugar, indigo, salt, earthenware, glass, paper, and spices. Great caution seems to have been employed lest any duties be raised so high that importing would be discouraged;[20] yet in a few cases where demand was judged to be inelastic, duties were sharply increased.[21] Whether any of the new duties were intended to give greater protection to domestic manufacturers is hard to determine, for although the duties on coal were increased 50 percent[22] and those on unwrought steel just a trifle less,[23] the duties on beer, candles, and nails remained unchanged. It seems reasonable to conclude, therefore, that the primary concern of Congress centered on increased customs revenues, and that the petitions were considered in terms of this basic objective.

The preoccupation of Congress in 1790 with fiscal matters is attested also by its decision to leave the tonnage act of 1789 virtually unchanged, even though spokesmen for American shipowners, particularly Fitzsimons of Pennsylvania, did their best to have the tonnage duties on foreign ships raised from fifty cents to a dollar.[24] It is quite

16. *Annals*, 1st Cong., II, 1583 [April 16, 1790]. Mustard had not been enumerated in 1789 and therefore paid 5 percent. In 1790, however, mustard was included in a grocery list subject to 10 percent.

17. Ibid., II, 1602 [April 30, 1790]. In the 1789 tariff, "paints ground in oil" paid 10 percent, whereas dry paints were unenumerated and therefore paid but 5 percent. The 1790 tariff made all "painters' colors" dutiable at 10 percent.

18. For their petition, see ibid., II, 1583 [April 16, 1790].

19. 1 *U.S. Laws*, 180–182, 1st Cong., 2nd Sess., ch. 39 [August 10, 1790].

20. Coaches, chariots, phaetons, chaises, and carriages which had paid 15 percent in 1789 were raised to 15½ percent.

21. The duties on wine were just about doubled; those on tea, coffee, and sugar were increased by 60 to 80 percent.

22. From 2¢ a bushel to 3¢.

23. From 56¢ a cwt. to 75¢.

clear, however, that in this case, petitions from merchants did not help the "maritime interest";[25] indeed they seemed to have succeeded only in solidifying the opposition of southern representatives to any further increase in tonnage duties. Smith of South Carolina brought up the old argument that higher tonnage duties would injure agriculture, "the primary interest of the United States," by imposing the equivalent of an export tax on southern staples.[26] The right policy, he declared, ought to be to facilitate, not to impede, the marketing of American farm produce, a view vigorously endorsed by Williamson of North Carolina[27] and White of Virginia.[28] Smith's severest criticism of the proposal to raise the tonnage duties, however, was that the maritime interest had asked for more than its share of governmental encouragement; indeed, in his opinion, the "navigating States" had already obtained more favors than either the manufacturing or the agricultural states and were entirely unreasonable in their demands. As for the petitions that had helped to precipitate the debate, Smith disposed of them with the devastating remark that it would be "an extraordinary proceeding" on the part of Congress to double the tonnage duties merely because a petition had been received "from some merchants in Portsmouth."[29] And so the southern opposition prevailed. Although the tonnage act was rewritten in order to define "coastwise traffic" more precisely, no changes were made in the tonnage duties;[30] the reenacted regulation of foreign trade became law exactly one year after the original tonnage act of 1789. This time the petitions of interested parties had merely prejudiced some members of Congress against the petitioners.

The next revision of the tariff, on March 3, 1791, was incidental to the passage of an excise act, and this may have been the reason why only two petitions having any bearing on commercial policy were

24. Fitzsimons argued that higher tonnage duties would encourage shipbuilding, an industry which would lead to the export of a limited amount of materials, and a large amount of American labor. *Annals*, 1st Cong., II, 1620 [May 12, 1790]. This argument had been often used by British advocates of protection in the seventeenth and eighteenth centuries. See my *Predecessors of Adam Smith*, chap. XV.

25. See the petition from "merchants and traders" of Portsmouth, New Hampshire, *Annals*, 1st Cong., II, 994–995 [March 26, 1790], and a similar one from "sundry merchants and traders" of Newburyport, Massachusetts, ibid., II, 1574 [April 9, 1790].

26. Ibid., II, 1610 [May 10, 1790].

27. Ibid., II, 1614.

28. Ibid., II, 1621 [May 12, 1790]. White charged that the pressure for higher tonnage duties justified the fears of those members of the Constitutional Convention who had foreseen the undue influence of "the commercial interest."

29. Ibid., II, 1611–1612 [May 10, 1792].

30. 1 *U.S. Laws*, 135–136 [July 20, 1790].

submitted to Congress in 1791.[31] One of these, however, constituted the spearhead[32] of a group of petitions submitted a year later by merchants of Philadelphia,[33] New York,[34] and Rhode Island[35] engaged in the China trade. The Philadelphia and New York petitions, separated in time by only one day and identical in their demands, indicated that the merchants of America's leading seaports had joined forces. But while the Philadelphia and New York merchants who were engaged in direct trade with the Orient sought higher duties on Far Eastern goods that came in foreign bottoms, the Rhode Island merchants asked that tea brought from Europe in American ships be admitted at the same duties levied on tea shipped directly from India and China. These somewhat conflicting requests gave Congress an excuse for disregarding the petitions entirely, which was extremely convenient since either course of action recommended by the petitioners would probably have reduced federal revenues[36] at the very moment when the fiscal exigencies of the government were so acute that recourse had to be made to much-despised excise taxes.

The excises imposed in 1791 soon brought a storm of protest.[37] Meantime Indian uprisings had necessitated greatly increased military expenditures that made larger federal revenues imperative. Once again the tariff was revised, on May 2, 1792, and this time the duties were increased all along the line.[38] But not a single petition was submitted

31. One, addressed to the Senate by "the masters of American vessels in the port of Charleston," asked for "some further regulations for the encouragement of the carrying trade to Europe." *Annals*, 1st Cong., II, 1801 [February 16, 1791].

32. Presented by Fitzsimons, it asked that additional duties be laid "on all goods imported into the United States from India or China in foreign bottoms." Ibid., II, 1921–1922 [January 20, 1791].

33. The Philadelphia merchants addressed petitions to both the House and the Senate. *Annals*, 2nd Cong., 427 [February 24, 1792]. Ibid., 98 [March 1, 1792].

34. Ibid., 431 [February 29, 1792].

35. Ibid., 477 [March 21, 1792].

36. It will be recalled that all goods from China and India (except tea) brought direct in American ships paid but 5 percent whereas goods brought in foreign bottoms paid 12½ percent. Higher duties on foreign ships would no doubt have decreased customs receipts. As for the request of the Rhode Island merchants that tea be admitted on equal terms whether it came direct from the Orient or by way of Europe, this would have meant a lowering of the duties from 16 to 25 percent on all tea imported from Europe.

37. See below, pp. 284–286.

38. 1 *U.S. Laws*, 259ff. Specific duties on beer and on some wines were increased 60 percent; distilled spirits about 25 percent; cocoa duties were doubled, as were also those on nails and spikes; unwrought steel was raised 33⅓ percent; coal 5 percent; commodities subject to 12½ percent ad valorem under the tariff of 1790 were charged 15 percent, while most imports paying 7½ percent were increased to 10 percent; unenumerated goods which had hitherto paid 5 percent were made dutiable at 7½ percent. Two new categories of goods were estab-

to Congress when this new revenue bill was being debated, and the only indication of the attitude of the public toward the new legislation is to be found in the vigorous opposition of one member of Congress who spoke in behalf of frontier farmers. The whole system of federal taxation, said John Steele of North Carolina, was tending to become more oppressive to the "landed interest";[39] high duties "on salt, nails, shoes, and other essential articles in husbandry . . . are seriously complained of" in the southern states. Steele's criticism had adequate justification: the salt duties had been doubled in 1790 to the disadvantage of the cattle raisers, while now, in 1792, Congress was about to double the duty on nails, to increase the duties on iron, unwrought steel, and fire arms, and to raise all nonenumerated articles from 5 percent to 7½ percent. Without question, the new tariff would operate to the disadvantage of frontier farmers. But the need for more revenue to meet increased current expenses and to service the public debt made a deeper impression on Congress than did this slight to frontier farmers; thus Steele's protest was in vain.

For the next two years, no changes were made in the tariff. Only a few petitions were presented to Congress praying for tariff changes, and most of these dealt with administrative or technical problems. The merchants of Charleston, for example, asked that the fees in the Court of Admiralty be reduced,[40] and within four months had the satisfaction of congressional compliance.[41] "Sundry masters and owners of coasting vessels" asked that the fees imposed on coasting vessels be reduced;[42] the "merchants and traders" of Wilmington requested a revision of the revenue laws so that drawbacks might be authorized on goods reexported from a customs district other than the one into which they were originally imported;[43] while the inhabitants of Hudson, New York, requested that their city be designated a port of entry, so that they would no longer be required to "register, enter, and clear their vessels at the port of New York."[44] Last in this series of minor

---

lished, paying 15 percent and 10 percent respectively. The revisions were consistently upwards except that a few commodities, formerly dutiable, were placed on the free list, notably copper and raw wool.

39. It is clear from Steel's remarks that he meant the small farmers rather than the large planters. *Annals,* 2nd Cong., 587 [April 1792].

40. They petitioned both the House and the Senate. *Annals,* 2nd Cong., 670 [November 5, 1792]; ibid., 610 [November 6, 1792].

41. 1 *U.S. Laws,* 332–333 [March 1, 1793]. The new legislation, entitled "An Act to Ascertain the Fees in Admiralty Proceedings," specified the maximum fees of the clerk and the marshal.

42. *Annals,* 2nd Cong., 728 [November 26, 1792].

43. Ibid., 752 [December 24, 1792].

44. Ibid., 790 [January 5, 1793].

items came a petition from "the merchants and inhabitants" of Norfolk and Portsmouth, Virginia, urging Congress to impose an additional tonnage tax in order to establish marine hospitals "for sick and disabled seamen."[45] The only petition in the 1792 crop that requested a change in a particular tariff duty came from a printer in Worcester, Massachusetts, who asked that printing type be placed on the free list.[46] Meantime Congress, without the goading of any petition, had removed impost duties "on horses, and other useful beasts" and had agreed to remit all duties that had already been collected on breeding stock.[47]

In 1793 one vague request for a general tariff revision[48] and a precise petition from Pennsylvania paper makers[49] (asking that imported rags be admitted duty free and that duties on paper be continued) were apparently shelved, inasmuch as Congress deferred any further general revision of the tariff until the Third Congress convened. The winter and spring of 1794, in contrast, brought a bumper crop of tariff petitions. The paint makers of Baltimore and Alexandria wanted duties on dry paints removed and higher duties imposed on "paints ground in oil," in order to encourage the grinding of paints within

45. Ibid., 868 [February 8, 1793]. Williamson of North Carolina, in recommending an additional tonnage duty on all American vessels that failed to carry a complement of apprentice seamen, also proposed that some of the revenue collected should be earmarked "for caring for sick and infirm seamen." Ibid., 695 [November 19, 1792]. The proposal that the federal government establish marine hospitals was probably an effort to transfer responsibility for the hospitalization of seamen from the states to the central government. Virginia had levied a tax on seamen for the purpose of maintaining a marine hospital; North Carolina had required sailors to make contributions to a relief fund; Georgia had collected funds for a seamen's hospital from tonnage duties. See 12 *Virginia Laws (Hening)*, 305 [October 1786]; ibid., 494–495 [December 20, 1787]; 13 *Virginia Laws (Hening)*, 158–159 [December 24, 1790]; 1 *Shepard S.L. Virginia*, 307 [December 25, 1794]; 25 *North Carolina S.R.* 56–57; I *Martin* 481 [December 22, 1789]; *Georgia Laws (Watkins)*, 351ff [February 10, 1787]; Ibid., 383f [February 1, 1789].

46. The petition came from Isaiah Thomas, whose printing indicates he had need of better type. *Annals*, 2nd Cong., 768 [December 31, 1792]. The tariff of 1790 had imposed duties of 1¢ per lb. on lead, and the tariff act of 1791 stipulated that this duty applied to any commodity made entirely of lead, or any commodity in which lead was the chief component. See 1 *U.S. Laws*, 180ff, 198ff. In 1795, a duty of 10 percent was levied on printing types. Ibid., 411.

47. See the House Resolution, *Annals*, 2nd Cong., 867 [February 7, 1793]; a message from the Senate, ibid., 893 [February 23, 1793]; and the act repealing the duties on "horses, cattle, sheep, swine, or other useful beasts, imported into the United States for breed." 1 *U.S. Laws*, 324 [February 27, 1794].

48. From "sundry merchants and traders of Providence . . . stating the disadvantage that attend the operation of the existing revenue laws of the United States, and praying that the same may be revised and amended." *Annals*, 2nd Cong., 881 [February 19, 1793].

49. Ibid., 881–882.

the United States,[50] but their petition was fruitless.[51] Two manufacturers of New York City,[52] who asked for higher duties on "house or hand-bellows," were more successful, since the duties on all leather goods were increased by 5 percent.[53] The opposition of the farm bloc probably explains why the petition of Thomas Perkins and Company, of Philadelphia, and a similar one from Joseph G. Pierson of New York, asking for additional duties on nails,[54] were disregarded. Congress did find merit, however, in the petition of Samuel Swann and others,[55] of Richmond, Virginia, for higher duties on coal, and raised the duty on coal to five cents a bushel.[56] But in spite of petitions from the leading members of the Boston Glass Factory,[57] from M'Clallen, MacGregor and Company, of Albany,[58] and from John F. Amelung[59] and his associates, of Frederick County, Maryland, Congress refused to increase the duty of window glass, although it did raise the duties on other kinds of glassware by 5 percent.[60] The iron manufacturers showed less unanimity than the glassmakers; a memorial from a group of Pennsylvania iron manufacturers urged that the existing iron duties be continued;[61] this may have been intended to offset a petition from "merchants, manufacturers of iron, and shipbuilders" of Philadelphia who importuned Congress to repeal the duties on bar iron.[62] Yet despite the disagreement between the petitioners,

50. *Annals,* 3rd Cong., 256 [January 22, 1794].
51. The 1789 tariff levied 10 percent on "paints ground in oil"; the 1790 tariff made the 10 percent applicable to all "painters' colors"; the 1792 tariff imposed 15 percent on "painters' colors, whether dry or ground in oil"; the 1794 tariff made no changes in the duty on paints.
52. *Annals,* 3rd Cong., 417 [February 3, 1794].
53. 1 *U.S. Laws,* 390ff [June 7, 1794].
54. *Annals,* 3rd Cong., 432 [February 6, 1794]; ibid., 458 [February 21, 1794]. No change was made in the 2¢ per lb. levied in 1792.
55. Ibid., 442 [February 10, 1794].
56. The coal duty went steadily upward, from 2¢ in 1789 to 3¢ in 1790, 4½¢ in 1792, and 5¢ in 1794.
57. *Annals,* 3rd Cong., 452 [February 13, 1794]. The Boston Glass Factory was already receiving bounties and other aid from the Commonwealth of Massachusetts.
58. Ibid., 453 [February 14, 1794].
59. Ibid., 456 [February 19, 1794]. Amelung made persistent efforts to obtain a loan of money from Congress for his glass works. See below, pp. 275–277.
60. It seems likely that the glass makers had an effective lobby in the 1790s inasmuch as the glass duties moved steadily upward, from 10 percent in 1789 to 12½ percent in 1790, then to 15 percent in 1792 and except for mirrors and window glass, to 20 percent in 1794.
61. This petition came from "Levi Hollingsworth and other proprietors of iron works." *Annals,* 3rd Cong., 474–475 [March 3, 1794]. It also requested that encouragement be given "to the erecting and improving furnaces and forges for manufacturing the said article within the United States."
62. *Annals,* 3rd Cong., 474–475 [March 3, 1794].

Congress increased the duties on cast, slit, rolled, and manufactured iron by 5 percent. It raised the duty on hats by an equal amount, thus gratifying the hat makers of Fredericksburg and Falmouth, Virginia, and those of New York, Pennsylvania, and Delaware, all of whom had asked for more protection.[63] The metal button makers of New Haven, who had requested higher duties,[64] also succeeded in getting an additional 5 percent, as did the stocking manufacturers of Newark, New Jersey.[65] All in all, then, the 1794 tariff was a field day for the petitioning manufacturers. But whereas the petitioners modified the details of the tariff revision, it was Congress that dictated the general design.[66] Indeed only one speaker[67] protested vigorously against the upward trend of import duties, and his complaint that the increased duties on nonenumerated articles would injure "the poorer class" of people failed to hold back the tide of sentiment in favor of higher import duties.

There was one other matter, in 1794, that concerned some businessmen. As British foreign policy became increasingly hostile, the earlier proposal for discriminatory tonnage duties on the vessels of those countries that had not entered into a commercial treaty with the United States was revised.[68] The problem was debated at great length.[69] Some of the representatives from the shipbuilding and shipowning states had urged discrimination against Britain and were accused of using the critical emergency to feather their own nests. Spokesmen for the mercantile interest recommended caution and patience, which led William Findley of Pennsylvania to say that the merchants had no interest in anything but the volume of business they were conducting with Great Britain.[70] On February 5, 1794, by a close vote (51 to 47), the House postponed action on the matter until March 15. The businessmen of Norfolk and Portsmouth, Virginia, seized the op-

63. Ibid., 478–479 [March 5, 1794]. Obviously Congress could not grant the second request of the Virginia hat makers for an export duty on beaver and other furs since this would have been unconstitutional.

64. Ibid., 481–482 [March 6, 1794].

65. See the petition of Michael Trappal, ibid., 522 [March 17, 1794].

66. Although the act of 1794 changed very few specific duties, it increased the ad valorem duties on several categories (for the most part by 5 percent) and it raised the duty on nonenumerated articles from 7½ percent (the 1792 rate) to 10 percent. See 1 *U.S. Laws*, 390–392 [June 7, 1794].

67. See the remarks of Jonathan Dayton of New Jersey, *Annals*, 3rd Cong., 459–460 [February 21, 1794].

68. See above, p. 258.

69. *Annals*, 3rd Cong., 174–430. For an excellent summary of the entire debate, see the remarks of Abiel Foster of Massachusetts, ibid., 413–417 [January 31, 1794].

70. Ibid., 431 [February 5, 1794].

portunity to petition Congress and to urge "further restrictions and higher duties" on British imports.[71] Indeed as Britain's naval policy became still more menacing, the attitude of southern representatives changed markedly. Thus Smith of South Carolina, who had persistently opposed any economic discrimination against nontreaty countries, not only admitted that appeasement had failed but proposed that an embargo be laid on all shipping in order to bring Britain to terms.[72] Now it was Theodore Sedgwick of Massachusetts who counseled patience. He asserted that American shipbuilders and manufacturers were trying to shape the foreign policy of the United States to advance their own selfish interests. He asked the House if it felt justified "in sacrificing to . . . a few ship-carpenters and other mechanics, the ease and comfort of that most useful and respectable description of men, the farmer and planter."[73] Most members of Congress, however, realized that much more was at stake than immediate business considerations. Ten days later (March 26, 1794) Congress laid a thirty-day embargo[74] on "all ships and vessels in the ports of the United States . . . bound to any foreign port or place," thereby establishing a precedent for several other embargoes,[75] and particularly for the embargo of 1807 which was to have tremendous political and profound economic effects upon the course of American history. Merchants kicked like steers at the embargo of 1794;[76] nevertheless it was extended for another month,[77] although clearances were authorized for ships engaged in the China trade.[78] Just before it adjourned, Congress authorized the president to reimpose the embargo during the summer recess if circumstances should make it necessary.[79] Here, then, was a case where Congress, in the interests of peace and national prestige, largely disregarded the importunities of businessmen and dealt courageously with a vexatious problem of foreign policy.

71. This petition came from "sundry merchants, mariners, tradesmen, and other citizens." Ibid., 484 [March 10, 1794].
72. Ibid., 506–508 [March 14, 1794].
73. Ibid., 517–518.
74. 1 *U.S. Laws,* 400 [March 26, 1794]. In order to ensure that coastwise ships would not engage in overseas operations a bond equal to twice the value of the ship and cargo had to be given to ensure the relanding of the cargo at an American port. Ibid., 400 [April 2, 1794].
75. See Herbert Heaton, "Non-Importation, 1606–1812," *Journal of Economic History,* I (1940), 178–198.
76. See the remarks of Samuel Dexter of Massachusetts, *Annals,* 3rd Cong., 588 [April 14, 1794].
77. 1 *U.S. Laws,* 401 [April 18, 1794].
78. The shipowners were required to post bonds which were to be forfeited if a ship unloaded before it had passed the Cape of Good Hope. Ibid.
79. Ibid., 372 [June 4, 1794].

Undismayed, the petitioners continued to send in their requests. A group of Philadelphia merchants asked Congress if they might export lead to India or China.[80] But no sooner had this petition been granted,[81] on the assumption that lead exports were essential for the continuance of the Oriental trade, than some New York City merchants asked permission to export "a quantity of cutlasses" to the West Indies.[82] These rather unusual petitions soon gave way to the more familiar kind. The ironmasters of Pennsylvania wanted additional duties on all iron imports;[83] the Massachusetts chocolate manufacturers asked Congress to repeal that portion of the tariff of 1794 which had imposed an extra two cents per pound on cocoa;[84] while the paper makers asked, once again, that imported rags be placed on the free list.[85] Meantime Congress had made a few minor changes in the tariff,[86] although there is no evidence to indicate that businessmen had anything to do with this relatively insignificant tariff law.

Little more need be said about the relation of businessmen to the growing fabric of tariff legislation. Petitions had increased in number, and efforts had been made to consolidate lobbying power. But as the petitioners gradually increased their pressure, Congress seemed to build up more resistance against their demands. When fiscal considerations were of paramount importance, petitions for tariff reductions were disregarded, while in other instances increases in duties were made that equaled or exceeded the demands of the petitioners. Thus, in the spring of 1794, when fundamental international rights had been challenged, Congress ignored the protests of the merchants and voted in favor of a punitive embargo. It should be remembered, of course, that the forthright and overt lobbying attested by petitions represented only a fraction of the pressure that was brought to bear upon Congress. Only one petition from the holders of government securities is recorded in the *Annals of Congress*,[87] although it seems not at all unlikely that the public creditors might have exerted a great deal of influence upon

80. *Annals*, 3rd Cong., 1061–1062 [January 6, 1795]. Because of the fear of war with England, an embargo had been laid on the exportation of all arms and ammunition on May 22, 1794. 1 *U.S. Laws*, 370.
81. *Annals*, 3rd Cong., 1093 [January 15, 1795].
82. Ibid., 1131 [January 26, 1795].
83. Ibid., 1146 [January 28, 1795].
84. Ibid., 1159–1160 [January 30, 1789].
85. Ibid., 1164–1165 [February 3, 1795].
86. 1 *U.S. Laws*, 411 [January 29, 1795]. Entitled "An Act Supplementary to the Several Acts Imposing Duties," the new legislation had as its main purpose the elimination of ambiguity in the laws already in force. A few duties were raised, however, those on printing type, girandoles, white sugar, and wines.
87. *Annals*, 1st Cong., I, 824 [August 28, 1789].

the decision of Congress to provide adequate revenues for the maintenance of public credit.

The Demands of Businessmen for Public Patronage

Requests for governmental encouragement of business enterprise were not restricted to petitions for tariff revision; another series of petitions raised extremely important questions about the proper relation between government and business. The first of these petitions, submitted to Congress in April 1789 by Baltimore businessmen, did little more than voice a hope that the new government might set in motion forces making for business recovery.[88] On the heels of this petition came another one from the shipwrights of Charleston, South Carolina, equally vague, but equally hopeful that the "National Legislature" might be able "to relieve the particular distresses of the petitioners."[89] Next came a memorial from "the mechanics and manufacturers of the city of New York," setting forth "the present deplorable state of trade and manufactures" and looking "with confidence" to the new government for "that relief which they have so long and anxiously desired."[90] The "tradesmen and manufacturers of Boston," whose petition was sponsored by Ames of Massachusetts also looked to "the wisdom of the National Legislature" to increase business activity,[91] particularly by increasing American shipping.

Aside from intimating that tariff and tonnage duties would be helpful, these 1789 petitions did not specify any precise measures the new government ought to carry out to revive business prosperity. The spring of 1790 brought another batch of coy requests. John F. Amelung described the difficulties he labored under in his glass works and solicited "the aid of the United States [government] in this important undertaking."[92] The proprietors of the Beverly Cotton Manufactory likewise sought "the patronage of Government," although what they really wanted was higher duties on cotton cloth.[93] Amelung's petition, in contrast, had a different purpose; the House debates reveal that what he meant by "the patronage of the Government" was an $8000

88. *Annals*, 1st Cong., I, 120–121 [April 10, 1789].
89. Ibid., I, 128 [April 14, 1789]. The main hope of the Charleston shipwrights was that Congress would pass a navigation act which would increase the demand of their services.
90. Ibid., I, 175 [April 19, 1789].
91. Ibid., I, 457 [June 5, 1789].
92. Ibid., I, 1016 [May 27, 1790]. This petition was addressed to the Senate. For his petition to the House, see ibid., II, 1672 [May 26, 1790].
93. Ibid., II, 1574 [April 9, 1790].

low prices of fish and the high expenses of fishing voyages.[107] "The business," said the *Report*, "is so nearly in equilibrio that one can hardly discern whether the profit be sufficient to continue it or not."[108] Since the fisheries were regarded as the chief "nursery of seamen" and therefore as a training ground for naval personnel, problems of national security were involved as well as the familiar question of the responsibility of the government toward an important interest. Jefferson's *Report* therefore informed Congress that it was the task of that body to decide what ought to be done to bring back prosperity to the fishing industry, and it suggested, rather cautiously, that federal taxes might perhaps be remitted "in the form of a drawback or bounty."[109]

This innocent proposal led to a blistering debate in the House; immediately after Jefferson's *Report* was presented, a resolution was introduced proposing that a bounty be granted to the cod-fisheries. William B. Giles of Virginia opened the debate; the burden of his argument was that although Congress had the right to regulate commerce and thereby to encourage any occupation connected with commerce, it had no right to grant a bounty to a particular employment, and, even if it did, the consequences would be disastrous. His objections were grounded on political, ethical, and economic theory. The payment of a bounty would mean, in the first place, that revenues collected from all the taxpayers would be given to a selected minority; this would be a violation of "the common right." In the second place, the tender of public money to a privileged minority would invest that part of the national community with "exclusive rights"; this would be unjust and oppressive.[110] Giles went on to outline what he thought ought to be the proper and just relation of the state to private enterprise, and in doing so he expressed the eighteenth-century doctrine of the individual's natural rights to property. "Under a just and equal government," said Giles, "every individual is entitled to protection in the enjoyment of the whole product of his labor, except such

107. It was estimated that expenses of £124 were incurred by a Marblehead fishing schooner while the catch sold for from £82 to £143, and that the federal taxes amounted to $5.25 per sailor, and that this was in addition to the state poll tax.

108. *American State Papers, Commerce and Navigation*, I, 9 [February 1, 1792].

109. "It will rest therefore with the wisdom of the Legislature to decide, whether prohibition should not be opposed to prohibition, and high duty to high duty, on the fish of other nations; whether any, and which, of the naval and other duties may be remitted, or an equivalent given to the fishermen, in the form of a drawback, or bounty." Ibid.

110. *Annals*, 2nd Cong., 363 [February 3, 1792].

portion of it as is necessary to enable Government to protect the rest."
Every bounty, every exclusive privilege, every monopoly granted by a
government violates this fundamental principle of government, because any bounty, exclusive privilege, or monopoly would signify
that "the product of one man's labor is transferred to the use and
enjoyment of another."[111]

Having stated the Lockean labor theory of property, Giles next explored the political consequences of any deviation from it. He asserted
that if the government could transfer the property of its subjects to a
chosen group within the community, then it followed that "the whole
product of the labor of every individual" did not really belong to the individual but to the government and could be "distributed among the
several parts of the community by governmental discretion." Under
such circumstances, "every individual in the community is merely a
slave or bondsman to Government, who, although he may labor, is
not to expect protection in the product of his labor." Consequently, if
authority is once given to a government to transfer the wealth of its
subjects, the ultimate outcome can be nothing less than a "complete
system of tyranny."[112]

In Giles's opinion the economic effects of bounties would be equally
hazardous. Since the wealth of a nation can be augmented only by
enlarging the "product of useful labor," bounties cannot help—indeed,
they actually hinder the increase of a nation's wealth. For "if an occupation is really productive," said Giles, it will have no need of subvention; it will give a return on capital, pay wages, and "yield a profit
besides"; in short, "it will support itself." And so, closely following
Adam Smith, Giles concluded that "all occupations that stand in need
of bounties, instead of increasing the real wealth of a country, rather
tend to lessen it";[113] all of which showed that his confidence in the
natural justice of the automatic market seems to have been as
complete as his fear of tyranny was undoubtedly sincere.[114]

William Vans Murray of Maryland brought the debate down to a
less philosophical level. He maintained it was incumbent upon the
"friends of the bill" to prove that the fishing industry "did not yield the
ordinary profit" on the "stock employed in it," that there was a naval

111. Ibid.
112. Ibid.
113. Ibid., 364 [February 3, 1792].
114. Giles did admit that the payment of bounties would increase employment in the cod-fisheries. But if this were to be justified on the grounds of training a naval personnel, he claimed that British experience had proven that subsidizing the fisheries for the purpose of training seamen had cost too much.
Ibid., 365.

program in contemplation which the fishing industry rather than any other maritime trade was expected to assist, and that the cod-fisheries had such a special claim to encouragement "as to leave far behind every consideration of the manufacturing interest, the agricultural interest," and any other claimants.[115] The "friends of the bill"[116] accepted Murray's challenge. But Goodhue of Massachusetts, who began the rebuttal, did not meet Murray's demands head on; he merely elaborated on the importance of fish as an export and on the usefulness of the fisheries as "a copious nursery of hardy seamen."[117] Ames, although usually direct and accurate in debate, also evaded Murray's propositions. He vindicated bounties for the cod-fisheries not only because they increased national wealth[118] and provided national security, but because justice "required" these "bounties." What the bill asked for, said Ames, was really not a bounty at all, but an adequate drawback on reexported salt. The word *bounty* had stirred up a mare's nest, and the Massachusetts delegation did its best to center the discussion on the drawback. There were fairly sound reasons for increasing the amount of the drawback, especially since Jefferson's report had shown that federal taxes had a good deal to do with the stagnation of the fishing trade.[119] But it proved to be difficult for the friends of

115. Ibid.
116. Except for Barnwell of South Carolina and Laurance of New York, the members of the House who spoke in favor of the bill were all from Massachusetts.
117. Ibid., 365–366 [February 3, 1792].
118. Ames brought the employment argument (see above, pp. 212–213) into the discussion by asserting that the cod-fisheries gave employment to 30,000 people. Ibid., 368.
119. Document No. 6 accompanying Jefferson's *Report* was entitled "An Estimate of the Duties Paid by the Proprietors and Navigators of a Fishing Vessel of Sixty Five Tons and Eleven Hands." To an estimated duty on salt of $80.25 it added $14.00 for duties on rum, $2.64 on tea, $3.03 on sugar, $.99 on molasses, $7.33 on coarse woolens, $2.09 on fishing tackle, $2.05 on sail cloth, $20.00 on cordage, $1.00 on iron, and $3.09 for tonnage duties to reach a total of $138.00 for all the federal taxes levied on an average fishing schooner. (*American State Papers, Commerce and Navigation*, I, 15.) The argument which this document was intended to reinforce was that federal taxes constituted the marginal item of cost that made the fisheries unprofitable. For even if the salt duties were all remitted there would still remain $57.75 in federal taxes, a sum which might easily have turned loss into profit. Had the computation been made on the 1790 rather than the 1789 scale of duties, total taxes would have been about $235.00 and after deducting the salt drawback the figure would have been about $75.00. This kind of statistical evidence, appropriate enough in Jefferson's report, which concerned itself with showing why the fisheries were not profitable, was scarcely usable in the House debates for the reason that any industry subject to import duties could argue that taxes were taking away the margin of profit. But the estimate is of interest because the "bounties" that were voted under the fisheries act of 1792 amounted to $162.50 on a sixty-five-ton fishing vessel, which is to

the fisheries to convince their opponents that all they sought was an adequate drawback on salt—difficult for the very simple reason that they actually wanted something more! Whereupon Robert Barnwell of South Carolina observed that "if the bounties should happen to exceed the drawbacks, by eight or ten thousand dollars [a year] the number of seamen to be maintained would be well worth that sum."[120] Gerry of Massachusetts still insisted that the only thing involved was a drawback, although he went on to say that if the proposed aid for the fisheries really were a bounty he would still favor it. All government assistance, he asserted, is, in effect, a bounty; "the landed and agricultural interest" has been given the equivalent of a bounty in the form of duties on hemp, beer, and ale, while the manufacturers have been even more generously dealt with in tariff legislation.[121] As for Giles's contention that public money ought never to be used to benefit a minority, Gerry alleged that Massachusetts had contributed at least $200,000 for the protection of frontier farmers, and hence it was eminently reasonable that the agricultural interest ought to bear part of the indirect costs of providing a navy.[122] Laurance of New York agreed with Gerry that tariff duties were indirect bounties, and that every argument advanced against bounties could equally well be levied against protective duties.[123]

This attempt to equate bounties with protective tariffs gradually turned the discussion back to the basic principles which Giles had enunciated at the beginning of the bitter controversy.[124] Williamson of North Carolina took Gerry to task for confusing regional expenditures for defense with grants of public money to a favored group of businessmen.[125] He pointed out that if Congress once began doling out money to beleaguered business groups, there would be no end to the demands that would come pouring in upon Congress. If the cod-fishermen needed a larger drawback, his advice was to give it to them; but under no circumstances should the government grant bounties to enterprises simply because they could not earn profits.[126]

At this point, when the debate seemed virtually deadlocked, that master politician James Madison once again cleared the way for congressional action. Tactfully he agreed with the New Englanders

---

say that the owners and navigators of such a vessel were given a rebate of about 70 percent of their total federal taxes.

120. *Annals,* 2nd Cong., 375 [February 3, 1792].
121. Ibid., 376.
122. Ibid., 377.
123. Ibid., 385 [February 6, 1792].
124. See above, p. 278.
125. *Annals,* 2nd Cong., 377 [February 3, 1792].
126. Ibid., 381.

that what they were seeking was really not a bounty, but "a mere reimbursement of the sum advanced."[127] He therefore urged the House to vote for the resolution. But as a concession to Giles, Williamson, and other opponents of the measure, he placed himself on record as opposed to bounties or any other expedients whereby public money could be distributed at the discretion of the government.[128] Madison's diplomacy, however, did not conceal the favoritism which the cod-fishermen were seeking. John Page of Virginia promptly pointed out that if the merchants engaged in the cod-fisheries were allowed draw-backs including the remission of duties they had paid not only on salt but on cordage, iron, rum, and other supplies, "they would have a preference to other merchants."[129] What Page disliked most of all, however, was the idea of governmental intervention with private enterprise. Where, he asked, would such a thing end? "May not Congress, with equal propriety undertake to regulate the tobacco, the rice, and indigo trade, as well as that of the fisheries?"[130] And if Congress had a right to "intermeddle in the business of sailors, why not in that of manufacturers and farmers?" Page therefore declared that whereas he stood ready to help all interests by any general legislation, he could not sanction a bill that selected the fisheries "as objects of more consequence than other branches of trade."[131] Whereupon his fellow Virginian Giles, who had opened the debate, once again called to the attention of Congress the dangerous precedent they would set if special consideration was afforded to the cod-fishermen. "Bounties in all countries and at all times," he said, "have been the effect of favoritism" and "have only served to divert the current of industry from its natural channel, into one less advantageous or productive." Then, growing more emphatic, he branded bounties as "nothing more than Governmental thefts committed upon the rights of one part of the community, and an unmerited Governmental munificence to the other."[132] Like Taylor of Caroline, Giles asserted that governmental preferences to any occupation would end in the creation of "a separate and distinct interest"—a creation not of natural forces but of law, which would divide the United States into two factions: the privileged and the unprivileged.[133]

127. Since the Massachusetts delegation asked for payments in excess of the salt duties, Madison's interpretation was generous to say the least.
128. *Annals,* 2nd Cong., 388 [February 6, 1792].
129. Ibid., 392 [February 7, 1792].
130. Ibid., 395.
131. Page laid the responsibility for the proposal that bounties ought to be paid to the cod-fishermen on Jefferson: "I take the liberty of saying, that his honest zeal, like that of the friends of the bill, has led him into a mistake." Ibid.
132. Ibid., 399 [February 8, 1792].

If the statistical estimates contained in Jefferson's reports are reasonably accurate, the opponents of the bounties finally won. By a vote of 38 to 21 the House approved a bill authorizing payments to cod-fishermen to be based not on the quantity of reexported salt but on the tonnage of the fishing vessels. Under the new arrangements drawbacks and bounties could have been blended in unknown proportions,[134] but the fisheries act, as finally approved by the House and Senate,[135] described the tonnage payments as a "commutation and equivalent" of the drawback allowances previously made. The computations based on the figures in Jefferson's *Report* also indicate that the new tonnage payments were very nearly equivalent to the salt duties paid under the existing tariff laws.[136] If these calculations are approximately correct, Congress had merely sanctioned a new method of paying drawbacks and had denied the cod-fisheries an outright bounty. The only evidence which might lead one to suspect that the cod-fishermen had benefited by the new arrangement was a petition addressed to the Senate by a group of mackerel fishermen "praying that the drawback allowed on the exportation of cod fish may be extended to pickled fish in general."[137] The matter of bounties, however, had not been settled. A petition from inhabitants of Salem, Beverley, and Danvers, Massachusetts, asked that the tonnage payments to fishermen be increased 20 percent, even though the salt duties had remained unchanged since 1790.[138] But opponents of the bounties continued to condemn that mode of encouragement: "bounties can never prove effectual," said Williamson of North Carolina, for although they might, if employed to aid agriculture, lead to the introduction of a few foreign plants, "they cannot produce industry or plenty."[139] Meanwhile Congress, ignoring Hamilton's recommendation that manufacturing enterprises be stimulated by the payment of bounties,[140] had

133. Ibid., 400. "The instant bounties or Governmental preferences are granted to [an] occupation, that instant [there] is created a separate and distinct interest."
134. Ibid., 400–401 [February 9, 1792].
135. 1 *U.S. Laws*, 229–232 [February 16, 1792]. "An Act concerning Certain Fisheries of the United States, and for the Regulation and Government of the Fishermen Employed Therein."
136. Jefferson's *Report* had estimated that a sixty-five–ton fishing schooner paid, on the average, $80.25 for salt duties. Since this was based on the 1789 rate of 6¢ a bushel, this figure would have risen to $160.50 after the 1790 rate of 12¢ a bushel went into effect. The fisheries act authorized payments of $1.50 a ton on vessels under thirty tons, and $2.50 a ton for vessels over thirty tons. A sixty-five–ton schooner would therefore receive $2.50 × 65 or $162.50, which would be a close approximation of the salt duties. See *American State Papers, Commerce and Navigation*, I, 15 [February 1, 1792].
137. *Annals*, 2nd Cong., 660 [February 21, 1793].
138. *Annals*, 3rd Cong., 561 [April 7, 1794].
139. *Annals*, 2nd Cong., 693–694 [November 19, 1792].
140. See above, pp. 220–221.

chosen to give indirect subvention to manufactures by increasing the tariff rates in 1792 and more particularly in 1794.

The Business Protest against Excise Taxes

In his *First Report on Public Credit,* Alexander Hamilton recommended that Congress should collect revenues not only by import duties but by imposing an excise tax on distilled liquors.[141] Although the *Report* was presented early in 1790, when it was already evident that the tariff of 1789 would not provide enough revenue, Congress sought to avoid recourse to excises. Accordingly, it contented itself with increasing tariff rates on August 10, 1790, hoping that substantial revenue could be obtained from customs to meet the payments of interest on the funded debt, a responsibility that was greatly increased when the state debts were assumed less than a week before the tariff of 1790 was passed.[142] When it became clear, early in 1791, that even more revenues would have to be collected by some means or other, Congress passed an act which was at once a tariff and an excise law.[143] That business interests would register bitter opposition to excise taxes had become manifest before the Excise Act was passed: Joseph Hiester of Pennsylvania, for example, had presented "a memorial and remonstrance" from "citizens of Philadelphia" against the proposed taxes on distilled liquors;[144] another petition, from Lancaster, Pennsylvania, had likewise urged Congress not to impose excise taxes.[145] Although forewarned of almost certain trouble, Congress nevertheless passed the Excise Act on March 3, 1791, thereby planting the seeds of the Whiskey Rebellion of 1794.

For a country where hard liquor had traditionally been abundant and cheap, for consumers the excise duties meant an increase in the retail prices of rum and whiskey; while for the distillers it brought not merely the prospect of decreased demand but the probability that a

141. *Political Papers* (McKee), pp. 37–38 [1790]. Hamilton argued that distilled liquors could properly be taxed because they were "pernicious luxuries," and that if excise taxes would reduce the consumption of distilled spirits the agricultural classes would be benefited by the greater demand for grain which the substitution of malt liquors for distilled liquor would bring.

142. Because interest payments on the funded debt were to begin in 1791, the increased duties imposed by the tariff of 1790 were planned in terms of this responsibility. The assumption of the state debts meant that even more revenues would very soon be needed, since the interest payments on that portion of the debt would begin in 1792.

143. 1 *U.S. Laws,* 199ff [March 3, 1791].

144. *Annals,* 1st Cong., II, 1926 [January 24, 1791].

145. Ibid., II, 1794 [January 28, 1791].

portion of the excises would be shifted back upon them.[146] The Act, moreover, was badly drawn; indeed some of the provisions could not be enforced, and Congress was compelled to revise the excise legislation in 1792, lowering the duties somewhat[147] and setting up more elaborate regulatory machinery to be enforced by an inspection system. It was this interference with the right of farmers in western Pennsylvania to process grain into a less bulky and more valuable product that ultimately led to open revolt. Two years before that occurred, however, distillers in both the East and the West had petitioned Congress to reduce or to appeal the liquor excises.[148] Nor was it long before disaffected businessmen found congressional champions. However much "ingenious theorists" may "refine upon the nature of indirect taxes," said Steele of North Carolina, "it must always be admitted that excises retrench the liberty of citizens."[149] Not only are excises "odious" to liberty-loving people, but they are unjust because they operate as a tax upon particular occupations. Steele characterized the act of 1791 as especially distasteful since it penalized distillers directly, and farmers indirectly, at the very moment when manufacturers were being subsidized by protective duties.[150] Disregarding the fiscal considerations that had led a reluctant Congress to impose excises, he argued that the growing controversy over such taxes represented "a struggle" between the agricultural and manufacturing

146. The excises on spirits distilled in the United States "wholly or in part from molasses, sugar and other foreign materials" ranged (according to proof) from 11¢ to 30¢ a gallon; those on liquors made wholly from domestic materials ranged from 9¢ to 25¢. To prevent foreign distillers from stealing the market from domestic liquor manufacturers (and also to increase federal revenue) the tariff rates on imported spirits were raised from 8¢ to 15¢ a gallon (according to proof).

147. 1 *U.S. Laws*, 267–271 [May 8, 1792]. The new duties ranged from 10¢ to 25¢ a gallon on domestically distilled rum and from 7¢ to 18¢ on domestically distilled grain. These rates applied to distilleries located in cities, towns, or villages. Country distillers were given the option of paying 7¢ a gallon on all liquor they distilled, or paying 10¢ for each gallon of still capacity for each month that their stills were in operation. The latter arrangement required the owner of a still to obtain a license, and a $200 fine was to be imposed on any distiller who failed to show a valid license when required to do so by an inspector.

148. See, as an example from New England, the petition from the "merchants and distillers of the town of Salem, in Massachusetts, praying a reduction of the duty imposed on spirits of domestic manufacture." *Annals*, 2nd Cong., 192 [November 16, 1791]; and, as an example from the West, a memorial from "the counties of Washington, Westmoreland, Fayette and Allegheny in the State of Pennsylvania stating their objections to an act . . . imposing a duty on spirits distilled within the United States." Ibid., 204 [November 22, 1791].

149. Ibid., 585–586 [April 30, 1792].

150. He charged, moreover, that the actual excise duties were so arranged that the effect of the law would be "to build up the rum distilleries upon the ruins of those employed by farmers for domestic uses." Ibid., 586.

classes, and that the passage of the liquor excises should be construed as a victory for the nonagricultural interests.[151] More and more this became the prevailing belief in western Pennsylvania, and by 1794, after futile petitions to Congress,[152] the frontiersmen attempted to prevent the enforcement of the excise law. The Whiskey Rebellion was promptly quashed, but the inglorious victory of the federal troops over country distillers did little to settle the basic issue, which was whether Congress might single out particular industries and jeopardize investments in them by imposing excise taxes upon products which entrepreneurs had found profitable to manufacture.

This aspect of the controversy was better illustrated by the debates over excise taxes on sugar and manufactured tobacco than by the Whiskey Rebellion. For the revolt of the western farmers became an act of lèse majesté which called for suppression, whether the complaints were real or factitious. Indeed the immediate consequences of the Rebellion were to make Hamilton even more determined to persist in employing excise taxes as a part of his fiscal program. Before the insurrection, however, primarily because the whiskey and rum excises had yielded far less revenue than had been expected, Congress had already discussed the advisability of imposing excises on manufactured tobacco, snuff, and sugar. Protests against the pending legislation came promptly: the tobacco manufacturers of Philadelphia urged Congress not to tax their products,[153] and the "sugar bakers" of that city voiced a similar plea.[154]

Because two members of the House owned sugar refineries, the debates on the proposed excises proved to be unusually incisive. To Samuel Smith of Maryland it seemed "very odd" that Congress should see fit "to crush American manufactures in the bud." He pointed out that "men of capital and enterprise" had "advanced large sums of money" to build snuff mills; just when they had begun "to reap the reward of their expenses and their labor," the government "souses down upon them with an excise, which ends not in revenue but in extirpation."[155] And when the tobacco manufacturers had been driven

151. Ibid., 588.
152. See, for example, the petitions submitted in April 1794. Ibid., 558.
153. *Annals*, 3rd Cong., 622–623 [May 2, 1794].
154. Ibid., 632 [May 5, 1794].
155. Ibid., 625–626 [May 2, 1794]. Smith argued that an excise of 8¢ a lb. on snuff would triple the working capital investment needed for a snuff mill since the excise would be "double the price of the raw material." Moreover, the additional bookkeeping he estimated would cost $300 to $500 a year. For these reasons, he said, the proposed excise would mean "great injustice to the manufacturers of tobacco."

out of business, the effect of the tax would be to diminish the market for tobacco, and hence the burden of the tax would be on southern farmers. To penalize the tobacco growers by this indirect method, Smith charged, would be as unfair as to lay an excise upon Connecticut onions;[156] F. A. C. Muhlenberg of Pennsylvania predicted that an excise on domestically refined sugar would have no less disastrous effects on that industry; it would "stop the business," he said, and induce the owners of refineries "to turn their capital . . . into other channels."[157] The tax on sugar, in Muhlenberg's opinion, would fall squarely on the profits of the refiners; therefore it was foolish to expect the sugar excise to yield $50,000 in revenue when the combined profits of the seventeen sugar refineries did not amount to that much.

Despite the gloomy predictions of Smith and Muhlenberg, Congress not only imposed excises on snuff and sugar,[158] but also levied new taxes on carriages,[159] liquor dealers,[160] and auction sales.[161] It was understood, however, that these taxes were temporary emergency measures that would be suspended at the end of a two-year period. When it was proposed, less than six months later, that the sugar and snuff taxes be extended, a storm of protest resulted. Identical memorials came from the tobacco manufacturers and the sugar refiners of Philadelphia,[162] asking that the excises on snuff and sugar be repealed. A House Committee was appointed to consider the complaints, and evidence was presented that the manufacture of snuff had stopped entirely,[163] and that the sugar manufacturers were bearing the excise on

156. Ibid., 625.

157. Ibid., 635 [May 5, 1794].

158. 1 *U.S. Laws*, 384–390 [June 5, 1794]. The excises were to be 8¢ a lb. on snuff, 2¢ a lb. on sugar. Manufacturers of either commodity were to file a declaration of all equipment and building used in their business and were to forfeit a $5,000 bond if they failed to keep complete daily records of their production and sales. To compensate for the excises, additional import duties were levied on sugar, snuff, and manufactured tobacco.

159. Ibid., 373–375. The carriage tax ranged from $1.00 on two-wheeled vehicles to $10.00 on coaches. But all vehicles "usually and chiefly employed in husbandry" were exempt.

160. Ibid., 376–378. A license fee of $5.00 a year was required of all persons selling wine or spirits in quantities of less than 20 gallons.

161. Ibid., 397–400. The taxes on auction sales were fixed at ¼ of 1 percent for real estate, livestock, farm tools, and ships, and ½ of 1 percent for "goods, chattels, rights, and credits." Auctioneers were required to hold licenses from state authorities or, where no state licensing system existed, from the supervisor of revenue; and to forfeit their $1,500 bonds if they failed to keep records of all the auctions they cried, or if they failed to deliver the auction tax proceeds to the federal government.

162. *Annals*, 3rd Cong., 1023 [December 29, 1794]; ibid., 1060 [January 6, 1795].

163. Apparently confirming the prediction of Smith of Maryland.

refined sugar.[164] Smith of Maryland once again asked the House whether it had the right to enact legislation which brought about "the destruction of a manufacture,"[165] while Findley of Pennsylvania called the excises on snuff and sugar "improper restrictions" which discouraged honest manufacturers and established "a precedent that would eventually lead to levying excises on all manufactures."[166] Page of Virginia, however, saw no inherent objection to a general system of excises; what he condemned was the injustice of singling out "particular objects for taxation," since such a policy meant the "ruin of individuals, who may be selected as persons on whom a burden of taxes may fall."[167] Any selective system of excise he branded as "contrary to Republican principles" and as an "act of oppression." But to Smith of Maryland, although he disavowed any "personal interest" in the debate, the sugar excises were something more than an academic matter: "he [had] thought it sufficient that the House had by one act shut up his distillery," but, not content with that, "they were now shutting up his sugar bakery." He accused Congress of encouraging investment in domestic manufactures by protective import duties, and then of destroying the investment by the imposition of ill-considered excises.[168]

Ames of Massachusetts defended the excises. He said the experiment with excise taxes had been undertaken for the benefit of the public, not in the interests of snuff manufacturers and sugar refiners. It was quite proper, he asserted, to tax snuff because it was "one of the most trivial of all luxuries," and he thought it equally fitting to place an excise on sugar because it was consumed for the most part by people "who have some pretensions to wealth."[169] He predicted that the snuff manufacturers and the sugar refiners would soon adjust themselves to the new taxes, and that the excises were already in the process of becoming a part of the price of snuff and sugar. To repeal the taxes would be to derange matters once again.[170] But all of Ames's forensic skill could not prevent a modification of the snuff and sugar excises. More petitions were presented: from the sugar refiners of Baltimore[171] and Philadelphia,[172] and from the snuff manufacturers of

164. See the testimony of John Nicolas of Virginia, himself a member of the Committee. *Annals*, 3rd Cong., 1084–1085 [January 14, 1795].
165. *Annals*, 3rd Cong., 1085 [January 14, 1795].
166. Ibid., 1086.
167. Ibid., 1102 [January 15, 1795].
168. Ibid., 1092 [January 14, 1795].
169. Ibid., 1111 [January 15, 1795].
170. Ibid., 1112.
171. Ibid., 1174 [February 5, 1795].
172. Ibid., 1244 [February 23, 1795].

Baltimore and Boston.[173] In the face of pressure from a strengthening lobby, Congress repealed the eight cents a pound excise on snuff, substituting for it taxes on machinery and equipment used in snuff manufacture.[174] The revision of the snuff tax, however, ought not be attributed entirely or even mainly to the lobbyists; so large a part of the snuff excise had been remitted in the form of drawbacks that the yield to the treasury had been disappointing,[175] and Congress hoped that the tax on equipment would prove more fruitful. Apparently the snuff mills had not been driven out of business, nor had they provided so large a market for American tobacco as their advocates had alleged.

The persistent and belligerent opposition of businessmen to the taxes on liquors, snuff, and sugar did not deter Congress from imposing excise taxes; and, once the excise laws had been passed, the opposition of distillers, snuff manufacturers, and sugar refiners brought only minor revisions. The adamant attitude of Congress can no doubt be ascribed, in the main, to the insistent need for revenue. But there seems also to have been a belief that it was quite legitimate for the government to single out certain industries for taxation if these industries produced articles of luxury such as rum, whiskey, snuff, or sugar. Indeed all the excises, except those on auction sales, could be described as luxury taxes. That such taxes were discriminatory, and that they jeopardized private investments, was never denied. They were simply fiscal expedients, dictated by the commitments that Congress had made by funding the debts of the federal government and by assuming the state debts. In back of the excise program, therefore, stood a strong, if undemonstrative, pressure group—the holders of public debt or, to use the language of the period, the "monied interest." No petitions attest to their insistence that the government raise ample revenue, but it is a reasonable assumption that they pressed vigorously for a fiscal policy that would ensure the payment of interest on the public debt.

The Congressional Attitude toward Speculation

As compared with the vitriolic attack of pamphleteers,[176] the attitude of Congress toward the "monied interest" was rather cautious and restrained. A few members of the House assailed the speculators in

173. Ibid., 1227 [February 16, 1795].
174. 1 *U.S. Laws*, 426–430 [March 3, 1795].
175. See Davis Rich Dewey, *Financial History of the United States* (New York, 1924), p. 108.
176. See above, chap. IV.

government securities, excoriating them, in moments of anger, as "rapacious wolves"[177] or, when sarcasm seemed more effective than insult, as "silent majorities."[178] For the most part, however, the congressional debates on the funding and assumption legislation were temperate; certainly the reported discussions in the House do not bear out Fisher Ames's statement that "the language of insinuation and invective has been exhausted."[179] It is true that the funding act could be introduced into a debate on any conceivable subject, and the frequency with which this happened, long after the problem of the public debt had been settled, attests a deep-seated resentment against the "monied interest."

Members of Congress obviously could not avoid taking sides in the controversy over funding. But whereas men like Madison of Virginia and Jackson of Georgia openly declared themselves as advocates of discrimination in favor of "original holders," others with similar convictions remained silent. Similarly, although men like Gerry and Sedgwick[180] from Massachusetts staunchly defended Hamilton's policy of full payment to all holders, many other members of Congress said nothing until they were called upon to vote. It does not follow, however, that every member who voted for the funding act can be accounted a henchman of the "monied interest." In the eighteenth century the defense of property rights was considered, by liberals as well as conservatives, a fundamental responsibility of government; and Hamilton's vigorous defense of the innocent assignee no doubt appealed to many staunch individualists. It is therefore futile, on the basis of congressional votes, to separate the partisans from the critics of the "monied interest." But it is possible from the debates to detect the general attitude of Congress toward the business of finance, more particularly toward speculation, whether it be in real property or in evidences of property such as government securities or bank stock. And this climate of opinion is of primary importance in any analysis of contemporary attitudes toward government and business, since in this case it actually was the failure of Congress to restrict speculative

177. See the caustic remarks of James Jackson of Georgia. *Annals,* 1st Cong., I, 1137 [January 28, 1790].

178. The words of Theodorick Bland of Virginia. Ibid., II, 1532 [March 30, 1790].

179. *Annals,* 3rd Cong., 1107 [January 15, 1795].

180. Sedgwick frankly indicated his position almost a year before the debates on the funding act by bitterly opposing an appropriation of $40,000 for negotiating Indian treaties. It appeared to him "totally incomprehensible" that so large a sum of money should be voted when no provision had been made for the public creditors." *Annals,* 1st Cong., I, 793 [August 19, 1789].

activities that constituted the governmental sanction of what already was and continued to be one of the chief aspects of American business freedom.

The presentation of Hamilton's *First Report on Public Credit* on January 14, 1790, precipitated the first serious congressional debate about what attitude Congress ought to take toward speculation.[181] Gerry of Massachusetts said that Congress need have no fear "of injuring the community by increasing the spirit of speculation," since that kind of business was "carried on between speculator and speculator" and served merely to determine the true value of salable property.[182] Thus the defense of speculation came to be based on the operation of the automatic market,[183] by means of which, presumably, a fair and equitable price would always be "regulated by common opinion." At any rate, it was argued that since merchandise found its true value in "the open market," public securities also would. From this acknowledged tendency of commodities to be properly valued in the open market, the defenders of speculation concluded that any governmental interference was inadmissible; "a diamond, a horse or a lot of ground might be sold too cheap or too dear," said Livermore, "but Government could not interfere without destroying the general system of law and justice."[184] For that whole market system was presumably based on the right to transfer property with unabridged freedom, and the lubricant which made such transferability regularly possible was speculation. Any restraints upon speculation, said Gerry, would do irreparable injury for the simple reason that "speculation gives currency to property."[185]

But while men like Gerry defended speculative business activity un-

181. There had been many attempts to introduce this subject into the House debates in 1789, but no sustained discussion took place. Thus on August 28, 1789, a memorial from sixteen public creditors was submitted by Thomas Fitzsimons of Pennsylvania, and this petition, which anticipated many of the arguments that Hamilton subsequently employed to justify the funding of the debt, led to some discussion of the merits and demerits of a public debt. See Ibid., I, 824 [August 28, 1789].

182. Ibid., I, 1141 [January 28, 1790]; ibid., II, 1327 [February 18, 1790].

183. See above, chap. VII, p. 207.

184. *Annals,* 1st Cong., II, 1338 [February 19, 1790]. His remark that "Essau sold his birthright for a mess of potage, and heaven and earth confirmed the sale" was no doubt intended to prove that the system he defended was beyond reproach.

185. Ibid., I, 1136–1137 [January 28, 1790]. Nor did Gerry see any reason why any distinction ought to be made between foreign and domestic speculators; the purchase of government securities by foreign speculators, he said, would increase the American money supply which would have the effect of "enlarging the operations of productive industry."

qualifiedly,[186] other members of Congress, although they insisted that speculation was legitimate, thought it might be carried too far. Boudinot of New Jersey, for example, said he would be sorry if the House should decide that speculation in government securities constituted "violations of either the moral or political law." He admitted, however, "that everything of this kind has proper bounds," and that if speculation became so extensive as to divert capital from "productive" enterprises, then the community would suffer.[187] Sedgwick of Massachusetts, who later was bitterly attacked as a leader of the monied interest,[188] took great pains to point out that he did not approve of unlimited speculation; indeed he declared himself in favor of governmental curbs if capital were withdrawn from necessary business activity and "employed in speculations no way useful in increasing the labor of the community."[189] But neither Boudinot nor Sedgwick offered any concrete suggestions about what the government should do to restrain the variety of speculation they signalized as unwholesome and "pernicious."

The enemies of speculation could find no middle ground. They accused speculators of taking advantage of the misfortunes of their fellow citizens,[190] of diverting capital from "productive industry,"[191] of depriving the dependents of soldiers of their legal rights,[192] and of creating a dangerous legislative lobby.[193] To these indictments they added other complaints against the increase in the public debt, which funding at full value had created; their argument was that not only had the "monied interest" profited by buying up depreciated securities and redeeming them at full value, but that the creation of a huge public debt had made speculation a permanent rather than a temporary institution.

From the debates in the First Congress we may detect the origins of one of our most typical governmental processes, the efforts of economic groups to shape legislation by exerting pressure upon members of the Congress. These activities reflect the pluralistic structure of the

186. "The right of speculators to purchase securities at the market price is undoubted, and their conduct in making the purchases and payments is unquestionable." Ibid., II, 1330 [February 18, 1790].
187. Ibid., I, 1139 [January 28, 1790].
188. See I. T. Callendar, *Sedgwick & Co., or a Key to the Six Per Cent Cabinet* (Philadelphia, 1798).
189. *Annals,* 1st Cong., I, 1136 [January 28, 1790].
190. See the remarks of James Jackson of Georgia. Ibid., 1137–1138
191. Ibid., 1214 [February 10, 1790].
192. See the only petition against the inequalities of the funding act recorded in the *Annals of Congress.* Ibid., II, 1952 [February 3, 1791].
193. Ibid., II, 1532 [March 30, 1790].

American economy and indicate the inadequacy of a system of congressional representation based on territorial apportionment rather than on occupational status. The consequence was a dual form of representation: a formal one structured on territorial space and population, supplemented by an informal and circumstantial arrangement which would more accurately reflect the wishes of the several "interests" within an ever-increasingly complex economic society. For better or worse, this is the governmental dualism we have inherited from the Age of Washington.

X

Pluralism and Public Policy
An Attempt at Recapitulation

Formal government makes but a small
part of civilized life; and when even the
best that human wisdom can devise is
established, it is a thing more in name and
idea than in fact . . . the more perfect
civilization is, the less occasion has it for
government, because the more does it
regulate its own affairs and govern
itself.

Thomas Paine

The Great Synthesis

IT IS NOT chauvinism or instinctive egocentrism that leads Americans to believe they have evolved a beneficent form of economic organization. For despite all its shortcomings, and, alas, they are all too many, our volitional economy has demonstrated a capacity to stimulate human effort, increase investment, improve productivity, and partly erode that greatest evil of all commonwealths, perceived since Plato's days: the coexistence of great wealth and abject poverty. It is therefore entirely appropriate as we approach the two-hundreth anniversary of American independence that we should examine the origins of our polity, for I am convinced that it was the conscious and unashamed acceptance of a system of politico-economic pluralism thirteen years after the beginning of the Revolution that made possible the vigor and the catholicity of our developing institutions. The play of these pluralistic forces again and again has saved us from hardened dogma, so that the real virtue of our history—political, economic, and intellectual—has been our flexibility, our capacity to adapt ideas and instrumentalities to tasks of high social urgency. In the process we have created an economy so complex that it almost defies description, but one so tolerant ideologically that it can be called essentially private by those who find happiness in that ascription, although there can be no burking the very obvious fact that it is today inherently socialistic. For whereas one can demonstrate statistically that two-thirds of all capital formation is private, by an equally plausible demonstration it can be shown that, adding corporate and personal income taxes only, more than two-thirds of the revenues of American enterprise are socialized. This mixed economy is, therefore, the great, ever-improving American invention, based on the quintessential content of our variant of democracy whose trinitarian elements have been well defined as shared respect, shared power, and shared knowledge.[1]

1. For this neat trilogy I am indebted to Ralph Gabriel, long on the Yale faculty.

How was this admirable creation spawned, granted that it has, like any other organism, undergone progressive morphological change? The answer, as we have just seen, is that it was conceived by eighteenth-century minds in one of the most complex acts of institutional parturition ever experienced, and one so unique that scholars from all over the world continue to appraise and reappraise this extraordinary achievement.[2] Indeed neither the terminology of biology nor politics is in any way adequate to describe the formative process that created this leviathan; its origins are as pluralistic as its components. It synthesized the shrewdness, the wisdom, the pragmatism, the decency, and that strange secular religiosity of eighteenth-century minds, thus creating a basis for a humanistic polity so flexible that its potential is limited only by the intelligence and the moral aspirations of its beneficiaries. How hard it is to trace the course of democratic thought! As I have said, it thunders through the tortuous gorges of political controversy and foams conspicuously in the defiles of constitutional quarrels; but, in strange contrast, it meanders unobtrusively through the meadowlands of business enterprise, taken for granted, unmeasured, almost unnoticed. Yet here was surely the emergent American democracy, the magnet that drew millions of immigrants to a rough, undeveloped country. But it is quite wrong to assume that ours was merely an experiment with the "obvious and simple system of natural liberty"; it was quite otherwise, a militant, pragmatic, conflict-fashioned variant of neo-libertarian public policy that compromised rather than harmonized the demands of existing and emergent "interests."

The Recognition of Societal Pluralism

Semantically, the key to the enigma of our policy origins is surely this word *interests,* which stalks through the pamphlet literature and the legislative debates of the Age of Washington.[3] Because every society is of necessity some better or worse amalgam of its constituent eco-

2. Only recently two more studies of the *Federalist* Papers have appeared, one by an Italian (Aldo Garosci), the other by a naturalized German (Gottfried Dietze). Meantime the *Centre International de Formation Européenne* is planning a new critical study on "The United States of America: Example of a Federation" with the object of finding guidance for the process of European political integration which the *Centre* champions.

3. For representative examples, see *The Federalist* (Lodge), X, 54; IV, 25; X, 55; XXXVII, 221; XXXV, 205–206; LVI, 354; XXI, 325–326. (Full bibliographical information for the following was given earlier, but is repeated here for the reader's convenience.) George Logan, *Five Letters Addressed to the Yeomanry of the United States* (Philadelphia, 1792), p. 8. Pelatiah Webster,

nomic components, democratic government is inescapably confronted with the question of which interests should be represented, and how far a solicitude for particular interests, however well or ill concealed, should be the guiding concern of public policy. This issue was publicized in pamphlets, debated in public forums, and, after 1789, belabored in the Congress. Would it be possible and expedient for a new plan of government to recognize formally the existence of interests? Or would this introduce discord, friction, and endless trouble? Madison said, ". . . a landed interest, a manufacturing interest, a mercantile interest, a monied interest" and other "lesser interests" grow up of necessity,[4] creating conflict, jealousy, and disharmony.[5] Hamilton looked to the members of learned professions for a reconciliation; they should be "impartial arbiters," a view shared by few writers and, as Hamilton was to learn so unpleasantly, by even fewer politicians.[6] And what of the "lesser interests," the mechanics and the fishermen, for example? Would they not be overshadowed by the larger interests? Even more contentious was the question whether interests were

---

Political Essays on the Nature and Operation of Money, Public Finance and Other Subjects (Philadelphia, 1794), p. 7. George Logan, *An Address on the Natural and Social Order of the World as Intended to Produce Universal Good; Delivered before the Tammany Society* (Philadelphia, 1798), p. 8. *11 Pennsylvania Statutes at Large,* 560, ch. 1159, sec. 1–3. Nathan Strong, *A Sermon* (Hartford, 1790), p. 22. John Taylor, *An Inquiry into the Principles and Policy of the Government of the United States* (Fredericksburg, 1814), p. 259. William Findley, *A Review of the Revenue System Adopted by the First Congress* (Philadelphia, 1794), pp. 52–53. John Taylor, *An Enquiry into the Principles and Tendency of Certain Public Measures* (Philadelphia, 1794), p. 37. George Logan, *Letter to the Citizens of Pennsylvania on the Necessity of Promoting Agriculture, Manufactures and the Useful Arts* (Philadelphia, 1800), pp. 16–17. James Bowdoin, *Opinions respecting the Commercial Intercourse between the United States of America and the Dominions of Great Britain* (Boston, 1797). Richard Henry Lee, *An Additional Number of Letters* (New York, 1788), p. 61. John Adams, *A Defense of the Constitutions of Governments of the United States of America* (London, 1787), p. 155. Noah Webster, *Sketches of American Policy* (Hartford, 1785), p. 6. James Sullivan, *The Path to Riches: An Inquiry into the Origin and Use of Money* (Boston, 1792), pp. 6–7. John Beal Bordley, *Essays and Notes on Husbandry and Rural Affairs* (Philadelphia, 1799), p. 385. *2 Delaware Laws,* 1122, ch. 53. C. Azel Backus, *Absalom's Conspiracy* (1798), pp. 24–25. Samuel Langdon, *The Republic of the Israelites: An Example to the American People* (Exeter, 1788), p. 11. Timothy Stone, *A Sermon* (Hartford, 1792), p. 19. Daniel Foster, *A Sermon* (Boston, 1790), pp. 13–14. Jeremy Belknap, *An Election Sermon* (Portsmouth, 1785), p. 20. Thomas Jefferson, *Notes on the State of Virginia* (1785), p. 213. Tench Coxe, *View of the United States* (Philadelphia, 1787), p. 29.

4. *The Federalist* (Lodge), X, 54.
5. *The Federalist* (Lodge), XXXVII, 221.
6. See Mitchell, *Alexander Hamilton,* especially chap. 12.

equally legitimate, or whether some were holier in the sight of God and man than others? Were some, like agriculture and fishing, "natural" and therefore cleaner, and for that reason deserving of political preference? Were others, such as moneylending and stockjobbing, "unnatural," tawdry, unclean, and unworthy of political recognition?

That controversy, fierce as it was before the adoption of the Constitution, became really violent when Hamilton proposed the funding of the debts of the central government, the assumption of state debts, and the creation of a national bank. John Taylor exceeded all his contemporaries in vituperation[7] with his scurrilous arraignment of the "untitled aristocracy of paper and patronage"[8] that had, by cunning and intrigue, perverted republican government into a fraudulent system of exploitation. But although Taylor led the attack on the "monied interests," and although his indictment was echoed by gentlemen farmers like George Logan, by scholars like Noah Webster, and by illiterate Shaysites in Frontier hamlets, the stain of illegitimacy, which the righteous defenders of the "natural" interests hoped to use to disqualify their opponents, did not quite stick. And soon thereafter compromise, that ugly but useful offspring of expediency and tarnished idealism, reluctantly admitted the "monied" interest to the concert of power segments wrestling with the tasks of formulating and implementing a new plan for a workable government.

Confronting these architects and pioneer politicians, then, stood the interests—"natural" and "unnatural," spontaneous or "factitious" —which represented both the rich and the poor, and hence were quite unequal in suffrage because an aristocratic heritage had been woven into a skein of law, one that had to be painfully unraveled in a second revolution. Explanation of that exciting chapter of our cultural, political, economic, and moral-intellectual history would involve a historical analysis far beyond the scope of this exploratory essay that has concentrated on little more than a decade of American history. My concern has been with the preconceptions that really made another revolution possible, with the seeds of insurrection that were beginning to sprout long before the muddy boots of Jackson's admirers were to dirty the White House floors.

So back, for a moment, to the interests. Except for John Taylor, who groped romantically for an organizing principle that foreshadowed Durkheim's "organic solidarity"[9] and who rejected the very

---

7. The condemnation of the "financial interests" pervades all his writings but is most elaborately developed in his *Principles and Policy.*
8. *Principles and Policy*, pp. 20–21.
9. Durkheim, *De la division du travail social.*

thought of according formal legislative recognition to the several interests, the all-engaging concern of the Founding Fathers was to find some fair and workable scheme for political representation at least for the major interests. But since every interest is of necessity self-centered, none could be trusted to enact laws for the general good.[10] Hence there were only three solutions: either the interests must be "balanced"; or an arbitral function must be assumed, as Hamilton urged, by an educated minority;[11] or one must simply hope that in a free democratic society so many interests would presently emerge, with so many varied ends and motives, that any "unjust combination" of them would be "very improbable."[12] But whereas Madison advanced this optimistic forecast, John Adams feared there could be no stability unless the interests were balanced ab initio, and therefore proposed that the very rich, whom he considered the most power-hungry interest, should be allowed to monopolize a weak Senate where they could do the least harm. But even if such a clumsy segregation might temper the problem of the rich and the poor, how could the disproportionate size of the agricultural, the commercial, and the Johnny-come-lately financial interests be equated with the insignificance of the manufacturing, the mechanic, or the professional interests? Hamilton was convinced that government itself, by transcending its "interest" motivation and by looking far into the future, would have to correct this disequilibrium. But sadly and reluctantly the brave hopes of balanced representation were abandoned, and unsatisfactory territorial and population aggregates became our electoral units, with no assurance that a rational occupational representation would ever result.

Thus the search for an appropriate franchise for occupational groupings (a search renewed much later with even greater hope by Weimar Germany, and again in a very different context by socialist Yugoslavia) was unsuccessful in the Age of Washington. Unsuccessful but not wholly fruitless, because the earnest thought given to the central issue, the honest if sometimes intemperate exchange of views, and the very posing of the unanswerable questions profoundly influenced the current of American political and economic thought. For there can be no doubt but that the sentiment of many of the founders of our government was well epitomized by the pamphleteer who asserted that the only "fair representation" is one wherein "every order of men in the community . . . can have a share," one that ensures

10. For an example of this argument, advanced by so many writers, see Lee, *An Additional Number of Letters*, p. 61.

11. *The Federalist* (Lodge), X, 205–206.

12. Ibid., XXXV, 53.

that "professional men, merchants, traders, farmers, mechanics, etc.,"
bring "a just proportion of their best-informed men respectively into
the legislature."[13] For in a democracy, public policy must have pluralistic sanction. But will the haggling between interests result in wise
policy? Will not "separate interests warily balanced" make it easy for
the few to exploit the many?[14] Must not the formulation of public
policy require legislators to transcend the narrow horizons of particular
interests and be inspired by the "general interest"? This elusive concept, this darling of dreamers, how should it be reconciled with the
crass purposes of egocentric interests? Would a "natural aristocracy"
emerge, representing, as Adams, and Hamilton thought, such "virtues
and abilities"[15] that its elite would rise above party and interest? Taylor led a blistering attack on the advocacy of such old-fashioned nonsense. Aristocracy was never natural, he averred; historically it has
been based on witchcraft and superstitions, on conquest, or on property and arbitrage. There could be little hope that the "public interest"
would be really protected by the rich and wellborn.

Read the long, acrimonious controversy over the legitimacy of interest representation, and one will begin to sense the preconceptions of
American libertarianism. The fear was that the general interest could
easily be frustrated, compromised, or ignored. By whom? The blameworthy interests were both historical and emergent. The British "landed
interest," the British factorage system—here were examples of "foreign interests" that must be exorcised. Meantime the controversy over
funding and the revelation of speculation in public debt, to say
nothing of the alleged injustice of full payment to purchasers who had
paid but a fraction of face value—all that made it easy for plain and
ordinary people to believe that they had "sold their birthright" to the
"monied" interest "for a mess of paper."[16] Democratic public policy
ought to prevent both old and emergent perversions. The fruit of labor
ought not be divided by chicanery, fraud, or onerous taxation, but by
some natural process that is just and, because it is just, one that creates
a "beneficent excitement of effort."[17] Democratic government must
protect the right of people to engage in socially useful labor unhindered by restraints imposed by "artificial" or "factitious" interests.

Here, then, is the vision of the good society where men will follow

13. Lee, *Letters from the Federal Farmer*, p. 10.
14. Taylor, *Principles and Policy*, p. 404.
15. See Adams, *Defense of the Constitutions*, pp. 106–107; *Works of Alexander Hamilton*, I, 401.
16. Taylor, *A Definition of Parties*, p. 6.
17. Taylor, *Principles and Policy*, p. 620. See also a parallel argument in
Sullivan, *Path to Riches*, pp. 5–6.

"honest and painful methods of earning fortunes,"[18] avoiding "chimerical ways and means of obtaining wealth by sleight of hand," forsaking quick speculative profits for the "slow and regular gains" that preserve social morality and "keep men employed."[19] By leaving distribution to the free play of "industry and talents," each producer will be paid in proportion to his contribution to the nation's stockpile of product and charged with only his share of public burdens.[20] Such a scheme of things should be the object of public policy. Nor would any elite group be required to formulate and implement public measures. Wisdom is not the monopoly of the wellborn; "the wise men made by nature are eternally overturning those made by law."[21] Moreover—and here the radiant confidence—"with the intervention of education" variations in talent will be "numberless" and the ever-developing abilities of the rank and file will demonstrate that a democratic society need not rely on a privileged few for wise leadership.[22]

But always the specter of threatening evil: "the clamorous importunity of partial interests"[23] and the moral blemish of group egoism, which was not peculiar to financiers but equally endemic among farmers and merchants. Hence the real danger was that agreements will be made and "interests combined."[24] It was all well and good to say that the money changers should be driven out of the temple,[25] but who would do the driving if one interest trades votes with another? This is the eternal dilemma inherent in the very idea of pluralism. Admit the omnipresence of interests, as the eighteenth-century realists did, and it then follows that interests cannot be driven out of legislative halls. If they cannot be balanced, and if individuals cannot, except in moments of national peril, transcend their interests, how then will the public welfare be served?

The theoretical answer, advanced by both Madison and Hamilton, was delectably attractive: the solution was to create "a will in the community independent of the [legislative] majority."[26] It was some

18. Pelatiah Webster, *Political Essays*, p. 290.
19. Noah Webster, *Collection of Essays*, p. 106.
20. Taylor, *Principles and Policy*, p. 282.
21. Ibid., p. 634.
22. Hamilton did not share this optimism. He admitted, rather grudgingly, that "there are strong minds in every walk of life that will rise superior to the disadvantages of situation." For that reason "the door ought to be equally open to all." But he did not think much upward mobility was likely. *The Federalist* (Lodge), XXXV, 207–208.
23. Logan, *Five Letters to the Yeomanry*, p. 23.
24. Findley, *Review of the Revenue System*, p. 128.
25. "The expulsion of paper men" was John Taylor's solution for ridding Congress of one pressure group.
26. *The Federalist* (Lodge), LI, 325.

such concept of rational solidarity, essentially akin to Rousseau's *volonté générale,* that John Taylor espoused with such passion: "A nation cut up into orders or separate interests," he said, "cannot exert national self-government because the national self no more exists than a polypus . . . cut into pieces, which forage in different directions or upon each other."[27] A nation must find its unity in rational solidarity springing from the "salutary restraint of accountableness" of legislators to a critical electorate that insists upon representation by alert, public-spirited, responsible, rational individuals.[28]

For most of the Federalists, however, the solution was not to be sought in the moral perfection of congressmen and senators but in some imprecise equilibrium that would result from the interplay of pluralism. Presumably in a country as varied in resources as the United States, so many separate interests would progressively crystallize that the unreasonable demands of one interest or of a few interests would be neutralized by still other interests. A variety of circumstantial solidarity would therefore emerge, grounded in reasonable and legitimate self-interest but tempered with some measure of appreciation for the general good. Like Adam Smith, the American political philosophers puzzled over the relations that should exist between benevolence and self-interest. The motto of every American, asserted George Logan, should be that of the French economists: *"faire le bien, c'est le recevoir!"*[29] This ethical overtone becomes increasingly audible. Self-interest, Noah Webster argued, must be enlightened, because "a selfishness which excludes others from a participation of benefits is . . . self-ruin."[30] Self-interest cannot be sovereign. The "right to gain all the property which vigilance and industry . . . can bestow" must not infringe the well-being of the community.[31] The true goal of public policy must be to "promote the general interests with the smallest injury to particular ones";[32] it must seek to "so unite and combine public and private interests, that they may mutually support, feed and quicken each other."[33]

Concepts of Freedom

It is, therefore, in this great debate about the relation of interests to republican government that one must search for our pristine American

27. *Principles and Policy,* p. 444.
28. Logan, *Five Letters to the Yeomanry,* pp. 19–20; Taylor, *Definition of Parties,* p. 5.
29. Logan, *Five Letters to the Yeomanry,* p. 24.
30. *Sketches of American Policy,* p. 48.
31. Sullivan, *Path to Riches,* p. 5.
32. Coxe, *View of the United States,* p. 29.
33. Pelatiah Webster, *Political Essays,* p. 499.

attitudes toward freedom and authority. But in this obscure, little explored area of our intellectual history the difficulties are legion, for although our economic freedom in 1790 was actual, widespread, and more deeply ingrained in social customs than in Europe, one seeks in vain for any formal description, or any analysis of a unified character such as had emerged in French or British writings. Hence one must painstakingly survey the pamphlets, essays, sermons, public addresses, and laws; here one finds clusters of ideas that have a rather different emphasis and flavor from their European counterparts. In these ill-organized suggestions (advocating, supporting, or defending public policies that interblend private and public action) lie the doctrinal origins of our mixed economy. Through this intellectual canebrake I have tried to blaze a trail.

The advocates of freedom of economic action formed neither a school nor a political party, since basically the attitude toward economic policy was interest-oriented. Farmers and planters dependent on export markets sang the praises of free trade. Merchants and shipowners railed against price-fixing laws that had hampered their operations during and after the Revolution.[34] Mechanics and craftsmen insisted that their freedom to follow an occupation ought not be prejudiced by governmental favors to corporate interests;[35] their contention was that legislative interference with the free choice of occupations brings only mischief and oppression. In contrast, a volitional allocation of the work force provides the best distribution of manpower, and the foolish efforts of legislators to "warp employment against its natural bent"[36] will inevitably impair the efficiency vouchsafed by a natural order.[37] Meantime the much-abused financial interests also championed economic freedom, asserting that private ownership of banks or other business corporations produced more social benefit than did government-sponsored ventures. Despite the rancorous attacks by the antifunding, antiassumption, antibank factions, unregulated speculation in private and public securities found a host of defenders. Freedom to invest and freedom to assume risk were goals of policy honored with Lockean and utilitarian accolades.

34. In his many writings, for example, the Connecticut-born, Yale-educated merchant Pelatiah Webster fulminated more against American price-fixing laws than against the British government.

35. In 1793 the Virginia legislature resolved that "a clause [be] inserted into the constitution of the United States . . . to prohibit any director of the bank of the United States from being a member of either house of Congress." *Session Laws* (Shepherd), 284 [December 11, 1793].

36. Bordley, *Essays on Husbandry*, p. 378.

37. This argument is found in the writings of Madison, Jefferson, and Coxe. See Madison, *Works*, VI, 96; Jefferson, *Works*, VIII, 13; Coxe, *View of the United States*, pp. 66–67.

The fierce controversy between the "natural" and the financial interests must not be construed as a struggle between advocates of *laissez-faire* and proponents of intervention. Each interest, natural or otherwise, supported that type of freedom which promised to advance the well-being of its constituents. Actually four separable varieties, of economic freedom were sought, together with scores of subvarieties. The export-oriented farmers wanted international free trade (*laissez-passer*); the commercial interest asked for freedom from governmental interference with the market mechanism (*laissez-faire*); the manufacturers and mechanics pressed for occupational freedom (which might be called *laissez-travailler*); while the financial and monied group championed the freedom to buy and sell rights to property (a type of liberty one could call *laissez-placer*).

But these four freedoms did not exhaust the libertarian importunities. The deep-seated Anglo-American fear and hatred of monopoly could be marshaled against Hamilton's projects,[38] simply because it had become a part of American folklore to believe that all monopolies are "odious," contrary to the spirit of free government, and hence "ought not to be suffered."[39] And because "free and fair competition," in all trades and industries, is "an inherent and essential right of the people," the argument was that a democratic government must protect citizens "against all monopolies and conspiracies." How prophetic were these words from the 1776 Constitution of Maryland and from the 1784 Constitution of New Hampshire, which enunciated principles of intervention destined to lead so programistically into that legal morass we call "antitrust." But it should be emphatically pointed out that no one interest and no party upheld the antimonopoly standard alone; and even though the Republicans stigmatized their opponents as monopolists, it can scarcely be suggested that the followers of Jefferson were the only paladins of American liberalism. They too were interventionists, as Heath's studies have so convincingly shown.[40]

The eternal dilemma of democratic government, then as now, derived from the awkward question: how much freedom, how much authority? Granted that self-love is the "spring of all action,"[41] it does not follow that public welfare can be ensured by giving selfishness free rein or by tempting man's latent immorality "by hopes of boundless

38. See Mitchell, *Alexander Hamilton,* chap. 12.
39. These words are quoted from the Constitution of the free state of Maryland (1776).
40. Milton Heath, *Constructive Liberalism.* See also his "Public Railway Construction and the Development of Private Enterprise in the South before 1861," *Journal of Economic History,* Supplement X (1950), 40–53.
41. Noah Webster, *Collection of Essays,* p. 382.

acquisition."[42] It is an inescapable duty of government to prevent deleterious consequences of unbridled cupidity, yet at the same time to preserve the force and the vitality that originates in reasonable self-interest. Norms of legitimate self-interest must therefore be established by law as occasion demands.[43] And the task of determining such boundaries will perforce be a matter of great delicacy calling for wisdom, judgment, and a sense of social morality. For the right to seek one's own well-being must be recognized as the most hallowed natural right, one which an individual does not relinquish on becoming a member of civil society.[44] But he may not abuse this privilege: he is free to promote his own well-being provided in doing so he does not injure the community.[45]

But how can government, itself the reflection of interests, establish the legitimate boundaries of self-interest, and how can it, conversely, carve out those areas of intervention that will be socially protective and collectively useful? Intervention was not something new, to be sure; hence one test of the overall thesis might be found in the "legislative will" to continue old laws or, oppositely, to repeal unwarranted legislative patterns of intervention. Here, alas, we move into another jungle! A weird tangle of state law circumscribed and limited entrepreneurial freedom. A maze of inspection laws governed the quality of goods offered for sale, and sometimes the prices at which they could be sold. Nor does the annual crop of state laws regulating enterprise show any sign of abating in the 1790s; if anything, the legislative harvest increases. Meantime, on the federal level, a policy of government assistance to enterprise was recommended in President Washington's first annual message,[46] and the Senate promptly agreed that agriculture, commerce, and manufacturing would "be advanced by all proper means in our power" while the House, not to be outdone by the Senate, promised "legislative protection" for the basic sectors of the economy.[47]

Theory and practice moved on different levels. Franklin, Witherspoon, Adams, Logan, Jefferson, and Taylor all sang the praise of international free trade, although presently Jefferson was compelled to adjust his views to meet unexpected political and diplomatic situa-

42. Taylor, *Enquiry into Certain Public Measures*, p. 61.
43. Noah Webster, *Sketches of American Policy*, p. 6; Sullivan, *Path to Riches*, p. 18; Pelatiah Webster, *Political Essays*, p. 290; Taylor, *Enquiry into Certain Public Measures*, p. 5.
44. Logan, *Letters to the Yeomanry*, p. 5.
45. See Robert Gray, *A Sermon*.
46. James D. Richardson, *Messages and Papers of the Presidents*, I, 57–59.
47. Ibid., I, 60–61.

tions,[48] reluctantly confessing that "an equilibrium of agriculture, manufactures and commerce" had become "essential to our independence."[49] In his sixth annual message, Jefferson was even more pragmatic; he urged that certain import duties be continued lest an advantage be given "to foreign over domestic manufacturers."[50] Even John Taylor, that knight errant of freedom to export and import, was prepared to restrict the right of farmers to produce export crops that destroyed the fertility of our landed heritage.[51]

A corresponding ambivalence characterized the discussion of competition and the virtues of an automatic market mechanism. Pelatiah Webster almost excelled Frédéric Bastiat's later panegyrics when he extolled the capacity of free markets to measure value, maximize production, improve the quality of goods sold, adjust supply to demand, ration factors of production, and elicit and intensify efforts to achieve efficiency in the use of a nation's resources[52]—all this without government supervision or coercion! Less extravagantly, Tench Coxe, Madison, and Jefferson praised an "open market."[53] But the readily admitted exceptions to the general theory reflect the pragmatism of shrewd men facing tough, unpleasant problems. Jefferson made it very plain that "protection from casual embarrassments" might require governmental intervention. Meantime, state legislatures still registered a distrust of competition by reenacting laws against engrossing.[54] Nor can one trust preambles; laws that pretend to further "the holding of an open market" (as was the case of a Pennsylvania law "in aid of the Callowhill Market")[55] may prove on closer inspection to be inspired by an effort to reduce the competition of street hawkers (who had not hired stalls in Callowhill Market). There is, in short, no clear trend: the tides of policy choice move in and out. Jefferson, the advocate of freedom of enterprise, recommends that private traders be driven out of the lucrative trade with the Indians by means of an expansion of government-operated trading posts.[56] Yet concurrently, in Pennsylvania, the assize of bread, which had regulated the price and

48. For details see Joseph Spengler, "The Political Economy of Jefferson, Madison and Adams," in *American Studies in Honor of W. K. Boyd*, p. 5.
49. Jefferson, *Works*, V, 440.
50. Richardson, *Messages and Papers of the Presidents*, I, 334.
51. Taylor, *Arator*, p. vi.
52. *Political Essays*, pp. 9–11.
53. Coxe's phrase; see *View of the United States*, pp. 164–165. See also Madison, *Works*, V, 342; for Jefferson's views, see Richardson, *Messages and Papers of the Presidents*, I, 318.
54. See *Delaware Laws*, 183, 249; *Maryland Laws (Kilty)*, chs. 17, 59.
55. *13 Pennsylvania Statutes at Large*, 225–226, ch. 1398.
56. Richardson, *Messages and Papers of the Presidents*, I, 340–342.

size of loaves for decades, was challenged as inconsistent with the "rights established by the [1790] Constitution" of the state, and, persuaded by this libertarian argument, the legislators proceeded to abolish this time-honored assize.

Meantime, the defense of occupational freedom, although well argued in terms of full employment and maximum production,[57] went beyond entrepreneurial considerations and became inseparably entwined with the mutations of democratic thought. Hence in its most extreme form it represents an heroic attempt of American social theory to uproot the traditional European theory of classes. This version is not typical, despite the clamor of Shaysites or frontier distillers. But the very earnest conviction that freely chosen occupations result in efficient labor pervades contemporaneous literature. Talents will thereby be adjusted to tasks,[58] the nation's limited capital stock will be optimally utilized,[59] and social contentment will be maximized.[60] But what about the imbalance between sectors of the economy, and among "interests," that can result from this planless allocation of the work force? Madison, for one, did not worry about this. Confident that the majority of native-born Americans and most immigrants would elect to be farmers, he was certain that complete choice of occupation would strengthen the agrarian character of the economy which he and Jefferson thought so eminently desirable.[61] Coxe and Hamilton sharply disagreed with the physiocratic ideals of their southern contemporaries and argued that freedom to choose one's occupation might correct the imbalance caused by an overemphasis on agriculture since it would make the recruitment of an industrial work force quite easy. If immigrants, for example, were assured the right to choose their occupations, artisans with skill and talent would be attracted to the shops and mills in the United States, and their technical contributions would hasten industrial development.[62] Here, then, in the third freedom (*laissez-travailler*) we find essential agreement. Free choice of occupation has a salubrious effect on the will to work, on total output, on the variety of economic activities, on capital formation, on immigration; hence it is a policy that should be favored because it is at once "wise and just."[63]

And now we come to the fourth freedom, which I have had the

57. Especially by Madison, *Works*, VI, 96–99.
58. Taylor, *Principles and Policy*, p. 282; Adams, *Works*, VI, 530.
59. Coxe, *View of the United States*, p. 143.
60. Pelatiah Webster, *Political Essays*, p. 24.
61. *Works*, VI, 99.
62. Coxe, *View of the United States*, pp. 239–240.
63. Taylor, *Principles and Policy*, p. 282.

temerity to call *laissez-placer*. Despite the fierceness of the great controversy over funding, a freedom to invest, to lend money at interest,[64] and to speculate becomes a cherished part of our economic philosophy. Actually the funding and assumption tempest was rather short-lived, and it constitutes a poor barometer of opinion largely because the critics of Hamilton's financial program were so much more articulate, emotive, and frenetic than the few defenders of this well-planned program that laid the foundations of our public credit.[65] The trouble with the funding controversy was that all manner of dissatisfaction confused the basic issues: Republican opposition to Federalist policies, antagonisms between debtors and creditors, between inland farmers and seaboard merchants, and of course the bitterness of the original holders of public debt who had sold their securities at large discounts and now saw "speculators" cashing the same securities at full face value. Despite all this, the right to invest was not challenged even though it was frequently argued that certain kinds of "speculation" should be either forbidden or regulated. But these intimations of future securities and exchange acts were vague, ill formulated, and evanescent.

It could not have been otherwise. The right to make shrewd investments, the right to hold lands or other property for appreciation had the approbation of merchants and planters, of Federalists and Republicans, frontiersmen and city-dwellers.[66] This freedom was really basic in determining the course of our history because of the general understanding that the investment process required a favorable political environment[67] since, as the authors of the *Federalist* so neatly put it, "an unstable government damps every useful undertaking." For "what prudent merchant will hazard his fortune in any new branch of commerce . . . what farmer or manufacturer will lay himself out" unless assurance is given that investments will be protected?[68] But whereas government should foster and encourage individual investment, should it look with equal solicitude on corporate ventures? This was an issue acerbated by Hamilton's proposal for a national bank and indeed by the whole funding controversy. Critics argued

64. The case for complete freedom to lend money was vigorously presented by Noah Webster in his spirited attack on usury laws. See his *Collection of Essays,* pp. 304–334.

65. Mitchell's chapters are brief but contain the essential details. See *Alexander Hamilton,* chaps. 3 and 4.

66. See Adams, *Works,* VIII, 294, for one view; Taylor, *Principles and Policy,* p. 282, for another.

67. See Beard, *Economic Interpretation of the Constitution,* p. 53.

68. *The Federalist* (Lodge), LXII (Hamilton or Madison), 390–391.

that unless the individual investor was protected against the "monied interests" the whole structure of republican government would be undermined,[69] while defenders replied by pointing out that only a "union of many individuals" could amass the capital needed for large-scale ventures and could distribute risks in a rational manner.[70]

And there, for all the clatter of debate and the mutual execration of the disputants, the matter stood. The channels of investment ought to be entirely free from governmental interference. No distinction should be made between investment (in the purchase-to-use sense) and speculation (purchasing to resell).[71] Nor should limitations be placed upon group investment provided such joint enterprises did not create monopoloid situations disadvantageous to other producers, other investors, or the public at large.[72] This ingrained fear of monopoly, derived from British tradition, had been intensified by the antagonism to the favoritism that had crept into colonial administration and by the incidence of the terms of trade on frontier communities. It is therefore understandable why the Hancock-Adams resolutions in the Massachusetts (ratifying) convention proposed an amendment to the Federal Constitution forbidding Congress from chartering companies and granting them "exclusive advantage," and equally plain why four other conventions made similar recommendations.

The Pattern of Public Policy

Out of this composite, interest-oriented, pragmatic cluster of ideas were our basic patterns of public policy derived. Born in controversy yet blessed with an inherent attraction that transcended party, class, and region, a body of principles took form in the Age of Washington which was so generally accepted that it is only meretricious to contrast Hamiltonian with Jeffersonian policy or solemnly to attribute interventionism to one party and libertarianism to another. In this con-

69. For an indication of the extent and degree of distrust of corporate ventures, see Livermore, *Early American Land Companies*, pp. 67–69.

70. All this is richly analyzed in Davis, *American Corporations*, I, 429–446.

71. "Speculators," said Robert Morris, "always do least mischief when they are left most at liberty." *Journals of the Continental Congress*, XXII, 435. Leave them alone, he counseled and they will "invariably counteract each other." Even the sharpest critics of speculation in public debt admitted that "stockjobbing" was not inherently evil; when such business "is conducted with truth, sincerity and fairness," said James Sullivan, "it may be considered as reputable and honorable." *Path to Riches*, pp. 10–11.

72. See Livermore, *Early American Land Companies*, pp. 5, 8, 12, 20, 36, 38, 62.

text, political history is an untrustworthy guide to the study of economic ideas or policy. Momentary circumstantial differences, to be sure, were legion; but great national policy decisions concerning economic development must be based on agreement not on discord, variance, or uncompromising truculence. What then were the real areas of agreement discovered in that decade of decision we call the Constitutional Era?

First comes the preference for a naturalistic process of development. But this very rarely becomes an object of worship or a fixation paralyzing legislative imagination. For although Jefferson's prescription was to "let things take their natural course without help or impediment,"[73] was it not he who authorized the construction of the National Road and who sent Lewis and Clark on their fateful survey? Oppositely, Pelatiah Webster's fulsome comparison of business with an "irresistible river" that "will ever run safest, do least mischief and most good, when suffered to run without obstruction in its own natural channel" represents a flamboyant Federalist advocacy of a natural order. Clearly, then, a climate of opinion existed which favored the largest measure of entrepreneurial freedom consistent with that vague, ill-defined, ever-changing concept: "the public interest." But if, on the other hand, the welfare of citizens required state action, no predilection in favor of a presumed happy natural order should stand in the way.

And just here we detect the second essential element in our basic polity. Noah Webster put it bluntly: since "vast inequality of fortunes" is not only inconsistent with republican government[74] but impairs the economic efficiency of nations, one of the first responsibilities of government is to frame "a fundamental law, favoring an equal or rather a general distribution of property."[75] Once again a principle is accepted by Federalists and Republicans, by patricians and plebeians. Jefferson,[76] Madison,[77] and Taylor[78] favored equal division of estates, but so did Webster and John Adams! And the purpose should not be to equalize fortunes, for that is impossible,[79] but to "insure constant revolutions of property," thereby stimulating "vigilance and industry" and "giving every citizen an equal chance of being rich and respectable."[80]

73. *Works* (Washington), II, 413.
74. *Collection of Essays,* pp. 331–332.
75. Ibid., p. 327.
76. *Works* (Washington), VI, 575.
77. *The Federalist* (Lodge), X, 54.
78. *Principles and Policy,* p. 621.
79. Logan, *Five Letters to the Yeomanry,* p. 12.
80. Noah Webster, *Collection of Essays,* p. 327.

But the democratization of economic practice ought not to be restricted to laws governing inheritance or land policy; it should pervade all legislation. Even Hamilton, who doubted the capacity of ordinary people, conceded that "the door ought to be equally open to all,"[81] thus agreeing at least in principle with his more optimistic countrymen[82] who recommended liberal apprenticeship, public assistance for the promotion of useful knowledge, simpler naturalization laws, and the right of foreigners to acquire property. In the vanguard were those who found the emergent democratic pattern too narrow and unimaginative, men who hoped to use taxation to correct the inequalities between rich and poor[83] or who proposed to exempt every "artificer's subsistence" from all possible deductions. Madison epitomizes the spirit and the conscience of this group of reformers: the primary policy of legislation, he said, should be to "reduce extreme wealth toward a state of mediocrity, and to raise extreme indigence toward a state of comfort."[84]

I cannot here attempt to catalogue or appraise the institutional arrangements whereby the public interest was to be furthered. That is another long story that has not been adequately told. But overriding I find a few principles of intervention that have shaped the nation's destiny. It should be the policy of government to aid and encourage "that industry, those occupations, and kinds of business, which most enrich, strengthen, and happify a nation,"[85] even as it is the inescapable duty of government to repress "those fashions, habits, and practices which tend to weaken, impoverish and corrupt the people." The art of government calls for an Aristotelian mean between complete liberty (which would be anarchy) and complete authority (which would be despotism); hence the object of legislation should be "to unite and combine" public and private action so they will "mutually support, feed and quicken each other."[86] Wisely conceived economic policy may therefore serve both the separate interests and the general interest. For national prosperity can be assured only when a nation possesses a proper complement of employments, and when each of these is efficiently organized. Where these goals can be attained by means of self-interest, there is no need for intervention. Where they

81. *The Federalist* (Lodge), XXXV, 207–208.
82. Coxe, for example; see his *View of the United States,* pp. 66–67, 74, 159, 214.
83. James Swan, for example, demanded the abandonment of the "cruel" faculty taxes and their replacement by luxury taxes. *National Arithmetick,* p. 60.
84. *Works,* VI, 86.
85. Pelatiah Webster, *Political Essays,* pp. 239–240.
86. Ibid., p. 499.

cannot, it becomes both wise and proper to employ the "fostering hand of government."[87]

This, then, was our great legacy from the Constitutional Era. For despite all the controversy, wrangling, and recrimination, there was a very genuine solicitude for the general interest and a prescience that public policy must be progressively adapted to changing tasks and problems. Every generation must, of course, redefine the public interest in terms of its cluster of cultural, intellectual, political, and economic values.[88] Whether the thinkers of 1790 had a proper appreciation of the essential meaning of the public interest might be a matter of dispute. But the earnestness with which they tried to relate the tasks of government to *their* concept of the public interest is a challenge to the ingenuity of future generations confronted with the self-same problem in different settings.

87. This phrase occurs repeatedly in congressional debates and in contemporaneous literature. See in the *Annals of Congress* the remarks of Mr. Hartley (I, 114), Mr. Madison (I, 118), Mr. Fitzsimons (I, 150), Mr. Ames (I, 230). See also Coxe, *View of the United States*, p. 357.

88. The following preamble to a 1949 law defines the public interest (insofar as housing is concerned) in terms that would have seemed very strange to the Founding Fathers: "The Congress hereby declares that the general welfare and security of the nation and the health and living standards of the people require housing production and related community development sufficient to remedy the serious housing shortage, the elimination of sub-standard and other inadequate housing through the clearance of slums and blighted areas, and the realization as soon as feasible of the goal of a decent home and a suitable living environment for every American family." *Public Law 171, 81st Congress*, sec. 2 (1949).

Index

Index

322

222, 223; primary, 215; product, 59; productive, 169, 282, 291n, 292; property, 60, 61, 71, 175, 185, 188, 302, 310; quality, 143; quantity, 143; rewards, 182, 192; shipping, 252, 253n; silk, 212; steel, 251; sugar, 287; taxes, 90n; wealth, 101, 104, 134, 186
Infant industries, 216n, 234
Inflation, 165
Infrastructure, 8
Inheritance, 51, 185, 186, 311
Inland farmers, 175, 308
Inland towns, 215
Innovation, 170n, 225, 233
Inspection, 85, 92, 97, 98, 147, 148n, 162, 244n, 285, 305
Insurance, 108, 109, 135, 179n
Interest, 16, 52, 82, 102, 106, 111, 113, 115, 122, 130, 131n, 133, 134n, 135, 136, 140, 148n, 150, 179, 180, 181, 206, 284, 289, 308
Interests, 69–71, 109, 158, 165n, 190, 195, 228, 239, 250, 253, 261, 265n, 278, 282, 283n, 286, 293, 296–297, 299–302, 305, 307, 311: agricultural, 74, 75–78, 81, 100, 108, 114, 156, 183, 204, 219, 222, 227, 240–242, 254, 255, 276, 280, 281, 299; amalgamated, 6; artificial, 22; balanced, 16, 48–51, 66, 67; basic, 197, 236; commercial, 7, 42, 43, 45, 46, 49, 51, 59, 79–81, 87, 100, 107, 155, 156, 199n, 208, 222, 227, 234, 243, 246, 254, 258, 262, 276, 299, 304; conflict, 41, 50, 65, 254; consumers, 97, 100; corporate, 303; divergent, 4; economic, 37, 51, 93, 170, 173, 235, 292; financial, 5, 7, 10, 33, 43–45, 55, 57, 62, 63, 65, 67, 73, 75–78, 84, 90n, 96, 102–116, 118, 120, 121, 126, 127, 132n, 135, 140, 141, 148–151, 155, 156, 175, 178, 182, 183n, 188, 200, 208, 227, 298, 299, 303, 304; foreign, 5, 44, 45, 76, 78, 83, 94, 97, 103, 108, 118, 125, 126, 129–131, 134, 142, 144, 147, 149, 166, 167, 178, 186, 197, 199, 204, 208–211, 216, 217n, 218, 219, 223, 231, 233, 234, 236, 240, 245, 249, 251, 253, 254, 256, 258, 259, 262, 265, 267, 273, 277, 283, 291n, 300, 306, 311; individual, 147, 193; landed, 40, 73, 74, 76, 150, 246, 269, 281, 297; major, 5, 10, 42, 211, 264; manufacturing, 14, 40, 81, 86,

88–92, 94–96, 114, 183, 219, 222, 227, 234, 248, 257, 259, 262, 280, 297; maritime, 244, 245, 254, 257–259, 267; mercantile, 40, 82, 85, 86, 114, 154, 219, 243, 252, 272, 297; moneyed, 40, 64, 96, 102, 103, 112, 150, 289, 290, 292, 297, 298, 309; natural, 55, 56, 58, 63, 72, 96, 112, 119, 238, 260, 298, 304; paper, 104, 107, 119; partial, 61, 63; professional, 96, 114, 222; propertied, 57; representation, 46, 47; theory, 9, 40, 118, 154, 260; true, 13; various, 11
Intermediate credit, 205, 206
International dealings, 114, 135, 274, 304, 305
Intervention, 9, 39, 153n, 154, 156, 157, 162, 163, 166, 167, 169, 182, 193, 195, 196, 199, 200, 208, 228, 233, 236, 260, 262, 264, 304, 305, 309, 311
Inventions, 38, 38n, 224, 295
Investments, 23, 24, 29, 32, 34, 35, 123, 124, 125, 126, 129, 133, 137, 140, 142, 150n, 151, 156, 157n, 163n, 175–181, 205, 235, 253n, 286, 288, 289, 295, 303, 308, 309
Iron, 83, 99, 125, 220n, 231n, 241, 248n, 263, 269, 271, 272, 274, 280n, 282

Jackson, Andrew, 56, 173, 298
Jackson, James, 239, 240, 256, 290, 292n
Jacobean monopolies, 178
Jamaica, 229, 230n
Jay, John, 9, 14, 17, 18, 26, 41
Jefferson, Thomas, 24, 34, 35, 51, 72, 169, 204n, 297n: agrarians, 9, 21, 307; agricultural credit, 205, 209; Bank of the United States, 127, 138, 141; emigration, 160; fishermen, 213n, 277, 278, 280, 282n, 283; free trade, 164–167, 172, 209, 305, 306; idealism, 16, 26; individual initiative, 7; laissez-faire, 153n, 157, 170n, 196; land policy, 185, 197, 212, 310; mechanic arts, 87; opposition to manufactures, 76, 88, 89, 165, 173; philosophy, 21; planters, 10, 19, 23; program, 18; revolution, 20; self-evident truths, 13; slaveholder, 22
Jeffersonians, 15, 23, 53n, 162, 165, 182, 304, 309
Jewelry, 231n
Judges, 152, 158

270, 271, 272, 273, 274, 275, 277, 283, 285n, 286, 288, 289, 291n

Petty, Sir William, 32

Pewter, 216n, 231n, 248n

Phaetons, 266n

Philadelphia, Pa., 10, 77, 205, 233, 246, 250, 264, 265, 266, 268, 271, 274, 277, 284, 286, 287, 288

Philosophy, 11, 12, 13, 52, 152, 153, 158, 302, 308

Physiocrats, 19, 23, 24, 74, 153, 164n, 307

Pickering, Timothy, 25, 202n

Piecework, 93

Piedmont, 3

Piers, 85n

Pierson, Joseph G., 271

Plantation, 10, 19, 23, 26, 87, 98, 203

Planters, 19, 22, 23, 84, 154, 209, 217, 250, 257, 258, 269n, 273, 303, 308

Plated ware, 231n

Plato, 295

Playing cards, 230n

Plebians, 16, 64, 65, 310

Pluralism, 4, 6, 7, 10, 39, 46, 118, 292, 294, 295, 296, 300, 301, 302

Plutocracy, 66

Poland, 218

Political: authority, 107; change, 111, 305; economy, 123, 148, 151, 164n, 211; emancipation, 4; environment, 175, 210, 219, 308; family, 70; history, 182, 273; ideas, 4, 51, 55, 107, 108, 109, 173, 217, 292; importunity, 91; innovations, 170n, 295; instability, 57; junto, 75; morality, 65; opportunism, 63, 90; party, 153, 181, 182, 303; priority, 45, 51, 52, 53, 55, 56, 57, 65, 73, 74, 80; privilege, 5, 57; recognition, 46, 217; representation, 6, 46, 73, 299; theory, 45, 54, 63, 71, 119, 123, 260, 278, 299, 302; tracts, 5, 99, 191; unity, 217

Politicians, 52, 157, 260, 297

Politics, 219, 296

Poll taxes, 186, 278n

Poor, 5, 12, 15, 17, 35, 50, 64, 65, 71, 77, 114n, 179, 180n, 186, 190n, 192n, 202, 204, 212, 239, 262, 272, 298, 299, 311

Population, 8, 35, 46, 47, 61, 73, 74, 75, 99, 131n, 160n, 166, 174, 203, 207, 212, 213, 215, 293, 299

Pork, 241n

Porter, 229, 230n, 241, 248n, 249

Ports, 62, 98, 165, 215, 235, 255, 264, 268, 269, 273

Portsmouth, N.H., 267, 270, 272, 277

Postlethwayt, Malachy, 9, 123, 131n, 208n

Potash, 203

Poverty, 112, 161, 182, 295

Power, 16, 21, 27, 46, 48, 49, 50, 53, 54, 55, 56, 57, 65, 71, 73, 79, 83, 89, 100, 105, 106, 107, 109, 110, 111, 114, 116, 117, 118, 120, 127n, 134, 144, 145, 146, 153, 155, 158, 167, 170, 211, 219, 231, 232, 245, 255, 276, 295, 298, 299

Preachers, 10, 35, 35n, 36, 43n, 52, 53, 65, 140, 159, 167, 197, 200

Preferences, 30, 56, 57, 161, 252, 282, 283n, 298

Premiums, 79, 184, 214, 220, 221n, 223, 224

President, 273

Pressure groups, 39, 61, 62, 63, 68, 263

Price-fixing, 13, 16, 22, 28, 29, 35, 109, 154, 156, 162, 167, 168, 182, 189, 190, 303

Prices, 52, 85n, 93, 98, 104, 122, 131n, 132, 136n, 137, 139, 154, 162, 167–172, 175, 180, 181, 183, 189, 190, 207, 209, 210, 216, 217n, 218n, 220–222, 244, 249, 256, 257, 278, 291, 292n, 305, 306

Primogeniture, 20, 160

Princeton, N.J., 10, 11

Printing, 91, 212n, 270, 274

Prison, 98, 106

Private citizens, 103, 152

Private enterprise, 7, 10, 62, 90, 91, 125, 162, 172, 176, 179, 183, 184, 191, 221n, 225, 278, 282, 289, 295, 302, 306

Privileges, 17, 21, 44, 50, 53, 58, 68, 71, 77, 82, 90, 116, 117, 159, 181, 184, 188, 191, 278, 279, 282, 301, 305

Produce, 51, 60, 88, 206, 207, 232, 240, 253, 254, 256, 258, 267, 286, 301

Productivity, 3, 23, 35, 88, 96, 103, 104, 124, 125, 126, 129, 134n, 143, 145, 151, 156, 161, 163, 169, 170, 171, 173, 174, 191, 192, 194, 200, 205, 206, 212n, 214, 222, 223, 225, 234, 236, 279, 291n, 292, 295, 306, 307

Professional men, 4, 5, 46, 66, 73, 81, 95, 96, 107, 114, 174, 299, 300

Unequal taxes, 239

United States, 5, 10, 11n, 20n, 21, 25, 28n, 30, 48, 50, 55, 73, 78, 84, 89, 93, 94n, 98, 103, 105, 113, 114, 117, 125, 126, 128, 135, 140, 145, 153, 154, 162, 164, 170, 174, 184, 197, 198n, 199, 204, 207, 209–212, 216, 217n, 219, 222, 223, 225, 226, 228, 232, 233, 235, 237n, 239–242, 245, 246, 248, 251, 253, 255, 258, 262, 265–267, 270n, 271–273, 275–277, 282, 283n, 285n, 302, 303n, 307

Usher, Abbot Payson, 38n

Usury, 12, 141, 142, 143, 178, 179, 180n, 181, 308n

Vats, 99

Vessels, 198, 211, 231, 233, 235, 244, 253, 254, 255, 257, 259, 268n, 269, 270n, 272, 273, 277, 280n, 281n, 283

Villages, 3, 285n

Vining, John, 276

Volonté générale, 67, 302

Wadsworth, Jeremiah, 250, 255, 256

Wages, 22, 52, 82, 87, 89, 93, 100, 164, 174, 183, 189, 217n, 220, 279

Walnut, 215

War, 3, 10, 31, 60, 74, 135n, 149, 157, 166, 167, 209, 212, 216, 219, 230, 236, 237, 274n

Warehouses, 3

Washington, George, 2, 10, 18, 33, 56, 67, 127, 141n, 158, 162, 163, 175, 196, 200, 203, 217, 293, 296, 299, 305, 309

Water, 199, 213

Wealth, 8, 17, 43, 45, 51, 53, 54, 56, 60–63, 65, 67, 68n, 74, 77, 80, 81, 83, 90, 91, 101, 104, 106, 110–112, 115, 117, 124, 126, 131n, 132n, 134, 137, 140, 143, 146, 153, 157, 163, 164n, 174, 176, 185, 187, 189n, 198n, 200n, 205, 210, 218, 219n, 279, 280, 295, 301, 311

Weaving, 87, 91, 92, 93

Webster, Noah, 11, 12, 45n, 47, 51, 57, 68, 69n, 70, 82, 86, 95, 96, 115, 122, 125 138, 158n, 178, 179, 180, 181, 184, 190n, 204, 218, 297n, 298, 302, 308n, 310

Webster, Pelatiah, 8, 10, 28, 29, 30, 42, 57, 58, 79n, 80, 81, 82, 97, 123n, 127, 136, 137, 144n, 147n, 148n, 154, 158, 167, 168, 169, 171, 174, 176, 186, 189, 193, 198, 199, 203, 297n, 303n, 306, 310

Weights, 172, 173

Weimar Germany, 299

West Indies, 165, 212, 246, 250, 253n, 274, 277

Whaling, 85, 220n, 221n, 256

Wheat, 83, 181, 190n, 195n

Whiskey, 27n, 195n, 284, 286, 289

Whiskey Rebellion, 27, 27n, 188, 284, 286

White, Alexander, 242, 265, 267

Widows, 137

Williamson, Hugh, 265, 267, 270n, 281, 282, 283

Wilmington, Del., 269

Window glass, 231n, 271

Wine, 201, 220n, 230n, 266, 268n, 274n, 287n

Witherspoon, John, 11, 12, 13, 26, 30, 152, 158, 164, 165, 171, 182, 190, 206, 305

Wives, 88n, 214

Wool, 126, 196n, 207n, 215, 223, 230n, 231n, 248n, 269n, 280n

Worcester, Mass., 69n, 270

Workers, 32, 35, 78, 91, 92, 99, 114, 155, 164n, 173, 175, 214, 303, 307

Working capital, 135, 139

Workshops, 3, 89, 164, 186

Yarn, 264n, 265n

Yates, Robert, 11n

Yeomanry, 12, 65, 77, 79, 112, 185, 202n

Young, Arthur, 9, 108n

Yugoslavia, 299